Apostles of the Alps

Apostles of the Alps

Mountaineering and Nation Building in
Germany and Austria, 1860–1939

TAIT KELLER

The University of North Carolina Press Chapel Hill

Publication of this book was supported in part by
a subvention from Rhodes College and with the assistance
of the Authors Fund of the University of North Carolina Press.

© 2016 The University of North Carolina Press
All rights reserved
Designed by Alyssa D'Avanzo
Set in Quadraat by codeMantra
Manufactured in the United States of America

The University of North Carolina Press has been a member of the
Green Press Initiative since 2003.

Cover illustration: "Auf der Hochebene"
(Signatur DAV NAS 39 FG/8/0), Deutscher Alpenverein e.V.

Library of Congress Cataloging-in-Publication Data
Keller, Tait, author.
Apostles of the Alps : mountaineering and nation building in Germany
and Austria, 1860–1939 / Tait Keller.
pages cm
Includes bibliographical references and index.
ISBN 978-1-4696-2503-4 (pbk   ) — ISBN 978-1-4696-2504-1 (ebook)
1. Mountaineering—Alps, Eastern—History—19th century.
2. Mountaineering—Alps, Eastern—History—20th century. 3. Alps,
Eastern—History—19th century. 4. Alps, Eastern—History—20th century.
5. Germany—History—1789–1900. 6. Germany—History—20th century.
7. Austria—History—1789–1900. 8. Austria—History—20th century. I. Title.
DQ828.K45 2015
943.64044—dc23
2015027999

Chapter 4 of this book is an expanded version of
"The Mountains Roar: The Alps during the Great War," Environmental
History 14, no. 2 (2009): 253–74. Used by permission.

For Mom and Matt

Contents

Acknowledgments xi

Note on Citations and Translation xv

Abbreviations Used in the Text xvii

Introduction *Disenchanted Mountains* 1

PART ONE | Opening the Alps, 1860–1918

1 Civilizing the Crags
Urban Adventurers Modernize the Mountains 17

2 Peaks and Progress
Alpine Reveries, Bourgeois Dreams, and National Fantasies 47

3 Young People and Old Mountains
Commercialism and Conservationism Tangle in the Alps 67

4 The High Alps in the Great War
Soldiers and Summits on the Alpine Front 89

PART TWO | Dominating the Alps, 1919–1939

5 Forbidden Heights
Lost Mountains and the Violence of Alpine Anti-Semitism 121

6 Mechanical Mountains
Movies and Motors Remake the Alps 152

7 Fascist Landscapes
Nature Lovers and Nazi Desperadoes on the Alpine Frontier 183

Conclusion *The Retreat of Nations* 213

Notes 223

Bibliography 249

Index 277

Figures

1. The Alpine region xx
2. Mountaineering and industrialization 29
3. Berlin's *Winterfest* 33
4. The dining salon in the Berliner Hut 37
5. The Lamsenjoch Lodge 38
6. The Kemptner Hut 39
7. Berliner Hut renovations 41
8. Scientists taking core samples of a glacier 42
9. The Münchner Haus and Observatory 44
10. Hiking on Plattenjoch 52
11. The Alpine front during the First World War 98
12. Eduard Pichl (1872–1955) 134
13. "So, now it is just us" 142
14. Molding mountains 169
15. Construction on the Grossglockner High Alpine Road 171
16. Sleek machines and rugged mountains 173
17. Grossglockner Visitor Center on Kaiser-Franz-Josefs-Höhe 174
18. The Nazi eagle rising over the Alps 210
19. "Over the Alps" 218

Acknowledgments

My debts are great. These few poor sentences that I offer are meager compensation when measured against all that people have done for me, and all that I have been given so that I might write this book. Red drenches the ledger of my life. Yet my gratitude and joy accrued are greater still and all the richer for the depth of what I owe.

First and foremost I thank my mentors. Roger Chickering suggested this topic to me and then suffered through numerous drafts of highly questionable quality. Though his famous blue fountain pen must have run dry—repeatedly—while correcting my prose, his encouragement and care never did. Under his rigorous tutelage and gentle guidance I have matured in ways that I hope make him proud. John McNeill has been just as important to me as I launched into the pools of the profession and then found myself in heavy water. I should have drowned but for John helping me to navigate the rapids with their hidden boulders, big waves, and sudden falls. I am fortunate indeed to have him as a guide. Tom Zeller never failed to provide reassurance and boost my confidence, especially when I needed it most. His enthusiasm for this project and thoughtful suggestions as it developed carried me through to its end. While wandering around a rummage sale, the late Richard Stites happened upon a copy of *The White Tower*. He bought it on the spot and wrote a kind note in it for me. When I see that book on my shelf I remember his jovial, generous spirit and consider myself lucky to have known him. Celia Applegate holds a special place for me for first inspiring me to study history when I was her undergraduate student. Without her support I could never have followed my aspirations. Now my friend, always my mentor, she is my model of the scholar and teacher that I strive to be.

This book would not have seen the light of day were it not for Chuck Grench's unflagging support from the start. I could not have asked for a more understanding, thoughtful, and encouraging editor. I am deeply grateful to Julie Bush for the care she took in editing my manuscript. Grants from the German Academic Exchange Service, the Austrian Academic Exchange Service, Georgetown University, and Rhodes College allowed me to conduct research in Europe. Funds from the Department of History at Rhodes enabled me to hire my gifted student Olivia Muehlberger to proofread the German phrases in the manuscript. The interlibrary loan departments at Georgetown and Rhodes aided me immensely, as did the staffs at the other libraries and archives where I conducted research. In particular I would like to thank the archivists at the Bavarian Main State Archive, Ulrike Feistmantl at the Salzburg State Archive, and Valerie Thoni at the International Climbing and Mountaineering Federation headquarters in Bern, who were all exceptionally generous with their time and expertise. The staff members at the German Alpine Association in Munich and at the Austrian Alpine Association in Innsbruck far exceeded my expectations. I cannot think of more welcoming places to conduct research than those libraries and archives. Martin Achrainer, Monika Gärtner, and Veronika Raich in Innsbruck and Klara Esters, Carmen Fischer, Ulrike Gehrig, Friederike Kaiser, Renate Lebmeier, the late Johannes Merk, and Stefan Ritter in Munich assisted me in countless ways.

Colleagues and friends have offered guidance, provided support, and read portions of the manuscript. Tim Huebner, Jeff Jackson, Charles McKinney, and Robert Saxe gave invaluable feedback on various drafts. David Blackbourn, Alison Frank Johnson, Tom Lekan, Christof Mauch, Scott Moranda, John Alexander Williams, and Jeff Wilson coached me along the way and offered outstanding models of environmental history. Mountaineering scholars and Alpine experts Marco Armiero, Mark Carey, Wilko Graf von Hardenberg, and Kerwin Klein helped me greatly to develop my ideas. Shelley Baranowski, Martin Geyer, Dagmar Günther, and Richard Kuisel made time to discuss the project with me. Christine Mueller and William Tudor leased to me their apartment in Vienna, which proved to be the perfect space to write a book. I thank Nannette Gills and Heather Walter for helping me manage all the logistics of finishing the manuscript and sending it off. Änni and Martin Gruner, Jan-Philipp Müller, Stephanie Naumann, Jörg Rohaus, Rich Stevenson and Anita VanBarneveld, and Ted Wiederhold made my stays in Germany feel like being home, and I cherish those friendships. I extend heartfelt thanks to my Georgetown cohort of Gregory Baldi, Gregory Caplan, Elizabeth Drummond, Marc Landry, Kevin Martin, Seth Rotramel, Chris Vukicevich, and Andrew Wackerfuss for their much-needed moral support, as well as to Andrew Denning and Brian Feltman, my German Studies comrades. Kristine Alexander caught mistakes with her careful eyes while lifting my spirits with her infectious laughter. Words will fail to convey all that Alex Merrow and Simone

Ameskamp, my big brother and super sis, have done for me. They have carried me through so many times.

Sacrifices are a part of every book project; sadness, too. I thank Catherine Taylor for giving all that she could; this book would not have been finished without her. Without the help of dear friends and family, I might not have recovered from the losses incurred while writing. In Memphis, Jennifer and Paul Sciubba, Tony Ludlow, and Betsy Mandel-Carley took care of me. Sohini Chowdhury, Hilary and Jon Davis, Katherine Jacobs, Sherilyn Klueber, Irene and Steve Lachance, Sarah Low and Mark White, Andrew Mitchell, and Gregg Roberts and Gale Segarra Roberts saved me from utter isolation with their open arms. Terry and Bonnie and the girls—Maria, Julieanna, and Isabella—lovingly teased me about hurrying up and finishing. Finally, this book is dedicated to the two nearest my heart.

Note on Citations and Translation

During the gestation of this book, the German Alpine Association, the Austrian Alpine Association, and the Alpine Association of South Tyrol overhauled and merged their archival collections. In 2006, the clubs opened the Alpine Historical Archive with materials located in Munich, Innsbruck, and Bolzano. As part of the restructuring, the German Alpine Association reordered its holdings, assigned all new file signatures, and created an electronic database with improved finding aids. When I first conducted research at the German Alpine Association's archive in 2001, reams of documents were simply bundled into bins for each chapter (for example, Berlin Karton). These papers now have specific file numbers. Where possible, I have indicated the updated file signature in the citations. When unavailable, I have listed the corresponding bin. Unless otherwise noted, all translations are my own.

Abbreviations Used in the Text

AV-Berlin	Deutscher Alpenverein Berlin
DAV	Deutscher Alpenverein
DBW	Deutscher Bergsteiger- und Wanderverband
DÖAV	Deutscher und Österreichischer Alpenverein
DRL	Deutsche Reichbund für Leibesübungen
ÖAV	Österreichischer Alpenverein
ÖTC	Österreichische Touristenklub
SA	Sturmabteilung
SAT	Società degli Alpinisti Tridentini

Apostles of the Alps

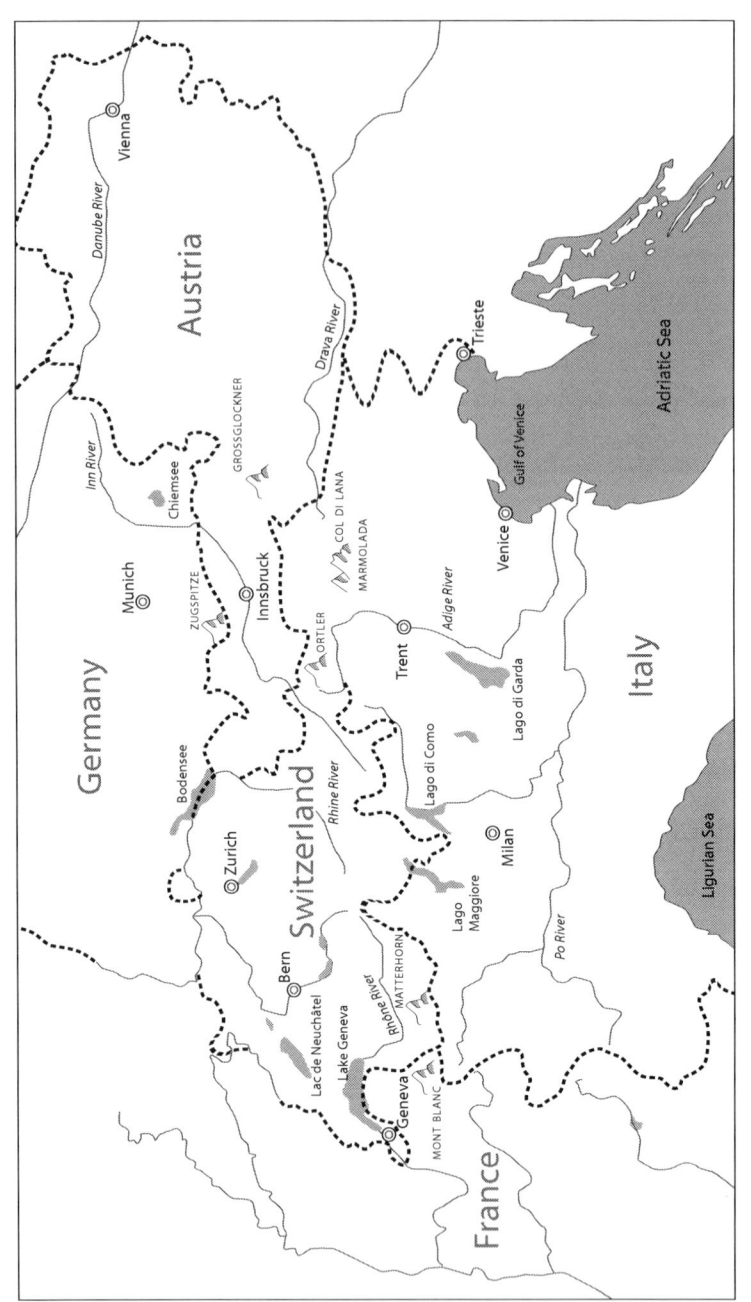

FIGURE 1 The Alpine region.

Introduction
Disenchanted Mountains

"European history in great outlines seems to be shaped by fights for the Alps or against them," wrote the German Jewish author Arnold Zweig in 1939.[1] Witness to Hitler's assumption of power, Zweig went into exile after the Nazis took over Germany and later found his way to Palestine in the 1940s. As the Third Reich's maelstrom of destruction swelled, he looked from afar to the Swiss mountains, the "stronghold of democracy," to preserve civilization: "Nature has formed a barrier against the aggression of Fascism from the South and Nazi tyranny from the North. The sense of freedom, now lost in Tyrol and the High Tauern, defends itself and the European civilization, though modern aviation and radio have given to the dictatorships undreamt-of possibilities. The watch on the summits of the Alps creates the last hope and safeguard of modern democratic civilization and freedom in the middle of Europe."[2] Zweig's portrayal of the Alps as bastions of liberty echoed the sentiments of eighteenth-century naturalists and philosophers who first attached civic virtues to the Alps, as well as nineteenth-century mountaineers who claimed relief from life's woes on their climbs. To these (mostly) men, the tough Alpine landscape promoted independence. Lofty meadows and stony palisades cultivated and protected democracy. The chill glacial air seemed to inspire peace. In their and Zweig's formulation, nature defined and gave meaning to nationhood.

Zweig conceded, however, that freedom and tranquility did not thrive on all the peaks. The Austrian summits had fallen, with the help of technology, to oppression. He recognized that humans could deliberately shape the environment's physical landscape and discursive meaning. Romancing the mountains also stirred darker dreams. Here the brutal terrain somehow fostered cruel politics. Canyons and crags apparently nurtured and sheltered fascism. Hitler's minions likewise saw the importance of controlling Alpine aeries for their own agendas. Struggling up the slopes hardened bodies for battle, and subjugating mountains whetted appetites of conquest. Gazing out across sweeping vistas aroused desires for *Lebensraum* (living space). Once a peaceful realm of deliverance, the mountains could also harbor violent drives of domination.

The Alps have always been a meeting place of opposites, right down to their stone bones. Geomorphic phenomena and human enterprise together have made for a landscape of paradox. Earth science teaches that mountains were the products of both constructive and destructive forces. Massive tectonic collisions crushed together continental plates, thrusting up the towers. While orogenesis uplifted and deformed the earth's crust, crumpling and piling rock strata into high relief features, mass-wasting processes of nivation and solifluction eroded their mantles. Frequent frost action reduced the ramparts, littering the cirques with scree. Weathering wrinkled the mountain face. Storms, avalanches, sudden seismic activity, and glaciers grinding down the slopes made the heights a dynamic, dangerous environment.[3]

Geological convolutions and natural cataclysms were not the only forces at play in the Alps. Humans, too, gave shape to the mountains, also through powerful constructive and destructive endeavors. German and Austrian alpinists engineered the landscape with designs to inspire an alternative sense of belonging and nationhood among their fellow citizens. Religion, ethnicity, and class, along with a strong tradition of localism, had formed the main girders of community in Germany and Austria during the late nineteenth and early twentieth centuries.[4] Yet those fundamental beams also supported the joists of bigotry, violence, and disunity. This uneven foundation stressed communal structures and unsettled nation-building projects in both countries. To buttress the shaky edifice of the nation, middle-class German and Austrian mountaineers sought out the massive stone pillars of the Eastern Alps. They attempted to use the mountains to construct an inclusive, pluralistic *Grossdeutsch* (Greater German) community that embraced all Germans and Austrians. Central to their aims was the idea that Alpinism—climbing or hiking mountains— would enable citizens to surmount their differences. When the largest mountaineering club in the world, the Deutscher und Österreichischer Alpenverein (German and Austrian Alpine Association) opened the Alpine frontier, its members altered the physical terrain to match their mental geography of the mountains. Climbers blazed trails over the highlands and erected lodges on the summits, inviting the broader public to the heights in hopes of bonding patriotic loyalties to a landscape that united Germany and Austria. But the peaks became convergent points for divergent interests as tourists carried their prejudices with them to the frontier.

While mountaineers set the Alps as a mighty national foundation that could both withstand political upheaval and support the weight of Greater German pluralism, their rhetorical contortions twisted and folded the Alpine space in ways that provoked social tremors, cultural convulsions, and environmental disruption. Alpine enthusiasts found themselves caught in conundrums of their own making. When German and Austrian tourists modernized the peaks, they politicized the mountains and bound their search for national wholeness and individual autonomy to a landscape defined by contradiction.

This book explores the paradox that Europe's seemingly peaceful "playgrounds" were battlegrounds where competing visions of Germany and Austria clashed. As more vacationers swarmed through the Alps, mass tourism became a vehicle for various ideologies that altered the physical topography and discursive geography of the mountains. Now pressures that had formed the contours of the modern state—political fights, social conflicts, culture wars, and environmental crusades—shaped the peaks. These borderlands did not reflect the struggles occurring at the center; they were the center of nation-building struggles. Contested mountains were the setting for three interwoven tales pivotal to the making of modern Germany and Austria. The first thread is the account of humans in nature. Beginning in the mid-nineteenth century, tourists packed the Alps, seeking respite from the stress and strain of industrial development and the hustle and bustle of city life. The Alpine allure proved particularly seductive for the emerging middle classes. Masses of urban pilgrims sought out what the pious still called "Holy Mountains" as a sanctuary from modern life. Yet congested summits prompted collisions of all sorts. Bourgeois alpinists spurned proletarian hikers. Male chauvinists resented the presence of female climbers in the Alps. Throngs of clumsy sightseers and careless skiers infuriated climbing aficionados. Racket from the crowds disturbed the search for individual serenity. The more people traveled to the Alps, the more such troubles defined the frontier.

This modern narrative of mass tourism braids together with the second thread of the story: humans shaping nature. Urban wanderers brought the modern world with them when they civilized the crags. Civic outdoor organizations paved the way for greater environmental transformations of the heights for the mass consumption of tourists. But swift skis and clunky boots by the millions trampled the delicate Alpine ecology. This distressed nature lovers, whose angst turned to alarm when more cable cars and automobiles took to the mountains in the early twentieth century. The emerging nature preservation movement fought desperately against rail line and highway construction in the mountains. It mobilized with such urgency because for conservationists, the "Holy Mountains" were the last preserves of "immaculate" nature free from the sins of industry.

What the mountains meant to different people ties in with the final thread of the story: nature as a national symbol. Recreational pursuits placed the Alpine periphery at the heart of the German nationhood question. Largely through the labors of "apostles" of the Alps—urban Alpine enthusiasts who preached the splendors of the highlands upon their return to the world below—the mountains retained their rank as sacred, but by the late nineteenth century they served as hallowed ground for the secular nation.[5] However, not all were welcome to worship in the Alps. Declaring the heights sacrosanct barred at different times various groups excluded from the national congregation. During the confessional culture wars of the 1870s, when Prussian officials expelled Catholics from positions of power and influence, Ultramontanists in Austria equated efforts to modernize the Alps with Protestant plots to colonize papal supporters. In the early 1920s, anti-Semite alpinists called for racially pure mountains and assaulted Jewish tourists in the Alps. A decade later, when the Nazi Party rose to prominence in Germany but was outlawed in Austria, reference to sacred mountains carried ominous overtones of annexation. Irreconcilable ideologies battled on the heights where despotic fantasies challenged democratic aspirations.

Nowhere were these tensions more evident than in the Eastern Alps. Located east of the Rhine, these mountains had long been a cluttered maze of political dominions, ecclesiastical dioceses, ethnolinguistic divisions, and natural rifts: fault lines of all sorts intersected and overlapped each other. Discursive fissures likewise complicated the meanings of the mountains. Religious beliefs, Enlightenment ideals, and romantic sentiments converged on the Alps. Early modern theologians like Thomas Burnet had ascribed mountain formation to the cracking open of the earth following the Deluge, making the Alps material projections of man's sinful nature. Yet the sight of the "inchanted [sic] Country" sent him into such "a pleasing kind of stupor and admiration" that he developed a theory of divine mountain building to alleviate his unease with nature's chaos.[6] Geologists later brought rationality, order, and measurement to what many viewed as the quintessential irrational landscape. Scientific methods organized nature but appeared to rob the mountains of their mystique, a modernization process that the German sociologist Max Weber later called the "disenchantment of the world."⁷ In response, romantics sought to "re-enchant" the once-magic mountains. Through art and literature they turned dreadful heights into delightful haunts and urged others to experience the sublime beauty of the Alps.⁸

Toward the late nineteenth century, German and Austrian alpinists likewise tried to "re-enchant" the mountains by styling the Alpine backcountry as the German heartland. Their efforts might seem strange when we remember that most Germans lived to the north, nowhere near the Alps. The majority of Austrians resided in or around Vienna, beyond the mountain chain's eastern foothills. The German-speaking Swiss secluded themselves from their imperial neighbors, who largely discounted the tiny country anyway. For both the German and Austrian empires, the Alps made up only a small percentage of the total land holdings. The peaks marked the margins. Yet despite the frontier's fractured topography and muddled history, by the early twentieth century, patriotic mountaineers proclaimed the Eastern Alps as "the most German of all the Lands," "ancient German earth," and the source of "sacred German feelings."⁹

We might assume that such an Alpine awareness must be something manifestly regional, but these mountaineers did not think in provincial terms. They were not looking for local metaphors.¹⁰ Instead, they saw the Alps as an apolitical "national landscape," a transcendent environment that would appeal to all Germans and Austrians. The creation of a German state separate from Austria in 1871 cleaved the Alpine frontier with a political border that was linguistically illogical and naturally nonsensical. As a German climber tried to explain when he toured through the Berchtesgadener group in southeastern Germany, "Politically-geographically our massif lay almost entirely on Bavarian soil," observing that "the border passed over the southern side of its ridge and cut so that only the southern peak, the Seehorn, was away in Austria."¹¹ An Austrian mountaineer demonstrated just how pervious the political border could be: "One foot in the German Empire, the other one in the *Heimat* [homeland]."¹² Any sense of statehood became increasingly vague as one wandered over the Alpine frontier. Such political ambiguities when combined with the appearance of natural solidity were precisely the attraction of the Alps. Rather than identifying the nation with one's *Heimat*, mountaineers wanted to forge a bond to a distinct landscape and environment, where sharp political boundaries became blurred and multifaceted identities could coexist. An Alpine allegiance offered a solution to German nationhood dilemmas that went beyond state lines and superseded the provincial loyalties. Like local *Heimat* advocates, mountaineers emphasized the importance of place but framed the Alps as a landscape with which any German or Austrian could identify. Mountains provided a geographical sense of self where being German was no longer an abstraction. Efforts to open the mountains and foster a Greater German community bound together tourism, the borderlands, and nation building in ways that regional *Heimat* organizations, sport clubs, or nature groups could not.[13]

This Alpine answer to the question of German nationhood was not, however, a rejection of modernity or a denial of political realities. Previous scholarship has argued that Alpinism in Germany and Austria nourished Nazism's roots. Some historians have blamed conservation groups and back-to-nature movements with their *Blut und Boden* (blood and soil) ideology for this supposed German infatuation with authoritarianism.[14] Sport historian Rainer Amstädter, for example, has used Alpinism to draw a direct line of continuity from nineteenth-century German idealism to anti-Semitism and fervent support of Hitler in the 1930s.[15]

Yet why should Alpinism lead to Nazism? Personal liberty, individual accomplishment, freedom, and autonomy—the values held dear by mountaineers—were anathema to Nazi ideology. A closer examination of hiking clubs, landscape preservation movements, and homeland protection groups in recent years demonstrates that outdoor organizations were not havens for reactionaries or agrarian romantics with antimodern tendencies that paved the path for the Nazis. Rather, these associations looked for ways to shape modernity, not reject it. Besides, plenty of other Europeans and North Americans criticized modernity, as did Leslie Stephen, the intrepid British climber, literary critic, and father of Virginia Woolf, in his 1871 bestseller, *The Playground of Europe*, when he characterized the Alps as "the natural retreat of men disgusted with the existing order of things, profoundly convinced of its rottenness," and as places "unspoilt or unimproved by the aggressive forces of civilization." Most Austrian and German climbers would have agreed with his remark that "the love of mountains is intimately connected with all that is noblest in human nature."[16]

The emotionally charged relationship that mountaineers shared with the Alps points to deeper connections between Germans and Austrians. This is more than just a story about the Alps. The landscape itself emphasizes Austria's pivotal, though often disregarded, place in German history. As the historian Charles Maier remarked, "Few historians really think it an obligation of conscience to write a modern German history that includes Austria," and fewer still write on the German-speaking Alpine region.[17] Yet to fully understand the two states' development, their histories need to be read in tandem. Drawing on original and overlooked evidence, this book thus emphasizes the borderland, the Alpine environment, and moves beyond the restraints of the nation-state framework to bring together these two national narratives.

Seeing Germany and Austria from the standpoint of Europe's Alpine Arc reorients our approach to the two countries. In her article "A Europe of Regions," Celia Applegate discusses the potential of subnational places to change "not only our sense of what matters but our overall understanding of what happened." "A renewed engagement with the regional level of experience," she suggests, "can productively destabilize our perceptions of European history."[18] Despite her encouragement, regional analysis remains mired in the framework of the nation-state. With the notable exception of Beatrice Ploch and Heinz Schilling, who define regions as "landscapes of action, of meaning, and of experience," most historians think of regions in political terms of state provinces or as cultural entities within a political system.[19] The Eastern Alps, however, are not an administrative unit. They are an "ecoregion" with an entirely different set of relations to political borders and cultural communities.[20] Examining an ecoregion forces us to rethink traditional national narratives in ways that typical regional histories cannot. Our new bearings also allow us to map the special relationship between the center and the periphery within both Germany and Austria.

Once neglected, peripheral places have received greater attention in recent years. Scholars have turned to the borderlands, where the interactions among different ethnic groups, the processes of modernization, and nation-building efforts are thrown into sharp relief. Historians of modern Germany and Austria have looked to the edges of their respective empires, to the East in particular, to illuminate, as Tara Zahra once remarked, the "importance of daily life on the periphery of German empires for shaping politics and culture at the center." Vejas G. Liulevicius has shown how the German fascination with the East revealed the "hopes and anxieties about Germany itself." He gestures to Frederick Jackson Turner's now infamous paper, "The Significance of the Frontier in American History," given at the Ninth Annual Meeting of the American Historical Association in 1893. In Turner's thesis, westward expansion forged a resilient American spirit. In some ways Manifest Destiny paralleled the German *Drang nach Osten* (drive to the East); both provided foundational myths. Turner maintained that American civilization "followed the arteries made by geology" with the frontier becoming "interwoven into the complex mazes of modern commercial lines." Civilizing "savage lands" led to the emergence of a single nation rather than to "a collection of isolated states." He compared the process to the "steady growth of a complex nervous system for the originally simple, inert continent." Similar to the American belief in Manifest Destiny, conquering mountains served as a baseline for measuring the world, a medium for historical progress.[21]

Borderland studies, traditionally, have focused on ethnic, linguistic, and political boundaries. An environmental perspective complicates those approaches. This book will show that not only were the dynamics of cooperation and conflict different in the mountains from what we find in the East, but also mass tourism brought extensive change to the Alps. To make the borderlands into the German heartland, a new landscape emerged. Tourism and environmental engineering in the Alps serve as our waypoints to navigate the tumultuous struggles on the borderlands outlined above. The mountains became central to modernization projects, but not the sort of state-led schemes that James Scott has described. Several historians have demonstrated how tourism became a way for nonstate actors to actively lay claim and give meaning to borderland space. Leisure activities could connect these places to larger communities or promote particular social or political agendas.[22] Rather than simplifying and reorganizing the natural world to make the terrain more "legible" from above, as was the case with much modern statecraft, the outdoor organizations used tourism to counterbalance the weight of the state and make the mountains accessible from below.

Mass tourism in the Alps was the conduit that connected the periphery to the center. Organized tourism first emerged in the mid-nineteenth century when Thomas Cook, committed teetotaler, part-time preacher, occasional cabinetmaker, and amateur publisher from the English Midlands, first began planning group excursions for his temperance society. Similar business enterprises offering package tours emerged across Europe.[23] For people who preferred to strike out on their own, a new series of travel guidebooks directed their way. Karl Baedeker's popular travel guides commanded the market. Based in Coblenz, he and his sons built their family-owned firm into a veritable publishing empire over the course of the 1800s. As Rudy Koshar has shown, Baedeker's handbooks shaped new patterns of consumption. Marketed toward the individual bourgeois consumer, sales of his guides matched Germany's boisterous economic growth during the late 1860s. The handbook, with its distinctive bright red cloth cover, could be seen protruding from coat pockets all across Europe. In his succinct style, Baedeker provided travelers with information for navigating local customs, avoiding unscrupulous hoteliers, and determining the best sights to see.[24] With a Cook Tour ticket or a Baedeker guide in hand, masses of vacationers headed out to see the world.

Group tours and guidebooks directed sightseers to natural wonders around the world, but current discussions on borderlands and tourism often overlook the land itself. The environmental context is crucial to understanding the dynamism of tourism and interactions on the frontier, especially in the Alps. A few environmental historians have explored changes to the land wrought by tourists, but typically in a declensionist light that emphasizes the degradation of nature while obscuring the cultural and social dimensions of tourism. Examining the efforts of a suprastate actor like the German and Austrian Alpine Association reveals the relationship of mountaineering and nation building while correcting the declensionist narrative. Changes to the Alpine landscape show how ecological and social systems have responded to each other over time, and not necessarily for the worst. Perhaps tourists were not "Thinking like a Mountain," to borrow Aldo Leopold's phrase on environmental ethics, but mountaineers certainly approached the Alps with a reverence that framed the peaks as icons of nationhood.[25]

Scholarship on mountaineering remains heavily tilted toward British climbers in the Western Alps.[26] True, these agents of empire (and their Swiss guides) first reached most of the higher summits. They established the first mountaineering organization in 1857, the British Alpine Club, whose members defined it as a "club for gentlemen who also climb," an explanation that expressed its social biases. More than half the members had attended university, and several had gone up to Cambridge or Oxford. Elitism was part of their creed. They sought the chill clarity of the mountains because, as Leslie Stephen wrote, "there we can breathe air that has not passed through a million pair of lungs."[27] To join the club, aspiring members had to submit a résumé of verifiable climbs in the Alps and stand for election. Acceptance based on accomplishment and fitness fed conceit. British mountaineers expressed a haughty self-confidence in their masculinity, class, and imperial endeavors. Equating "fittest" with "best" also suggested a social Darwinian approach to mountaineering that first applied to individuals but then eventually to nations.[28] Leisure activities became national imperatives.

Soon similar Alpine clubs sprang up across Europe. A group of Viennese university students and professors established the Österreichischer Alpenverein (Austrian Alpine Association) in 1862, largely in response to British feats in the Swiss Alps. The Club Alpino Italiano (Italian Alpine Club) was founded in 1863, as was the Schweizer Alpenclub (Swiss Alpine Club). In 1869, the Deutscher Alpenverein (German Alpine Association) started in Munich and within a year had chapters as far north as Hamburg and Berlin. The Club Alpin Français (French Alpine Club) was created in 1874, the same year that the German and Austrian clubs completed their merger and became the supranational German and Austrian Alpine Association. Cadres of cosmopolitan men, representatives of their bourgeois milieu, chartered the various clubs with the intent of introducing their fellow citizens to the Alps. The Swiss viewed the mountains as a national edifice, and its Alpine club sought "to gain a better knowledge of our Alpine landscape, especially with regard to its topography, natural history, and social implications."[29] The French club gathered "all enlightened men who care about the future of France."[30] More egalitarian than the others, the German and Austrian Alpine Association encouraged any man or woman interested in the Alps to join. Theodor Trautwein, an antiquarian book dealer from Munich and charter member of the German club, explained that his organization "demands no particular achievements, only a keen interest in the Alpine World." Unlike the British, who had no qualms about rejecting poseur mountaineers, the German group was expressly "not an association of mountain climbers."[31]

Therein lay the rub. Many mountaineers viewed the Alpine landscape as impervious to the collective currents of modern mass society that eroded individualism. The Alpenverein sought to rescue those left adrift by offering them firm footing in the Alps. With its open membership and dual aims of increasing knowledge about the Alps while facilitating travel to them, the German and Austrian Alpine Association made the mountains accessible to the masses. But doing so aggravated Alpinism's inherent contradiction between the individual and the collective. Contemporaries often expressed this tension in terms of "good" travel, with its connotations of an authentic experience—derived from its root, "travail," which indicated exertion, toil, and suffering—and "bad" tourism, superficial and inauthentic, although such distinctions reflected social conceit more than anything else.³²

Hard-core mountaineers could certainly be snobs. For them, the people who effortlessly rode a cable car to the summit rather than struggled to the top could hardly claim an authentic Alpine experience. Most tourist organizations recognized this paradox and addressed it in different ways. The British seemed to have no problem conflating individual prowess in the mountains with imperial power. Conquering distant places in the name of the empire applied equally well to Swiss peaks as it did to the African savannah and Indian jungle. The German and Austrian Alpine Association, however, found itself facing an altogether different dilemma. Mountaineers endeavored to use the Alps to assuage political divides by inspiring a collective cultural identity among Germans and Austrians while still emphasizing the heralded individuality of mountaineers. That meant, however, that this particular dissonance between the individual and collective would become increasingly shrill as nationalistic tensions in Europe sharpened.

....

"The value of mountains," Edmund Alden explained at the Tenth Annual Meeting of the American Historical Association in 1894, "is dependent on their structure, height, average height, width, length, relation to the lowlands and to the coast, direction, and grouping." He neglected to mention that a mountain's value also depended largely on the meanings that people gave to it. Alden listed how mountains had influenced human society by furnishing natural resources, modifying climate, acting as barriers, and serving as "conservators of the past, as aids in the development of freedom, as powerful stimulants of the imagination." His paper, "Mountains and History," opened the convention's closing session and expressed many of the same sentiments held by Alpine enthusiasts in fin-de-siècle Europe. He also emphasized the importance of topography to historical inquiry and urged his readers to spend fewer hours doing "arm-chair study" and more time rambling through the hills with a knapsack strapped to their backs. He may have been overly optimistic, however, when he commented, "Where the political divisions of historic import lie close together in complicated and perplexing arrangement, as in Germany, Italy, Greece, and various portions of central and southern Europe, it is safe to affirm that the tangle becomes wonderfully straightened out after a journey of several days through the intricate regions."³³

Yet members of the Alpine Association hoped that touring the Alps would untangle the knots of nationhood for Germans and Austrians. In identifying "Alpinists" in this book, I borrow Alden's point that "the term mountaineering does not necessarily signify the scaling [of] the Matterhorn, but rather active life among the mountains."[34] I take "active" to be the consumption of the Alps by tourists and include day hikers and casual sightseers alongside serious climbers and determined scientists. My approach, however, has its limits. The Alps were not blank spaces on the map. People had lived and worked on the slopes for generations.[35] But alpinists from the metropoles were the ones who first transformed the Alps from a landscape of labor to one of leisure. It was urban tourists, not local dairy farmers or salt miners, who attempted to "re-enchant" the backcountry, often while objectifying the peasants who lived there. German and Austrian mountaineers climbed all over Europe's Alpine Arc, but their clubs concentrated efforts on the Eastern Alps and typically in the higher regions above the climatic timberline. This book follows their lead. While the topics of hydropower, agrarian practices, and skiing do appear in the following pages, this study focuses on climbing and hiking activities in the mountains. Last, the labels "German" and "Austrian" give the impression of more concrete identities than was often the case. The Alpine Association used the terms to distinguish between citizens in the German Empire and those in the Austro-Hungarian Dual Monarchy. Contemporary sources used "Austrian" in reference to German-speakers in Cisleithania, the Austrian part of the empire. My study does the same.

The book comprises two parts. Part I, "Opening the Alps, 1860–1918," includes the first four chapters and follows developments in the Eastern Alps from the mid-nineteenth century through the First World War. Part II, "Dominating the Alps, 1919–1939," contains the final three chapters that examine the aftermath of the First World War in the Alps, the explosive growth of mass tourism, and the abuse of the Alpine landscape by the Nazi dictatorship.

The first two chapters center on the second half of the nineteenth century. Chapter 1 analyzes the structural changes to the Eastern Alps, with a focus on economic and environmental transformations. These developments related to larger currents of the *Gründerzeit* (founding years) in Germany and Austria, during which the two countries underwent tremendous political and economic upheaval in the 1860s and 1870s. Chapter 2 shows how bourgeois values colored the Alps in the nineteenth century. The Alps served as a proving ground for individual and social/collective bourgeois notions of progress. But attempts to use the mountains to meld heritage, history, and geography into a progressive "Greater German" identity produced mixed results.

Chapter 3 moves the narrative forward to the early twentieth century, when fears about mountaineering's environmental impact revealed the inherent conflicts of nature tourism. At the same time, the growing popularity of downhill skiing and motorcars on the heights threatened traditional mountaineering norms. Some believed that the only way for climbers to secure the future was through youth education and nature preservation, while they emphasized the importance of the Alps to the strengthening of Germans and Austrians, the Volk. These developments were not innocuous.

The First World War was a turning point in the history of Europe and the Eastern Alps. Long-standing disputes between Italian irredentists and Austrian nationalists erupted in armed conflict in May 1915, creating a battlefront that crossed the Dolomite, Carnic, and Julian Alps. Like the landscape itself, mountaineering ideals were militarized during the conflict. In the aftermath of war, the political reorganization of central Europe recast perceptions of the Alps, particularly among the defeated.

Chapters 5 and 6 examine developments during the interwar years. Political antagonisms and anti-Semitism shaped Alpinism in the 1920s. The tense situation in South Tyrol resulted in restricted or closed access for Germans and Austrians to the Dolomites. Meanwhile, automobile tourism and blockbuster *Bergfilme* (mountain films) popularized the Alps. The number of visitors to the mountains increased exponentially, aggravating mountaineering anxieties. Male chauvinists correlated the growing presence of women to the invasion of machines and condemned both. Most Austrian and some German mountaineers openly regarded socialists and Jews as undesirables and agitated to restrict their access to the Alps. Shadows of the racialized mountains loomed over the political and cultural landscapes in the German and Austrian republics.

The final chapter narrates the story of the Alps under the Nazi dictatorship. Many mountaineers flocked to Hitler's banner, praising his apparent desire to protect the Alps. But not all alpinists had cordial relations with the Nazi Party. Their sense of individualism clashed with Nazi notions of collectivity. The mountains' position on the borderland made their *Gleichschaltung* (synchronization) with the Nazi state in Germany challenging. Only with the *Anschluss* (annexation) in 1938 did the Alps become monuments of Hitler's new order.

This book tells the story of mountaineering and nation building. Others have written about the history of climbing, its evolving techniques and tools, and the institutional history of Alpine clubs. Instead, I explore how Alpinism changed the borderlands both physically and discursively and analyze what these Alpine intersections meant for Germans and Austrians. The Alps staged the struggles that fundamentally shaped Germany and Austria, and yet the mountains get overlooked as places of meaningful historical change. Romantic visions of the Alps as timeless places that history forgot still inform views of the mountains. Others, through eyes of affluence, see the summits as playgrounds, habitats for the very rich, surrounded by picturesque dairy land where poor but apparently contented farmers still reside. Popular literature and Hollywood films frame towering peaks as the setting for tall tales of high adventure, although mountains typically serve as the dramatic backdrop for either the narrative's climax or resolution and little else. Even in scholarly writings, most historians rarely consider the Alps in their analyses; the real historical action seemingly took place elsewhere. However, nation building is not just discursive practice but environmental as well, and that action is on the frontier. Understanding that seemingly distant mountains played a central role in modernization processes compels us to use a different locus when measuring central Europe's historical development. Seeing how civic tourist organizations, like the German and Austrian Alpine Association, transformed the mountains and attempted to turn the Alpine highlands into the German heartland likewise obliges us to reconsider nation-building efforts in both Germany and Austria. German and Austrian mountaineers tried to nationalize a transnational space but in a way that could accommodate pluralistic notions of nationhood and mitigate difference. That these efforts went awry makes their enterprise no less significant.

PART ONE

Opening the Alps, 1860–1918

1

Civilizing the Crags
Urban Adventurers Modernize the Mountains

> The form and the outer appearance of the mountains are caused
> by two factors, namely: the nature of the rocks of which they are composed,
> and the intensity of the forces that shaped them.
>
> —Edouard Desor, *Der Gebirgsbau der Alpen* (1865)

"Wandering across glaciers has lost its harrowing repute and is now reckoned as almost humdrum," Paul Grohmann noted with regret in 1864, "and in recent years many of the high peaks have lost their reputation of remoteness."[1] One of the founders of the Austrian Alpine Association and credited with several challenging first ascents in the Eastern Alps, Grohmann recognized that Alpinism had changed. The following year, Edward Whymper led the famed first ascent of the Matterhorn, an event that traditionally marks the end of Alpinism's so-called golden age. By then daring mountaineers had climbed—or "conquered," as most wrote—nearly all the major peaks across the Alpine Arc. Now came the era of mass tourism in the Alps and with it environmental change on an unprecedented scale. Solitary climbers summiting distant peaks may not have substantially altered nature, but these pioneers opened the way for larger crowds and more systemic transformations of Alpine ecologies.[2] What started as a trickle of tourists and academics in the early 1860s turned into an avalanche of vacationers, investment schemes, and heavy construction projects a generation later. Though located on the fringes of empires, the Alps loomed large in the imaginations of urbanites across Germany and Austria. Voluntary civic groups, most notably the German and Austrian Alpine Association, experienced massive growth as would-be mountaineers swelled the ranks. These civic clubs transformed the landscape and tamed the heights for urban wanderers. A massive network of blazed hiking trails soon crisscrossed the peaks. Bridges, ladders, gangways across glaciers, and chiseled stairs along stone ridges provided greater access to remote places. Highly detailed maps of the Eastern Alps with climbing routes turned mysterious crags into a series of rational contour lines. Clubs published travel aids and certified tour guides to escort novices. With convenience came civilization. Construction sites dotted the peaks. Fancy chalets replaced weather-beaten huts. Through their prodigious efforts, civic mountaineering organizations transformed the economies of the Eastern Alps and changed the "fabric" of the mountains.

• • • • • • • • • • • • •

Contrary to romantic musings on pristine wilderness, the Alps had felt the human touch for millennia. Neolithic hunters, like Ötzi the Iceman, had braved the heights.[3] Roman merchants once frequented the passes along the Brenner watershed. Smelting and mining in the region stretched back to late antiquity. During the medieval and early modern eras, iron ore works stood atop mountains, harnessing the wind and harvesting forests to power the forges. Miners hollowed out mountains and willfully felled trees for pit timber in the tunnels. As early as the twelfth century, local land managers raised concerns about deforestation. By the mid-nineteenth century, around the same time that civic mountaineering clubs first took shape, Alpine forests supplied nearly a quarter of the timber needs for Austria's entire coal mining industry. Clear-cutting hindered reseeding and reduced the biodiversity of the region as monocultures of spruce pine trees replaced mixed stands. The denuded slopes raised the risk of avalanches, mudslides, and seasonal flooding.[4] But dairy farmers, *Senners*, also took advantage of the open hillsides for grazing. In the Alpine provinces of Tyrol, Salzburg, and Carinthia, pastureland accounted for 75 percent of productive land, and most of the population worked in agriculture.[5] Almost the entire social economy of mountain dwellers revolved around the Alpine meadows, the "Alp" or "Alm," where cows, goats, and sheep found fodder.[6] The sheep and goats spent their days on the upper, less fertile fields. Cows occupied the lower, lusher stretches.

Adherence to tradition and internal regulatory mechanisms did seem to maintain a somewhat homeostatic equilibrium on the farmsteads.[7] Scarce resources demanded careful management. Fertile loam was precious, and Alpine cultivation and animal husbandry extended only as far as the highest meadows. The farmers followed a careful system of transhumance, rotating cattle to different portions of the pasture over the course of the summer. A village's "Alp-master" oversaw the schedule. His task was to prevent pastures from going to ruin. In addition to supervising cattle rotation, he checked the stone walls and borders of the fields, dictated the precise day when the wild hay was ready to mow, and kept tabs on both the exact number of cows munching in the fields and their owners. Burghers of the village had the sole rights to pasture, *Kuhrecht*, but laws allowed a farmer to keep only as many cows in the winter as he could put to pasture in the summer, unless he paid for extra hay or owned extensive meadowland.[8]

Although the Alps acted more as a filter than a barrier for much of human history and were more deliberately regulated than most other landscapes, their crags were still forbidding places at the start of the nineteenth century. Even those who lived on the mountains had no love for the barren heights. Since *Senners* often managed several scattered land parcels located at varying altitudes, they held little interest in what lay beyond the vegetation zone. The peaks offered stone, ice, and the "vague idea of endless cold and desolation." "Above the last green mountain terrace of rock, silent as death, sublime as eternity, looms an unknown land," waxed one traveler in the early 1800s, "where man and the nature suited to him find no home."[9] Reaching a summit demanded exertion that was better spent elsewhere, and farmers had little incentive to climb any higher than they needed. Many high places were inaccessible anyway. The few highways skirted around hulking mountains, and most railroads avoided the rugged regions. Only the occasional mule track wound its way along the ridges. People far from the mountains had few options for reaching the Alpine frontier until industrial developments during the first half of the nineteenth century opened the way for the masses.

The onset of mass tourism in the Alps began with coal. Coal commanded central Europe's industrial energy regime. More coal meant greater iron output, steel manufacturing, and more steam-powered machines as factories grew and mines expanded. By the mid-1860s, industrialization and urbanization were gearing into full swing across most of central Europe. The coal and metal sectors dominated Germany's industrialization. Belching smokestacks signified progress as the country evolved into an economic behemoth. Austria's industrial growth was not nearly as impressive as its neighbor's but present nonetheless.[10]

Coal fueled trains, which in turn drove the economic boom of the 1860s. More numerous powerful locomotives required miles of steel track. The expanding web of rail lines soon laced through the Alps, opening remote valleys. Austria's railroad network increased from just over five thousand kilometers in 1869 to more than ten thousand kilometers in 1875.[11] Prior to this expansion, getting to the Eastern Alps from the north was expensive and difficult. People in Hamburg, Hannover, Bremen, or Magdeburg had an easier time traveling to Switzerland and the Western Alps than to Munich. As one traveler observed, hotel guest books in the Swiss Alps had more signatures from northern Germans than did lodges in the German Alps.[12] But new tracks changed that. Distant cities now had better connections to the mountains. The Vienna-to-Munich line with connections to Linz and Salzburg was completed in 1860, the Brennerbahn opened in 1867, and the Salzburg line with connections to Zell am See and Innsbruck began operating in 1875. The Pustertalbahn, which opened 1871, traveled from Villach across Tyrol to Bolzano. Along with the Rudolfsbahn line from Ljubljana to Villach, which began operations a year later, the Salzkammergutbahn and roads over the Stelvio Pass connected the Eastern Alps to ports on the Black Sea, the Adriatic, and the North Sea. Even tourists from across the Atlantic could reach the little towns of Gmünd, Mallnitz, and Heiligenblut.[13] With improved connections, journeys that once took weeks could now be accomplished in days.

Rail networks stimulated heavy industry and contributed to the construction sector's explosive growth. Cities bulged beyond their medieval walls as their populations swelled. New factories, housing tenements, and public buildings crowded the skylines. Rail lines also provided labor mobility. Most European countries had also eased travel restrictions, increasing social movement and the flow of traffic. Migration from the countryside to the city added to the ranks of urban workers. Berlin's population doubled from 1850 to 1871 to over 820,000. Vienna's citizens numbered well over half a million, and Munich contained more than 170,000 residents when their Alpine clubs rose to prominence.[14]

The timing was no mere coincidence. Urbanization set the mountains apart from the metropolis. With prosperity came pollution. Coal fires made cities dark with smoke, soot, and grime. Foul air was the hallmark of urban centers, along with sprawl, squalor, and the lack of sanitation. The lag in waste management technology meant that most people wallowed in their own filth. Only plumes of sulfur dioxide and other chemical by-products covered the stench of open sewers. Citizens suffered. Health ailments were myriad. Horrible living situations provided a haven for infectious disease. Cholera epidemics and typhus outbreaks raged through the cramped quarters with devastating results. Cities acquired reputations as gloomy, dirty, rank, and teeming with the unwashed masses. The Alps formed a natural antithesis to the growing cityscapes across Europe. The unfiltered light of the peaks, crisp glacial air, and seemingly pristine snowfields played against the dark alleyways, suffocating atmosphere, and grimy urban existence. Visions of "empty" mountains drew those who wanted to escape the crowds and expanded the memberships of civic Alpine clubs.[15]

Eduard Fenzl was right when he called the Austrian Alpine Association a "child of its age" during his opening address at the club's first official convention in November 1862.[16] A respected professor of botany at the University of Vienna and the association's first chairman, Fenzl exemplified the club's social composition and academic orientation. His speech lasted for the better part of an hour and exalted the club's future contributions to scientific progress and civic life. He knew his audience. With industrialization, the nineteenth century witnessed the emergence of a confident and influential bourgeoisie in Germany and Austria that steadily grew in size and strength. Economic development brought wealth, and with it the bourgeoisie exuded a sense of achievement and self-importance. The growing preponderance of bourgeois values centered on notions of progress and self-improvement was essential to the success of civic groups, especially Alpine clubs.[17] Numerous voluntary associations now abounded across Germany and Austria. In the 1850s, both regimes had kept a close eye on civic clubs after the turmoil of the 1848 revolutions, and in Austria the organization of overtly political clubs was outlawed. But by the 1860s, restrictions had loosened and the number of voluntary associations grew steadily, particularly among middle-class Germans and Austrians.[18] Most of them belonged to some such club or another. Membership required time and money, particularly for mountaineering clubs. Only people with disposable incomes and room for leisure could afford recreational trips to the Alps.

Railways and wealth provided the means for popular Alpinism, and city living typically the incentive, but organized Alpine tourism first began under the guises of scientific inquiry and social progress. Two men in particular embodied these drives: Eduard Suess, a professor of geology at the University of Vienna, and Franz Senn, a curate in the tiny Tyrolean village of Vent. Senn's interest in tourism stemmed from his concern for his impoverished parishioners. He had already introduced manure and other improvements to increase harvest yields in the early 1860s, but Vent's economic plight remained dire. Such a situation was not unusual for rural inhabitants of central Europe. Although agricultural productivity increased during the mid-1800s as agrarian science improved, new land came into cultivation, markets diversified, and seed prices dropped, most German and Austrian peasants still led hard lives.[19] The Alpine regions fared particularly poorly. Mountain villages also suffered from significant depopulation during the nineteenth century when their young people sought out better, more exciting lives in the cities.

Yet what dairymen in villages like Vent had, which farmers in the Hungarian Alföld, that vast central European plain, or peasants on Junker estates in East Prussia did not, were the Alps. Vent lay to the southwest of Innsbruck, in the Ötztaler Range, among the more massive groups of the Eastern Alps. Wildspitze (3,770 m), one of the highest peaks in the region, towered nearby, providing a sense of majesty to the poor valley. Nestled on the forested floor near the confluence of the Niedertalbach and Rofenache Rivers with a view of the two largest ridges of the mountain group, Vent's panorama was stunning. The inhabitants, however, had not always considered the view inspiring. The high summits felt oppressive. More pragmatically, erosion threatened the tenuous hold of already narrow meadows with poorer, rocky soil. Senn, known to locals as the "Glacier Priest," realized that tourism was the key to long-term prosperity. In the years ahead, thanks partly to Senn's efforts, the high mountains became a "veritable gold mine" for hamlets like Vent, more valuable than the meadows had ever been. "For it is the peaks," as one tourist later observed, "and not the pastures that attract visitors from below to the Alpine glens, and these visitors leave much gold behind them."[20] But for the time being, Senn contemplated ways of generating broader interest in the Alps.

So did Eduard Suess. The young professor was well known among Alpine circles and had firsthand experience wandering in the Alps. In 1854, following a Swiss academic conference for natural scientists in St. Gallen, the twenty-three-year-old Suess and some colleagues hiked to Bregenz, located on Lake Constance about twenty miles away, and then onward over 125 miles across the Arlberg mountain range to Innsbruck. Considering that few Alpine lodges existed and that tracks for the Arlberg line, the first railroad to run east-west across the Alps from Innsbruck to Bludenz, would not be laid for another twenty-six years, the journey must have been arduous. The mountains certainly made an impression on Suess. Upon returning to Vienna, he committed himself to establishing an educational Alpine organization. In the summer of 1856, he participated in the Meeting of German Nature Researchers and Doctors in Vienna, where he proposed the creation of an Alpine Geological Society that would focus on Europe's entire Alpine region, "from Lyon to Vienna." Although the participants held high hopes, the international character of the program proved too cumbersome to manage. Suess left the conference disappointed, still wanting an Alpine research organization. Increasingly, he referenced the Alps in his lectures. One of those lectures was not only interesting enough to keep one particular student, Eduard von Mojsisovics, awake but inspired him as well.[21]

Mojsisovics and two fellow students, Paul Grohmann and Guido von Sommaruga, had been eager to establish an Alpine explorers club ever since they had a few chance encounters with members of the British Alpine Club. Now with a professor's support, the students, all in their early twenties, moved forward with their plans. In the spring of 1862 they recruited respected mountaineers to their cause: lawyer Anton von Ruthner; city councilman Achilles Melingo; and scientist Friedrich Simony. Suess brought along several other academics with professional interests in the Alps. Announcements for the new club ran in newspapers, circulars, and professional journals. The advertisement in the trade publication *Petermann's Geography Notices* was a typical example. The note reminded readers of the British Alpine Club's "daring activities" and of how school textbooks rejoiced that no impenetrable place in the Alps was safe from such intrepid explorers. "But where were the Austrian men?" the advertisement chided. The flier then explained that a group of men had established a club that combined scientific research with bold ventures across the Alps. *Petermann's* editors added a final note, hoping that soon this club would have the strength to match its "English Rival."[22]

Appealing to a certain sense of adventure while challenging Austrian manhood and invoking a degree of national jealousy proved effective. Upon its establishment at Vienna's Academy of Sciences in November 1862, the Austrian Alpine Association (Österreichischer Alpenverein) counted more than 630 members, all men. The Austrian organization was the first Alpine club on the continent. Unlike the British Alpine Club, where a person had to apply for membership, the Austrian Alpine Association maintained open admissions, insofar that a person could pay the rather expensive annual dues. Early members were educated men from Vienna, though some hailed from other Austrian provinces, and a few German academics also joined the ranks. Women were allowed to join but made up only around 4 percent of the total membership in the 1860s, a trend that continued well into the twentieth century. Many were the wives, daughters, or sisters of current members. The Austrian Alpine Association was heavily centralized. Proposals to register chapters in Salzburg and Linz were rejected, and the empire's capital remained the club's center. The club did open small branch offices in a few other cities, but all answered to Vienna.

The club's activities reflected the membership's academic background. Members typically attended monthly meetings, where guest speakers gave lectures on a wide variety of topics related to the Alps. A lecture in February could focus on Alpine flora, and the talk in March might discuss the Alps in literature. Select lectures might be published in the club's proceedings. Several members contributed to the revised edition of Adolf Schaubach's popular series *The German Alps: A Handbook for Travelers*, first produced in the years 1845 to 1847. In most ways, the club behaved like a scholarly association, not a tourist organization. The association's educational orientation partially fulfilled its primary purpose: "To increase knowledge about the Alps, in particular cultivate love for the Austrian Alps, and facilitate travel to the mountains."[23]

Improving travel to the Alps, however, received less attention from the members. They had other priorities. During his opening speech, Fenzl explained that the club sought to develop the "material interests" of the lower classes while increasing the enjoyment of the educated middle-class life and paving the way for specialists to conduct their research.[24] His remark about social improvement applied to situations like Senn's, where tourism could help raise the standard of living. But the chair's appeal fell on deaf ears. The attendees cared mostly for their own scientific research. All were upper-middle class, many were academics, most had a liberal outlook, and they defined the club's orientation. Subsidies to assist improvement projects or building infrastructure, such as hut and trail construction in the mountains, constituted only a marginal part of the club's annual budget during the first decade of its existence. Rather than fund such developments directly, the club took a laissez-faire approach and deferred to private companies and individuals. Such an approach typified late nineteenth-century Viennese liberals, who saw no need to increase government spending. The association paid lip service to assisting those less fortunate, but the members' real interests were self-centered.

Senn learned this lesson the hard way. Thanks to his friendship with Anton von Ruthner, Senn knew of the Alpine Association's formation, though he missed the ceremonies in November. Instead, he traveled to Vienna the following spring with a proposal to establish a trail and mule track over Hochjoch Pass. His project did not seem to have a downside. It would connect the northern part of Tyrol with South Tyrol, thus improving traffic and trade across the mountains while reducing the danger of such travel. The trail would also afford tourists a spectacular view of the region's glaciers. And the landscape's shape itself was conducive for path construction. The locals had already raised a significant amount of money to support the development. That they could not fund the entire project was the reason for Senn's trip to Vienna. There he found himself caught between the centralized nature of the club and the members' liberal orientation.

Since the Austrian Alpine Association did not have individual chapters, Senn had to appeal directly to Vienna for financial assistance. He could not rely on a local Tyrolean chapter, which would likely have had greater appreciation and sympathy for his project. Within the Austrian Empire, significant cultural and political divides existed between the imperial city and its Alpine provinces. The club's hesitation to directly invest in development projects outside the capital reflected in part these differences. At the same time, the Viennese liberals advocated greater individual autonomy. This stance seemed to contradict that club's organization. But to members' thinking, the association's minimal involvement in provincial affairs meant greater independence and self-sufficiency at the local level. Hence the decision to provide Senn with only a small percentage of the funds he requested. To Senn and his supporters, it appeared that the Austrian Alpine Association was all talk but no action.[25]

The club was a lot of talk. Most members were men of the mind, not necessarily men of action. The vast majority of the club's expenses covered its publications and lectures. The association did manage to erect a rustic lodge near Kaprun, located to the north of Grossglockner (3,798 m), the highest mountain east of the Brenner Pass. Built in 1868, the hut was simple, small, and the first erected by a local club. A couple of members used private funds to build Alpine lodges, like Johann Stüdl, a businessman from Prague, who built the Stüdl-Hut on one of the ridges along Grossglockner. But these men were the exception. The membership had discussed organizing the Alpine tour guides. But most tour guides worked part time, farmers or the sons of innkeepers who gave tours to earn some extra money on the side, and organizational efforts proved difficult. Besides, in accordance with their liberal leanings, the majority of members stood against centralized regulation of tour guide operations. Most members were content to attend the monthly meetings, pay their dues, publish articles, and read the journal. With the construction of just one hut and only a handful of trails, the Austrian Alpine Association's existence made little material impact on the Eastern Alps.

The club's apparent disinterest in actual Alpinism frustrated the founders. Mojsisovics, Grohmann, and Sommaruga had wanted something more akin to the British Alpine Club, where membership entailed death-defying adventures in the mountains. Instead, they found themselves listening to long lectures, which was like being back in the classroom. As frustration grew, personality conflicts intensified. Several quit the club. A few had attempted to organize another group in Vienna but with limited success. The association's inaction also aggravated individuals like Senn, who sensed that Vienna's control hindered development in the Alps. Prioritizing the club's publications meant that little money made it to the impoverished mountains. The heavily centralized nature of the association also bothered Senn, who envisioned more independent, self-governing chapters, like those of the Swiss Alpine Club. The factions and discontent within the Austrian Alpine Association pushed those who wanted something different toward Germany. Senn led the way. Dissatisfied with the Viennese, he began contacting friends in Bavaria, including young Karl Hofmann, a law student in Munich, about establishing a new club.

Bavaria provided fertile ground for a new Alpine club. In the late 1860s, mountaineering circles in Munich encompassed an ever-increasing number of citizens. The Bavarian king had recently loosened strict laws governing voluntary associations. Informal groups of Alpine enthusiasts, along with many other sorts of civic groups, took shape and began to meet regularly. In May 1869, Hofmann, Senn, Stüdl, and Theodor Trautwein, a book antiquarian, along with some thirty other men, founded the German Alpine Association (Deutscher Alpenverein) in Munich. Soon thereafter, they placed a newspaper advertisement in most major cities across Germany. They directed their announcement, titled "A Call to All Friends of the Alps," to those "in all German regions on the Danube and on the Rhine, from the North Sea and the Baltic Sea to the Adriatic, who feel a deep rapture for the most marvelous part of Germany, the Alps."[26] The posting resonated across Bavaria, throughout Austria, and even to the north in Prussia. That year witnessed the establishment of additional chapters in Leipzig, Salzburg, Frankfurt, Heidelberg, Stuttgart, Innsbruck, Lienz, Berlin, and Bolzano, as well as in a few other smaller Bavarian and Tyrolean towns.[27] The association elected a central committee headed by club president Gustav von Bezold, a minister in the Bavarian government, issued its bylaws, prepared the annual budget, and organized a press for its publications.

The club's aims were nearly identical to those of its Austrian cousin: increasing knowledge of the Alps while facilitating Alpine travel and exploration. Hofmann, now the deputy-secretary of the German Alpine Association, explained that the heart of the club would lie in the individual sections.[28] Trautwein, editor of the club's journal, further stipulated that the Alpine Association must not be excessively centralized; the organization should instead encourage strong, semi-autonomous chapters, a clear difference between it and the Austrian Alpine Association.[29] The dissimilarity reflected prevailing political realities. The German lands were a patchwork of principalities that would not be unified for another two years, unlike the German-speaking part of the Austrian Empire, which operated under a central government. Individual German chapters were thus responsible for the care and upkeep of their own specific mountain lodges, maintaining independent budgets, and organizing outings to the Alps. Executives deliberately designed the club's decentralization to appease the resilient provincial identities and loyalties across the various German principalities.

They calculated correctly. The German Alpine Association's appeal was powerful. As one member remarked, the Alps themselves served as "natural propaganda."[30] By the end of its first year, the club counted more than 700 members in sixteen chapters. A few years later, when the Hohenzollerns established the German Empire in 1871, the club had 1,584 members (721 Germans and 863 Austrians) in twenty-six chapters (twelve German and fourteen Austrian). Meanwhile, the Austrian Alpine Association's membership hovered steadily around 1,400.

The two clubs shared a number of commonalities, which encouraged talks of merger. From its inception, the German Alpine Association coordinated its activities with the Austrian Alpine Association, as the two organizations had similar aims and shared mountains. However, some Austrians viewed the relationship with misgiving. For them, their German neighbor appeared more as a rival than a collaborator, and several resisted the idea of joining forces. But as the German club's membership quickly matched and then dwarfed that of the Austrian Association, the Viennese acquiesced to a merger. The primary reason for the union was fiscal expediency. By pooling their resources, the clubs could better finance their scientific endeavors, increase publishing capacity, and coordinate hut and trail construction to accommodate the explosive growth in tourism. At the annual conference in Villach, Carinthia, in 1872, German and Austrian members discussed the future name of the combined clubs, suggesting that the society should be called the Central Association for Alpine Affairs (Central Verein für Alpenkunde).[31] But the name did not have quite the same ring and recognition as did the Alpenverein. Some Austrians still resisted the marriage. For reasons that will be explored in greater detail in the next chapter, they perceived the German club as a threat to things Austrian. But by the following year, the majority of members favored the merger, and the two clubs changed their name to the German and Austrian Alpine Association (Deutscher und Österreichischer Alpenverein) in August 1873 at the annual meeting in Bludenz, a town in Austria's Vorarlberg region. Six months later they formally united.[32] More precisely, the German Association incorporated the Austrian Alpine Association as a single constituent chapter, Section Austria, with its office in Vienna.

Now a single, more efficiently governed entity, the association metastasized across Germany and Austria. On its silver anniversary in 1894 (members counted 1869 as the founding year), the club comprised 214 chapters (124 German and 90 Austrian) with 31,358 members (21,262 Germans and 10,096 Austrians). In this period, the Alpine Association grew on average by eight chapters a year. The German membership increased on average 58 percent annually and the Austrian membership 47 percent. The numbers, however, are a bit deceptive. Over the course of a quarter century, the rate of annual growth for German members steadily increased from around 40 percent to upward of 65 percent, while the Austrians gradually dropped from a high of 62 percent down to 32 percent.[33] Suffice it to say that the club grew at an exponential rate. By 1909, the association boasted 86,200 members in 253 German and 131 Austrian chapters. On the eve of the First World War, the club broke the 100,000-membership mark with 72,965 German and 28,595 Austrian members and comprised over 400 chapters. The German and Austrian Alpine Association had rapidly become the largest civic Alpine organization in the world.

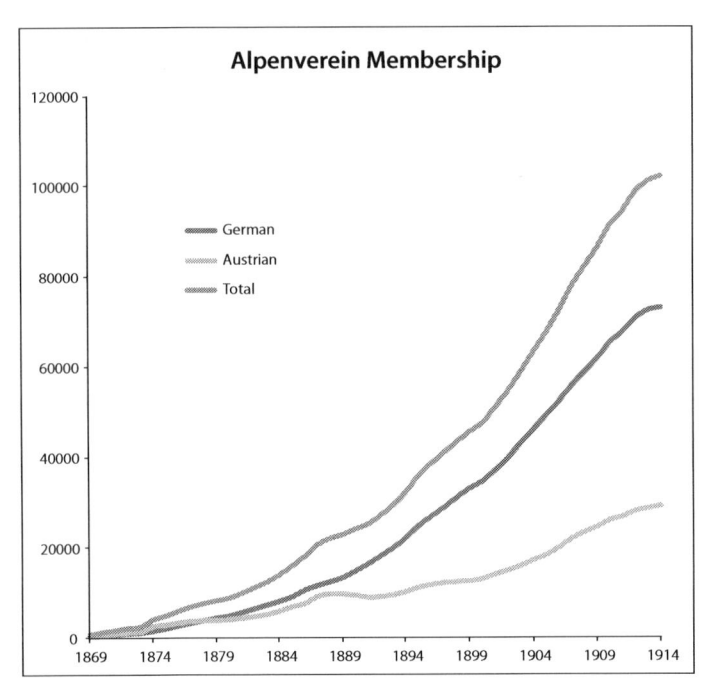

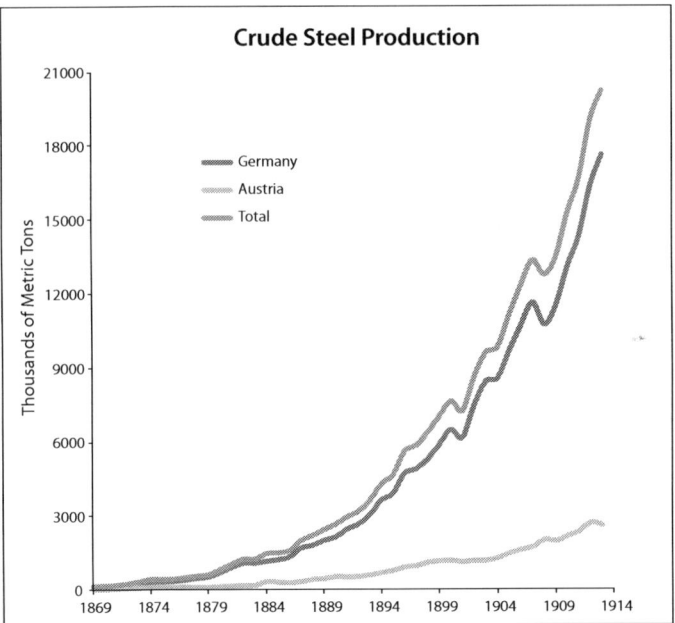

FIGURE 2 Mountaineering and industrialization.
Sources: "Anlagen zur Vereinsgeschichte" and Mitchell,
International Historical Statistics, 507–8.

The merger's success stemmed largely from the similar social composition of the Austrian and German membership. With annual dues as high as ten marks a year in 1900—a sum well beyond a lower-class budget—the club's appeal was selective. Time also acted as a limiting factor. Monthly meetings, summer excursions, and holiday banquets required careers that afforded leisure opportunities. Initially, more than half the membership came from the upper-middle class, and one-third of the membership were midlevel civil servants and merchants. A small percentage worked in agriculture, and a good number were university students.[34] The German and Austrian Alpine Association was the only European Alpine club to allow women to join, although in keeping with its decentralized nature, individual chapters could determine whether or not to accept female members. Vienna and Munich did; Berlin did not. But even with chapters that allowed women to join, the Alpine Association was a male-dominated club and portrayed the mountains as male spaces. Middle-class sensibilities, based on affluence and the need for achievement, formed the basic building blocks for the club's success in the late nineteenth century. Its social composition matched the membership of other tourist clubs, nature associations, and *Heimatschutz* (homeland protection) groups.[35] The club's general social makeup changed little in the years before the First World War, except in overall numbers. Thus a certain social constituency defined the early years of Alpine tourism.

Members also exercised democratic practices, which shaped the club's culture and enhanced its broad appeal. Johannes Emmer, the designated historian of the association in 1895, observed that the original aristocratic tendencies of mountain climbing, as seen with the British, had become "democratized," and these democratic ideals had formed into a common heritage for members of the Alpenverein. All members of the association belonged to a specific chapter, where they had the right to vote on chapter policies, run for office, and participate in chapter activities. Annual meetings in particular afforded members the chance to practice democracy.[36] Every year chapters sent representatives to the annual conference to vote on propositions and elect the executive board and executive committee. The gathering allowed for discussion and debate on the association's activities, provisions, and direction. Every attendee at the annual meeting could submit a petition for consideration at the general meeting. For Germans, this practice of democracy reflected the broader participation in democratic culture. With the creation of the German Empire came direct, equal, universal manhood suffrage in federal elections. Germany's law created the most progressive franchise in Europe. In this sense, the Alpine Association's procedures exemplified the degree to which democratic practices suffused bourgeois civil society. In Austria, where universal male suffrage did not exist until 1907, the Alpine Association kept warm the embers of reform, particularly at the local level.[37]

Chapters remained the center of life and the foundation of the association, as most organizational activities of the Alpenverein took place on the local level. The chapters differed in size, in urban and rural settings, and in political and confessional circumstances. Yet chapters were remarkably similar in their operations. While the chapters' appeal, interests, and vitality reflected local conditions, all chapters conformed to the aims and culture of the association. The most common activity was the monthly chapter meeting. Members gathered, consumed copious amounts of food and drink (Munich held its monthly meetings at the local brewery, Löwenbräukeller—one of the benefits of membership), gave talks about their mountain experiences, and hosted speakers from other chapters. In keeping with the association's aims, the talks were educational, though typically not overly scientific; rather, they were meant for the well-informed layperson. Most lectures discussed a particular peak or range.[38] Talks that featured newfangled technology, like picture slide shows of Alpine adventures, were especially popular. Humorous poems, plays, and caricatures sometimes provided additional entertainment. Nearly every chapter organized outdoor group activities, such as local jaunts in the countryside or longer excursions to the Alps. Sections closest to the mountains, like Munich or Innsbruck, might lead several short tours of nearby peaks throughout the year, whereas chapters in Berlin, Hamburg, or Prague might offer only a single, longer trip during the summer. The lectures, outings, and other events at the local level were intended to create a common culture of Alpinism across Germany and Austria.

The eagerness to share in the Alpine culture adopted curious forms. Most chapters celebrated the Christmas holiday with a banquet or *Winterfest* to close the year. Northern chapters used their annual banquets to reinforce stereotypes about German Alpine culture and to allow members in the north to feel connected to those in the south. Invitations were often printed in Bavarian dialect with typical images of Alpine life. Berlin's *Winterfest* announcement featured dances from the Alpine region and Tyrolean games. Hamburg's invitation to its banquet displayed the image of a woman wearing the traditional dirndl, a distinctive Alpine style of dress, with a mountain peak in the background. These urban members found the rural Alpine culture appealing for what they perceived as its simplicity and quaintness.

Chapters spared no expense to create an "Alpine atmosphere" in the banquet hall. Decorations were extravagant. Large canvases with painted scenes from an Alpine village covered the walls. Props on the stage included Alpine flora along with small Alpine huts and the mountains as the backdrop. Attendees were required to wear the regional dress of Alpine inhabitants. The Berlin chapter mailed to its members explicit directions on what was appropriate to wear—"only that from our mountains!" The banquet committee made clear that the *Winterfest* was not a formal "costume ball." Men were forbidden to wear dress gloves and women were strongly encouraged to "leave their diamonds at home," a nod to the members' social standing. Bicycling and tourist clothing were not allowed. The banquet committee included with its directions a list of books containing pictures of Alpine inhabitants that members could peruse to ensure accuracy of their dress. Attendees could dress as anyone who "played a role in the life of a Tyrolean mountain village," including priests, teachers, local officials, soldiers on vacation, hunters, farmhands, foresters, mountain guides, guesthouse proprietors, Alpine dairymen, and various merchants. The goal was to create the impression that the attendees "really found themselves in an Alpine valley."[39]

That organizing committees went to such measures suggests that a good number of urbanites had no idea what living in the mountains actually meant. These gatherings tell us much about the way many association members viewed the Alpine landscape and its inhabitants. In their portrayals of mountain life, members romanticized the Alps as a realm of recreation rather than as a landscape of labor. While they tried to dress the part, they deemphasized the place of peasants even as the participants extolled the virtues of the rural world and the agrarian way of life. Most of the association's members did not live along the "Alpine backbone." People had toiled in the Alps for generations, but to urban tourists the Alpine landscape appeared unscathed, a static "mausoleum ... of immemorial time."[40] In their eyes, little had changed during the *longue durée* of human habitation in the mountains. Alpine peasants still led subsistence lives in much the same way as their distant forebears, but missing from the celebrations were the real privations that defined the *Senner* world. The association was not the only climbing club to paint the countryside with selective colors, but it was the largest and most influential.

FIGURE 3 Berlin's *Winterfest*. As part of the festivities, attendees could slide down a "mountain shoot" erected on the stage at Kroll's Theater.
Source: *The Graphic*, 18 January 1902.

Individual chapters shaped attitudes about the mountains and played a decisive role in opening the Alps for mass tourism. Expenditures told that story. Huge sums of money went toward construction projects on the mountains. In the forty years from 1874 until the outbreak of the First World War in 1914, chapters built or renovated more than 300 mountain lodges and expanded countless miles of hiking trails, climbing routes, and walking paths. Affluent and influential members provided the club with the clout and resources for such massive enterprises. The Central Range of the Eastern Alps, which cuts across the middle of Austria along an east-west axis through Styria, Carinthia, East Tyrol, and the lower half of North Tyrol, contained the most huts, exceeding 130. The Northern Limestone Range that runs from Vorarlberg across the Bavarian frontier and through Salzburg, Upper Austria, and Lower Austria counted more than 110 huts. The Southern Limestone Range, which occupies most of South Tyrol, the lower edge of Carinthia, and parts of Slovenia, had the fewest huts, with less than seventy. The lower number indicated both the region's tough terrain for building lodges and the increase of non-German-speaking districts that privileged Italian clubs over the Alpenverein.[41] More than half of all the huts were built before 1900. The 1880s in particular witnessed construction on a massive scale all across the Eastern Alps. The acoustics of the landscape amplified the sounds of hammers and saws across the vales; the banging and clamoring echoed for miles.

That the mountains sounded like one large construction zone was no surprise, given that the primary goal for nearly every chapter was to erect a lodge. Building one demonstrated a chapter's affluence and conferred legitimacy. When constituted, and in consultation with the association's executive board, each chapter selected an *Arbeitsgebiet* (work region) in the German or Austrian mountains. A chapter could possess one or several work regions, although each work region belonged to only one chapter. Work regions differed in size and geological characteristics with borders that tended to follow the contours of the landscape and certain natural features such as streams, glaciers, or ravines. Work regions were not laid out in any systematic fashion; rather, they took shape in an ad hoc manner as chapters formed. Some chapters bought the land outright, while others concluded a land-use agreement with the local community. Since local townships tended to view the highlands as "unproductive, meaning without a tax base," they often granted chapters development rights for a nominal fee. The 1901 agreement between Academic Section Graz and

Pitztal, a small Tyrolean community forty miles west of Innsbruck, specified the precise parcel of land the chapter could use. Since Pitztal's zoning board considered the land "worthless," it did not charge a fee for the land, except for a one-time five-kronen payment. However, the agreement stipulated that dairymen maintained their *Kuhrecht* on the nearby pastureland and that only with the zoning board's approval could the section chop firewood from the forest.[42] Most chapters used their *Arbeitsgebiet* for hut construction, a "work region" in every sense. Large chapters, like Munich and Austria, had the financial capacity to construct several lodges. By 1912, Section Austria managed eight Alpine huts. Smaller chapters could petition the association for monetary assistance.

In 1879, as construction escalated along with grant requests, the club organized an ad hoc "Hut and Trail Committee" to wade through the growing pile of subsidy petitions. The association's budget included a line item for lodges and trails, which accounted for 30 percent of the club's annual expenditures. To streamline the process, the committee proposed building codes for paths and lodges. Chapters that applied for grants had to demonstrate how the money supported the club's aims. For trails, a chapter submitted a map together with a short description, a statement from the local municipality that the trail would be for public use, and a budget. The application for hut construction was more exacting. Chapters had to provide detailed blueprints and maps specifying accessibility to fuel sources and potable water, a construction schedule including a budget and how the chapter intended to obtain materials, an environmental impact assessment, a maintenance plan, and the proof of building rights to the land, such as a public record of sale. Should a chapter cease functioning, the club would assume ownership of the hut. In keeping with the club's decentralized nature, chapters that covered their own costs for large projects did not need to receive approval from the committee or even provide notice. However, the executive committee encouraged chapters to keep it informed of such construction projects so that it might prevent possible "collisions" among them.[43]

Collisions occurred anyway. Such clashes betrayed inherent tensions in Alpinism. A number of chapters, Munich and Austria in particular, interpreted the codes as an infringement on the property rights of corporate entities. The state laws on the subject with respect to voluntary associations were vague in this respect. Nonetheless, both Munich and Austria made the argument that the Alpine Association lacked legal standing to "control" chapter affairs. The two largest sections agreed in theory with somehow rationalizing hut and trail subsidies but not the approach. They were the loudest in their criticism, for they had the most to lose. Up to this point, they had been among the largest beneficiaries of the club's money. But as the largest chapters, they also contributed the most to the club's coffers. From their letters, members of both chapters bristled at the thought of capricious supervision over their affairs.[44] Others did not want the executive committee to have any say at all; some proposed that the general assembly should approve and vote on subsidies for new construction. Only with the creation of the permanent Hut and Trail Committee with elected positions, and substantial revisions to the proposed codes, did the membership adopt subsidy regulations. The incident highlighted a fundamental tension within the association: the rights of the chapters versus the rule of the club. Stress mounted as more chapters took shape and as established chapters grew larger and richer. The passage of the subsidy regulations mollified tempers, but the club's systemic volatility remained.

With procedures now in place, chapters petitioned for money in droves. In any given year, the executive committee received more than one hundred requests for assistance.[45] To further standardize the process, the club issued the Klagenfurt Resolution in 1897. This agreement stated that the association would not subsidize more than 50 percent of construction costs, to a maximum of 20,000 marks.[46] But generally, if a chapter made a strong case for its project, it received support. In 1899, the committee awarded 2,000 marks to the Academic Section Berlin for its hut construction in the Wild Kaiser Range. Section Gastein received 850 marks to repair damage to its hut caused by seismic activity. The committee granted Section Innsbruck 950 marks to complete its hiking trail from the Franz Senn Hut to the Dresdner Hut and presented Section Lindau with a whopping 3,000 marks to build its Lindauer Hut in the Vorarlberg Alps. Projects in Tyrol, Salzburg, and Bavaria received the bulk of subsidies, with Tyrol commanding nearly 50 percent of the funds.[47] The committee remarked on the necessity of these projects for tourism in general, as well as on the benefits for the adolescent club.

As the association grew, subsidies became increasingly complicated and politicized. Larger chapters requested more money, since they had more members. Smaller chapters demanded assistance to offset the economic power of chapters like Munich and Section Austria. And not every petition met with success. The committee began rejecting those proposals that it considered unimportant or frivolous, like Section Lungau's

FIGURE 4 The dining salon in the Berliner Hut.
Source: Historisches Alpenarchiv Deutscher Alpenverein, Munich.

application to build a hut on Preber Lake in the state of Salzburg. A number of hotels and guesthouses already bordered the lake. The committee was usually unequivocal in its dismissal. "On no account whatsoever," one committee member fumed, "can I understand how someone would expect to receive money for this petition."[48] Several requests met Lungau's fate.

Even with rejections, the money spent on construction projects was staggering. In 1874, the club had allotted close to 4,300 marks. By 1914, the amount was over fifty times higher at nearly 230,000 marks. In those forty years, the club granted well over 3 million marks in hut and trail subsidies.[49] To put these numbers in perspective, the average annual income in the 1890s was only around 740 marks.[50] Chapters, too, spent vast sums. In 1872, Section Villach spent over 15,500 gulden to build its Villacher Haus in the Carinthian Alps and then 25,000 marks to renovate it in 1908.[51] Most chapters balanced their budgets around hut construction, especially those distant from the Alps. As the years went on, construction costs inflated. The Nürnberger Hut located in the Stubaier Group in Tyrol cost 6,600 marks to erect in 1886. In 1908, the chapter paid 67,000 marks for renovations.[52] But larger chapters could absorb the costs. In 1909, Section Berlin reported that its earnings exceeded 75,000 marks with more than 42,800 marks in expenses and 343,212 marks in

FIGURE 5 The Lamsenjoch Lodge.
Source: Historisches Alpenarchiv Deutscher Alpenverein, Munich.

its reserves.[53] No wonder that the Berliner Hut in Austria's Zillertal Range was among the most extravagant lodges in the Alps, complete with chandeliers, a dining salon, sixty individual rooms, a hundred mattresses, and a glass veranda. In the decade before the First World War, the chapter added a darkroom for photographers, a post office, storage sheds for gear, a telephone connection to the valley below, and hydroelectric-generated power for the lights.

The Berliner Hut was excessive even by luxury hotel standards. Most lodges were modest in size and appearance. Before its renovations, Berlin's lodge was more typical, like Section Innsbruck's Franz Senn Hut, built in 1885. The first story included a cramped kitchen with a wood-burning stove, an open dining room with several seven-foot-long tables and benches, and a few private bedrooms. A narrow wooden staircase outside led to the attic, which also served as sleeping quarters for a dozen or so people. Behind the lodge stood a storage shed and a simple latrine.[54] Other building projects, such as the Lamsenjoch Lodge in the Karwendel Range and the Kemptner Hut in the Allgäu Alps, used similar blueprints.

Hut construction fueled the tourism industry. Alpine architects drew up blueprints. Lumberyards and quarries prepared the building materials. Construction firms transported timber and stone to high altitudes and

FIGURE 6 The Kemptner Hut.
Source: Historisches Alpenarchiv Deutscher Alpenverein, Munich.

provided the labor to put it all together. Engineers determined location and layout, often based on water access, although they sometimes failed to account for avalanche routes in their calculations. But then insurance companies offered coverage in the event of natural disasters or vandalism. By the early 1900s, an increasing number of chapters hired part-time caretakers to staff the huts during tourist season. More huts meant more tenderfoot travelers in the Alps. Under the auspices of the association, tour guide operations became better organized. The club assigned guides to specific regions and eventually required that guides attend training seminars. In 1893, the association offered fifty-three courses with 1,171 participants. Only certified guides received recognition (and publicity) from the club. Travel agencies saw profits on the horizon. New shops went up that advertised all-inclusive trips to the mountains, designed for the single adventurer, young couples, or the annual family vacation.

As construction techniques improved, chapters sought to build huts at higher altitudes and established trails across the more desolate "wastelands of the high regions."[55] Yet even as builders gained proficiency with experience, constructing any hut was still a major feat. Men and mules hauled materials on their backs to nearly two thousand meters above sea level. Erratic weather patterns confounded building schedules. Workers might face heat exhaustion one day and hypothermia the next. Precipitation could be disastrous. The summers in the late 1870s and early 1880s were particularly wet. Even in July, snow sometimes appeared at the higher elevations.

To celebrate success, chapters threw huge parties to debut a new hut. In August 1894, Section Freiburg hosted a banquet and invited local dignitaries up to the dedication of its new lodge, the Freiburger Hut in the Vorarlberg Alps. The festivities included fireworks and live music, despite cloudy skies and periodic light drizzle. An official from Bludenz remarked that by their efforts, the "Freiburgers have earned the *Heimatrecht* [right of residence] in our Alps." The next day, over 180 people gathered for the hut's christening, which included a long retelling of the hut's construction. Participants toured the hut and found it "small and simple, but pretty nice and practical." The parlor had room for twenty people, and the guests particularly enjoyed the imported cuckoo clock from the Black Forest. Then the rain returned and the party ended.[56]

When Section Berlin completed an addition to the Berliner Hut in 1892, the party lasted for four days. The program included food, drink, music, songs, dance, a light show on the peak, and fireworks. A lengthy poem commemorating the occasion was written with the urban tourist in mind. The poem was odd; it explained, in rhyming sextain, the debates behind the renovations. According to the author, upon realizing that the flood of tourists to the Alps filled the hut to the rafters, the chapter decided to enlarge the building. Draftsmen presented sketches of a new structure that had all the comforts of home. But sharp conflict arose over the financing. In the end, members agreed to issue bonds and borrow. "The great states borrow for cannons, for soldiers," the poem rationalized, "then we borrow, when we borrow, we borrow for Nature!" The next stanzas then exalted what the chapter's gold had wrought: a big house in the Alps that offered "peace, joy, and merriment." The poem announced that if the time should come when the new lodge proved too small, "then Section Berlin moving quick and without delay will just build a bigger house!"[57]

Besides facilitating tourism, hut construction contributed to the latest scientific research. Some lodges served as labs for wandering geologists and meteorologists. Classifying and ordering the Alps was part of the Alpine Association's civilizing mission. Scientific methodology and detailed research divided and tamed the mountains. The club prided itself as a "nurturing haven of science."[58] Articles in the first volumes of

FIGURE 7 Berliner Hut renovations. *Above*, the Berliner Hut in 1874; *below*, the hut in 1892. Source: Historisches Alpenarchiv Deutscher Alpenverein, Munich.

its journal on Alpine botany, geology, mineralogy, meteorology, and glaciers gave the association a scientific hue.

Scientific research on the Alps reflected the broader developments within the natural sciences during the late nineteenth century. In addition to achievements in medicine, biology, and chemistry, German and Austrian scientists led the field in Alpine studies. Most research projects

FIGURE 8 Scientists taking core samples of a glacier in the Ötztaler Alps, 1911.
Source: Historisches Alpenarchiv Österreichischer Alpenverein, Innsbruck.

examined glaciers. The ice giants fascinated scientists, who spent summers poking and prodding them. Some teams placed markers on a glacier's restless tongue to track its creep up and down the moraines. Others drilled into a glacier's body to measure its depth and study its core.[59] These studies marked the first serious undertakings into Alpine climatology. By measuring glaciers, the "sum effects of various and slow acting causes," researchers could better understand climate change. According to forward-thinking newspaper editors, these studies were of the highest importance because they concerned the security of future generations.[60]

Interest in the climate, along with improvements in hut construction, spurred the building of meteorological observation towers in the Alps during the 1890s. Here also the Alpine Association took the initiative. Since the club worked on mountaintops, constructing weather stations was a natural fit. The stations benefited both science and tourism. Meteorologists used the facilities to conduct research; travelers relied on the towers for weather predictions. With support from the Bavarian government, Austrian state, and various academic institutions, the club built high-altitude observation posts in Carinthia and Salzburg. The association constructed Europe's highest such station at three thousand meters on the Sonnblick Peak, located near the spa town of Bad Gastein in Salzburg.[61] The club's most notable station was its observatory on the Zugspitze, Germany's highest mountain. Members first proposed the project to the Bavarian Chamber of Deputies in the spring of 1898. Although the chamber supported the construction in the name of science, some raised concern about the feasibility of the project. The minister of the Interior reminded the deputies that the state's budget already contained provisions for additional weather balloons, the standard equipment that meteorologists used. He was still inclined to support the construction but doubted that the club could staff the facility. "Who would be willing to spend four winter months," he asked, "indeed even longer, locked up on the Zugspitze?" His question was rhetorical, but the point was well taken.[62] Further reservations surfaced about the project's hidden costs, such as maintaining telephone connections to the observatory. A few doubters questioned the reliability of the instruments in the extreme environment and suspected that the data would be corrupt. Others simply opposed spending state funds on the construction and planned to make it an issue in Bavaria's upcoming parliamentary elections.[63] The skeptics won the day.

Throughout the summer, scientists campaigned for the observatory. They sent letters to government officials and published articles in various newsletters. Supporters praised the advances in science that the station would bring. They provided a detailed analysis of how the Zugspitze's location and topography set it apart from Sonnblick and Säntis. Others outlined the shortcomings of low-floating balloons. Since the weather "comes from above," clearly the heights offered unparalleled advantages. Some catered to German pride. As the highest peak in Germany, the Zugspitze deserved to be "crowned" with such a station. One patron took a different tack and advocated the construction for health reasons:

FIGURE 9 The Münchner Haus and observatory. *Above*, sketch for the Münchner Haus, 1895; *below*, the completed Münchner Haus and observatory in 1910. Source: Historisches Alpenarchiv Deutscher Alpenverein, Munich.

since rheumatism and respiratory ailments were so prevalent in southern Bavaria, knowing weather patterns would improve the quality of life for those sufferers.[64] Personal well-being stretched the argument a bit, but the club's efforts paid off. The leaders of the Center and Liberal Parties, the two largest parties in Bavaria, eventually supported the project, as did other "highly placed people." In June 1900, the association entered into a contract with the Bavarian government, and construction on the tower began.[65]

Development in the Alps fulfilled Suess's scientific aims and Senn's hopes of social improvement. When a local newspaper in Innsbruck sang the Alpine Association's praises in 1876, it did so to the tune of progress. From the editors' perspective, the club's efforts brought prosperity, "and prosperity affords development, and development generates progress."⁶⁶ The editorial implied development in a moral sense, as well as economic. Money from tourism allowed formerly isolated Alpine villages to build better schools and afford professional teachers and opened insular places to the wider world. Huts and paths stood as a testament to material improvement. They made "desolate" land useful and invited further development. The association's members congratulated themselves for introducing "backward" villagers to the modern world and continued to work with missionary zeal.

Karl Baedeker's well-known *Handbook for Travelers* series praised the association's efforts for upgrading the mountains. The *Eastern Alps* volume was in its thirty-fourth German edition and twelfth English edition in 1911. The book contained numerous maps, current exchange rates, timetables, and hotel ratings, along with a complete list of trails, huts, and local attractions. For those unfamiliar with Alpine etiquette, regulations, and insider knowledge, Baedeker's guide proved indispensable. "The accommodation afforded by the chalets of the Alpine herdsmen is generally far inferior to that of the club-huts," the 1911 edition advised. "Whatever poetry there may theoretically be in a bed of hay, the traveler will find that the piercing cold night-air through abundant apertures, the jangling of cow-bells, and the grunting of pigs are little conducive to refreshing slumber." Baedeker noted that the popularity of the Eastern Alps had grown because of the efforts of the "public-spirited" German and Austrian Alpine Association, and he congratulated the club for increasing the pleasures of the higher ascents.⁶⁷ Many others agreed. As one writer believed, "The mountains would lose half their charm if the small huts, the tokens of man's supremacy amidst the most savage wastes, were absent." Even Leslie Stephen felt that the beauty of the Alps was "amazingly increased when a weather-stained chalet rises in the foreground."⁶⁸

Not all celebrated the changing landscape. Some, like Paul Grohmann, felt that the mystique of the mountains had diminished. When the Austrian climbers Robert Hans Schmitt and Johannes Sautner conquered the last impregnable peak in the Alps, the Fünffingerspitze (Five Finger Peak) in 1890, they closed an era. Located about twenty miles east of Bolzano in South Tyrol, the peak was infamous among climbing circles; its highest summit, the middle finger, stood as a defiant salute to the defeated. Schmitt and Sautner's triumph caused a sensation. Humans had wrested Europe's upper reaches.⁶⁹ Serious alpinists despaired. All that now remained for them in the Alps were technical challenges, such as conquering the Eiger's treacherous north face. But casual hikers and amateur climbers rejoiced.

Outdoor organizations like the German and Austrian Alpine Association exuded confidence that scientific inquiry into the making of mountains, along with economic aid for impoverished Alpine vales, would somehow direct the reckless energies of modernization toward more enlightened ends. Largely through the efforts of the Alpine Association and countless anonymous individuals, tourism in the Eastern Alps now rivaled that in the Western Alps. Lands perceived as "wild" and populated by "backward" people were "improved" and "modernized" by urban alpinists. Impoverished Alpine hamlets became prosperous villages, and even though mountain inhabitants played an equally important role in the service industry to mass tourism, hard-working dairy farmers appeared like props on nature's stage. Members of the Alpine Association remade the mountains in their own image and then disseminated that through its conduit of chapters. Physical alterations changed how people perceived the landscape. Mass tourism transformed the ecologies of the Alps. Where agriculture had once regulated the tempo of life, now tourism set the seasons. Yet skirmishes of all sorts accompanied the opening to the Alps. As we shall see in the next two chapters, tourism and technology inscribed new pressures on the palisades, the effects of which can still be felt today.

2

Peaks and Progress

Alpine Reveries, Bourgeois Dreams, and National Fantasies

> Insofar that we might thus see the whole of mountain building
> as the solidification process of Earth's surface.
>
> —Eduard Suess, *Die Entstehung der Alpen* (1875)

The Alpine allure was powerful in the late nineteenth century. Aided by improved railway connections between the city and the countryside, millions visited the Alps each year seeking elation in elevation. Some found serenity in mountain climbing. The rugged terrain at once tested the bounds of human frailty and bestowed strength. Some enjoyed the danger of death on the heights. Many praised the recuperative qualities of the mountain's rarefied air, whose properties reportedly healed feeble lungs, disturbed minds, and troubled hearts. The Alps served as the sanatorium for the human condition. Others viewed the mountains as the ultimate natural realm, home to untamed nature, a wild arena, and a sacred, ancient place where men were made. These were intimate spaces. For those tired of crowded cities, lonely crags offered solitary joy. "The single wanderer," one alpinist mused, "can forget the world and dream."[1] In his famous novel *The Magic Mountain*, Thomas Mann compared the effects of Alpine tourism to the powers of time. Like time, space induced forgetfulness. Standing on the summit placed a person "in a free and pristine state—indeed, in but a moment it can turn a pedant and philistine into something like a vagabond."[2] In the Alps, bourgeois dreams of vagabond wandering became possible. Fantasies of escape and freedom drove many middle-class men, and a few women, into the embrace of the mountains.

Standing on the summit feeling like a vagabond was meant to be temporary; the effects, however, were not. Tourists could experience the (civilized) Alps and then return home fortified from their time on the heights. Outdoor organizations spent terrific sums of money to manicure the mountains and make that temporary stay as comfortable as possible. Many clubs did so because they viewed mountaineering as necessary for individual improvement. The Alpine Association in particular defined Alpinism as a key component to bourgeois notions of *Bildung* (personal edification). At the Section Augsburg meeting in 1870, a member gave a typical speech titled "Alpine Travel as Means of Intellectual Development," which underscored a particular bourgeois understanding of the natural world, especially the "cult of individuality" that nineteenth-century liberalism promoted.[3] Working-class organizations, on the other hand, viewed Alpinism as a cure-all for proletarian ills. In any case, touring the Alps provided a coping mechanism for weary urbanites. A rigorous climb supposedly steeled a person to withstand better the traumas of modernity, be that sitting at a desk or standing on the factory floor.

Mountains did more than just soothe. For the Alpine Association, bringing people to the Alps not only developed individuals but also cultivated a particular understanding of German nationhood; the two worked in tandem. These German and Austrian Alpine enthusiasts did not think in terms of regional identities. They did not want a regional answer to the question of German nationhood. Rather, they turned the traditional ideas of *Heimat* and regional loyalties—being Bavarian or Tyrolean first and German or Austrian second, for example—on their heads by using tourism in the Alps to construct a Greater German cultural identity.

But these Alpine apostles did not convert all with their gospel of progress.[4] Opening up the mountains invited discord. When the culture wars between Protestants and Catholics raged in Germany in the 1870s, clerical hostility in Austria toward the association turned ugly. Critics in Austria's western provinces accused German climbers of importing a hidden Prussian-Protestant agenda and of colonizing the Alps in the name of Bismarck. Other Austrian tourist organizations charged the Alpine Association with not being Austrian enough. For a region where states and nations had never coincided, the club's portrayal of the Alps as the natural expression of a pluralistic German nation garnered uneven acceptance. The result was a fractured landscape where resentments festered amid hopes for unity.

· · · · · · · · · · · · ·

Mountaineers believed that Alpinism offset the negative influences of a "modern livelihood."[5] A common thread running throughout many climbing narratives was the desire to escape the modern world—the city—and rediscover "pure existence" in the Alps. Mountaineers often contrasted the organic empowerment of nature against the "loud and empty machinery" of the city, a curious comparison given the enthusiasm for heavy construction in the Alps.[6] Nevertheless, Alpine enthusiasts placed the mountains as a "powerful counterweight" against the metropolis.[7] Most contrasted the dark, stifling atmosphere of the city with the crisp air and brilliant light on the peaks: "A large city. How the street appears bustling with a thousand quick feet, the shouts, raves, wheezes, roars; chaos, in which people dance like marionettes on a thousand invisible threads of their life's duties. A gloomy, diseased, discolored atmosphere covers all; and a single face is in all the pasty, careworn faces: haste, miserable discontent, insatiable craving for what they call Culture. And they call their city the precious temple of progress, the heaven and hell of modern life, the shrine of the Nation!"[8] Plenty of critics throughout Germany and Austria gestured to the city as the symbol of modernity's depravity. They believed that cities bred corruption and anguish. The crowded streets and the crushing urban environment created the malnourished, modern man, starving for something more meaningful in life.

Compared with urban torpor, existence on the heights was invigorating. The mountain atmosphere "roused the drowsy burgher" to action.[9] The glacial air also served a medicinal purpose. Doctors praised the Alps for their "virtuous purity" and their rejuvenating effects.[10] Tuberculosis, a common affliction in the nineteenth century, brought affluent people to the mountains, as did asthma, bronchitis, and other respiratory ailments. The Swiss Alps were famous for their mineral springs around which exclusive sanatoriums and hotels were built.[11] Advertisements for health resorts and spas sold the Alps as a pristine world.

To fully benefit from the Alps, one had to physically experience nature in the raw. The path to enlightenment and well-being was not easy. While the peaks were conducive to medication and invited a person to linger, the steeps required *Kampf* (struggle). Climbing the heights demanded courage, strength, energy, and the will to victory. "It is true that there [on the peak] dwells peace ... and solitude," one German climber observed, "but for us men there is only one path to there: the hard struggle."[12] The battle to reach the summit was as seductive for bourgeois mountain climbers as the peace and solitude of the peaks. For die-hard alpinists, the joy of struggle was an essential element of genuine Alpinism.[13] Only through one's own strength and physical effort could a person reach the pinnacle. The greater the exertion, the more meaningful the experience.

Members of the Alpenverein contrasted action in the Alps with their dull lives at home. Some admitted to reveling in Alpine daydreams while sitting at work, musing about a place where "Sunday lasts forever."[14] A never-ending Sunday, a day without work, in the mountains was their ultimate fantasy. Yet these longings betrayed the vanity of urban living and a certain bourgeois conceit. Middle-class mountaineers generally lived sedentary lives of comfort and financial security. That they could afford travel to the Alps reflected affluent income levels and the sort of jobs that made weekend travel or summer vacations possible. They were not farmers. The white-collar world took a thoroughly urban view of the heights. Only someone from the city would see the Alps as a playground and overlook locals toiling to scratch out a living on the slopes. Urban adventurers were neither coal miners nor factory workers. None faced real hazards on the job. They might suffer mental fatigue but never muscle soreness from hard manual labor, much less the loss of life or limb. Bourgeois tourists could boast so freely about the sheer exertion to climb a mountain because they faced such low physical demands in their daily lives.

Working-class narratives about the Alps, on the other hand, rarely discussed the struggle to the summit. Proletariats did find emancipation atop mountains, though their freedom was of a different sort. For most of the 1800s, strict government censorship had impeded the establishment of socialist clubs in Germany and Austria. But in the last decade of the nineteenth century, state regulations relaxed and voluntary worker organizations emerged to form what Vernon Lidtke called an "alternative culture" in both countries.[15] Such was the case with nature organizations. Workers created their own alternatives to middle-class outdoor leisure. Social Democrats in Vienna established the Naturfreunde (Friends of Nature) in 1895, which later spread to Germany in 1905 and then on to Switzerland and other European countries. Like the Alpine Association, the Friends of Nature comprised constituent chapters, held meetings, published a newsletter, built lodges, and organized outings. Instead of the salutatory "*Berg heil* [hail mountains]!" of the Alpine Association, its members addressed each other with "*Berg frei* [free mountains]!" The relationship between the bourgeois association and the socialist Friends of Nature vacillated in the years before the First World War. The respective executive boards acted in a professional manner toward each other; however, local chapters of the two clubs frequently quarreled, typically because they refused to share mountains.[16]

Both groups enjoyed the benefits of Alpinism but did not share intended beneficiaries. Rather than a retreat for those who suffered middle-class malcontent, the Friends of Nature presented the mountains as a haven from working-class woes. By 1914 the organization had more than ten thousand members. Annual dues were purposely low, only two kronen in 1901. Club officers hoped that the discounted fees would appeal broadly to workers and induce them to get out of the "dead-end atmosphere" of bars and into the "clean air" of the mountains.[17] "What could be better and cheaper," one member asked, "than drinking the air and sunshine here above, and so strengthening one's limbs anew for the factory?"[18] Proletariat hikers frequently contrasted the peace on the heights with the buzz, whir, and worries of the workshop. The purity of nature cleansed the body of factory filth. Wandering around the wild with like-minded people deepened camaraderie among laborers, hence the club's motto: "Hand in Hand through the Mountains and the Land."

Working-class nature narratives did not expressly concern themselves with *Bildung*. That was for the bourgeoisie. Instead, standing aloft mountains gave workers back their humanity. "As for us," one worker declared, "we do not want to be tools and dead equipment." The middle class escaped the machinery of the city; workers fled from being machines. Making the Alps accessible was of vital importance. The stakes were escape from bondage. Thus "true friends of the mountain world" were also "good social democrats." Not only could workers find emancipation on the peaks, but this freedom was transferable. "Free mountains" descended down to the valley, creating "free peoples" and a "free world" for humanity.[19]

Freedom, in whatever form, came at a price. In the Alps, danger was paramount. The mountains were unforgiving; death was only a misstep away. One alpinist warned about "losing your grip on handholds and footholds, slipping on stone, ice or grass, falling rocks and lightning strikes ... along with sudden falls, avalanches, and extreme weather."[20] Even with blazed trails and experienced tour guides, climbing a mountain was a serious undertaking that required physical fitness and mental alertness. Ascending the steep mountain face, dangling above the void, and crossing the deep splits in a glacier by means of a flimsy ladder required calm nerves. "The border between existence and nonexistence," one mountaineer wrote, "is in many spots only a foot wide."[21] Death was ubiquitous, but its proximity nurtured a deep sense of comradeship among mountain climbers. A person often relied on partners

FIGURE 10 Hiking on Plattenjoch.
Source: Historisches Alpenarchiv Deutscher Alpenverein, Munich.

to live. After an especially perilous climb, one young man remarked on the profound affection he felt for his climbing companions, which grew out of the dangers they faced. Another mountaineer described a frightening incident when a storm threatened: "Surging fog blew in from the north and south and swelled and pooled around us into an immeasurable vastness. We silently grasped hands. Each read in the other's eyes that mountain friendship lasts through life and death!"[22]

The close embrace of death acted as an Alpine aphrodisiac, but selectively so. Working-class wanderers rarely talked about putting one's life in danger. Bourgeois climbers, however, described the acute sense of awareness that comes from a brush with death. Even as peril forged bonds among alpinists, it strengthened an individual's sense of self. The quest to conquer the mountain helped a person "to realize, test, and develop one's own slumbering strength"—"in other words," one contributor to the club's newsletter wrote, "the striving for self-realization and self-improvement."[23] This focus on individuality defined middle-class narratives. Climbing was a formative and deeply personal experience, all the more so because of danger and death.

Alpine stories were not simply tales about conquering mountains. Like an ersatz bildungsroman, the accounts described a mental and physical transformation that took place as one overcame adversity to reach the peak. The Alps educated individuals in ways that the pedagogy of grammar schools and universities never could. The lessons were formative. One young man remembered a day he and some friends spent in the Alps. The afternoon was "full of dangers and full of pleasantly tiring progress," he reminisced. "We indulged in the magic of the magnificent landscape, which had born, bred, and made us into men, and which we carry deep within us."[24] This was the power of the Alpine experience; the mountains made the man.

Alpinism contributed to the bourgeois *Bildungsideal* in other ways besides danger and death. A large number of the early members of the German and Austrian Alpine Association were academics, which may explain why half the club's budget covered publishing costs. Given the length of the club's journal—the first issue alone numbered more than seven hundred pages—and the strict schedule for the monthly newsletter, 50 percent of the budget seemed modest. The journal was professional and clearly intended to be educational. For a time, the publication included a regularly updated bibliography on all things Alpine. Often the journal arrived on doorsteps with new maps of a particular mountain attached. Throughout the 1870s, subscribers could read the annual report, find new members, and review chapter activities. When the sheer size of the club became unmanageable for the editors, they cut the updates from the journal and placed them in a newsletter. The monthly mailing included short essays, letters from members, pages of advertisements that illustrated the growth of the tourism industry, and obituaries. Chapters also published newsletters, which typically imitated the association's circulars. The chapter chairman outlined upcoming events, members contributed stories, and local businesses promoted their mountain gear. The journals, and especially the newsletters, offered open forums for informed discussions about climbing techniques, hiking routes, and equipment reviews.

Other publishers picked up on the trend. Soon the association's journal and newsletter were the big stars in a large constellation of Alpine weeklies. *The Austrian Alpine Newspaper* began publication in the late 1800s, as did the version in Germany. The *Alpenfreund* and the *Alpenland Monatshefte* appeared around the same time. When smaller, local clubs took shape, like the Niederösterreichischen Gebirgsverein

(Lower Austrian Mountain Association), their mailings added to the mix.

Widely circulated publications played a crucial role in broadening common knowledge about the Alps. The world of print also helped sell the mountains to the general public as consumer goods. Marketing executives knew that readers were consumers. Advertisements for clothing and equipment became increasingly enticing. As circulation widened, certain outdoor clothing brands became fashionable, particularly for men who wanted to appear rugged and tough, especially if they were soft city folk leading safe lives. Tales of daring climbs, scientific commentaries on exotic flora, and sketches of sweeping vistas induced more tourists to visit the Alps. For the right price, anyone could share in the Alpine experience. The association's publications were just as important as trains in transporting people to the Alps. Heightened awareness increased the attraction of the heights.

The growing body of literature found a home in the newly established Alpine Library. In 1900, the explorer and adventurer Willi Rickmer-Rickmers donated his collection of nearly five thousand volumes of books, maps, and pictures to the association. His endowment formed the core of the library, located in Munich. Two years later, the collection held fifteen thousand books, two thousand travel maps, five hundred panorama maps, and more than ten thousand pictures.[25] With generous contributions, the Alpine Library grew in size and importance. Anyone could borrow books, plan trips with the maps, or simply spend an afternoon perusing pictures. Publications by English explorers, French writers, Italian climbers, and American observers filled the shelves.[26] The proliferation of books and tourist magazines on the Alps contributed to the growing body of Alpine knowledge. Climbing parlance entered everyday vocabulary. The various mountain subgroups and their principal peaks became familiar terrain for urbanites, something that had not been true a generation earlier.

In 1911, the Alpine Museum opened next door to the recently built Deutsches Museum, located on the Isar River in Munich. The Alpine Museum displayed paintings, pictures, climbing equipment, scientific paraphernalia, mineral samples, antique maps, models of huts, and other Alpine affects. It told the story of progress. Like its neighbor, the purpose of the association's collection was for education. It brought the mountains to the city. After touring the exhibits, a person could "speak with full appreciation about modern Alpine regional history."[27] Although small, the collections attracted more than ten thousand people in the first four months. In another four months, the number more than doubled to twenty-five thousand.[28]

Mountaineers had institutionalized the Alps. The library and museum worked in tandem with the Alpine experience. As one alpinist concluded, "These days, knowing the Alps is considered as an imperative for general Bildung."[29] Yet simply appreciating the mountains was not enough to sustain a person. A devoted climber should "learn about and understand its [the mountain's] mysterious works, so that when he is out in the open air he sees and learns not just as a sight-seer but as a knowledgeable and progressive thinking lay person."[30] This writer drew a critical distinction between the boorish vacationer and the cultured alpinist. For the Alpine Association, being a "progressive thinking" mountaineer also meant viewing the Alpine world as a means of "edification for the entire Volk."[31]

. . . .

"The founding of the Association was not only a time of growing enthusiasm for the Alpine world," one mountaineer recalled during Section Austria's fiftieth anniversary celebration; "it was also a moment of political renewal."[32] That was a generous way to describe a time of civil war and political partition. Otto von Bismarck's Kleindeutsch (Lesser German) approach had divided Germans and Austrians in 1866, following the short Austro-Prussian War, and created a German state separate from the Habsburg Empire in 1871. After this, Austrians faced, as the Social Democrat leader Otto Bauer later explained, "a conflict between our Austrian and our German character."[33] Some Germans wavered between their allegiance to the Prussian-dominated Kaiserreich (German Empire) and loyalty to a provincial community. Many Germans, particularly liberals, considered Austria part of Germany. The states in southern Germany were especially sympathetic toward their neighbor. Editors of the German club's first journal attempted to mediate division, asserting that "the German Alpine Association does not recognize political boundaries—just as it gradually intends to bring the entire German Alps into the realm of its research, so should the club, on the other hand, embrace all the German peoples who inhabit Germany or German-Austria."[34] The club's perception of the Alps envisioned Austria, the South German states, the free cities, and other German provinces on equal terms with Prussia. Austrian and German alpinists saw the mountains (and themselves) as the physical bond between the two countries.

One did not have to imagine the Alps. Real stone fastened together Germans and Austrians in an ancient, elemental way. Many mountaineers claimed the Alps as the universal symbol of *Deutschtum* (Germandom), a broad cultural community tied to a distinct landscape. Yet promoting a Greater German identity seemed at odds with the newly minted German state. Somehow, love for the mountains translated to devotion to one's nation, although how one made that discursive connection was left deliberately vague. Two points were clear to the Alpenverein: Austrians and Germans belonged together; and the Alps made that so.

Constructing identity through nature was something familiar to Germans and Austrians in the late nineteenth century. Essayists drew connections between particular features of the natural landscape and the peculiar characteristics of its inhabitants. Wilhelm Heinrich Riehl articulated such ideas in his famous work *The Natural History of the German People*. Similar books included W. Klein's *Alpinism and Character* and J. Kutzen's *The German Land in Its Characteristic Traits and Its Relationship to Human History and Life*, among many others. Klein identified Alpinism as an ethical system while Kutzen wanted to "stimulate patriotic knowledge and a patriotic way of thinking" by understanding the "nature of our fatherland and its influence on the history and life of humanity."[35] Meanwhile, local *Heimat* groups celebrated nature as a testament to regional distinctiveness together with a national identity. Both the Alpine Association and *Heimat* groups used the natural world to articulate a certain sense of belonging, but the association used the mountains to inspire a passion for the homeland in its broadest cultural sense. A person did not have to live in the mountains to appreciate them or feel a sense of *Heimat* when visiting them. For members of the club, *Heimatgefühl* (sense of home) was not tied to the region of someone's birth. Instead, the feeling was fostered through engagement with the Alpine landscape.

The German Alpine Association's second annual meeting, which took place in Salzburg in 1871, reinforced the club's particular vision of the Alps. Speeches defined Germans and Austrians as "ethnic brothers who, without regard for political borders, are members of a single family... and the German Alpine Association is one of many of the connecting links which authenticates the solidarity of the German peoples."[36] The club's secretary, an Austrian, began his business report with a comment on the Franco-Prussian War. After expressing his sympathies for the German cause, he listed the members of the association who had been decorated or killed during the war. The most prominent name among the dead was Karl Hofmann, who fell in the Battle of Sedan. During his remarks, the secretary placed the Alpine Association in the middle of Germany's search for geographic integrity and political power. He went so far as to equate Austria with the German cause. "We Austrians also felt like German men," he declared; "we were well aware of our ethnic community, and followed with feverish attentiveness the feats of our brothers."[37] It was a strange statement to make. Such notions of unity were not universally shared among the broader populace in either country after the Austro-Prussian War.

Yet members hoped that the German and Austrian clubs' merger would remedy the wrongs of 1866. Mountaineers seemed to have succeeded where statesmen had failed. Hearty toasts to the association's achievement met with resounding cheers at its first meeting after the merger. One member gave a speech that illuminated the new club's idea of progress: "It is lamentable that the Germans have always been divided among themselves. . . . The Assembly still remembers well the Thirty Years War, Napoleon's campaign, and the War of 1866. It is wished that the members of the German and Austrian Alpine Association will aspire to progressive endeavors as they climb up the mountains, and that they transfer these aims to their civic life with the same persistence and tough perseverance: Upward to the Light and Forward to Freedom!"[38] But while this speaker hoped that the association could unite Germans and Austrians, memories of internecine war and bitter feelings lingered.

Resentment within Austria toward Prussia had smoldered since 1866. In the 1870s, Germany's *Kulturkampf*, the Protestant culture wars that forced Catholic Germans out of positions of power and influence, set Catholic Austrian passions ablaze. The climate of anticlericalism and secularization in Germany created the perfect conditions for combustion. When Prussian officials violently arrested priests and seized church property, Austrian ultramontane anger flared, particularly in Salzburg and Tyrol.

Although not expressly Protestant, the Alpine Association had a subtle connection to the *Kulturkampf*. Beneath the harsh cacophony of anticlerical rhetoric was the insistent undertone of progress. Advocates of progress portrayed Catholicism as an obstacle to their endeavors. In its efforts to improve living standards in "backward" Alpine villages, which tended to be heavily Catholic, the Alpine Association revealed similar biases. According to one member, the club's efforts awakened farmers from their "vague indifference towards the modern zeitgeist" and acted as a force of modernity against the Alpine vale's insularity.[39]

The yellow press in Austria quickly conflated the Alpine Association with Prussian Protestantism and directed its fury toward the club's projects in the Austrian mountains. Several tabloids in Salzburg and Tyrol served as clerical mouthpieces and criticized the association. With its slogan "For God, Emperor, and the Fatherland," the Neue Tiroler Stimmen was among the most outspoken critics. The paper was thoroughly Catholic, bluntly anti-Semitic, and vehemently opposed to the liberals in Prussia, as well as to those in Vienna. Everything that the Alpenverein did seemed to desecrate the Alps in the eyes of those editors. Following Karl Hofmann's death, the association laid a plaque on the Grossglockner, one of the highest mountains in Austria, commemorating his work as an Alpine pioneer and heroic soldier. Erecting a memorial to a fallen German on Austrian territory stung. "And what about the sons of Austria," the editors seethed, "who not long ago were killed in the thousands by Prussian bullets?" To add insult to injury, the club changed the name of the Johannes Lodge, christened after a popular Tyrolean archduke, to the Hofmann Hut.[40] The editors of the paper howled when the association opened the Glockner House by singing the German national anthem and planting a large German flag on Grossglockner's peak. Loud protests later forced the flag's removal.[41]

Flippant attitudes on the part of tourists toward Tyrolean piety also offended Catholic Austrians. For the devout, forcing local tour guides to miss church services because sightseers wanted to climb on Sundays was tantamount to damnation. One newspaper contributor reflected that the association's gospel of progress seemed to require losing one's religion. He doubted the club's mission of "carrying the flame of Bildung and enlightenment to our dark mountains." If being cultured meant prowling around with sheep and goatherds in the mountains and eating meat on fasting days rather than worshipping in God's house, then this contributor preferred to be branded as crude. Here again the motif of Protestantism and progress stood against Catholicism and backwardness. In this article, however, progress represented all that was ill with the world. The author also took the opportunity to dismiss the club's scientific endeavors. "Science is a word that has caused much mischief," he declared, "and the Alpine Association has played a fair part in that."[42]

The stone that had started the avalanche of rancor was a short brochure, Prussia and the Alpine Association, written by an anonymous "Austrian patriot" in 1876. The author railed against Prussia and accused the Alpine Association of "smuggling" Prussian culture and customs into Austria. The simple fact was that one could not be a "good Prussian" and a "good Austrian" at the same time. The club was an "anomaly" within the Austrian monarchy, and with its supposed "Prussian tendencies," the association "sucked out the blood of patriots." Such bile spewed for several pages. Everything about the club angered this author, from the pictures of Kaiser Wilhelm and Bismarck and the portraits of General Helmuth von Moltke and Prussian war minister Albrecht Graf von Roon hanging in its lodges to the fact that "German" preceded "Austrian" in all the club's publications. The "pernicious" club called itself German, held conferences in Austria, and interwove Austrian with German territory. "In what other country in the world," the writer begged, "does this happen?" In the eyes of this patriot, Prussians had colonized the Austrian Alps, and the occupation held dire religious consequences. The writer insisted that the association's metaphor of bringing light to darkness was code for de-Catholicizing the Alps and establishing "Prussian colonies" of Protestantism in the valleys. The club's activities, particularly lodge construction and scientific research, were mere elements of the German imperialist/Protestant agenda. "Prussianization and national-liberal swindle," the writer fumed, "that is the intention of this Alpine alliance." The flood of German tourists and the club's rapid growth within Germany reinforced this person's concerns. "What we search for in vain," the author bemoaned, "is a truly Austrian Alpine Association."[43]

Some other Austrian mountaineering organizations agreed. During the late nineteenth century, nationalist rhetoric infused tourism groups.[44] The Alpine Club Austria (Alpenclub Österreich) clashed with the association over such differences. A group of Viennese climbers established the Alpine Club Austria in 1879 with explicit "Alpine patriotic aims." Its members believed that Austria deserved its own Alpine club, just like the British, French, Italians, and Swiss. No one mistook the unspoken accusation that the association was not an Austrian club. Tensions between the two groups reached such a crescendo that "loyal" members from one club were prohibited from interacting with the other club.[45] The Austrian Tourist Club (Österreichische Touristenklub, ÖTC) asserted that the Alpine Association's latent political agenda undermined Austrian interests. The ÖTC, established in 1869 in Vienna, had similar aims, projects, organization, and social composition as the association but not its Greater German orientation. During the 1890s, the Alpine

Association held a near monopoly over tour guide operations in Tyrol. To break the association's hold, the ÖTC appealed to Austrian patriots. The ÖTC argued that Germans outnumbered Austrians nearly four to one in the association's membership rolls and thus controlled the club. In its "form and content," the German and Austrian Alpine Association was really just German, making it a "foreign" club, and full of Protestants at that, unlike the wholly Austrian and almost entirely Catholic ÖTC. Moreover, the association's headquarters had recently moved to Berlin (Prussia), adding fuel to the ÖTC's patriotic fire. In this instance, the spark was a coat pin. Tyrolean tour guides had to wear the association's badge, which the ÖTC denounced as the insignia of "hegemony and autocracy of the Alpine Association." The ÖTC accused Germans of acting like "lords and rulers" of the Austrian mountains, noting that not even the English behaved in such a fashion in Switzerland, even though they had spent far more money there than the Germans had in Austria. Echoing the sentiments in the anonymous brochure, the ÖTC called on "Tyrolean patriots" and "friends of the Austrian Fatherland" to avoid the association's lodges and hire only ÖTC-certified guides.[46]

In response to attacks on the Alpine Association, its supporters closed ranks. The liberal press, especially the *Innsbrucker Tagblatt*, was the most vigorous defender of the club. Editorials appealed to rationality and common sense. They chastised the clerical newspapers for their "venomous" and close-minded patriotism that labeled critics as traitors. "Blind obedience" was not the measure of one's national loyalty. "Supporting progress" became the touchstone of patriotism for the club's advocates. According to the editors at the *Innsbrucker Tagblatt*, the real tragedy would be if patriotism were the exclusive domain of those who thanked God that they were not "one of those liberal-minded people of progress."[47] "Our bigots and reactionaries," another contributor testified, "hate nothing more than progress and enlightenment." When the anonymous "patriot" accused the Alpine Association of treachery, liberal editors condemned the person as a "medieval Rome-ling from the dark ages," a Catholic country bumpkin who disliked outsiders, particularly "Jews, free masons, Prussians, and Protestants," and who clearly opposed Austria's prosperity.[48] The competing worldviews centered on conflicting visions of progress. These beliefs were not merely a matter of praising railroads over making confession. What the battles made clear were the deep divisions within Austrian society, as well as the significant divides between Germans and Austrians.

The association's galas became a means to mitigate political cleavages. Festivities during the annual conference turned into patriotic rituals. To celebrate the association's self-ascribed "glowing patriotism," lavish decorations, flaming garlands, and blinking edelweiss stars surrounded the banquet hall.[49] Flags and banners in the association's colors—yellow, black, white, and red, symbolizing the "brotherly alliance between the Germans in both empires"—covered the walls and hung from the ceiling. During the 1911 meeting in Coblenz, the attendees watched an impressive fireworks show. Hundreds of rockets shot up from the shores of the Rhine while cannons fired from the surrounding hills, reminding the German participants of the "glorious battles from 1870."[50] Many of the observers spontaneously began to sing the German national anthem. But the celebrations overlooked the gory reality. No Austrian would have qualified the 1866 Battle of Königgrätz as glorious. In all the talk of a "brotherly alliance," no one mentioned that one brother overshadowed the other. That anonymous Austrian "patriot" had a point when he accused the club of ignoring the Austrian past.

The Alpenverein tried a different tack in 1913 by celebrating the centennial of the Wars of Liberation against Napoleon. Patriotic songs filled the air, large paintings from the German liberation movement lined the halls of the convention center, and fireworks dazzled the night skies while massive cannon salutes invoked victories on the battlefield. Delegates held ceremonies at the Befreiungshalle, the large memorial on the Danube River that commemorated the German victory over Napoleon, and toured Walhalla, a neoclassical temple that served as a German hall of fame. Rousing speeches made direct connections between the Alps and Germany's war of liberation. Club executives portrayed the mountains as a source of national strength and the abode of freedom. The very landscape "cultivates the mind for independence." There existed an affinity between the battles against Napoleon and the association's campaigns in the Alps.[51] The comparison was clumsy, but this did not stop the participants from bursting into patriotic songs—"Das Lied der Deutsche," with its famous refrain, "Deutschland über alles" ("a proud song set to music by an Austrian, written by a north German")—and Ernst Moritz Arndt's famous "The German Fatherland." The salient point of the speech was Napoleon's importance. His actions fomented a sense of solidarity among Germans and Austrians. Without him, the club would not be the same. At Walhalla, music set the mood. Richard Wagner's "Voices from the Heights" and Felix Mendelssohn's "Lift Thine Eyes to the Mountain" greeted the participants as they arrived. During a wreath-laying ceremony, club executives praised Bismarck and Emperor Wilhelm I as the founders of the German Empire and cocreators of the German-Austrian Alliance.[52] Members reveled in selective memory. They ignored the fact that a good number of Germans had fought for Napoleon and that Bismarck had viewed the Habsburgs as his great rivals. These were also distinctly German memorials. Once again, the association emphasized the "German" part of its Greater German identity.

Nevertheless, during the business meeting the following day, a couple of Austrian chapters tendered a proposal to make the association "more German." They wanted the newsletter and journal to use the German Fraktur script and not the Latin letters. Others then added amendments to the proposal: all of the club's publications, including trail markers and maps, should use Fraktur script; foreign words should be stricken for all official club documents; and instead of *Sektion* the words *Ortsgruppe* (district group) or *Zweig* (branch) should designate the constituent chapters. A delegate from Innsbruck invoked the perspective that members had gained from visiting the Befreiungshalle: "Yesterday we celebrated the memory of the Wars of Liberation; today let us immortalize the occasion through the liberation from all that is un-German in script and words." Backers of the bill maintained that it did not represent a political agenda. As one supporter explained, "The German and Austrian Alpine Association is, in its character, through-and-through a German association; it is fully entitled to build its signs along German lines. That is not an infringement on the political arena."[53] Patriotism had nothing to do with politics, although the aforementioned anonymous Austrian "patriot" might gainsay that point, even while agreeing that the association was indeed thoroughly German.

Arguments over linguistics and typography within the Alpine Association reflected the larger so-called font debate, which was widespread across Germany and Austria during this time and becoming increasingly divisive. Most popular newspapers had switched to the Fraktur script, but the large publishing houses and most scholarly journals had not. The proposal before the club's general assembly did not go uncontested. Josef Donabaum, a liberal Jew from Vienna and member of the association's executive board, believed that it would be presumptuous of the club to change its font before a national consensus had been reached. Moreover, technical difficulties might make such a change expensive. A professor from Frankfurt worried that the association might alienate its foreign readership, particularly within the scientific community, if it changed fonts. While he recognized the value in using "real German script," he felt that the petition was premature. Few voices spoke out against the petition, but they represented the majority of voters. Although the measure failed to pass the general assembly, the debate revealed the sharpening jingoistic attitudes within the club.

The Alpine Association's "glowing patriotism" burned brighter and hotter in the early twentieth century. While a Greater German identity was not explicitly xenophobic, it opened the club to more virulent forms of nationalism. Advocating an inclusive cultural identity planted the seeds of its own undoing. At the turn of the century, a small number of German and Austrian chapters established explicit racial restrictions in their statutes. Mountaineers disgruntled over the presence of Jews in their sections formed new groups out of the association's largest chapters in Berlin, Munich, and Vienna. Anti-Semitic chapters were in the minority, but they were located in the association's most important cities.

In Germany, a group of Berliners founded the Section Mark Brandenburg exclusively for "adult Christian men" in 1899.[54] Mark Brandenburg was like any other chapter, with an executive board, monthly gatherings, a newsletter, and two lodges in the Alps, except that a person had to apply for membership. Within a few years it had over one thousand members.[55] A group of university professors and students likewise established the Academic Section Munich in 1910 for "academically educated gentlemen of Germanic ancestry." Only men who had attended a German-speaking university could apply for membership. This chapter was serious about mountain climbing. Its founding members were frustrated with Section Munich's continual catering to Alpine dilettantes. Applications required three recommendation letters, and members were obligated to submit "tour reports" every year.

The "Germanic" orientation of these chapters, however, did not sit well with the association's executive board. Investigation into the matter uncovered that Academic Section Munich was indeed "against Jews," and some club officers sought to "remedy" this situation.[56] They worried that Academic Section Munich's membership clause gave a bad impression of the association as a whole. The board voted to recognize the chapter on the condition that it removed "Germanic ancestry" from its statutes.[57] Academic Section Munich complied. The records concerning discussions about Section Mark Brandenburg's orientation are absent. One can only speculate on the extent to which the club's executive board discussed the matter. What is known is that Section Mark Brandenburg's requirements for membership did not change.

Disturbing trends in Alpine tourism reflected larger troubling tendencies in central Europe. In 1879, German publicist Wilhelm Marr had introduced the term "anti-Semitism" into the political lexicon when he established the Antisemiten-Liga (League of Anti-Semites). He based his political concept of anti-Semitism on the supposed racial characteristics of Jews and not on religious differences, which distinguished his hate from earlier forms of anti-Jewish hostility. That Alpinism and anti-Semitism both emerged in the late nineteenth century is not entirely coincidental. In a sense, both were reactions to the era's anxieties.[58] As it gained respectability in Germany and Austria, anti-Semitism grew in popularity and soon became a political tool for extremist organizations. Germany's Pan-German League used anti-Semitism as a rallying cry. Austrian Pan-Germans, led by Georg von Schönerer, employed anti-Semitism in their fight for a political *Anschluss* (union) with Germany, even though such a union implied the end of the Habsburg dynasty. The empire's economic conditions and social structures in the 1880s and 1890s proved conducive for the spread of Schönerer's anti-Semitism. But after 1900, his Pan-German movement fell out of favor. His stint in prison and association with "roughnecks" contributed to the movement's demise. Many Austrians had grown weary of Schönerer's boorish agitation, his incessant charges of libel, and his attacks against the monarchy.[59]

Yet Schönerer's bigotry remained attractive in some circles. Those most susceptible to his ideas were often members of student fraternities at the University of Vienna, including Eduard Pichl. Born in 1872 into a thoroughly middle-class home, Pichl's immediate family was not particularly political in nature, although he displayed right-wing tendencies during his teenage years. His mother once confided in a friend that Eduard was a "Schönerianer." He styled himself as "an adversary of Jews in word and deed." His anti-Semitic activities as a university student brought him to Schönerer's attention, and eventually the two became close friends. A natural athlete, Pichl belonged to a *Turnverein* (gymnastics group) and the Alpine Association; he served as the pipeline for Schönerer's hate to infiltrate these clubs. Pichl had introduced the "Aryan paragraph" in his *Turnverein* for what he called "the start of national cleansing" and later did the same in the Alpine Association.[60]

Pichl was an outspoken Alpine anti-Semite, and he was not alone. The Austrian Mountain Association (Österreichischer Gebirgsverein), formed in 1890 as the Lower Austrian Mountain Association and then renamed in 1904, was explicitly anti-Semitic in orientation. It aimed to collect all "German-minded mountaineers" under its banner, by which the club meant only "German Aryans."[61] That old anonymous Austrian "patriot" had believed that no "Christian, patriotic persons" held elected positions in the Alpine Association, and he equated Jews with Vienna's "liberal swindle" in his vitriolic remarks.[62] Some thirty years later, many drew the same conclusions. Members like Pichl grew increasingly antagonistic toward the liberal old guard of Section Austria, such as the chairman, Josef Donabaum. Dissatisfied with the supposed "absence of sociability" but really with the third of the membership that was Jewish, a group of Viennese mountaineers left Section Austria to establish Section Wien in 1905. Another group, the Academic Section Vienna, also became known as a chapter for anti-Semites. Pichl, who had first joined Section Austria, transferred his membership to the Academic Section Vienna. Significant tension existed between Section Austria and the other Viennese chapters, which often also had lower membership fees. Although the two new Viennese chapters were tiny compared to Section Austria, they became increasingly influential.[63]

Nevertheless, in the 1870s, the Greater German identity of most mountaineers differed from that of the extremist Pan-Germans, with their hate, their visions of domination, and their demands for the political unification of Germany and Austria. The Alpine Association offered a gentler cultural identity, one more palatable to the majority of middle-class Germans and Austrians. But by the start of the twentieth century, abrasive chauvinism challenged the club's stance. Not all members were blind to the dangers that such inclinations posed. In 1909, Otto von Pfister, the outgoing president, warned of the pressures the association faced, one of which was the desire to align with the "nationalistic-political" elements in Germany and Austria. In his farewell address, he cautioned against political pursuits; otherwise the club would lose, as he believed, its "moral" standing. Others concurred. "When someone stands on the peak of a mountain," one climber remarked, "he does not ask which region of the German lands a member comes from, he does not inquire about political convictions."[64]

・・・・・・・・・・・・

On the eve of the Great War, one alpinist described the mountains as "the magic land of longing."[65] His words resonated with those who wanted a fuller life. With their "eternal presence" and "almighty strength," the jagged edges of civilization promised relief from cultural despair. Imposing heights offered a firm foundation and sense of security, something that many found lacking on the slippery slopes of modern life. Beckoning peaks conveyed the feeling of escape from city life and all its troubles. Only by clearing one's head of daily concerns could a person fully develop into a mature, well-rounded adult. The value of *Bildung* and emphasis on individual accomplishment colored the mountains in bourgeois hues.

Middle-class mountaineers served as the apostles of the Alps. They presented a certain vision of the mountain landscape contrary to the one offered by the American geographer Ellen Churchill Semple. She had studied under Friedrich Ratzel at the University of Leipzig and was well known among geographers in Germany. As one of the worst protagonists of environmental determinism, she declared, "The important characteristics of plains is their power to facilitate every phase of historical movement; that of the mountains is their power to retard, arrest, or deflect it" and concluded that "man ... feels always the pull of gravity."[66] But for German and Austrian mountaineers, the attraction was upward, not downward. Ascending the Alps meant moving forward, closer to political unity. Far from retarding, arresting, or deflecting progress, Alpinism and the Alps fostered a sense of a heroic, individual accomplishment and personal space while still allowing one to feel connected to a broader, more meaningful cultural community.

When members tirelessly preached the gospel of progress and national unity, some in the congregation were bound to convert, often fervently so. Pfister had a point when he warned against siding with the nationalistic camp. The Alps tied together the multitude of symbols into a cultural identity, which may have blurred political borders but also supported conflicting political leanings. A heady mix of confession, politics, regional loyalties, and national allegiances entangled the landscape. Some of these conflicts lost their furor over time. The bitterness of Austrian patriots following 1866 had largely mellowed by the start of the twentieth century. Although not extinguished, confessional ardor had also cooled. But some battles still raged and new ones opened. Class divides deepened. Working-class clubs now also claimed rights to the Alps. Although the Alpine Association had wealth and numbers and controlled sizable tracts of land in the peaks, the Alps clearly did not belong to any one organization. When anti-Semitism found its way into Alpine tourism, most prominently in fin-de-siècle Vienna, it became clear that defining the Eastern Alps as "German" was not so easily done.

3

Young People and Old Mountains
Commercialism and Conservationism Tangle in the Alps

> In our Alps, which following their formation have naturally not
> stood a single day untouched, the ravages of time have gnawed powerfully.
>
> —Franz Wirth, Die Entstehung der Alpen (1909)

Fin-de-siècle tourists stormed the Alps. Membership in the Alpine Association continued to rise, as did the number of visitors to the club's huts. In 1874, the club's 14 huts received 1,451 visitors. On the eve of the First World War, the association counted more than 230 huts and 260,000 visitors. In one summer season alone, over 7,000 individuals packed the 7 huts maintained by Section Austria.[1] The Ortler-Hochjoch Hut at 3,635 meters, the highest in the Eastern Alps, had nearly 100 guests in 1911, a significant number given its altitude.[2] Travel vouchers and discounted hut rates for members of tourist clubs offered further enticements to head for the hills. By the early twentieth century, travelers could hop on a train to the mountains, hike to the top, spend the night in a hut, and be back home in time for dinner the next day. No wonder that thousands made the trip.

Crowded mountains raised serious social and environmental concerns. Many feared that hordes of city folks bumbling their way up the slopes would ruin the peaceful mountain ambience and upset the delicate Alpine ecology. Hard-core climbers fretted that the Alps were already overdeveloped and sought to drastically reduce any further construction in the mountains. Others elsewhere in Germany and Austria echoed similar misgivings about mass tourism and the commodification of nature. Individuals like Ernst Rudoff, founder of the Deutscher Bund Heimatschutz (German Homeland Protection Society), an organization that largely matched the Alpine Association in social composition, decried mass consumption of the natural landscape. Such critiques reflected nature tourism's inherent conflict between consumption and conservation.[3] Similar divides ran deep in the Alpine Association, where discord over the club's aims and orientation illuminated anxieties about fin-de-siècle mass society and its attendant consumerism. Some members wanted a larger, open tourist organization, others a smaller, more restricted mountaineering club. In keeping with the founders' aims, the majority believed that every German and Austrian should have access to the Alps, so long as they were mindful of nature and hiked with care. Yet against the onslaught of the masses, extreme climbers doubted that such standards could be maintained.

Open mountains complicated the debates. "Alpinism had become popular," one mountaineer remembered, "and had penetrated into the social strata that previously had stayed far away from the mountains."[4] New tourists increasingly came from the lower middle class—teachers, civil servants, and modest businessmen. Generational differences also became apparent. New ways of thinking about the mountains took hold.[5] Enjoying the struggle to reach the peak, the sense of solitude, and the simplicity of modest Alpine lodges had become old-fashioned sentiments. At the same time, nostalgia for more rustic and risky mountains crept into Alpine clubs. The association faced a dilemma of its own making. To preserve the Alpine ecology, the club had to cultivate a love of the mountains. But for that, it needed to bring more people to the Alps. Yet greater numbers of tourists constituted the very threat to the mountain environment. In reaction to the pressures of mass tourism, mountaineers attempted to resolve the inherent contradictions of Alpinism. A new rhetoric of nature preservation entered the Alpine lexicon as concerned citizens lobbied to establish nature reserves in the Alps, but with the purpose of barring industry from the mountains, not people. Other alpinists devoted themselves to training adolescents as means to both educate and accommodate the masses. Conservation efforts and youth development sought the same end: to protect the Alps from becoming lost.

・・・・・・・・・・・・・

Extreme mountaineers raged against commercial development and mass tourism in the Alps. They believed that the high peaks were never intended for the general public but only for those fit (and wealthy) enough to climb the heights. "Promenade paths" and opulent lodges attracted the type of people whom serious climbers loathed. Urban tourists brought to the

Alps the very attitudes and way of life that earlier alpinists had sought to escape: "the philistine existence of the sprawling city." The Alps had become so commercialized that many Munich mountaineers refused to hike on Sundays, having no patience for the "swarms and queues" of "non-alpinists" and "dawdling" tourists.[6] "Those who seek that holy mountain peace will have to look elsewhere," an Innsbruck climber lamented, "and perhaps not even there." Many shared his grief, wishing for a place where "Alpine mobs" would not "cramp, aggrieve, and disgust" them.[7] That these tourists lacked appreciation for nature was perhaps pardonable, but that they brought "mischief, coarseness, clumsy impudence, and triviality" to the mountains was unforgivable.[8]

Die-hard climbers protested the hordes of tourists but directed their rancor toward the Alpine Association itself for capitulating to the whims of mass society. Their resentment escalated to hyperbole. "The end of Alpinism would come," one mountaineer bristled, "when the Alpenverein forgets that it is not a tourist association, when it sees its primary task in path and trail construction instead of mountain climbing."[9] They accused the club of "profaning" the Alps with "gymnastic scaffolding" and ruining the rock faces for "proper" alpinists. "Not only do climbers feel impeded by the trail constructions," another seasoned member fumed, "but also cables, iron works, path markers, warning signs, and so on, pain the many who climb mountains solely to pursue the joy of pure nature."[10] Bitter mountaineers targeted the type of "luxury" huts now being built as the harbingers of such change.[11] Given the large sums that the association spent on huts and trails, the critics had a point. In the first decade of the twentieth century, the association distributed well over a million marks in subsidies. Demand for comfort had also inflated prices. Erecting "modern huts" for under fifty thousand marks was "utterly impossible." Yet one old-timer dismissed "luxury huts" as excessive. "We all have grown old in the Association," he groused during a convention, "without the present comforts in the lodges." People who found joy in the mountains did not need modern amenities. "A young man is not going to die from sleeping on straw sacks and pallets," he declared to the sound of riotous applause.[12]

Section Bayerland, an exclusive mountaineering chapter located outside Munich, had long rejected the commercialization of the Alps and refused to renovate its Meiler Hut near the Dreitorspitze in Tyrol—that is, until 1909, when an Austrian businessman filed a complaint against the chapter for refusing him admittance to the lodge. The details of the altercation are vague, but the matter was serious enough for the chairman of Section Innsbruck to contact Bayerland. He first chastised the members for their rash actions—"Just imagine . . . Austrian authorities lodging an official protest against the Bavarian chapter concerning the business enterprises of an Austrian citizen on Austrian territory"—and reminded them that the purpose of the association was to promote tourism, not impede it. If Bayerland wanted to keep its hut public, then it needed to enlarge it, or "at the very least act like it would." Innsbruck's chairman asserted that the Dreitorspitze was hardly the "reserve of extreme mountaineers." The paths were easy and the climb light. Wanderers of all sorts visited the region, especially with the recently opened Innsbruck-Mittenwald-Garmisch rail line.[13] To maintain its presence near the popular peak, Section Bayerland had to accept the demands of mass consumerism.

Hard-core climbers often found themselves in the minority. "Extreme alpinists are not entirely in the wrong," one climber observed, "when they complain that they are being edged out."[14] Most tourist club members believed that the mountains existed for all to enjoy, whether they were extreme mountaineers or just persons seeking a pleasant afternoon excursion, and admonished hard-core climbers to be less "hypersensitive" when casual tourists also found the Alps enthralling.[15] Some went further and accused the elitists of "intolerance, egoism, and doctrinarism" and of being blind to the progression of Alpine tourism. The opening up of mountains and the construction of lodges "automatically followed the development of high Alpine tourism."[16]

Yet even proponents of open mountains wondered if hut construction had reached the point of diminishing returns. Too many cabins dotted the peaks. A hiker might come across three or more huts on the way to the summit, some only a two-hour march apart. With new train stations redirecting tourists, once popular lodges had fallen into neglect.[17] During the general meeting in 1896, the Hut and Trail Committee suggested that chapters curb their hut enthusiasm.[18] Since most chapters simply ignored the suggestion, the committee announced measures to limit construction projects a year later. It planned to review future proposals with a much more careful and critical eye. The committee's guiding question would be that of necessity. Was the proposed location in a region heavily visited by tourists, or would the hut be built in an Alpine wasteland? Was the hut the right size, not too big? The committee planned to reduce subsidy allocations, and cabins that appeared as hotels would not receive funds.[19] Yet hut construction continued unabated. In 1911, the executive committee further reasserted, "In the future it will give preference to such huts that fulfill a high need" and to trails that "really serve a practical need."[20]

The announcement seemed to exacerbate matters. A "high" or "practical" need was vague enough to allow a "petty business sense" rather than "noble Alpine enthusiasm" to direct commercial development in the Alps. Rivalries among chapters grew fierce. Attracting more tourists meant more revenues. "In the neighboring lodges a person no longer sees common aspirations and activities of sister sections," one executive of the Alpine Association lamented, "but tiresome competition."[21] During one general meeting, the Hut and Trail Committee found the need to remind members that everyone belonged to the same club. Should misunderstandings in work regions occur, the committee urged chapters to resolve the situation in a "friendly, open, Alpine way."[22] Clearly, some had not.

In 1911, during his last speech as the club's president, Otto von Pfister warned against the "growing superficiality of tourism," especially its detrimental impact on the Alpine Association.[23] He had a point. Mass tourism revealed latent fractures in the club that the patriotic rhetoric of cultural community and unity had tried to conceal. But Pfister's remarks also betrayed his own male bourgeois biases for what defined a sublime experience in the Alps. Tourism certainly brought the pressures of modern consumerism to bear on the Alps, but the Alpine Association mitigated the worst of those impacts. Rather than thousands of boots trampling all over nature, trails and lodges directed and concentrated hikers. As for its superficiality, mass tourism brought more money and people into contact with the Alps but also raised environmental awareness among enough sympathetic Alpine enthusiasts to drive nature conservation campaigns in the early twentieth century. Pfister really worried about the club's place in the twentieth century. By 1911, skiing had arrived on the scene and challenged the dominance of the Alpine Association. The new sport gathered the energies of mass tourism to transform the winter Alps. Skiing's wild popularity unsettled the older generation of climbers to the point where they doubted their own efforts in opening the Alps. They had yet to accept the irony that the Alpine Association's successful mission was the very cause of their anxiety. Whatever the future held, this much was certain: a lot of money had saturated the mountains.

• • • • • • • • • • • • •

With the injection of affluence, sleepy Alpine hamlets awoke as luxury spa towns and ski resorts. The Swiss Alps were home to several of the more famous spa towns, like Davos. But Austria also had a large share of resorts. Little places like Sölden, Ischgl, and Kitzbühel now became world-class ski venues. Once a utilitarian means of crossing snowbound lands for hunters and mail carriers, skiing emerged as sport in the late 1890s. As with mountaineering, the wealthy were the prime movers. The predominance of the Nordic style and of long skis made for practical cross-country travel gave way to the Alpine downhill approach, with skis like blades, instruments to slice the slopes.[24] The new style altered how people used the wintry Alps. For Nordic enthusiasts, the mountains were no place to ski. One did not hurtle down sheer inclines at terrifying speeds. And mountaineers shunned the peaks in winter for fear of freezing to death. But when Mathias Zdarsky, a Bohemian Austrian, published his manual on Alpine skiing in 1896, *The Lilienfelder Ski Technique*, he turned downhill skiing into a phenomenon.[25] Using a single pole and shorter skis, Zdarsky and his students rocketed down slopes. What unnerved Nordic skiers thrilled devotees of the Alpine style. The dreadful steep became a winter wonderland. By the early 1900s, one Munich paper estimated that some thirty-five thousand to forty thousand Germans and fifteen thousand Austrians skied for sport. The German Ski Association was established in 1905, as was the Austrian Ski Association, although local clubs that had formed in the 1890s preceded both.[26]

Initially, some mountaineers embraced skiing. They did so for a number of reasons. Some thanked skiers for opening the winter Alps to tourists and encouraged others to try "the newest, most modern form" of Alpine sports. Even local residents, supposedly "skeptical of innovation," found value in skiing. Novices gushed about the "awesomeness" of the mountains in winter, the "shimmering palaces" and the "glittering" landscape.[27] Others compared the sport to the golden age of mountain climbing. The two activities shared several affinities; both required athleticism and entailed danger, excitement, perseverance, love of nature, and knowledge of the mountains. Skiers frequently borrowed the exact words and images that mountain climbers used to describe their experiences.[28] Many climbers viewed skiing as a solution to the negative impact of summer tourism. Additionally, winter tourism restored the necessity of struggle and fitness.[29] Skiing was the perfect fitness activity for mind and body. Not only did it strengthen the body, but it also developed the "masculine characteristics of our Volk," although whatever benefits skiing might have held for women went unremarked by male commentators.[30] Others translated their passion for the sport into a sense of patriotism.

The frost-tinted rocks, icy air, and frozen steams threw the depth and power of the Heimat into sharp relief. The Alpine experience in winter was far more intense than a summer excursion to the mountains and, according to some, created a deeper appreciation for the homeland.

Still others took a broader approach and extolled the virtue of winter sport as a "remedy for modern decadence." Critics failed to elaborate on what exactly that affliction entailed, though the condition seemed related to urban living. One well-known mountaineer and writer, Eugen Guido Lammer, employed a pseudo-psychological approach to diagnose the illness. At issue was the conflict between the individual and modern civilization. "The person of today stands quite alone in a completely atomized society," he ventured; "this eternal tension, this isolation, this constraint continually makes the ego anxious."[31] Apparently, Alpinism was therapy. For those who enjoyed risking life and limb, winter sports soothed the neuroses of modern life. The aesthetics of skiing were timeless and boundless. Speeding down the slopes projected a feeling of dominion over space and time. According to Lammer, skiing created valuable interpersonal bonds and thereby fostered a strong sense of community.

Except when it did not. No sport did more to aggravate more members of the Alpine Association than skiing. Alpine skiing became an increasingly popular pastime, especially among college students. Young people packed the peaks during the winter break. Tensions quickly arose between ski clubs and the Alpenverein over who had rights to the mountains. Most serious alpinists did not appreciate Alpine Sportlers. In their minds, winter sport meant competition; they viewed climbing as contemplation. Mountaineers characterized skiers as unruly kids interested only in sport and lacking appreciation for the beauty of the Alps. They dismissed skiing as youthful indiscretion. Those who belonged to the older generation had been taught that the Alps were all the more treacherous in winter and could not understand the appeal of winter tourism to young people. Skiers, on the other hand, saw mountain climbers as stodgy traditionalists who wanted to keep the mountains for themselves. To many ski adherents, the Alpine Association appeared stagnant and old-fashioned.

Such criticisms were not entirely lost on members of the Alpine Association. As one official remarked, "We are old men, but we do not want to become an old man's club."[32] Several members feared that the Alpine Association was already becoming "decrepit."[33] Extending the seasonal calendar of activities to the winter months would transfuse young blood into the ailing club. Some chapters, like Freiburg, had already assembled ski groups with the hope of attracting young people. The association could educate them, imbue them with a sense of respect for the mountains, and, at the same time, rejuvenate the club. In typical fashion, association executives established a committee, the "Committee for the Promotion of Ski Tourism," to help the process along.[34]

If it hoped to survive in the twentieth century, the association needed to open its doors. Progressive-minded members meant that in a real sense, that is, making the club's huts available to skiers. Most huts closed in late autumn and did not open again until late spring or early summer. But if the chapters kept their huts open during ski season, they might win new friends. Others argued that the association had, in fact, a moral obligation to make its huts accessible during the winter season; Alpine huts might be the only refuge for injured skiers, frostbitten hikers, or climbers suffering from hypothermia. These individuals cited the "German Civil Code" to defend their proposition that legally the association had to keep its huts open in the winter. Austrian law was essentially the same. Supporters also contended that keeping the huts open year-round allowed members who seldom had the chance to travel to the Alps greater opportunity to visit their own huts.[35] Some members even suggested building winter lodges specifically for skiers. Academic Section Munich petitioned that trail markers list the addresses of chapters whose huts were not sufficiently furnished, directing tourists to cabins that had adequate provisions (usually those of larger, wealthier chapters). In 1909 a member from Section Austria proposed that "all chapters of the German and Austrian Alpine Association be required to furnish all of their shelters and huts with a heated room with cooking and sleeping facilities for several persons, for travel outside the standard tourist season."[36]

The timing for such a proposal could not have been worse. Many older mountain climbers conflated the debates about hut renovations with opening the huts to skiers in the winter. One elder from Berlin accused those who supported skiing of dismissing the excessive and often prohibitive costs of hut renovation, vandalism repair, and constructing a room for winter use. He railed against the renovations and amenities in Alpine huts:

> We older mountain climbers used these primitive huts for forty
> years, with two lights from small lanterns, dry cold bread from the

backpack, and a sip of brandy to warm you on a cold summer night. And in the morning, with clothes still wet and with wet shoes we set off once more on the unpaved path up to the peak. Sometimes we faced delay caused by weather, and sometimes we did not have enough food. But one was proud to have reached the goal and look back on the hardships one had to overcome. . . . These skiers should be satisfied with what they get, which is more than we got in the 70s.[37]

Based on his description, it was a near miracle that more people had not died of hypothermia. But he had a point. For smaller sections that lacked the financial capabilities to offer provisions or pay for costly renovations, outfitting a hut for winter use was impossible. A number of the older lodges lacked insulation and heating, and some offered only the most minimal of cooking facilities. Even the few huts that did have indoor heating and an adequate kitchen had no winter supplies, such as food and fuel or an on-site manager. Representatives also felt that the proposals gave preferential treatment to larger chapters. Negative experiences and violent clashes with winter tourists added to the doubts. Damage caused by pools of melted snow on the floor, broken windows from misplaced skis, and cracked plates and chairs from drunken revelry or outright vandalism became a heavy financial burden for chapters with huts. Although most chapters had property insurance, compensation was meager. Extensive damage could force a smaller chapter to close its hut or even plunge it into bankruptcy.[38]

Despite the reluctance on behalf of climbers to share their cabins, skiing made a permanent mark on the mountains in the years before the Great War. Mountaineers had conquered the peaks for summer workouts; skiers opened the slopes for winter fun. Here was yet another way of thinking about the Alps that translated into material change. New resort hotels that offered discount travel packages and ski passes seemed to appear overnight.[39] Where trails crawled up the mountainside, pistes now ran down. Not wanting to waste hours climbing to the top of the runs, skiers sought out resorts that employed chair lifts. People had used ropes and pulleys to haul goods up mountains for centuries, and the development of steel cables during the Industrial Revolution had improved transport technology; now metal and motors made the transportation of people feasible. The first cable car in the Eastern Alps opened in 1908; the Kohlererbahn traveled one and a half kilometers from Bolzano up to

Col di Villa in South Tyrol. Each carriage carried six people, and within two years thousands had braved the ride. Adolf Bleichert and Company, based near Leipzig, became a world leader in cable car construction. The firm renovated the Kohlererbahn in 1912, adding steel supports, a new motor that whipped carriages along at two miles an hour, and larger wagons that held seventeen people. Bleichert strung ski lifts all along the Alps; one of the first was built near the city of Merano.[40] Resort owners invested heavily in such mechanical features, which acted as lightning rods for storms of wealthy skiing enthusiasts. The attraction worked. Skiers swarmed the Alps, and cable cars hauled people up mountains by the thousands.

Most mountaineers found the merits of the cable cars suspect. Only a small minority acknowledged them as a necessary evil. Motorized lifts did allow those physically unable to climb to the peaks to partake in the Alpine experience. Still, most alpinists generally viewed cable cars as the industrial invasion of the heights, something that they feared more than the hordes of tourists. A cleared trail was one thing, but a permanent ski lift with its clanging machinery was quite another. Tourists could now reach the summit, but "without self-effort, without willpower, without love and perseverance." What was the mountain experience without sweat and suffering? The pious damned cable cars as profane. As one devout mountaineer explained, "For the true mountain climber the entire mountain (not just the summit) is a living being . . . for us the high mountain ranges . . . are a sacred shrine."[41] Standing on the peak was merely the reward; the purpose lay in the struggle. If hut construction raised a racket in the club, then erecting cable cars caused an uproar. Like those who cursed mass tourism, some predicted that industrial incursion into the Alps would be "the end of Alpinism altogether."[42]

Fears of a machine invasion were not entirely misplaced. New cogwheel trains mounted the first sortie. Mountaineers felt conflicted about trains in the dales. New railroads, like the Karwendel train, significantly decreased the time required to get from one trailhead to another. But the trains also disgorged ever-greater numbers of bothersome tourists.[43] Yet in some instances the Alpenverein supported such infrastructure development. It backed proposals for the "modern" Ortler line, which would run through the Fernpass, connecting Bavaria with South Tyrol.[44] However, climbers had no mixed feelings about cogwheel trains that crawled right up the slopes. In the late 1890s, Swiss engineers began construction in the Western Alps on the Jungfrau cogwheel train, the first of its kind in the mountains. The Jungfrau project set the mountaineering world afire with anger and anxiety. So too did plans in the Eastern Alps.

Proposals to lay tracks up Bavarian mountains horrified members of the Alpine Association. The most alarming project was the Zugspitzbahn. Just as the Jungfraubahn began operations, bids for an electric cogwheel train up Germany's highest mountain became public. Initial plans required significant excavations to support tracks and burrowing over two thousand meters up to the peak.[45] Some versions included blueprints for a grand hotel near the mountain. Monthly reports in the association's newsletter closely tracked the proposals' progress through the labyrinth of Bavarian ministries. The club mounted a ferocious offensive against the train with Section Munich leading the charge. Members invoked similar arguments used against mass tourism, with the added point that diesel engines belched smoke, polluting the clean mountain air.

Proponents identified immediately the hypocrisy in the association's stance. The Zugspitzbahn was a "natural consequence" of the club's efforts, part of a trajectory that had begun in 1820 when climbers first reached the summit and included the construction of Münchner Haus decades later. Supporters recalled that Section Munich still faced tremendous criticism for its work. Members had done so much to ease travel up the mountain that they should recognize, "without rancor," these "progressive endeavors." "Let us hope," one editorial remarked, "that by 1910 they will be ready to accept the locomotive with good grace."[46] But the association won by default. Financial setbacks delayed the Zugspitzbahn project, and then the outbreak of war suspended it completely.[47]

Meanwhile, in 1910, the industrialist Otto von Steinbeis received approval from the Bavarian government to build the Wendelstein cogwheel train. Unlike the more infamous Jungfrau and Zugspitze lines, the Wendelstein garnered less attention. Short blurbs in the association's mailings mentioned Steinbeis's project, but the club remained fixated on the Zugspitzbahn. Once it began, work on the Wendelstein line lasted only two years, a breakneck pace considering the amount of effort required. Explosions shook the mountain as hundreds of workers hammered and cut their way across the rock face. The original track ran nearly ten kilometers, crossed two bridges, and traveled through several tunnels.[48] It opened in 1912 as the first operating cogwheel railway in the Eastern Alps.

While railroads latched on to the peaks, highways festooned the mountains. Alpine thoroughfares were not new. In the early 1800s,

Napoleon had laid down roads in the Western Alps for better access to Italy. The Habsburgs built the Stelvio Pass in the 1820s, which reached the altitude of over 2,700 meters and was for a time the highest road in Europe.[49] But instead of helping horses, paved roads now prepared the way for automobiles. In the late nineteenth century, German and Austrian engineers, like Karl Benz and Siegfried Marcus, were at the forefront of automotive technology. By the early 1900s, auto manufacturers were firmly established in both countries. Cars excited passions. Motor vehicles represented the wave of the future, even if they were still toys for the rich. The internal combustion engine unleashed an avalanche of change in the Alps. Highways remade the mountain landscape. First built for postal trucks and military vehicles, the roads were soon lined with tourist buses.

Some chapters anticipated motoring tourists. To accommodate the thousands of hikers who flooded the Grossglockner region every season, Section Klagenfurt decided to build a "gently rising, drivable, modern street" from the village of Heiligenblut up to its lodge. Plans for the nearly twelve-kilometer-long private road took shape in the 1890s. State and local governments, banks, a train company, private donors, and the association's Hut and Trail Committee provided funds.[50] Construction began in 1900 and ran immediately into obstacles. Locals opposed the road, the landscape thwarted it, and legal battles delayed it. Costs trebled. Critics called it the "one-hundred-thousand-Gulden-highway."[51] Three hundred thousand would have been more accurate. The road drove Klagenfurt to near insolvency.

Such grandiose projects proved too great for civic groups, even those as large as the Alpine Association, but not for states. In 1891, a year after Robert Hans Schmitt and Johannes Sautner had reached the top and not far from the Five Finger Peak, civil engineers broke ground on a massive highway across the Austrian Dolomite range. The road, one of several projects in the Eastern Alps, rose over a mile high as it wound its way through punishing terrain from Bolzano to Cortina d'Ampezzo. Construction finally ended nearly twenty years later in 1909, the same year that the German and Austrian Alpine Association celebrated its fortieth anniversary. The completed Dolomite highway represented the concerted effort by state and local officials to strengthen commercial ties between Austria and Italy, as well as the growing need for concrete infrastructure to support the burgeoning number of drivers. Motorists took to the Alps with such gusto that climbers complained about the constant "dust clouds" and "gasoline vapors" from the cars, as well as irksome noise and traffic jams. How one could balance the "utility value of automotive travel" with the "quiet contemplation of nature" remained entirely uncertain.[52]

....

To tip the scales in its favor, the Alpine Association weighed in with youth development and nature conservation. At first some members focused on publications as a means to educate the general public, harkening back to the club's academic orientation in the 1870s. During the 1912 annual meeting, one climber suggested that the club issue a general book on the Alps. "We old-timers have read Schaubach," he said, referring to Adolf Schaubach's handbook for travelers, "and through those books we became not only alpinists, but also friends of Alpine nature, Alpine inhabitants, and all that exists in the Alps."[53] A new handbook, which would contain information on the land, people, plants, and all that the Alps had to offer, might appeal to young people. The proposal also echoed deeper concerns over stagnation within the association. The club, with its aging membership, was becoming antiquated. If it refused to regain the initiative in publishing material on the Alps, it might just pass away with its dying members. The membership was moribund. Likewise, "the literary propaganda of Alpine nature has arrived at a dead end." Languishing Alpine publications reflected a "sense of decay and petrifaction of Alpine sensibilities." By publishing a book on Alpine "geology, flora, fauna, history, culture, art, populations, anthropology, folklore, and sagas," the club could return to its founding ideals while attracting new members.[54]

But books were not enough. One mountaineer dismissed such proposals with the observation that "one throws the newsletter in the waste paper basket and sets the journal on the bookshelf."[55] Instead, others urged the association to foster a heightened environmental awareness, particularly among adolescents. Chapters thus made a concerted effort to attract and educate young people about Alpinism. Their goodwill was part nature conservation and part self-preservation. In his talk on uncontrolled tourism and the need to educate those who traveled to the mountains, Pfister concluded that the club's "only hope remains with the budding youth."[56]

Youth was a source of both hope and despair in the early twentieth century. Rebellious children distressed parents. Much adult worry centered on uninhibited adolescent sexuality and imagining what might happen among unsupervised teenagers alone in the woods. The Wandervögel movement was a particular source of suspicion. In the late 1890s, informal youth hiking groups had organized in a suburb of Berlin. In 1901, the groups coalesced and formally established the Wandervögel organization. Within a decade, constituent clubs existed across Germany. Hiking in the rural countryside constituted the groups' primary activity. Wandervögel expressed neo-romantic attitudes about nature. Frolicking in the forests and across fields was liberating. Out from under the eyes of watchful grown-ups, young people could discover themselves on their own terms. Nearly fifty thousand young people belonged to a youth organization on the eve of the First World War, almost half of whom were Wandervögel.

While some adults, notably Social Democrats, praised the youth movement as a force of change, many feared it for that very reason. Most parents agreed that adult-organized *Jugendpflege* (youth cultivation) projects were the best means to properly socialize teenagers. Youth group directors advocated hiking, but with adult supervision. As one teacher stated, "Just as the sciences are promoted in the schools, students also need to hear about the promotion of nature sensibilities . . . and that can happen best through nature hiking."[57] In 1911, "youth cultivators" established the National Federation for Youth Hiking and Youth Hostels.[58] Excursions got young people out of the city, gave them a sense of purpose, and instilled in them a love for the homeland.

The Alpine Association conformed to a broader trend when its members described the mountain ranges as a "school for life" that prepared young people for adulthood.[59] One mountaineer in particular, Ernst Enzensperger, a schoolteacher, took these ideas to heart. Years earlier he had lost his older brother during a climbing accident in the Alps. Still driven by his brother's death, he now campaigned vigorously to establish formal youth groups within the Alpine Association. He wrote two books about two young boys who traveled to the Alps and there learned the value of comradeship, nature awareness, and personal development.[60] In the stories, an older tour guide, who acted like a knowledgeable uncle, taught the boys through his careful manner and depth of Alpine knowledge. The books served two purposes: the first was to foster a sense of Alpine enthusiasm and curiosity among school-age children; the second was to demonstrate to older members of the association that they had the ability (in Enzensperger's opinion, the obligation) to teach youth in the ways of the mountain.

In 1912 and 1913, Enzensperger visited several chapters in his crusade to establish youth groups. Although men dominated most sections and therefore understood youth to be boys, Enzensperger also included girls in his plans. He admitted that, at first glance, youth and Alpinism did not belong together. For all the cleared trails and mountain huts, hiking in the Alps still involved serious risk. There were good reasons why the association had entered into an agreement with an Austrian insurance company in 1910 and accorded accidental death insurance to members.[61] Most alpinists had been groomed to think that the Alpine experience was an adult one, filled with hardship and struggle, danger and death. Few, if any, twelve-year-olds had the physical strength or mental fortitude to reach a high and challenging Alpine peak. But Enzensperger advanced a new mindset. He agreed that climbing could be dangerous, but involving teenagers in the Alpine experience taught them to respect the mountains. The Alps could make a formable impression on young minds. By channeling their enthusiasm, teenagers would mature into future "Alpine heroes" who carried a love of nature and appreciation for the Alpine world. More important, Enzensperger sought to develop healthy German youth who would mature into well-adjusted adults and who could weather the storms of human existence.[62]

Enzensperger's supporters also made a strong case. They emphasized that teenagers should not be dragged into the mountains; for the experience to have any meaning, young people needed to travel to the mountains under their own volition. They also pointed out the differences between chapters from the flat lands and those from mountainous regions. The association needed to be careful with those young people who had never seen the Alps before and should first encourage them to learn about their own local *Heimat*. Alpine youth hikes were not to be extreme Alpine excursions. Young people were not ready for the rigors of intense mountain climbing, nor should they be. Proponents repeated that the goal of Alpine youth groups was to educate and encourage and not to pressure or dismay. They also advocated open mountains. Middle-school students, vocational students, and elementary school pupils should all have equal opportunities to enjoy the Alps. There should be no distinction between rich and poor; each participant had the same rights and obligations. Others hoped to instill a connection to the German *Volk* by encouraging youth to explore and experience the Alps. They wanted not only to develop healthy, well-adjusted Germans but also to reinforce a natural connection to the Greater German cultural community. And, not the least important, many members viewed Alpine youth groups as a means to rejuvenate the Alpine Association. When the Munich and Hochland chapters submitted a proposal for the formal establishment of Alpine youth groups at the 1913 annual meeting in Regensburg, the general assembly overwhelmingly approved it.[63]

Almost immediately, a number of chapters took advantage of the available funds to create Alpine youth groups. Some of the larger, wealthier chapters had already started organizing the children of members. Austrian sections in particular had encouraged youthful engagement with the mountains long before 1913. Nonetheless, the Regensburg decision now provided formal regulations and fiscal support. The Hochland chapter near Munich was among the most active; it sponsored several youth excursions to the Alps in 1913. Pupils climbed midsize Bavarian peaks and spent nights in the chapter's huts. Organizers remarked that the Alpine excursion imbued participants with "eagerness, joy, and understanding" and encouraged cooperation among the different social classes. Altogether, close to one hundred youth participated in Alpine hikes.[64] The numbers are paltry compared to the Wandervögel, and it was unlikely that youth from different social classes mixed on the outings. But considering that 1913 was the inaugural year for organized Alpine youth groups, the attendance was promising. The Innsbruck chapter wasted no time and instituted the Alpine Youth Hiking Committee, which comprised thirty-three members (twenty-eight men and five women) that same year. Located at the feet of the Nordkette, Patscherkofel, and Serles peaks, Innsbruck pupils knew the mountains. But now the chapter could play a much more significant role in youth education programs. The committee sponsored Alpine excursions, certified youth group leaders, and served as a general administrator to these groups. Like other sections, Innsbruck sought to "influence the spiritual and physical development of young people, heighten their love for the Heimat and the Alpine world, deepen their knowledge of the Alps through travel, and expand their understanding of the Association's endeavors."[65]

The challenge that youth organizers faced, however, was finding accessible peaks that were not overdeveloped. The association wanted to inspire young people with the "inexhaustible sources of physical and spiritual well-being," not the debris of mass tourism.[66] The urge to preserve the Alps for future generations grew into the desire to protect the mountains. The language of youth found its way into the discourse of nature conservation. One member wrote that the promotion of nature conservation should spread to all levels of society, "but especially [to] the youth through the awakening of the love for nature."[67] However, advocating nature protection was a sensitive matter in the Alpine Association, given the organization's aim to encourage travel to the mountains. The riddle of how to preserve the Alpine environment while promoting Alpine tourism baffled members.

The Alpine Association was not the first organization to advance nature protection. As with its work in the youth movement, the club's conservation efforts connected to larger trends. When industrialization and urbanization transformed Germany and Austria, concern for environmental degradation grew. Print material on the dangers of pollution multiplied. The frequency with which Reichstag deputies discussed industrial waste increased. Professional associations intermingled as doctors and scientists held conferences in common to address toxic contaminants and public health.[68] In the filth of industrial waste, the nature protection movement bloomed into a bouquet of private organizations and state agencies. New groups took up the banner of *Naturschutz* (nature protection) or *Heimatschutz* and counted thousands of members by the early twentieth century. The two branches followed slightly different aims. *Naturschutz* clubs tended to focus on certain natural features of a landscape or on particular plants and animals. *Heimatschutz* groups took a totalistic approach, incorporating nature as well as human history and custom in their vision of the natural world. Both groups shared much in common with the Alpine Association; the various clubs were largely middle class and used parallel language when describing crimes of industry against the natural world.[69] The groups directed much of their efforts toward lobbying state governments to pass environmental regulations, raising public awareness, and supporting research. These organizations often adopted a nationalistic stance. They advanced the proposition that the natural environment shaped national character. Patriotism became an intrinsic part of nature preservation.

When protecting nature took on national importance, state governments got involved. Under the German constitution, environmental regulation fell generally within the purview of the states. The Prussian legislature adopted laws to restrict the destruction of the countryside in 1902. Two years later, the Bavarian Ministry of the Interior invited delegates from the Alpenverein and botanical, geographical, architectural, and engineering associations to establish the Landesausschuss für Naturpflege (State Committee for the Care of Nature), which Professor August Rothpletz, a member of the Alpine Association, chaired. As a club executive, Rothpletz had advocated conservation legislation, and he had lobbied state and local governments to establish official agencies charged with protecting the environment.[70] He was the government's logical choice. Although the committee was an impressive gathering, its mandate was limited. The ministry asked it to prepare expert reports, work toward the vaguely phrased "awakening and propagation of the feeling for *Naturpflege*," and coordinate efforts with other conservation-oriented organizations. Successes were small, and Rothpletz soon resigned in frustration. Within ten years, the committee existed only on paper.[71] Comparable initiatives in other states met similar fates. Business interests were powerful and often stymied regulations. Faith in technological progress had more believers than the converts to nature conservation. Overall, government intervention was minimal.

The Alpine Association's initial investment in nature protection was also modest. In 1900, following the example of groups in Italy and Switzerland, nature enthusiasts established the Association for the Protection and Care of Alpine Plants (Verein zum Schutz und zur Pflege der Alpenpflanzen) in affiliation with the Alpine Association. The practical aim of the new group was to protect Alpine flora from fumbling feet and thieving hands. It also hoped to "make new friends of plants" and increase knowledge about Alpine flora. It set about planting botanical gardens near mountain lodges, where ecologists could conduct studies and plant lovers could appreciate nature's bounty. Members also began work on an "Atlas of Alpine Flora" and a traveling exhibition of protected flowers. The group served as a clearinghouse for information on Alpine plants and had ties to a host of nature and outdoor recreation clubs in Austria and southern Germany, such as the Bavarian Botanical Society, the Austrian Tourist Club, and the Naturalist Society in Bamberg. The group also helped draft legislation, such as the Bavarian and the Austrian laws protecting edelweiss. But the organization was small. At the end of its first year it had around two hundred members; within a decade it counted close to a thousand.[72] Its few botanical gardens were quaint, certainly pretty, and hardly effective at preventing damage to the Alpine environment.

Concerned alpinists realized that the only way to protect mountains was to close them. Trains and automobiles had already gained a foothold in the Alps; to prevent industry from obtaining any more ground, conservationists favored the creation of a nature reserve in the Alps, taking their cues from the United States and Switzerland. The establishment of Yellowstone National Park in 1872 had drawn attention from all across Europe. Observers discussed the possibility of establishing similar parks in Europe, though on a much smaller scale. Plans to build a tourist train up to the summit of the Matterhorn mobilized Swiss scientists to action in the early 1900s; they constituted a Committee for Nature Protection that eventually established a national park in the Alps. Unlike the American model, which set aside land for people's enjoyment, the Swiss wanted "total protection" from the general public. The newly named National Park Commission found a region with no permanent settlements in a remote part of Lower Engadin, near the country's eastern border. Starting in 1909, the commission signed a lease with the local communes, which the federal government took over in 1914. The compromise was that people could visit the park, but hunting, fishing, logging, and farming were banned inside the grounds. Armed wardens patrolled the land and ensured that visitors abided by the rules, such as never straying from the few marked trails. Some sections of the park were open to mountain climbers, but most of it was reserved for scientific research.[73]

Following in these footsteps, a group of concerned citizens in Munich, some of whom were members of the Alpine Association, established the Verein Naturschutzpark (Association Nature Reserve) in 1909 with its headquarters in Stuttgart. Its purpose was to establish parks around the country in a variety of regions where the "primitive state" of nature would be safeguarded against the "progression of culture."[74] As a counterpart to the club in Stuttgart, Adolf Ritter von Guttenberg, a professor of forestry in Vienna, former chair of Section Austria, and member of the club's executive board, established the Austrian Nature Reserve Association in 1912, the same year that the Wendelstein train began operating. With its base in Vienna, his group also lobbied for the creation of a nature reserve in the Alps, where the "original character" of the landscape would be preserved.[75] But unlike the Swiss, these groups wanted to preserve landscapes so that citizens could enjoy them. Nature reserves were to be places free from industry and "jaded train-, bus-, and car-tourists" but open to the public.[76] Within a couple of years, the

Stuttgart group secured land in the Lüneburger Heide near Hamburg and looked to lease land in the Austrian Alps near the Niedere Tauern mountain chain in Styria.

In early 1914, the two clubs instead successfully negotiated a nature reserve in Salzburg's Pinzgau region. For about one hundred thousand kronen, the Association Nature Reserve purchased approximately ten square kilometers of land (the Austrian group lacked the funds to make the purchase). The location was ideal: the nearby pinnacles of the Glockner and Venediger mountains attracted tourists away from the Pinzgau, the vales were sparsely inhabited, and the landscape was "hardly touched" by culture. The reserve promised "unspoiled" nature, where even the trees and flowers were apparently protected from grazing sheep and goats. The property was meager, especially when compared to Yellowstone or the Swiss National Park. Still, the Alpine Nature Reserve represented a moment of triumph for conservationists.[77]

Members pushed the Alpine Association to do more. The Alpine Nature Reserve was a start, but it protected only a tiny fraction of the Eastern Alps. Articles on nature conservation began to appear in the club's publications with increased regularity and portrayed the mountains in a state of emergency. The rhetoric turned militaristic. Members believed that the club should maintain its "occupation" of the high regions of the mountains and fend off the "invasion" of industry.[78] Austrian members in particular expressed a sense of urgency, often standing at the forefront of the environmental movement within the club. Guttenberg was among the more outspoken. In a speech before the club's general assembly in 1913, he emphasized the importance of nature conservation and outlined a number of points on which the association could increase environmental awareness. The club should organize movements to protect natural monuments and demand state governments to do the same, he declared, and members should promote laws to protect Alpine plants in provinces where such laws did not exist. He emphasized the environmental education of schoolchildren, especially about their native plant and animal world. He wanted to add nature protection to the tour guide training curriculums. In sum, he urged the club to take a more active role in the protection of the "Alpine flora and natural monuments, the animal world, and the pristine beauty of the landscape." At the same meeting, the Innsbruck chapter submitted a petition for the "Protection of Alpine Plants and Natural Monuments," which contained nearly all of Guttenberg's points.[79] But the efforts were not enough. So-called robber barons and their enterprises, along with thousands of lumbering tourists, continued to occupy the Alps on the eve of the First World War.[80]

....

The years before the Great War were both exciting and frustrating for Alpine enthusiasts. Mountaineers had succeeded in opening the Alps to the broader public. But serious doubts overshadowed Alpinism. Its success threatened the very essence of the Alpine experience—struggle and peace. Concerns over tourism's environmental impact, the accelerated building of huts, the clearing of trails, the alleged betrayal of the ethos of danger and struggle, and the loss of Alpine solitude produced heated debates. Since the late nineteenth century, two divergent trends had taken shape within the climbing community—Alpine populism and mountaineering elitism—and arguments erupted between mountaineering purists, whom many qualified as "snobs," and those who favored a populist orientation, whom the extreme climbers termed "heretics."[81] Alpine populists celebrated the fact that in 1907, Payer-Hut on the Ortler (Austria's highest peak) had 2,300 overnight guests; on some days, over 100 people stood on the peak. Mountaineering elitists shuddered. The one commonality that the two groups shared was the belief that Alpinism made for a strong, united *Volk*. The *Volk* notion served as the glue to fill in the club's growing social and generational cracks. Members used the image of a healthy *Volk* in the attempt to mediate the latent tensions of nature tourism. The result was a slow shift in the club's emphasis away from individual development and toward collective well-being. Nineteenth-century tales of Alpine adventure had focused on individual accomplishments and narratives of personal triumph over danger and nature. By the early twentieth century, essays in the association's publications now also began to emphasize the relationship of Alpine tourism to strengthening the *Volk*. Most representative of this shift was the attention paid to educating youth in the ways of Alpinism.

But few climbers were willing to admit how shaky the edifice of Alpinism had become and how strong its inherent contradictions were. Alpinists, whether populist or elitist in orientation, were unable to reconcile these tensions. Even attempts to use the idea of a robust *Volk* to reinforce the cracked edifice produced conflict. Debates were turning vicious when war descended upon Europe. By 1915, armies occupied the Alps. The realm of serenity turned into a landscape of slaughter. In part, the efforts of the Alpine Association made that possible. Open mountains invited invasion. Yet the First World War gave temporary respite from the external pressures and internal crises that mass tourism had brought to the mountains. At the same time, the conflict expanded and made lasting the material transformations to the peaks. The rancor and tension incurred by opening the Alps remained permanent fixtures of the landscape. This animosity lay dormant while Germans and Austrians redirected their hostilities and battled the Italians on the heights, but it would awaken with greater violence in the interwar years.

4

The High Alps in the Great War
Soldiers and Summits on the Alpine Front

> In other respects, however, the Föhn turns out to be a mighty destroyer when its irresistible force annihilates the works of human hands, huts and houses, devastates forests, sets fires ablaze.
>
> —Rudolf Deschmann, *Der Föhn in den Alpen* (1914)

"It was not so long ago since the first tourists had declared this landscape as a point of destination," one Austrian soldier recalled about the Dolomite Alps, "and already it began to bear an increasingly militaristic imprint."[1] Antagonisms between Italy and Austria created an environment of unease in the Alps. Throughout the second half of the nineteenth century, the two were traditional enemies. Italy's unification in the 1860s came at Austria's expense. In 1859, the Habsburgs paid for defeat at the Battle of Solferino with Lombardy. The costs of Prussia's triumph over Austria in 1866 included losing Venetia to the new Kingdom of Italy, a Hohenzollern ally. In the early twentieth century, influential Italian nationalists still had their eyes on Austria's South Tyrol and the Trentino.[2] Both governments dispatched troops to the Dolomite passes. Austrian and Italian army vehicles began to sweep along newly built highways. Military forces conducted maneuvers near the borders. Officers appeared in hotels. Signs were posted forbidding photography and rest stops by wanderers. Karl Baedeker's guidebook for the Eastern Alps advised tourists about such travel hazards. The situation along Tyrol's border with Italy was especially tense. Besides photography equipment and hunting knives, even "playing-cards, almanacs, and sealed letters" were liable to confiscation. "Sketching or photographing in the neighborhood of fortifications," Baedeker warned, "also is sometimes attended by unpleasant consequences." Soldiers exercised their mandate with such severity that "harmless vacationers" were often restrained. Complaints filtered up to the Tyrolean government, and tourism's pace in the region slowed noticeably.³ It came to a halt in 1915.

On the eve of war, the Alps represented not only peace, solitude, and escape from the modern world but also excitement, danger, and death. The Great War resolved these contradictions as it scarred the mountains. The ways in which Germans and Austrians idealized the Alpine world represented their values, which, as we have seen, included an array of conflicting ideological positions before 1914. The war temporarily alleviated those divides as well. At the same time, the conflict created new problems. Industrialization of the Alps intensified with the vast expansion of roads and railways and the migration of war machinery and troops to the peaks. Erecting new military bases taxed forest reserves. Army boots trampled pastureland. The wastes of war polluted watersheds. Hostilities disrupted the Alpine ecology. That the landscape withstood the onslaught of destruction reinforced the preconceptions many people had of the Alps as muscular. The impregnable citadel-mountain came to symbolize the German nation's indomitable strength. Unvanquished, the stone towers held the promise of future triumphs. As a result of the Great War, the Alps, once the realm of serenity, now also provided a foundation for national fantasies of future conquest.

In turn, the Alps shaped perceptions of the conflict and of the men who fought on the peaks. On the Alpine front, the interactions between humans and the extreme environment were far more complex than in other theaters. Soldiers in all sectors faced harsh conditions. But as one alpinist argued, those fighting in the lowlands could not imagine the bitter existence in the mountains, where men faced subfreezing temperatures, ferocious storms, rockfalls, avalanches, and dreadful heights.⁴ Combatants who fought above acquired the heroic stature of the Alps. In the crucible of war, the ideals fostered by civilian alpinists—the hardening of the individual will against overwhelming odds, cultivation of personal vitality through struggle—were militarized. The martial and mountaineering ethos became one.

The militarization of mountaineering accentuated prewar motifs. When the German and Austrian Alpine Association had declared in 1914, "The struggle with the power of the Alpine nature has steeled us for the battle with our enemy and against the hardships of the approaching era," it echoed sentiments long held by many climbers.⁵ The death-defying struggling against nature, the freeing of oneself from the destitution of urban life and the boredom of middle-class existence, and self-renewal and cultivation in the mountains had attracted throngs of adventurers to the Alps before the war. These same allurements played into the romantic aesthetics of war in 1914. War and Alpinism had much in common, bound in "blood and iron"; both offered renewal and an end to degeneration. As one mountaineer remarked, "When the alpinist now exchanges his ice ax for the sword, his efforts remain devoted to the same ideals. It is cultural work now as before."[6] This blending of Alpine aesthetics with military values diminished distinctions between civilians and combatants not only during the conflict but also in the years that followed.

・・・・・・・・・・・・・

Property disputes in the Alps preceded Italy's war against Austria. When the peninsula transitioned from a collection of principalities to a nascent nation-state, Italian nationalists demanded expansion. In their vision, all ethnic Italians belonged within the new kingdom. This view pertained primarily to the *Welschen*, the Romance-speaking inhabitants of southern Switzerland and southeastern Austria. Like nationalists in other countries, these Italians defined ethnicity by language. While the more ardent among them desired the Swiss Cantons of Tessin and parts of Graubünden, most called for the seizure of the Trentino and South Tyrol provinces, as well as of the Dalmatia and Littoral crown lands from Austria. For Italian nationalists, the idea of Habsburg control of these regions was intolerable. They named the lands *Italia irredenta*—unredeemed Italy. To "restore" the land, Italians had to "repossess" these territories, although except for Napoleon's victory over the Austrians in 1805, the Habsburgs had ruled most of these regions since the late 1300s and had received Dalmatia during the Congress of Vienna in 1815. Such legalities were no matter for irredentists. They spoke in terms of reaching the country's "natural borders," which was their code for ethnic boundaries, and the Dolomite Alps served as their linguistic filter. In 1914, between 520,000 and 540,000 German speakers and around 380,000 to 390,000 Italian speakers lived in Tyrol, a region slightly smaller than present-day New Jersey or the state of Israel.[7] The majority of ethnic Italians lived in the Trentino and some in South Tyrol. To irredentists, this made the land rightfully theirs.

Professional geographers joined the fray. Italy's leading geographer, Giovanni Marinelli, addressed the question of "natural borders" in his 1883 grand treatise, *La Terra*, arguing that Italy's northern boundaries should follow the main watersheds, leading to the Adriatic Sea. His son Olinto, also a geographer, elaborated on his father's work and illustrated that much of Italian land lay under foreign (Austrian) domination. Other non-Italian scholars concurred. In his presidential address to the Royal Geographic Society in 1915, Douglas Freshfield asserted that the Trentino and South Tyrol were "geographically" Italian, showing that the Brenner watershed boundary conveniently overlapped the ancient bishopric border that had existed since before the Reformation.[8]

But then Albrecht Penck, a professor of geography in Berlin, made clear that political currents rather than actual rivers shaped "natural borders." This was particularly true in the Alps. The Dolomites presented political geographers with a host of challenges. Situated at the junction of empires and ethnic groups, the fractured terrain did more than make neat survey lines impossible. Penck posed the question, "What exactly do the features divide?" Some mountain chains bisect different ecological systems, like the Cascades in the Pacific Northwest, which separate the temperate rain forest from the semiarid steppe. In such regions, the label of "natural borders" makes ecological sense. But the Tyrolean ranges did not do this. What the Eastern Alps did distinguish was the Austro-Hungarian Empire from the Italian nation-state. In Penck's opinion, Italy could exist without encompassing all Italian speakers. But Austria, that fat agglomeration of ethnic groups, needed "natural borders" to hold it together. Facing "centrifugal forces" of national dissolution and weakened after defeat in 1866, Austria's "binding element" became the land itself, especially the Alps.[9]

If Penck believed that the mountains held the multiethnic empire together, then he was mistaken. The topography of the landscape confounded not only professional geographers but locals as well. Title deeds and property lines were often contested. The land dispute involving the Alpine Association's Bremer-Haus, a newly built hut in the Bocca di Brenta, illustrated the confusion. In 1910, Section Bremen commenced plans to erect a hut in the Brenta group, a mountain range in the Trentino. Since the chapter's building site sat in both the vegetation and tundra zones, ownership of the property was vague. Usually, the local county owned the productive montane and sub-Alpine pastureland, and the state controlled the upper Alpine biome. Bremen reached a compromise by acquiring a construction permit for the vegetation area from the local government, Molveno County, and by signing a lease with the Austrian state to build in the tundra zone.

Workers broke ground in June 1911 and troubles began immediately. San Lorenzo, a neighboring county, declared that it actually owned the land rights, and its commissioners asserted that the Bremen chapter lacked permission to build there. A month later, the Italian mountain club Società degli Alpinisti Tridentini (Society of Trentino Alpinists, SAT), an organization saturated with irredentists, sided with San Lorenzo and filed suit against Bremen, claiming that the Germans took property already leased to the SAT. The Italians also realized that their meager Tosa hut, which sat nearby and had the reputation for being unfriendly to Austrian and German tourists, could not compete with Bremen's luxury lodge. The land deeds were so confusing that the county court appointed a surveyor to resolve the matter in 1912. By this point, the entire Alpine Association was following the matter closely, as were Austrian state officials. The lawsuit's outcome carried far-reaching consequences for property rights in the ethnically mixed Dolomite Alps.

The surveyor determined that San Lorenzo owned the land. He based his reasoning on ecoclines, not established property lines. Most of the land parcel was karst. But San Lorenzo owned the adjacent grassy slopes of the Croz del Rifugio and the Cima Brenta Bassa, where sheep grazed. Strips of the green bands extended into Bremen's construction site. From the surveyor's logic, the Bremer-Haus sat on a large bald spot, whose vegetation patches were part of the lower pastureland and were substantial enough to fodder sheep. As such, the property belonged to San Lorenzo.

Bremen protested the report. Its lawyers argued that the patches in question were scanty. And in any case, the grazing animals were picky eaters and snubbed 90 percent of the edible plants. Still, with testimony from locals who had supposedly witnessed the occasional sheep munching on the contested land, the Italians won their lawsuit. Bremen appealed the decision in district court, which eventually ruled in the SAT's favor. In 1913, the case went to the supreme court in Vienna, whose judges upheld the lower court's verdict. Observers noted that the case had been without precedent; the supreme court had issued a landmark decision. The ruling compelled Section Bremen to surrender its hut to the SAT.[10] The legal battles left the chapter nearly bankrupt and the Alpine Association with a score to settle. More important, the Italian club's successful lawsuit jeopardized the association's other holdings in the region.

Demanding compensation for Austrian transgressions became a useful stratagem for the Italians. In 1882, the kingdom had entered into a defensive military accord with Germany and Austria-Hungary, the Triple Alliance. If one member came under attack, the other two promised mutual aid. Italians were generally not keen on an alliance with their traditional enemy. When Austria's conflict with Serbia escalated to a European war in 1914, Italy remained neutral, citing the defensive nature of its pact with the two Central powers. Not only did it refuse to commit troops, but the Italian government insisted on compensation from the Austrians. As a member of the Triple Alliance, Rome had not given consent for Vienna's intervention in the Balkans. Austria's aggression thus obligated it to Italy. This was a ploy by the irredentists to finally grasp the "unredeemed" territories. For its neutrality, Italy expected the Trentino and an adjustment of the border along the Isonzo River, at a minimum. A pamphlet later surfaced in 1918 that made public the irredentist prewar aims. It claimed that in the age of mass armies, nations needed "natural obstacles," behind which they could securely mobilize their forces. Italy thus had to reach its "natural confine" and "possess" the Alps as its first line of defense. If it did not, then the nation's enemies would occupy the littoral, and Italy would find itself backed "against a strong high wall of enclosure belonging to the enemy." The pamphlet concluded that "one war follows another always with the same net, precise and irrevocable aim; Italy wants to reach the Alps."[11]

Secret negotiations within the Triple Alliance continued into the spring until a newspaper reporter leaked the story.[12] The Central powers had offered Italy the Trentino but withheld the northern part, the Alto Adige. Details were sketchy. No one was certain how far such talks would go. The journalist may have embellished the article to excite readers. If so, it worked on the Alpine Association, whose members reacted forcefully to the news. Having just lost the Bremer-Haus, they feared that the Italians would confiscate their other huts if given the chance. The association owned fifteen huts in Italian-speaking regions, although it always tried to build in "friendly communities" and avoid areas rife with irredentists. The club's material losses would be severe if Austria ceded territory to Italy. In addition, any such agreement would force the club to forfeit a lucrative theater of tourism.[13] Chapters in Tyrol responded with particular vehemence. Innsbruck's chairman accused the Italians of charging Tyrolean property as the price for peace. "Those romantics cannot take a piece of the German state that has been German for a thousand years," he bellowed, "not without a sword stroke!"[14]

The Italians and Austrians were not the only ones rattling their sabers. When hostilities started in 1914, the Swiss army mobilized. Generals deployed the bulk of their forces in the Jura near the French border, but officers also worried about the country's eastern flank. The region was subject to irredentist avarice and vulnerable to opportunistic military commanders on either side. Strong fortifications guarded both the Austrian and Italian positions. To penetrate enemy lines, an army would have to perform a flanking maneuver, similar to the Germans' Schlieffen Plan in the west, the strategy named after Alfred von Schlieffen, who designed it in 1891 when he was chief of the general staff. According to his plan, Germany's armies were to sweep across neutral Belgium to the north while German forces to the south were to feign retreat, creating a "revolving door" effect and trapping the French. With a successful execution of the strategy, German generals believed they would avoid a two-front war. In the Alps, such an operation meant going through Switzerland. Austria's quagmires with the Serbians and Russians made its action in the Alps unlikely. But the better road connections between Switzerland and the south, along with the aggressive rhetoric of irredentists, presented a real danger with Italian forces. The Swiss had watched what happened to a neutral country that haplessly stood in the way of a determined army in 1914. They feared the same fate.[15]

Yet few military commanders among the belligerents had considered the Alps a potential battleground when hostilities erupted in August 1914. Generals deemed action on the crags unfeasible. Armies had matched the mountains before, most famously when Hannibal and later Napoleon's forces crossed them. But these troops marched through the Alps; they did not wage war on the heights. Even in 1809, when Tyrolean peasants mobilized under the leadership of Andreas Hofer to fend off the Bavarians and their French allies, the battles were fought in the valleys because the invaders rarely left the passes. The standard practice of operational maneuvers across wide battlefields was impossible when pressed against the slopes. The German High Command held to Carl von Clausewitz's belief that the peaks were unsuitable for a modern army: "The crowns of the higher Alps are so inaccessible and inhospitable that it is impossible for them to be occupied by strong bodies of troops. When one wants to have armed forces in the mountains, so as to master them, there is no choice but to remain in the valleys. At first sight this seems flawed, because according to the usual theoretical concepts one would say: the heights dominate the valleys. But this is not so since the ridges are only reachable by a few paths that, with rare exception, are only for light infantry. The roads are in the valley." When the Austrian General Franz Kuhn successfully defended South Tyrol from the Italians in 1866, he did so by heeding that advice. Kuhn's proof of Clausewitz's theorem instructed the next generation of officers in calculating the Alps in their grand strategies.[16]

But new factors had changed the equation. Despite the mindset at army headquarters, the years of work by Alpine clubs had, however unintentionally, served a military purpose. The ever-expanding network of trails and lodges, along with the construction of Alpine highways and expansion of rail lines, had made the mountains accessible. At the start of the war, one commentator estimated that over 150,000 German and Austrian citizens were members of a mountaineering club, two-thirds of whom belonged to the Alpine Association. Another 80,000 paid dues to a ski club. The Swiss held about 14,000 men in its Alpine club, the Italians counted more than 8,000, and the French numbered just over 7,000. Alpinism had become the "pacemaker" for the formation of elite mountain troops.[17] The Italian army had organized elite units of soldiers, the Alpini, who were familiar with the rugged terrain. The French had their Chasseurs Alpins. The Austrian Kaiserjäger recruited heavily from Tyrol and Vorarlberg and reinforced the local militia units, the Landesschützen. A few Austrian tacticians developed instructions and strategies for mountain warfare. Ski instructors offered combat courses to the troops. In 1907, the Alpine Association signed a military agreement with the German government for use of its Alpine huts in the event of war.[18]

Still, the Central powers were woefully unprepared to fight in the Alps. With the outbreak of war in 1914, the German army had no special units for mountain warfare. Most Prussian generals felt little need to organize auxiliary mountain troops. In November 1914, though, the Bavarian Ministry of War formed the Bavarian Snowshoe Battalion No. 1, under the command of the well-known mountain climber and writer (and influential member of the Alpenverein) Major Alfred Steinitzer. The company was small and comprised mostly middle-age men and some college students from Munich. The volunteers undertook little more than practice maneuvers in the Bavarian mountains on the weekends. The Austrians were better situated than the Germans, but only slightly. The Kaiserjäger were already deployed to the east. The home guard, including the

Landesschützen, numbered around 30,000 men. Prior to the outbreak of war, most militia groups in the Alpine villages had functioned as male social clubs, in which older boys learned to handle firearms and munitions before they entered the army. During community events, adult members wore the militia's regalia and marched in parades or played in bands. In the autumn of 1914, those of military age were enlisted in the Carpathian campaign against the Russians. Few of the citizen-soldiers left behind were conditioned to face the Alpini.

Tensions reached the breaking point when the Italian government expelled German and Austrian journalists from the country, recalled its military attaché from Berlin, and gathered its forces on the Friulian plain in the spring of 1915. The Austrian High Command ordered the Tyrolean militias to the mountain passes. The Swiss General Staff took immediate action. During a special session of the Swiss Federal Council, General Ulrich Wille, supreme commander of the army, painted a grim picture: he expected Italy to soon declare war against Austria. His officers felt that the situation was more perilous than the initial outbreak of war back in August. The possibility of invasion was now much higher, even though Wille had mobilized more divisions with mountain brigades and stationed troops along the Tessin and Graubünden borders.[19] The Swiss were right to act. Negotiations between the Austrians and Italians collapsed in early 1915. After signing a secret pact with London that promised extensive Austrian territory, including the Trentino and South Tyrol, Rome joined the Entente and let loose its armies.

・・・・・・・・・・・・・

Italy's declaration of war on Austria on 23 May 1915 created a five-hundred-kilometer-long Alpine front that extended from Switzerland to the Adriatic Sea. It reached heights of more than three thousand meters above sea level and crossed the Dolomite, Carnic, and Julian Alps. The region around the Tonale Pass held the highest trenches in the First World War on the Ortler (3,902 meters) and the Königspitze (3,857 meters).

Along the Alpine front, the Italians assembled thirty-five divisions against fourteen Austrian divisions and one German division.[20] The Italian offensive against Austria, led by General Luigi Cadorna, began two days after the declaration of war; he focused on the Isonzo Valley. This region of the Julian Alps, where the Isonzo River runs southward toward the Adriatic Sea, was less difficult for an offensive. Once renowned for its beauty and solitude, the Isonzo Valley suffered under twelve major

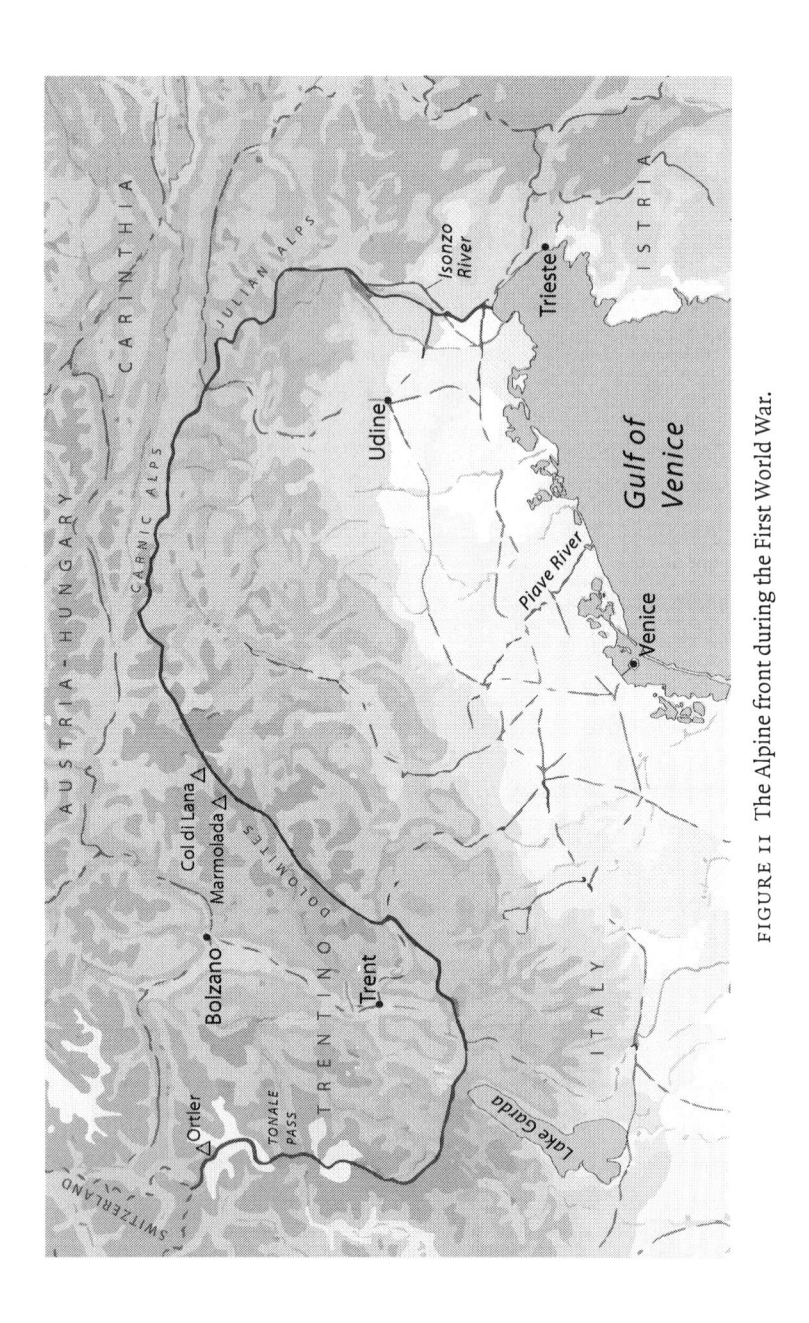

FIGURE 11 The Alpine front during the First World War.

battles during the war. Cadorna concentrated his forces on the Giulia plateau, with the objective of reaching Trieste and then crossing the plains to Vienna. From May 1915 to October 1917, the Italian army undertook eleven offensives, and Cadorna never deviated from his frontal assault strategy. In twenty-nine months of fighting, the Italians suffered

1,100,000 casualties, the Austrians 650,000. With each successive failure, Cadorna increased the manpower and artillery, but his armies were as far from Trieste in 1917 as they had been in 1915.[21] While large-scale battles raged on the Adriatic plains, Italian forces also threatened the mountains of Tyrol. For a mass army, the Alpine terrain was impossible. Along much of the front, only elite and well-equipped Alpine troops could operate among the precipitous slopes, jagged rocks, and dark crevasses; Cadorna's numerical superiority was negligible. The vertical limits, not the distances, proved to be his undoing. The Italians had the numbers, but the Austrians held the heights.

The new front created a logistical nightmare for German and Austrian armies already engaged elsewhere. Caught off guard and unable to redirect troops from the east to meet the new threat in the south, the Austrian High Command called upon local militias and all men with mountain experience (alpinists, skiers, mountain guides) to defend the border. With Italy's entry in war, the youngest and oldest members of the militias donned their uniforms, oiled their rifles, and prepared to face the Italians.[22] At first the Germans could offer little help to the Austrians. Then General Erich von Falkenhayn convinced the kaiser to form the German Alpine Corps under the command of the previous head of the Bavarian general staff, General Konrad Krafft von Dellmensingen. The allure of the special force was powerful, and the corps comprised volunteers from across Germany and transfers from the trenches on the western front. Most members were Bavarian, but many were from northern Germany.[23] All were familiar with the Alps.

The hasty mobilization to defend the mountains seemed to foster a distinctive sense of community. Alice Schalek, a correspondent for the Viennese newspaper *Neue Freie Presse* and the only female embedded journalist during the war, reported from the Tyrolean Alps and the Isonzo Valley and commented on the spirit of unity. In her observations, she appropriated the sentiments of mountaineers from the previous century. From her perspective, only up above in the mountains, free from inhibitions, far from the life of luxury, and distant from the demands of social etiquette, could these men strengthen their bonds to each other.[24] Age and status seemed of little concern to the defenders. Fathers fought next to their sons and civil servants stood shoulder to shoulder with farmhands. Many soldiers described the warm feelings between the "gray-haired" members of the Landesschützen and the younger soldiers of the German Alpine Corps. Official reports confirmed that the militias integrated easily with the corps.[25] Relations between officers and soldiers were reputed to be friendlier and demonstrated the characteristic "mountain comradeship" among those who served on the peaks. These proclamations of goodwill were what one might expect from different armies on joint missions. Yet real differences in customs and traditions existed between the Austrian and the German officer corps. The Austrian High Command had to remind its officers that successful integration depended on their cooperation with the Germans.[26]

The call to arms supposedly softened the ill will between the provinces and the central government and cemented allegiance to the imperial crown. Viennese observers sometimes remarked on the provincialism of Tyrolean peasants, insinuating shaky loyalties on their behalf. According to one reporter, farmers apparently loathed the central government, as personified by the tax collector. But when the kaiser called upon "his Tyrolers" to defend the land, they answered.[27] When the Tyrolean militias mobilized, they recalled their struggle for independence in 1809, albeit with selective memory since they were now battling the Italians and not the Bavarians. Fighting off foreign invaders from the native soil served as the discursive connection between the two conflicts. Soldiers wrapped together their overlapping, sometimes competing loyalties to family, land, and empire into the symbol of the "holy mountain."[28] The rhetoric of protecting the homeland found particular resonance throughout the region, precisely because Austrians and Germans were on the defensive in their own territory. Homes became headquarters. Town halls were converted to command centers, hospitals to triage barracks, and guesthouses to officers' mess halls. Bolzano, once the staging area for climbers, had become the "anteroom of war" with soldiers stationed throughout the city. To one reporter's eyes, the "difference between the martial and the civil had disappeared."[29]

Likewise, the German and Austrian Alpine Association now designated itself as a *Schutzverein*, a civil defense society. In response to the heightened sense of national duty, the association introduced the Fraktur script in all of its publications, ending the club's internal debate about font. The arguments against changing the script became hollow when concerns about international opinion appeared unpatriotic after August 1914. The executive committee also decided to continue publishing the club's newsletter and journal during the war as a way to maintain morale. The club's correspondent, Heinrich Hess, wrote a regular feature on the war in the Alps for the newsletter. The association gave money to assist the war effort, though executives were often uncertain as to how best to donate the funds. Some wanted to support field hospitals, others suggested sending warm clothes to the troops, and a few wanted to establish a rest home for wounded warriors.[30] As an organization, the club donated thousands of maps, blankets, and bedding, along with first aid and rescue equipment. Individual members sent equipment to the front lines in the form of care packages, including ice axes, mountaineering poles, backpacks, lanterns, rope, sunglasses, boots, mittens, compasses, towels, sweets and preservatives, baked goods, and lots of cigarettes.[31] One dedicated member traveled across Germany and Austria giving lectures on the Alpine front and donated all proceeds to the war effort.[32] The association also provided troops with trained mountain guides, expanded its network of trails, made its huts available for military use as observation posts and barracks, and printed detailed leaflets instructing the troops in mountain survival.[33]

But the war took its toll. Battles in the mountains ended tourist excursions to the Dolomites. Italian artillery targeted the club's lodges, which had long been a source of irritation for the irredentists. By September 1915, Sections Nuremberg, Bamberg, and Leipzig had lost huts. Italian soldiers had burned down Academic Section Berlin's hut, which had been well stocked with food and equipment and whose meter-thick walls had withstood many a winter storm. The war's demands shrank the association's coffers and sapped its membership. The executive committee canceled the annual meetings from 1915 through 1918, though it still convened once every year. Chapters continued to submit activity reports to the association's central office. But these simply listed the chapter's managing board and the names of members who had died a "hero's death" on the "field of honor." Most chapters held intermittent meetings, during which chairmen designated funds for the war effort, speakers discussed major battles, and members read aloud letters from those on the front. As one chairman observed, the war had brought associational life to a "near standstill."[34] As a tourist organization, the club receded into the background. As a self-appointed *Schutzverein*, however, the Alpine Association stood at the forefront of the national cause.

The Alpine expertise of its members became the club's most important contribution to the war. Overcoming the dangers in the mountains required an "iron soldierly spirit," and Alpine soldiers needed to be "men of iron" to survive.[35] Commanders requested troops with a strong set of lungs, healthy hearts, and the intelligence to contend with the demanding environment—men conditioned to fight in the Alps.³⁶ The club's Austrian and German chapters provided them. The characteristics of true alpinists were the qualities of a good soldier. Strength, will, tenacity, and courage were essential to both. Younger members of the association had enlisted with the outbreak of war in 1914. Eduard Pichl received a commission as a lieutenant and fought against the Russians in the Carpathian Mountains, where he was wounded and captured. After spending thirty-three months in a Siberian prisoner-of-war camp, he returned to Austria in a disabled prisoner exchange. He then traveled to South Tyrol and aided the war effort as a course instructor in a mountain guide division.³⁷ Many of the club's older members served as *Alpinen Referenten*, consultants to the troops on the Alpine front. Almost fourteen hundred Alpenverein mountain guides served as noncommissioned officers on the front. The consultants gave their expert opinion on all matters Alpine, including clearing paths, erecting barracks on the slopes, setting up cable transports, and addressing safety concerns with avalanches and rockslides. They taught soldiers the proper techniques for climbing mountains, what equipment to use, and how to secure themselves with ropes and harnesses. Men like Gustav Renker were indispensable. Renker was a member of the Alpine Association and among the better-known consultants. He was also a Swiss citizen. But he donned the Austrian field gray not out of sympathy for the Austrian monarchy—"for a democratic Swiss and a republican that would be impossible"—but rather in cultural solidarity with Germandom.³⁸ Officers praised alpinists, calling men like Renker "people of strength, full of daring, full of desire to test their abilities against nature's might."³⁹

The extreme mountain environment demanded such men. The heights of the Alpine front distinguished it from the western or eastern fronts. Soldiers called it a "different sort of war," where men fought along both the horizontal and vertical planes.⁴⁰ While battles in the west and the east dealt with masses of men, the war in the high mountains took place on a much smaller, more intimate scale. What struck reporters who had spent time on the western front was "the emptiness of the battlefield" in the Alps. "At first glance one sees nothing of trenches or positions," one correspondent recalled, "also no smashing impacts, no machine guns hammering, indeed not a single whipping rifle shot disturbed the paralyzing stillness[;] with the indefatigable thunder of the Western Front still in my ear, I was at first almost disappointed."⁴¹ Troops who transferred from the western front were at first surprised by the seemingly primitive nature of warfare in the Alps, compared to the "modern" war in other sectors with the mass armies and heavy artillery.

Unlike the open marches in the east where vast plains allowed movement across hundreds of miles, the Alpine front was cramped space with the "fury of war in a concentrated form."[42] The stone and ice, chasms, and snowfields made large-scale troop movements difficult. The war in the Dolomites evolved into a battle of squads. Small groups of soldiers patrolled sectors of the mountains like the Marmolada in search of enemy soldiers. Located to the east of Trent, the Marmolada was the highest mountain in the Dolomites and sat on the border between Austria and Italy. Austrian patrols frequently climbed its peak, Punta Penia, tracking the Italians.[43] Here individual soldiers played a pivotal role. As Renker explained: "The elemental force of war is, despite all the assistance of science, man himself and more so than anywhere else this is the case with the fighting in the high mountains."[44] Combat in a primeval landscape returned battle to the chivalrous age of war, before technology had diminished the role of individual warriors. Hand-to-hand fighting fit romantic notions of combat. In this sense, action on the Alpine front was easier to understand than the immense battles on the western front.

War in the Alps was no less terrifying. Nighttime was always the worst. Enemy soldiers often attacked under the cover of darkness.[45] The pitch black of the mountains amplified uncertainties as to the foe's movement. One contributor to the Alpine Association's newsletter described his harrowing experience while on guard:

> Listen! A metallic noise sounded. It could be the soft jingle of the steel of an ice pick or an ax. . . . Two guards carefully raise their heads above the cover. They listen tensely, holding their breath, hands to the ears to hear better. After a while, one points to the southwest. From there came the noise. The second swings himself silently over the balustrade of the cover. . . . A knife and hand grenades are his only weapons. Carefully he crawls across the shimmering snowy surface towards the southwest. . . . The other listens. . . . Anxiety-filled minutes pass. The soft jingle of the ax and the whirr of the ice splitter continues. Then, a short rattling scream of terror that immediately dies away. Deep stillness. The devout Tyroler above grips a cross, "Take pity oh Lord on this poor soul," his lips whispered.[46]

Identifying the slight sounds of the night made the difference between life and death. Even an experienced mountain climber like Walter Schmidkunz, a respected member of the Alpine Association, felt skittish on night patrol: "A footstep? Only a falling fir needle. A distant thud? No!—a stone falls up there in the cirque. . . . There! A roving light! Lanterns? Patrols? Ach, only a single star bathes itself in running water down in the valley below! How that wears you down! How that sucks on the nerves!" Soldiers who had spent time in the Dolomites during peace found it odd to fight on the same ground. Fears of ambush, the dark solitude, silence, and the uncanny features of the mountains at night unnerved the toughest of men. Schmidkunz likened the mountains at night to a crypt: "Like the lid of the marble sarcophagus, the dreadful mountain mass presses on the mind."[47]

Both sides struggled to overcome the landscape. Cadorna plied sheer numbers to the obstacles. Italian batteries shelled the Austrian positions, and then a surge of Alpini troops struggled up the mountainside. But only in rare instances did they break through. Usually, they were slaughtered.[48] The challenges of positioning cannons on the slopes and coordinating fire with an infantry advancing upward, not forward, exasperated more than one German artillery commander. The large, train-drawn guns common to the western front were too heavy and cumbersome for the rails in the Alps.[49] Instead, troops hauled up smaller cannons designed in the mid-nineteenth century. The Alps hosted an old-fashioned war. Soldiers even employed packs of hardy mountain dogs to carry munitions.[50] One minor innovation on the Alpine front was the use of the "roll bomb," which, once fired, rolled down the mountainside into the enemy's position. Some commanders attempted to use airplanes to dislodge defenders. The new technology had proven somewhat effective on the western front. Renker stood stock-still in amazement when he first saw an observation plane in the Alps.[51] But while novel, planes were usually of little use in the high mountains, where dense clouds and heavy fog blinded pilots. Engineers struggled to find suitable clearings for airstrips. Unexpected mountain downdrafts sometimes dashed fliers to earth. Even with greater accessibility, the Alps remained largely a barrier to the new machines of war.

Big guns may have had problems getting around the mountains, but people did not. Tourists were still permitted to enter Switzerland from the Austrian or Italian sides, except those wearing a military uniform or insignia of any type. Vacationers in civilian clothes could visit freely, although border guards refused anyone whom they suspected of espionage, and their definition of "suspicious" was broad.[52] To move troops quickly in the event of an invasion, the Swiss army kept open the passes. Its strategy supported the tourist industry but also provided opportunity for uninvited guests. Smugglers, deserters, and spies managed to sneak over the lines. Austrian and Italians squads willfully crossed neutral territory. One daring Austrian officer disguised himself as an Italian soldier, infiltrated enemy positions, and then successfully escaped.[53] Flagrant breaches of the border led to diplomatic showdowns. The Italians accused the Swiss of being sympathetic to the Austrians by allowing their patrols through. Given that Renker's sense of loyalty was not altogether uncommon among his Swiss compatriots, the Italians may have had a point. The Swiss army High Command repeatedly issued strict orders to prevent such encroachments, but the frequency of these orders suggested their ineffectiveness.[54] Illegal crossings continued.

The Swiss outpost on the Dreisprachespitz (Peak of Three Languages) witnessed the most violations. Located not far from the Stelvio Pass in the Ortler chain, the Dreisprachespitz stood at the nexus of the three armies. Here the Swiss border jutted into the front line, forming a salient between the Austrian and Italian defenses. Proximity to the fighting endangered Swiss troops stationed there. For political reasons, their government had decided against expanding outer defenses.[55] Soldiers could only speculate and curse what those reasons might be. Writing to his division commander, one Swiss officer warned that his emplacements were not strong enough to prevent intrusions. His patrols and guard posts had already come under fire. Italians and Austrians took aim at each other across the Swiss salient, and belligerent bullets had no respect for borders. He reported no casualties, but that could change if the opposing sides used grenades. He asked what to do if his men were wounded or killed. In response, battalion headquarters issued orders to return fire.[56]

The tense situation did not deter those sick of war from seeking asylum in Switzerland. Cloaked in mountains, deserters used the Dreisprachespitz as a primary transit point. The majority of deserters were from Cadorna's army. Not all Italians had favored their country's entry into the conflict. One Italian POW remembered protests in Torino against the declaration of war.[57] Cadorna's single-minded approach and his harsh disciplinary punishments did not help matters. To dissuade would-be deserters, the Italian regime strung barbed wire across parts of its border with Switzerland in 1916. Sentries patrolled constantly with orders to shoot on sight.[58] But each month some disheartened soldiers still risked imprisonment or death. What began as a trickle in late 1916 turned to a steady flow in the last two years of the war. In July 1917, one Swiss company received twenty Italians, four Austrians, four Serbians, and one Montenegrin. Fifty Russian refugees also crossed the border, an abnormally high number reflecting the turmoil in that country. During the last two weeks in February 1918, the same Swiss detachment took in eight Italian and eight Austrian deserters, six Russian refugees, one Serbian refugee, one Austrian soldier who had fled from an Italian POW transport, and seven intrepid Italian POWs who had escaped from a camp in Hungary and stole their way to Switzerland.[59] The Swiss generally accepted the asylum seekers. All deserters immediately underwent lengthy health examinations, and those diagnosed as contagious (with venereal disease, scabies, typhus, influenza, and so forth) were quarantined.[60] The anxiety about disease hinted at the dismal conditions along some sectors of the front more than at a Swiss fondness for cleanliness.

Desperate days on the Alpine front contributed to the sense of disconnection that combatants felt. Yet soldiers on the peaks interpreted these feelings of disconnection differently from those at lower altitudes. Renker described the impassive acceptance of death by men on the Alpine front as a form of valor. Just as water "gnaws away at limestone" and as "rocks gradually crumble," those who sat above could see the coming end. "That," he claimed, "is the courage of the mountain war!"[61] Others were more somber. Many soldiers remembered feeling surrounded by death and the sense of impending ruin. Most felt cut off from the world. Elitism combined with melancholy. The Alpine world at once elevated the soldier with its majesty and crushed him with its burdens. The emotions and sensations experienced by soldiers on the Alpine front resembled those of mountaineers in the years before the war. In this respect, civilians of the German and Austrian Alpine Association believed that they understood the needs and fears of soldiers better than politicians and families back home.

In many cases, the disconnection felt by soldiers on the heights from those on the home front fell along gender lines. In his memoir of fighting in the Alps, one veteran described the experiences of being on leave in Vienna. After spending a day with his family, he attended a war film, which he found to be mawkish, kitschy, and completely unrealistic but which captivated the civilian audience. Such drivel was appropriate for "women and weaklings," he thought, not for soldiers.[62] In a way, civilians back home idealized the war, just as climbers had romanticized the mountains in the nineteenth century. The two worked in tandem. Alice Schalek did much to perpetuate the view of the mountains as a hypermasculine realm. "It is unfortunate that we all, old people, women and children, could not spend at least a short time there," she remarked in one of her reports.[63] But like urban tourists from years earlier, Schalek saw only what she knew from her comfortable bourgeois upbringing in Vienna and overlooked the local inhabitants. In fact, farmers' wives and peasant girls played an essential part on the Alpine front. They carried food supplies, firewood, and potable water from the valleys and up the mountainside. Desolate peaks could not sustain human life for long periods of time. Renker mentioned a serendipitous moment when Italian artillery shelled a nearby lake, killing the fish and providing the Austrian soldiers stationed there with an unexpected feast.[64] The Imperial Office for National Defense instructed troops on how to prepare for summer water shortages in Tyrol by collecting snowmelt.[65] But without the support of local women, soldiers stationed up on the barren wastes would have starved, frozen, or died of thirst. Several Tyrolean women even donned men's clothing and attempted to join Standesschützen units.[66] When discovered, those women were sent back home. Even though women played a key role in the war effort, their activities were restricted to a traditional understanding of gender roles: men fought and women provided.

Soldiers on all fronts discussed the tensions between the front lines and the home front, the sense of belonging to a front community, and the pervasive feeling of death. But the mountain landscape forged a particular frontline community in the Alps. Those who served on the Alpine front had a unique perspective on the world below. While soldiers in the east felt forlorn in the vast empty spaces and combatants in the west felt like troglodytes, those in the Alps stood on the peaks above. The extreme environment developed physical prowess and mental fortitude. Clausewitz had noted, "The national spirit of an army (enthusiasm, fanatical zeal, faith, opinion) displays itself most in mountain warfare, where every one down to the common soldier is left to himself." In his opinion, mountainous country was the best campaigning ground for popular levies.[67] The perilous landscape elevated common soldiers to heroic stature. Even men who had no formal military training turned into "heroes" in the Alps. Many described the soldiers on the Alpine front as "our heroes," as "true heroes of the high mountain war," or as "simple men" who had answered their country's call. Others compared the steadfastness of the soldiers to the "ancient rocks" of the mountains.[68] Alpinists felt that the natural environment engendered a common "Alpine mentality" on the front, which bound Germans to Austrians.[69] Soldiers saw themselves as witnesses to the great struggle between human defiance and nature as they stood on the heights. Schmidkunz, not lacking a sense of self-importance, felt that his patrol was situated "at the pivotal point of the world, we stood at the center of all happenings, indeed the history of the world must have hinged upon us, yearning eyes all looked to us."[70] The Alpine environment elevated the experience of battle to a nearly existential yet nonetheless material level.

. . . .

While the mountains raised soldiers above the world, the war wreaked havoc on the Alpine landscape. The environmental impact of the First World War in the Alps was colossal. The rapid growth of Alpine tourism in the years before the war had raised the concerns of conservationists, who had worked to guard the mountains against the "depopulation, desertion, impoverishment, and deforestation" wrought by industry.[71] The war in the mountains brought to realization their deepest fears. The migration of armies to the Alps accelerated developments that had begun in the nineteenth century. As on the other fronts, trains played a crucial role in moving soldiers. In the preparation for war, existing lines in the Alps were expanded and new connections built. Isolated valleys became integrated within a sprawling military network. Those additions included more cable cars and lifts that zipped up the slopes like stitches. Streets were widened to accommodate heavier volumes of traffic. Military construction dwarfed the earlier efforts of the Alpine Association. The government spent thousands building large camps in the valleys, which included barracks, stalls for pack animals, and supply depots. For the best portage, artillery officers established munitions dumps near rivers, where harmful chemicals sometimes mingled with the flowing water.[72]

The army renovated the hills as well as the dales. To turn the Alps into functioning fortresses, engineers drilled and dug into the rock face to build command centers, set up electric generators, and establish observation posts. Others planted rows of iron spikes in the rock walls and attached metal ladders to the cliffs. Several new barracks clung to the mountainside and to some looked liked "swallows' nests" at a distance.[73] The army had a tacit understanding that the Alpine Association would assume ownership of the new buildings after the war.[74] Although previous construction projects had immersed the club in heated debates, no one voiced criticism now. Telephone wires crossed the peaks. The mountains hummed with the new sound of military machinery. Hermann Czánt, a colonel in the Austrian army, found the changes difficult to grasp. "How electrified the Königspitze was," he remarked, "was really hardly imaginable."[75] The guts of glaciers, like those on the Marmolada, became a jumble of shafts and tunnels carved out of the ice, crawling with soldiers. Entire companies lived inside the icy mammoths. Giant spotlights altered the perception of the mountains. Used to track enemy movements, the spotlights created eerie images on rock faces at once bathed in unnatural light and sheathed in darkness. All the aspects of the modern world that mountain climbers had sought to escape were now a permanent part of the Alpine scenery.

The wages of war in the Alps were ecological degradation. Movie star and veteran Luis Trenker remembered the environmental destruction and how "exceedingly bloody the rings around the especially important mountains were."[76] The Col di Lana, like the Marmolada, was one such mountain. Situated at a critical point along the Dolomite highway, the Col di Lana afforded key artillery observation and defended vital railway lines. The Austrians called it the "mountain of iron"; Italians called it the "mountain of blood." The exact number of those killed remains unclear, but more than eighteen thousand Italian soldiers and nearly as many Austrians died on its slopes. Although the battles on the Col di Lana did not match the scale of action on the western front, they were as intense. In a last-ditch attempt to take the summit, the Italians tunneled under the Austrian position and packed the chambers with over five metric tons of explosives. On 17 April 1916, the Italians detonated the mine. One Austrian survivor described what followed:

> The peak of the Col di Lana burned like a pillar of fire in the night sky. The mountain trembled and shook. It opened up. It rose. The peak tipped over, lost its shape, broke in on itself together. Here a chasm opened, there another closed. Rocks, snow, earth, human bodies, gun supports, covers, shelters, barracks, steel plates, machine guns flew light as feathers upwards, rained and raged heavily down. . . . Balls of fumes and thick smoke unfolded, rolled before the wind and were driven forward, sank, tattered, dissolved. When the smoke, which had long hovered low, faded away, one saw through the rain of ash the mutilated peak. Was that the Col di Lana? Who should recognize its well-known shape?[77]

Although few peaks were as mutilated as the Col di Lana, the landscape suffered everywhere. Artillery and other machines of war marred the countryside. Barbed wire scarred snowfields. Farmland and vineyards were ruined.

The woods bore the brunt of war. Artillery fire splintered trees. The loss of protective bark exposed stands to pests, rot, and blight. Wood was the fundamental construction material during the war. Trenches, barracks, bridges, transports, and cooking fires consumed forests. Out of concern for maintaining timber reserves, the German Alpine Corps received detailed instructions for obtaining lumber. Troops were to first use trees that had already fallen or were stripped of bark. Orders expressly forbade soldiers from felling trees along the timberline, which was a protected zone. The men were to avoid making large clear-cuts but were rather to distribute the cut areas in a "chessboard-like fashion." To avert landslides, the directive warned not to remove trees along the banks of streams. Trees also had to be cut in a certain way. If sawed down improperly, threat of mudslides and avalanches increased. Since lumber was not to be substituted for firewood, officers were expected to familiarize themselves with the trees in their sector and know the appropriate uses for each species. The corps designated timber experts to travel to the various "impact points" and provide assistance. But despite their efforts, troops leveled forests anyway to have unobstructed lines of fire and to prevent ambush. Deforestation led to a greater danger of avalanches in the winter and of soil erosion and flooding in the spring and summer. Some species of flora were pushed to the edge of extinction. Plants that survive at high altitudes are simultaneously hardy and delicate. They reproduce slowly. If enough are picked or plowed under, then those that remain are likely to fail.[78]

The environmental transformations wrought in war reinforced the preconceptions that urbanites had of the Alps. Soldiers groomed by the culture of the Alpine Association viewed mountains as pristine nature, however inaccurate, now ruined by war. Photographers and war correspondents captured the devastation wrought by artillery and further strengthened this view. In one image the mountain rose up and seemed to overwhelm the viewer with its appearance of strength. At the summit, smoke furled into the air, sending debris crashing down on the viewer below. The mountain looked like a volcano. The stone ramparts stood impervious to the blast. The blinding sun, which lay behind the explosion, threw the mountain into sharp relief and gave the scene a biblical quality. Here it seemed that the mountain defied the impact on its peak. A picture of another mountain gave a different impression. In this photograph a large plume of black smoke dominated the mountain and polluted the air. The mountain appeared to have fallen to its side, as if humbled and broken by the explosion. Unlike the brilliant sky in the first picture, dark gray clouds covered the horizon and deepened the sense of gloom. Barbed-wire fences crisscrossed the rock face and looked like stitches on the ailing mountain.

While loud explosions were dramatic, the silent miles of barbed wire were equally shattering. As in France and Belgium, barbed wire stretched across the Alpine front. The lines of dark twisted metal stood out in the pure white snowfields and looked like a scar on the Alps. In one photograph, the snows covered the mountain and reflected the sun. Towering peaks in the distance gave a sense of profound space, and the entire picture presented the impression of unspoiled nature but for the barbed wire running across the mountain face, which stretched across the entire view. A second photograph offered the same impression. Instead of displaying a proud peak, this picture showed a snowfield cluttered with barbed wire, guarded by Austrian soldiers and their dog. A mountain towered behind them. Layers of barbed wiring acted as a barrier between the viewer and the massif.

Seeing the landscape scarred by war threw into sharp relief the image of a peaceful world under siege. But this world fought back. Soldiers found themselves confronted not only by the Alpini but also by a harsh and unforgiving landscape. The Alpine environment presented soldiers with difficulties not experienced on the western or eastern fronts. Fighting at high altitudes was a singular experience. Combat along the vertical axis added additional elements of physical demand where moving forward meant climbing upward. Gravity constituted a constant threat. Every day troops faced avalanches, lightning storms, and rockfalls as well as heavy rains, blinding snow, and thick fog. Soldiers suffered from exposure, altitude sickness, snow blindness, sunburn, hypothermia, and frostbite.[79] The cold weather sapped immune systems and made the soldiers more vulnerable to communicable diseases. In the eyes of the combatants, nature could turn the Alpine paradise into hell. Many were convinced that natural disasters accounted for more casualties than combat. Renker overheard one flatlander mutter, "How nice it would be if the mountains were not here."[80] Another soldier voiced the despair held by many: "This monstrous front will devour us all."[81]

In winter, the mountains did just that. Soldiers called death by avalanches, snowstorms, or freezing "white death." Deep chasms and fissures hidden by snow also complicated military operations and increased the risk of military injury or death. During the winter the situation was intolerable. By late September big snowfalls smothered the Alps. Troops required a long list of proper apparel and equipment. They could expect isolation. Soldiers needed to collect enough wood to last the winter and learn how to conserve food, since transports would be unreliable. Ice might damage telegraph and telephone lines, cutting off communication with the valleys. The cold claimed thousands of lives. The heavy snows buried roads, and those who did not succumb to "white death" faced starvation. Some planners recommended building more permanent barracks with insulation to better withstand the elements.[82]

The struggle against environmental conditions and the tedious daily labor to repair damage done by the weather weakened troop morale. One could feel Renker's misery when he observed that in the Alps, snow fell for weeks, not for hours or days, and it was not the "graceful, sparkling flakes, dancing before one's window," he explained, "but teeming, whooshing gusts."[83] The sun too disappeared for weeks. The nights in subzero temperatures and the days with continuous overcast skies made for a maddening existence. Soldiers in field gray lived in a gray-clouded land; the mute and colorless world numbed the mind. The images of light and freedom found in mountaineering stories before the war seemed more like fairy tales in the wintry gloom. The war in the Alps became a gray hell. On the occasions when the sun did shine, it threatened soldiers with snow blindness. When the storms calmed, the deep snow had a muffling effect, absorbing sound but for the crystal tinkling of ice and the occasional rumble of avalanches. Lectures by winter survival experts were designed to brace the uninitiated. Yet even seasoned alpinists were despondent over the dual struggle with the weather and the war. Huddled in the barracks and listening to the freezing wind howl outside, Schmidkunz wondered who would triumph: the "men of iron" or the "mountains of ice."[84]

The first winter on the Alpine front was severe; the winter of 1916–17 was catastrophic. Snowfalls hit record highs and temperatures reached thirty-year lows. In some sections of the Alps, snow banks were more than ten meters deep, while temperatures plummeted well below freezing. Men returned from patrol frostbitten and incoherent.[85] Most of those who died during this winter fell victim to the massive powder-snow avalanches, which were more destructive than the wetter avalanches in previous years. Soldiers recalled this winter with bitterness. They often awoke to find the barracks doorway blocked by snow, and they spent the day digging themselves out.[86] Blizzards hid trails in chest-deep snow and made passageway to food depots and isolated barracks perilous. Going on patrol was insufferable. In the vain attempt to engage the enemy, soldiers trudged through blinding snow flurries along tortuous paths and heard only the wind and the pattering of ice particles against their helmets. The contours of the landscape amplified air currents, which blew with gale force against the mountainside. As Schmidkunz bemoaned: "Here, around us, the mountain roars."[87] Winter weather brought fighting to a standstill. Soldiers could do little more than assume defensive positions on the mountain summits. The deadly conditions of the high mountains in winter enforced a natural peace.[88] Fighting against Italians held the potential for victory, but battling against nature meant almost certain defeat.

While the storms brought despair to soldiers, they repaired the damaged landscape. The deep snows covered the scars of war. Avalanches swept away barracks, batteries, and barbed wire, leaving little trace of men or matériel and returning the mountains to what soldiers thought was their "original state."[89] Troops depended on the *Alpinen Referenten* to detect potential avalanche sites and to steer patrols away from hazardous areas, although even the most experienced alpinists found the conditions to be deadly. Renker described a near-death experience when an avalanche buried his patrol:

The storming avalanche tore at me, pulled and shook me—but
in mad mortal fear I held on. And then it raged around me, white
waves surged, lifted my feet from the ground . . . higher and higher
climbed the tide over my legs, over my chest, my breath failed as if
a clamp had been placed on my nose and mouth. Now it is covering
me—this is the end! Suddenly everything is still, only to the left
is there rushing like a torrent from the mountain. I could breathe
again and sucked the air like a man dying of thirst drinking water,
but I cannot move, can see nothing. . . . Then a voice pulls me out
of the hypnosis. From up above the First Lieutenant calls, "Doctor
are you still alive?" and a pale face with large, staring eyes looked
down on me. "That was close," I said slowly and with difficulty.
"Yes," he replied, "but where are the others?" "They are all dead," I
murmured to myself.[90]

The devastation of avalanches matched the destruction wrought by artillery. A single avalanche killed three hundred men in the Marmolada region. One soldier remembered "White" Friday the Thirteenth of December 1916, when thousands of soldiers died in avalanches. Another described the "Black Thursday" in the same month when the human and material costs of avalanches rivaled losses in the spring offensive.[91] Winter's wrath led soldiers to believe that those who fell to avalanches died a hero's death.

The summer months presented their own dangers. Perched on the summits, soldiers sat exposed to the naked sun, often with burns to show for it. Barracks and observation posts acted as lightning rods during the summer storms. To the combatants, the lightning flashes immersed peaks in a "sea of flames" amid tremendous thunder, the mountain's own artillery fire. The proliferation of metal machinery on the peaks heightened the peril. The slightest sign of a storm sent soldiers scrambling to dismantle the phones and remove metal objects as far from the barracks as possible. While resting in the barracks, one lieutenant experienced a lightning strike firsthand: "Suddenly a tremendous blow and crash—next to us was a green-golden flame and then the entire place was in flames! Holy God! Have we been blown up? Just outside across the burning rubble, everyone screaming, a wild tangle of humanity. . . . Over there the dugout is in flames, cries for help, wounded, pieces of the barrack fly about, windows rattle. The bright lightning and the claps of thunder—I want out!"[92] Although the units suffered fewer casualties from lightning strikes than avalanches, the summer drama fed the vision of the Alps' retaliation.

The Alps were an arena of redemption as well as death. Soldiers offered conflicting impressions of the mountains. They saw the war as destructive yet formative, and they believed that the Alps offered at once annihilation and asylum. Nature's towers and ramparts protected the Germans and Austrians who defended the heights. For soldiers, the Alps stood "for something very real . . . absolutely invincible fortresses, *our fortresses*," a "natural bulwark," and an "unshakable front" stronger than "modern armor."[93] Many located the "will to victory" in the Alpine landscape during their service.[94] In some accounts, the elemental force of avalanches and lightning storms strengthened soldiers. Surviving an avalanche or a lightning strike made some more resilient and gave others a new sense of self. Nature's tempests in the mountains proved just as formative as any factory-milled metal storms on the western front. Persevering on the

Alpine front developed a person, just as mountain climbing had in the years of peace.

While the mountain's fury unleashed death, the overwhelming beauty of the Alpine landscape provided respite from the machinery of war. Certain areas of the Alpine front did witness destruction and constant bombardment, but broad sectors did not. The Alps were not the desolated, ugly plain of no-man's-land. For soldiers on the western front, the pervasive images of mud, trenches, and gore shaped their perception of the war. The mountains stood in contrast to the unrecognizable morass of industrial destruction. The snowcaps, vertical heights, and precipices, though deadly, were beautiful. Even "white death" conveyed an image of purity. Soldiers wrote of how the towering white peaks and the vast blue sky made them forget for a moment that they were in the middle of a war. In contrast to the gloom of the world below, the peaks offered light of such brilliance that soldiers felt transported from battle. For all the destruction wrought by avalanches and storms, the dreadful mountains helped reverse the despair of war.

• • • • • • • • • • • • •

The Alps could not save the German and Austro-Hungarian Empires from collapse. The Central powers had trounced the Italians during the Battle of Caporetto in October 1917, but their joy was short-lived. The Battle of the Piave in June 1918 marked the turning point. Prompted by German demands to launch an offensive across the Piave River, the Austro-Hungarian army initiated its last major attack. The battle was a comprehensive failure for Austria. The defeat signaled the beginning of the end of the Austro-Hungarian Empire. Strikes and riots broke out in cities across the empire. Members of Hungary's parliament expressed open dissatisfaction. Although mutinies did not take place until late October 1918, the non-Austrian regions of the empire abandoned the Habsburg cause, and non-German soldiers deserted the army.[95] The situation on the Austrian side was dire: morale was low, food rations were often inedible or at starvation levels, clothing was inadequate for winter, and fuel was in severe shortage. The poor harvests in Hungary and Romania resulted in a food crisis along the Alpine front. In one Austrian division, the average man's weight was fifty kilograms. From July to October 1918, the Austrian army on the Alpine front shrank from 650,000 to 400,000 because of illness and desertion. The Battle of Vittorio Veneto, which began near the end of October 1918, was the empire's last gasp. Although the Italians met with stiff resistance, they eventually defeated the remaining vestiges of the Austro-Hungarian army. The Italians and Austrians signed an armistice on 3 November, and hostilities concluded the next day.[96] Austria's war was lost.

Defeat further complicated the meaning of the mountains. War-weary Franz Karl Ginzkey, a novelist and soldier on the Alpine front, described a psychotic episode he experienced during his train ride home to Vienna. As he rode "with the soldierly turmoil in the soul," he gazed out the window at the passing Alpine landscape, wondering if he would ever find peace. For a moment the beauty of the glaciers and snowfields transported him from his pain. But as he sat half awake, a large fly flew in front of his window and blocked his view. The sight disturbed him. The fly's dark silhouette seemed to travel at the speed of the train. To Ginzkey's eyes the hideous shadow grew immense and terrible until it blotted out the entire glacier. His vision expressed the feelings held by many that defeat had darkened the mountains.[97] For others, within the anguish of defeat hope was sustained. As Renker explained: "The mountains may have lost their purity, their Alpine ideal, so they have become something different to us, which I at least would estimate just as important: powerful monuments to a heroic era, witnesses to unheard of loyalty and self-sacrifice. The heroes, who in the winter storms and summer lightning strikes, lived, fought and died there above, have engraved on these mountains the mighty features of their own nature." The fallen appropriated the timelessness and heroic stature of the mountains. The Alpine ossuary gave meaning to the dead and offered the living a piece of eternity. For those of Renker's mindset, the mountains had played an important role in the war for Germany and Austria and would play an even greater role in the future. "Upon new paths will a new people, a powerful, victorious generation, climb to the heights," Renker continued; "the wounded, struck down by the war, will be healed and new life will bloom out of the ruins."[98]

A cult of memory grew up around the mountains. The battered landscape itself served as a memorial to the conflict. Stone better preserved the contours of war than sod. As one writer had predicted, thousands of people now went on pilgrimages to the former front, aided by the recently expanded infrastructure.[99] A series of combat memoirs and war films converted more devotees to the Alps. Soldiers toured their old battlegrounds. One veteran shared his experience of visiting the Plöcken Pass in Carinthia, where he had fought during the war. Being back in those mountains felt like hiking in a "lost world." The contrast between the past and present was unsettling for him and induced flashbacks. The nearby villages had been repaired, painted, and decorated. Where piles of burned rubble and blackened gables once smoldered, few traces of the war now remained. But when the former soldier looked to the peaks, he still saw Austrians and Italians fighting. He found it strange to drive along a serene highway that he recalled as a deadly road used for ambush. Passing old wire entanglements, shell holes in the rock, dilapidated trenches, and the graves of fallen friends added to the surreal sensation. Later, as he climbed the mountain, the memories overwhelmed him. Jingling cowbells triggered the cacophony of battle in his mind. Flares and spotlights flashed before his eyes. Across the sunny meadow he watched patrols crawl through the darkness as artillery ripped apart men and rocks with "iron claws." Walking along the ridge he remembered sinking in the deep snow during long marches and laboring for hours digging a path to the barracks. Yet it was summertime. Lush grass and bright flowers carpeted the slopes. All he could picture was winter, feeling cold and weary, soaked from head to toe, and having little to eat except crusts of bread. As he sat alone on the summit he thought about his old comrades and wished that they were there with him to share in the memories. He came to realize that everything had changed, and nothing had.[100]

The troubled veteran was not alone. Many struggled to rectify the past with the present in the Alps. People turned to the Alpine Association for direction. When climbers had redefined the Alpine Association as a *Schutzverein* during the war, they also revised the original purpose of Alpinism. In the nineteenth century, mountaineering emphasized personal development. Many had drawn a distinction between the dangers in mountain climbing for pleasure and the perils of battle. "Here now appears the difference between war and peace," one veteran had observed; "one is duty-bound to put one's life on the line for the Fatherland [in war], but to sacrifice oneself for a gamble [in peace] is without worth."[101] After 1918, the club took this veteran's criticism to heart. Visiting the Alps now meant much more than just going on vacation. Just as combatants shared the traits of mountaineers, alpinists acquired the soldierly sense of duty to the *Volk*. In the prewar years, struggle had meant that an individual matched his or her might against the mountains. After the war, it implied a national movement against the forces of cultural disintegration. Yet these same developments animated Alpinism's inherent discord, which had hibernated during the war. With its increased chauvinism, the club's growing anti-Semitic elements caused profound disagreement among the chapters in the decade after the war, as did attempts to restrict membership to bona fide climbers. Further industrial development in the mountains amplified nature conservation concerns. The Great War had alleviated some tensions in the Alps as it exacerbated greater divides in Alpinism.

PART TWO

Dominating the Alps, 1919–1939

5

Forbidden Heights

Lost Mountains and the Violence of Alpine Anti-Semitism

> Tremendous movement from the southeast to the
> northwest dominated the building of the Alps.
>
> —Hans Jenny, *Die alpine Faltung* (1924)

Although the 1918 armistice established a military truce, culture wars continued to rage on the peaks for the next two decades. These battles did as much to transform the Alps as armed conflict. Resentment toward the peace treaties, political extremism, and class antagonisms, issues that tormented the German and Austrian republics during the interwar years, beset the peaks. Italy's acquisition of the mountains south of the Brenner watershed infuriated German and Austrian alpinists, and Mussolini's campaign to "Italianize" South Tyrol mobilized them into action. They fought to maintain the region's German identity through tourism and charity. Yet while mountaineers rallied against Mussolini's fascist agenda, irreconcilable ideological differences had crystallized among them. Fierce debates erupted over who had rights to the Alps. After the war, many Austrian climbing clubs, including several chapters of the Alpine Association, adopted the so-called Aryan paragraph in their statutes, which banned Jews from membership. The uproar that followed transformed Alpinism. Although the Alpine culture wars made little direct material impact on the mountain environment, they fundamentally shaped how Germans and Austrians perceived the heights in the early twentieth century. The peaks became a hallowed sanctuary for some, sheltering and strengthening dreams of empire. Others blamed the Alps for cultivating the reactionary forces that later hastened the demise of the republics. In both cases, anti-Semitism had become a defining facet of Alpinism.

・・・・・・・・・・・・・

"Our mountains?" asked one mountaineer in his report on the Alpine Association and the First World War. "Can we still call them ours?"[1] In early 1919, German and Austrian alpinists had good reason to be anxious. Peace settlement talks began that year, and discussions focused on the new border between Austria and Italy. Irredentist desires for "natural borders" drove Italian demands. Italian envoys called for the new border to run along the main watershed in the Eastern Alps, the Brenner watershed. Some of the more chauvinistic circles pushed for possession of the ridges on the north side of the Etsch valley, but military planners ruled that out. The high peaks and narrow gorges on the southern side made the region easier to defend than the more open basins to the north. Passageways along the canyons were also easier when traveling from north to south, and therefore army strategists deemed control of South Tyrol and its German-speaking population essential for national security. Geological formations allowed realpolitik-minded politicians to justify the romantic irredentist bluster.

With the Italian army occupying the land with troops stationed as far north as Innsbruck, the Austrians had little room to negotiate. Still, they tried to keep South Tyrol. To work with the Italians and perhaps limit their gains, the new republic established a border commission, whose delegates included members of the Alpine Association, military officers, state officials, and representatives from Germany.[2] Much of the commission's work dealt with the minutia of moving a national border. Besides assisting in the negotiations, it marshaled public support for South Tyrol's cause. The Alpine Association's newsletter relayed information from state agencies to the public. When asked what role individuals could play, the Austrian Foreign Ministry advised climbing and hiking clubs to flood South Tyrol with German tourists.[3] Patriots emphasized the region's deep German past and Austria's ancient rights to the soil. One alpinist paraphrased Ernst Moritz Arndt, who once said, "The Rhine is Germany's river, not Germany's border." Likewise, "The Tyrolean Central Alps are Germany's mountains, not Germany's border," an awkward interpretation since those mountains had never been part of Germany proper.[4] But such particulars mattered little, especially when others claimed that "no other German land produces such affection the way the Alps do." "We love the German South Tyrol," gushed one contributor, "the land and people, just like our own nearest *Heimat*, perhaps even more."[5]

Alpine enthusiasts did more than write passionate essays. In the spring of 1919, they organized large protests against the hypocrisy of the Entente. The victors disregarded the rights of self-determination when it suited them. Wilson's Fourteen Points (number ten specifically addressed the peoples of Austria-Hungary) made a handy tool to break apart the Habsburg Empire. But where Italy's demands were concerned, the claims of ethnic sovereignty were conveniently ignored. By most accounts, the more than 230,000 German-speaking inhabitants of South Tyrol had no desire to become Italians. The largest demonstrations took place in Vienna and Berlin. Josef Donabaum gave the keynote speech at the Vienna protest. His talk emphasized the terrible plight of South Tyrol and the profound connection that the "German race" felt to the Alps. He disparaged the Italians as a people incapable of experiencing "mountain joy." That the country's national Alpine organization, Club Alpino Italiano, had only eight thousand members, a paltry number compared to the Munich or Vienna chapters alone, was evidence enough.[6] The demonstrations garnered a fair amount of publicity, but the efforts were to no avail. Italy secured its claims with the Treaty of St. Germain. Signed in September 1919, the treaty made good some of the promises that London had given to Rome. Italy obtained the Trentino and South Tyrol. The Brenner watershed along the Etsch valley became the new border. The ceded territory left holes in many mountaineering hearts. After hearing about the peace treaty, one member of the Alpine Association despaired, "Even in our fantasies, we cannot image what the future will bring in humiliation, suffering, and deprivation."[7]

The peace settlement created a legal morass in the Eastern Alps. When the Italians acquired the land, they confiscated Austrian and German private property, namely the Alpine Association's lodges. The government gave most of the buildings to the reconstituted Società degli Alpinisti Tridentini (SAT) but kept the lodges near the border as customhouses and troop barracks. Almost fifty huts in the German-speaking parts of the region and twenty huts in the Ladin-speaking areas were seized. More than thirty chapters lost property. Most of these chapters were German, and therein lay the problem. The Treaty of St. Germain did not address German property, only Austrian possessions. The Treaty of Versailles, which did concern German property, did not discuss South

Tyrol. The German huts had fallen into legal limbo. By rights, the Italian government was not allowed to liquidate German assets. Yet chapters like Landshut, Karlsruhe, Magdeburg, Düsseldorf, Zwickau, and others complained that Italian officials commandeered their huts.[8] The Alpine Association attempted to reach a solution through diplomatic channels, but Rome rebuffed its inquiries. The Italians had no intention of returning the prized lodges. The most the German Embassy could do was seek assurances that German alpinists could use the huts without hindrance. Angry mountaineers formed the "Committee for the German Huts in the Lost Regions," which accomplished nothing. It submitted documentation to the Imperial Office for War Damages but never received compensation for the lost huts. The Alpine Association then tried a new tack to get back its "stolen" property: it claimed that its motives were purely altruistic and that as an apolitical organization, it sought merely to open the Alps and encourage tourism. But the Italians were not fooled, and German property was never recovered.[9]

The legal fiasco exacerbated bitter feelings on both sides of the Brenner watershed. As late as 1922, neither the Austrian nor the Italian border commissions had yet issued maps of the new boundary. Getting lost in the fog and accidentally crossing state lines was common. So was being ushered out of the country under military escort. Italian patrols promptly arrested German and Austrian mountaineers who unknowingly crossed the border. Criminal treatment added injury to insult for alpinists, who out of "German pride and German piety" wanted to visit war memorials and military cemeteries in the Dolomites. Climbers were required to have a special Italian visa, and even then they could hike only in designated "neutral zones." But with Austria's financial woes in the early 1920s and the lopsided exchange rate between the Austrian krone and Italian lira, the visa was unaffordable anyway.

Byzantine bureaucracy did not help matters. Appeals to the Italian consulate in Villach had to travel through the convoluted innards of officialdom to Rome and back.[10] What little goodwill that had flowed between Italian and Austrian mountaineers in the nineteenth century had evaporated by the twentieth. Section Cassel warned other German chapters not to expect any cooperation from the SAT, which had been hostile to the Alpine Association even before the war and now refused German and Austrian hikers entry to its former huts.[11] Some of the Alpine Association's dissolved chapters in South Tyrol, like Bozen, reconstituted themselves as self-standing clubs. But the Italian regime prohibited those groups from having any formal relationships with German or Austrian organizations. These new Alpine clubs did not last for long, in any case. The SAT accused groups like the Bozen Alpine Association of Pan-Germanism, giving authorities enough reason to ban them.[12]

The situation worsened with Mussolini's rise to power. Troubles began in early 1921, when fascists attacked a traditional German costume parade in Bolzano, resulting in several casualties. By the autumn, thousands of Mussolini's followers occupied the city, which had long been the center of German life in South Tyrol. Harsh measures attempted to throttle the region's German culture. Businesses had to use the Italian language and employ only Italian workers. Church services could be conducted only in Italian. Fascists revised school curriculums and removed all references to Andreas Hofer and other Tyrolean patriots from textbooks. Mussolini's Black Shirts jailed private tutors who dared to teach their pupils German, outlawed traditional Tyrolean songs, and suppressed associational life and the press. Austrian reading materials were forbidden. In 1923, using the German designation "South Tyrol" became illegal; one had to use the Italian "Alto Adige." The same was true for most place names. Surnames were also Italianized, even those on gravestones. Hired thugs enforced the changes through terror. They vandalized Tyrolean memorials and cemeteries, assaulted those who openly spoke German, and threatened innkeepers and hoteliers who catered to German-speaking foreigners. Tourism plummeted, and the region's economy faltered. The promises made by Italian delegates during the peace negotiations that the region's language and culture would be protected proved empty.

Alarmed by the stories of harassment, distress, and dire economic conditions, civic organizations moved into action. As one member of the Alpine Association observed, "No other *Auslandsdeutschtums* [German community abroad] suffers as much as those in South Tyrol."[13] The club called for a boycott of all things Italian—fruit, fish, meat, wine, olive oil, and so forth, including any travel to the peninsula.[14] Hiking organizations engaged in "tourism propaganda" through newspaper articles. A number of mountaineers traveled across Germany and Austria, giving popular lectures and slide shows like "The Wonder World of the Dolomites."[15] Several groups organized fund-raising events, such as banquets or concerts. The charity organization Andreas Hofer Bund formed soon after Tyrol's division and served as a "spiritual bridge" between the south and the north. It published a monthly magazine, *South Tyrol*, whose articles spoke of the "desperate battle" taking place only one hundred kilometers from Innsbruck.[16] Tourist groups worked closely with the Andreas Hofer Bund to raise public awareness about the situation in the south. They exhorted fellow citizens to visit South Tyrol, despite the heavy costs of doing so.

The Andreas Hofer Bund also offered a series of guidelines for tourists, advising visitors to speak only German, to use German place names, and to patronize German businesses. To aid in this, the Alpine Association provided a list of German businesses and hotels, along with an index of Italian place names and their German equivalents. Tourists should be observant, avoiding talk about politics and not drinking too much. "Do not act arrogantly," admonished one memorandum, "but be German." Visitors should make a point of talking to locals in German, especially children, according to the guidelines. In addition, travelers to South Tyrol should also bring German newspapers, magazines, or even a farmer's almanac to leave in hotels for the locals, and vacationers should stay as long as possible, perhaps even the duration of the summer holidays.[17]

The advice applied equally to young people. Newsletters and speeches bombarded Alpine youth group members with images of Germans under the yoke of foreign occupation.[18] Youth were taught that these were German lands and that their return was critical to Germany's future rise to power. One advice column for those traveling south of the border offered "ten commandments" to follow in South Tyrol. As with adults, youth group hikers were to remember their "German sense" and "national feelings," always to speak German to the inhabitants of South Tyrol, and only to use German shops and youth hostels. Young people were obliged to visit South Tyrol and to explain to the Italians that the "theft and enslavement" of South Tyrol undermined the friendship between Germany and Italy, though just how convincing a teenager could be in such a situation remained uncertain.[19]

In 1927, the Alpine Association undertook a new, more subversive approach. In a highly confidential letter to the chapter chairs, the executive board outlined a plan to have individual chapters sponsor a county in South Tyrol. With nearly four hundred chapters in the club and around two hundred counties in the province, the math seemed feasible. The board hoped to recruit "energetic personalities" from each chapter who would work as consultants. They would serve as the links between the chapter and the county, encourage fellow members to visit the district, and establish a relationship with local innkeepers to covertly set aside rooms for German guests. The aim was to create a sort of "chapter colony" within each county.[20]

Several chapters responded to the request. Those most quick to reply were typically chapters that once owned huts in the region. Chemnitz stood ready to assist the counties of Luttach and Ritten, which bordered its former holdings. Bremen offered to sponsor Gossensass and St. Valentin, as well as Branzoll. Pforzheim was prepared to fund a consultant. Even little chapters did their bit. Bergfried, a small chapter near Munich, agreed to support the Corvara commune. But not all chapters shared in the enthusiasm. Due to financial hardship, several could not commit to sponsoring a county. Linz suggested that German chapters were better suited for this program since they received a more favorable exchange rate and had more economic resources than the Austrians. Also, according to the Linz chairman, Germans tended to travel with families whereas the Austrians were mostly mountain climbers. Serious alpinists apparently had no desire to stay in a single county every season. Some mountaineers simply viewed the program as unfeasible. One member reminded the board that hotels had to accept Italians; otherwise, authorities would intervene. Another cautioned that if the fascists got wind of this plot, which was likely, given their extensive spy networks in South Tyrol, then Alpine Association members would be completely barred from the Dolomites. As it was, climbers were forbidden from wearing the club's silver edelweiss pin while on Italian soil. A few years later, letters from the executive board still mentioned "colonies" of members in South Tyrol.[21] The stimulus program did not exactly fail, but its successes were meager.

Wherever German and Austrian tourists hiked in the Alps, they were reminded of South Tyrol's plight. "When you stand on mountains," one flier charged, "remember your brothers in the south."[22] Mountain lodges provided visitors with magazines about South Tyrol and free maps of the province. Journals that once avoided political issues, like the *German Alpine Newspaper*, now devoted large portions of each issue to South Tyrol. Only in 1932 did Italy and Austria finally reach an agreement about climbing along the border. Restrictions lessened somewhat. Mountaineers could cross state lines within certain "free zones," although only from June through September. They still had to have a pass, but now needed only a stamp and not the more expensive visa.[23] The province's woes lasted for several years, long enough to cement enmity. Before the war, serious German and Austrian mountaineers might have belonged to several organizations, such as the Swiss or Italian clubs, in addition to the Alpine Association. Now most German or Austrian climbers found it reprehensible to join an Italian club.[24]

Expressions of solidarity assumed a variety of forms among Alpine circles. During the immediate postwar years, mountaineers spoke of Austria's unification (*Anschluss*) with Germany. Following defeat, with the dethronement of the Habsburgs and Hohenzollerns and the breakdown of any notion of dynastic tradition, the creation a German-Austrian state seemed possible. Many felt that with the downfall of empires, union was the only natural solution to maintain stability in central Europe. The Alpine Association designated itself as the herald for the cause, the "symbol of *Anschluss* thoughts," and the representative of German and Austrian unity.[25] At the same time that alpinists provided aid to South Tyrol, club events and chapter meetings promoted hopes for a "powerful union" of Germans and Austrians in a "homogeneous realm."[26]

Politicians on both sides of the border initially shared those dreams. In a speech before the Reichstag in October 1918, Gustav Stresemann stressed the cultural unity between Germans and Austrians and anticipated a union of German-Austria with the Reich. Other German officials felt that the inclusion of Austria might offset the losses of war. The movement was especially strong in German-Austria, the rump republic. Following the Habsburg downfall, the empire broke apart along ethnic lines. In October 1918, parliament deputies had affirmed the right to self-determination for other national groups and also demanded the "unification of all German areas of Austria into a German-Austrian state."[27] The following month, Austrian Germans announced the creation of the German-Austrian Republic and declared with a constitutional law that German-Austria was a constituent part of Germany. The Austrians knew that President Woodrow Wilson was considering the prospect of such an Austro-German union; his secretary of state, Robert Lansing, had issued a memorandum instructing American delegates to the future peace conference to propose just such an agreement.[28] Social Democrats saw *Anschluss* with Germany as a means to allay the disintegrating tendencies within the republic. Karl Renner articulated the feelings of many when he remarked, "Overnight we have suddenly become a *Volk* without a state."[29] Otto Bauer, another influential Austrian Social Democrat, convinced his party to add the creation of the German-Austrian Republic to its platform.

Many others were less sanguine. Although in a unanimous vote on 24 February 1919 the German national constituent assembly adopted a resolution stating, "Germany and Austria form an inseparable unity," most German politicians held misgivings. Count Botho von Wedel, the German ambassador to Vienna, and Count Ulrich von Brockdorff-Rantzau, the German foreign minister, doubted the validity of the Anschluss declaration; currency, tariff, industrial, and legal questions were considerable.[30] German officials faced enough difficulties without the added demands of a starving Austrian population and an economically weakened Austrian state. The spring 1919 elections in Vienna indicated that many Austrian voters had lost interest in the Anschluss issue as well. For all of Otto Bauer's efforts, many Social Democrats remained skeptical of the idea. Preliminary negotiations with Social Democrats in Germany left both sides feeling frustrated and reaffirmed doubts.

Wary of a united Germany and Austria, the Entente powers precluded any union between the two nations in the Treaty of St. Germain. The treaty also changed the actual name of the republic from "Republik Deutschösterreich" (German-Austria) to "Austria." Forced to accept these stipulations, along with the loss of territory, many Austrians harbored resentment toward the settlement. One outspoken critic called it a "mockery of the proclaimed right of self-determination." To prove that point, some of the former Alpine crown lands held plebiscites on the matter. In Tyrol, 145,302 voted for a union with Germany with 1,805 voting against the proposal. More than 103,000 voters in Salzburg accepted the proposal and only 800 rejected the idea of Anschluss.[31] Despite political realities, some Austrians and Germans continued to entertain hopes of a future unification.

Those individuals found their home in the Alpine Association. Members from Tyrol's capital, Innsbruck, took the club's rhetoric to heart. During the 1920 annual meeting, they proposed changing the name of the club to simply the German Alpine Association. In their view, if the club represented Germandom and the Anschluss ideal, then it only made sense to rename it. "The word 'Austria' is today no longer necessary," they argued. The name change was a historical imperative, what they called the völkisch duty of the association. Since the peace treaties had made the creation of "Alldeutschland" politically and economically impossible, the movement for unification in the state legislatures collapsed. Civil organizations now had to exert their influence and voice public sentiment.[32]

Yet the name "Austria" still held meaning for many mountaineers. Although some alpinists proclaimed that they did not differentiate between Germans and Austrians, this sentiment was not universally shared. Prussian hegemony had established a separate identity decades earlier, which had evolved into accepted custom for most Germans by the twentieth century. The Viennese lived among the still-standing edifices of a fallen empire, which served as reminders of past greatness and of an identity separate from Germany. Those in the former imperial capital tended to view the idea of a union with Germany with less interest than did populations in the former Alpine crown lands. Even Otto Bauer later admitted, "The tradition of the vast majority of the German-Austrian bourgeoisie is old Austrian, Habsburgian."[33] Outside observers felt that most Germans and Austrians were not attentive to the idea of *Anschluss*; the general population wavered between tacit support and uninterested ambivalence for a union. Other Austrians within the association questioned the name change. All but Innsbruck's three chapter representatives rejected the proposal.[34]

Innsbruck's petition seemed like a minor affair. The delegates discussed its merits, voted, and moved on, as they did with several proposals that day. But the initiative to change the club's name was the surface ripple of much deeper and stronger chauvinistic undercurrents. Alienated Alps and the search for national unity in a fractured natural landscape had made an indelible mark on Alpine tourism, particularly among the Austrian climbers. The *Anschluss* rhetoric and the South Tyrol programs worked in tandem to define the mountains as exclusive territory and the club as "German above everything else."[35] When Innsbruck called upon the delegates to do their *völkisch* duty, it echoed sentiments expressed before the war. Then military defeat and territorial dissection amplified the rhetoric beyond mere jingoism. A writer from Linz declared, "We are not only a mountain climber club, rather a German, *völkisch* association, fighting for our German cause. . . . It [the association] stands on the pinnacle of the *völkisch* movement in Germany."[36] This was a curious statement coming from an Austrian, and a telling one. These alpinists attempted to identify *völkisch* as patriotic, not political. But in light of contemporary developments, this was a distinction without a difference. With the growing preponderance of political splinter groups, *völkisch* sentiments became the litmus test for far-right sympathies. Some tried to neutralize the acidic rhetoric with more basic notions of belonging. "The Alpine Association was born from the German soul," mused one writer; "German is the desire to roam, the spirit of adventure, the irrepressible urge for the heights, for freedom, the love of nature."[37] But such characterizations played into chauvinistic hands. Delegates rejected Innsbruck's petition, but the underlying interests remained very much alive.

Anschluss fantasies did not diminish in the Austrian Alps. To one climber from Dresden, talk about a union and a fascination with Germany seemed ever-present when he traveled through the mountains in 1925. Local newspapers had appeared filled with articles on the events in Germany and editorials supporting the *Anschluss*. Everyone he met on his hikes had expressed the desire to become a part of Germany. One Austrian remarked, "I am a good German and I feel as German as those proud gentlemen . . . from the Spree [a river in Berlin]." The experience touched the Dresdner. As the youth group leader for his home chapter, he worked to impress on the minds of the youth group members the importance of the *Anschluss*.[38] Assertions of German-Austrian unity grew more insistent with Mussolini's actions against German culture in South Tyrol. At a gathering of Austrian chapters in March 1926, speakers emphasized that the desire for union with Germany had not abated and that Germans were still receptive to the idea.[39] Most Germans outside of the Alpine Association did not, in fact, give much thought to unification in the 1920s. They faced more pressing domestic challenges. But as Germans turned away, Austrians pulled back with greater force.

・・・・・・・・・・・・・

"It could not be avoided that social and cultural opponents clashed violently in the mountains," remarked one journalist after the war, "and that political parties found a new battlefield there."[40] Tourist organizations around the Eastern Alps also found themselves caught in nationalistic conflicts. Right-wing mountaineers in several countries condemned the presence of "outsiders" on the heights. Italy's irredentists filled the ranks of tourist clubs like the SAT and directed their hate toward German speakers. The Slovenian Alpine Association brawled with the newly reconstituted Carniola (Krain) Alpine Association, a group that was previously an Austrian chapter. The Swiss confronted the so-called foreign infiltration of their alpine club; chauvinistic members feared that foreigners placed the club in "grave danger" by diluting its "Swiss character." "We have to decide whether we are going to give up another piece of our Swiss culture to cosmopolitanism," announced one member, "or whether we hold to our convictions and fight for the legacy of patriots." Others railed against the "parasites" in the club, those Swiss who used the organization for their own financial gain. Zealous alpinists sought to "cleanse" the Swiss Alpine Club of such "unclean" members.[41] German and Austrian sport clubs echoed Swiss concerns, but in explicit anti-Semitic tones. The Austrian Tourist Club, the Austrian Mountain Association, most German gymnastic groups, and several ski clubs banned Jews.[42]

Within the Alpine Association, the conflagration began in the 1920s when firebrands like Eduard Pichl, a known rabble-rouser and anti-Semite, kindled hatred and ignited nineteenth-century bigots into twentieth-century fanatics. He and his cohorts spewed the typical sort of compulsive anti-Semitic nonsense, but with an Alpine twist: they claimed that Jews had played no part in opening the Alps because that "requires manly courage and noble ardor that this race does not have." Austrian anti-Semites spoke in racial terms of blood and defined Jews as a foreign *Volk*. Preventing people of "foreign blood" from infiltrating the mountains was imperative. "It would be a crime," one bigoted climber from Graz spat, "to let these people, with the filth of their *Unkultur*, in the pure temple of our mountains."[43] Their language drew a connection between Jews and the negative aspects of city life, with references to materialism and pollution as code for Jewry. Alpine purity became a metaphor for racial purity.

Other tourist organizations faced internal dissension during the interwar years, but the Alpine Association stood apart. The club's sheer size and transnational organization placed its strife on an entirely different scale. With over two hundred thousand members in 1923, the Alpine Association was ten times as large as the Swiss Alpine Club and twenty times bigger than the Club Alpino Italiano. The Austrian Tourist Club and the Austrian Mountain Association combined were still smaller. Section Austria alone counted close to fourteen thousand members. While German *Heimatschutz* groups tended to represent local conditions, the Alpine Association's network of over four hundred constituent chapters stretched across two countries and incorporated a wide range of settings. Those chapters sympathetic to Pichl's cause served as a conduit for his propaganda.

The crusade against Jewish mountaineers began in Vienna. The fall of liberals from power, defeat in war, and the collapse of the empire all contributed to the swelling of anti-Semitism in Vienna. Jews were easy targets. Preexisting hatreds shaped the perception of "profiteering Jews" as "parasites" during the war. Jewish migration into Vienna further increased anti-Semitic agitation. Austrians leveled their frustration against Yiddish-speaking refugees from the east, who often arrived hungry and penniless and who aggravated the already severe shortage of provisions. Of the 137,000 refugees from Galicia who found asylum in the capital, 60 percent were Jewish; the city's Jewish population grew by half during the war years.[44] Residents like Pichl blamed the refugees for Vienna's woes. During and after the war, he campaigned against the supposed preponderance of Jewish influence. He lobbied to ban Jewish immigrants and limit the number of Jewish establishments in the city, and he argued that laws should protect the economic well-being of "honest working" Germans against the influence of foreign Jews.[45] He was not alone. Following defeat, all major parties focused their efforts on making citizenship impossible for Jewish refugees in German-Austria. Several politicians argued that Jews contributed to divisions among the Volk. Thunderous applause greeted a prominent Christian Socialist when he announced at a Tyrol Farmers' League rally in Innsbruck that "only a fundamental break with the spirit of Jewry and its disciples can save the German Alpine lands."[46] By 1921 legal barriers and intense resentment had forced all but twenty-six thousand refugees to leave Vienna.[47] Those who remained were ostracized, including acculturated Jews.

Although in the nineteenth century, Section Austria had been known for its cosmopolitan culture and liberal orientation, and assimilated Jews, like Josef Donabaum, played an important role in the chapter's life, now some Viennese mountaineers agitated for the expulsion of Jewish alpinists from the Alpenverein. To this end, they recruited Pichl to champion their cause. In early 1921, he transferred his membership to Section Austria and then introduced legislation to include the "Aryan paragraph" in the chapter's statutes. His proposal first came to a vote during a special meeting of Section Austria in February 1921. Even though Pichl won the clear majority, he faced the opposition of the current chairman and lacked the three-fourths margin required to change the statutes. But he had enough supporters to get elected chairman himself, and by October he garnered enough votes to adopt the "Aryan paragraph." Pichl called it a victory for "völkisch thought."[48]

Following Pichl's nomination to the chairmanship in the spring of 1921, hundreds of members left Section Austria and formed Section Donauland. The new group claimed that it was not an "opposition

FIGURE 12 Eduard Pichl (1872–1955). Source: Historisches Alpenarchiv Deutscher Alpenverein, Munich

chapter" and did not seek to engage in any "polemics" or "feuds." Unlike Section Austria, which openly continued down a "thoroughly national-chauvinistic and anti-Semitic track," Donauland intended to pursue "purely mountaineering and absolutely nonpolitical goals." In his first speech, the chairman of the new chapter reminded his fellow citizens that Donauland members had fought and bled for Austria in the war and had also done much for the Alpine Association.[49] His point that Donauland's members were accomplished climbers and loyal Austrians did nothing to assuage anti-Semitic hostility in other chapters. Private prejudices became public policy. As more Austrian chapters adopted the "Aryan paragraph," Donauland became the club's de facto Jewish mountaineering ghetto. New members, like Richard Fischer, found their way to Donauland after being turned away by other chapters. As a bank employee and a former captain in the Austrian army, Fischer fit the social profile of a typical member in the association. However, as he explained in his letter to the association's administrative offices, his attempts to join Section Mark Brandenburg and Section Austria left him with the impression that many chapters adhered to an "Aryan paragraph." Very few German chapters actually imposed the "Aryan clause" restriction on membership, but Fischer's feelings were telling. He wondered what chapter might accept a "dissident" and a "former Jew" like himself.[50]

Almost no Austrian chapter would. Invoking crusader-like imagery, Pichl called upon those with "flames of holy wrath burning in their mountaineer's hearts," men who were devoted to the Volk and to the Alps, to defend the "sacred mountains" from Jews.[51] He directed other Austrian chapters to include an "Aryan paragraph" in their bylaws, declaring that it was the "*völkisch* duty of German-Austrians" to force out Jewish members and preserve the Alpine Association as "an emblem of German unity." By 1923, ninety of the ninety-eight Austrian chapters had adopted the "Aryan paragraph." Letters to the association's executive board disclosed Austrian hate. In a tiresome litany of its issues with Jews, the Board of Viennese Chapters, which comprised the city's eleven other chapters, claimed Section Donauland's existence posed a grave danger. Its formation was like "a punch in the face," and the Viennese promised to refuse hut access to Donauland members.[52] Tyrolean groups maintained that a marriage between edelweiss and Jewry would damage the club's reputation in Austria. Others accused Donauland of being a gateway for foreign elements. Some proposed that the Jews establish their own Alpine club and not belong to the Alpine Association. All saw Donauland as a threat.[53]

In contrast, the vast majority of German chapters did not. Only 9 out of the 278 German chapters rallied to Pichl's banner. Some chapters like Section Berlin, along with Essen, Mainz, Hanover, Leipzig, and Breslau, became his staunchest opponents. They claimed that Pichl's agitation split Germany and Austria. In a broad sense, this was true. The Austrian chapters were nearly unanimous in their support of Pichl; all but a handful stood behind him. One Berliner remarked on the latent divides within the club between "those along the Association's Alpine backbone [Austrians and southern Germans]" and those to the north.[54] But the divisions within Germany were not so clear. Of those nine active supporters, three were located in Munich: Hochland, Oberland, and the Skiclub-Munich chapter. Sections Bergfried and Traunstein were also Bavarian. Yet Rosenheim, Augsburg, and chapters in the Allgäu supported Donauland. Frankenthal, from the Rhineland, sided with Pichl, but nearby Mannheim and Kaiserslautern did not. Berlin was one of Pichl's biggest foes. Sections Hohenzollern and Mark Brandenburg, both based in the capital city, were among his most notable supporters. The Hanseatic city Rostock, a seaport on the northern coast, enthusiastically backed the Austrians, while Hamburg and Kiel stood against them. Both sides included urban and rural chapters. The front lines beggared order.

The association's executive board split almost down the middle. Gustav Müller, a civil servant, chairman of Section Hochland near Munich, and an all but open anti-Semite, argued that the "Jewish chapter" would break apart the association by bringing the "battle against Jewry" into the club. Others believed that the board must consider the Austrian position since the country's other large civic groups, like the Austrian Tourist Club, had already adopted the "Aryan paragraph." Some conveyed that the Alpine populations, those "rooted in the soil," could not understand why the board would side with Donauland, given all the supposed "Jewish mischief" in the mountains. Karl Sandtner from Vienna rather pathetically added that Austrians could not be held accountable for disliking people of different races. Donauland supporters retorted that membership should not be dependent on "national, confessional, or social moments." Johann Stüdl, the last surviving founder of the association, accused Section Austria of "arrogance, intolerance, and brutality." Others reminded Donauland's detractors that the chapter was a legally incorporated entity. It adhered to the aims and purpose of the Alpine Association, and the board had no standing to disband it. If the board rejected Donauland, then by that logic it must also prohibit the Aryan paragraph. But while the board stood divided, few supported Donauland with enthusiasm. In the end, the executives decided that "the lesser evil is to admit Donauland" and voted fourteen to twelve to approve its charter.[55]

The board's shaky acceptance marked the start of Pichl's relentless three-year campaign to dissolve Donauland. He immediately initiated proceedings to have those executives who supported Donauland censured. He tendered a bill of no-confidence in Josef Donabaum and eventually forced him out of office. Raimond von Klebelsberg, a professor of geology at the University of Innsbruck and a vocal anti-Semite, took his place. Most other executives provided Donabaum with little support, and the club's bulwarks of decency began to crack. Pichl's troops charged the breach with incessant proposals to oust Donauland. They forged a large voting bloc, the Deutschvölkische Bund, in 1922 under Pichl's command.[56] Armed now with leverage, his forces bombarded the club's general assembly with resolutions and motions. Chapters Hochland and Oberland proposed that all new chapters require a two-thirds majority approval from the general assembly rather than a simple majority from the executive board. They also put forward an apparatus, should the need arise, to dissolve a chapter. Gustav Müller spoke in support of the motion, claiming to represent "those in South Germany [who] feel more affinity for Austrians than perhaps those in [the] north." He invoked the specter of a communist chapter, which would go against the "nation's world view." The implied communist threat was code; Pichl's supporters often equated Jewry to Bolshevism. "We in Munich especially understand the Aryan paragraph," he continued, conflating the current Donauland dilemma with communism and his city's short-lived "Red moment" after the war when it became the Munich Soviet Republic. Section Austria submitted a resolution for the dissolution of any chapter that "endangered the traditional German character and thereby the unity and the tranquil development of the Association." Proponents asserted that the motions did not concern Donauland but that they would also be thankful if, in the interests of the association as a whole, Jews voluntarily withdrew from the club. "After all, to be German means—as we have learned in the hard times—to be able to make sacrifices," a statement of bitter irony considering that Pichl and his ilk denied Jews a German identity in the first place.[57]

Some withstood Pichl's siege. In response to ravings that "we German Austrians recognize only Jews or Germans," Karl Arnold from Hanover made a point of distinguishing between German-born Jews and Jewish refugees from the east. Chapters in the north had Jewish members who had done much to support "Alpine aspirations." Furthermore, the work of Austrian anti-Semitic agitators "dampens the enthusiasm among the educated and the unprejudiced in Germany for *Anschluss*." A member from Leipzig spoke for several other northern German chapters when he simply declared, "Politics do not belong on the mountain."[58]

Mountaineers from the Ruhr valley and the Rhineland were especially forceful on this point. Their cities were then under French occupation. They invited the Austrians to spend six weeks with the French guns to learn what political really meant.[59] Philip Reuter from Essen described the grim situation in the "Rhine-Westphalia prison." From the perspective of "terrible economic, political and psychological misery," Pichl's battle against Donauland seemed like an "artificial dispute." In the face of real adversity, Austria's imagined struggles smacked of the most offensive form of vanity and self-righteousness to those in the Ruhr. Worse still, Pichl betrayed a core mountaineering value: the desire for escape, relief, and peace. Reuter recognized that heavy industry in his region was "certainly not Jew-friendly" but still argued that issues of politics, religion, or race had no place in the Alps.[60] "For us mountain climbers," he explained, "mountaineering belongs to the highest, the most beautiful, the most pristine realm that we can imagine." However, Austrian politics had stained the one "cultural landscape" that had remained free from politics, at least in Reuter's eyes. Those who sought simplicity and respite were now forced to carry their political creeds with them in the mountains.[61]

The Alps offered no asylum. A modicum of civility dictated behavior during the debates, but not on the peaks. Quarrels and assaults against Jews in the mountains were not uncommon. Austrian chapters made every effort to lock Jews out of the Alps. Section Donauland faced resistance as it sought a work region and tried to purchase a hut. Several Austrian chapters conspired against it. Lienz, Klagenfurt, and Villach convinced Alpine farmers, communities, and church authorities not to lease property to the chapter. Klagenfurt also instructed other Carinthian chapters to prevent Donauland from obtaining a work region. Donauland members felt there was a "witch-hunt" to keep them from purchasing land. The chapter filed a complaint against the Carinthian group, but nothing came of it. The only way that Donauland managed to acquire the Glorer-Hut was through a proxy. Since Austrian chapters refused to do business with Donauland directly, it used anonymous agents to make purchases.[62]

Owning the hut was more than a matter of prestige for Donauland; it was a question of survival. As more Austrian chapters adopted the "Aryan paragraph," more closed their huts to Jews. In 1920, the Central Association for German Citizens of the Jewish Faith advised that closing huts to "non-Aryans" compromised the Alpine Association's cherished political neutrality, but the warning failed to act as a deterrent.[63] Members of Donauland found themselves barred from several huts. Section Villach bragged that all the huts of the Carinthian chapters had posted notices declaring, "Jews and members of Donauland are not welcome here."

Section Austria either denied Donauland members entry to its huts or refused to offer the membership discount.[64] The story of an older married Jewish couple and their son from Section Breslau, who were denied access to a Section Wien hut, was familiar to Donauland supporters. The family was forced to spend the night in the horse's stall after suffering verbal abuse. Representatives from Section Wien maintained that the hut was meant only for mountain climbers, not day tourists climbing "in city shoes with handbags."[65] Yet accomplished Jewish alpinists also encountered the same bigotry.

The treatment of Section Donauland called into question mountaineering and Christian ethics. According to anti-Semites, Donauland somehow defied "Alpine customs and Alpine integrity."[66] But it was the Austrians who denied weary climbers access to shelter. Socialist publications emphasized the association's hypocrisy. "Is it Alpine custom to throw people out of huts," asked one observer, "even when they helped build them, or deny entry to people even though they are dead tired?" The *Worker Newspaper* portrayed the typical Pichl supporter as a fat, blustering, and pompous-looking man in lederhosen, complete with a swastika pin: "We'll throw out anyone who doesn't like the swastika," read the caption; "we'll show 'em Alpine manners."[67] While spending the evening in one of the association's huts, a Friends of Nature member stumbled across a sardonic poem written in the guest book:

> Jesus! Listen and remember well
> By your law they do spurn
> Were you to come, you born Jew
> Then you would stand outside too.

In the last stanza, the poet expressed relief to be a nonbeliever and not be grouped with such "Christians."[68]

Other publications tried a less aggressive approach. A cartoon in one magazine showed the image of Christ, with his crown of thorns and shepherd's crook, standing before an Alpine hut. Above the door hung the notice "German and Austrian Alpenverein, entry for Aryans only!!!" Christ responds, "This is not what I sought."[69] An article in the Donauland newsletter used the climbing rope as a metaphor for mountaineering ethics and Alpine solidarity. Climbers relied on each other for support when confronted with deadly situations. On the peaks, true alpinists did not care about a person's background or politics when dangling over the void or when pulling their partners up from the abyss. This was more than a safety harness; it was the physical bond of a much deeper spiritual connection. Climbing the rope symbolized the progression from "feeling detached in the drudgery of everyday existence to feeling like kindred on the open heights." The rope crossed time and space. Comradeship forged in danger and love for the mountains made for lasting relationships, an intimacy that only alpinists could know. Those who betrayed the bond and cut the metaphorical rope disgraced the "word and idea 'mountaineer.'"[70]

Pichl had his knife at the ready. His assurances that he did not wish to replace the club's edelweiss emblem with the swastika rung hollow as his thugs defaced Alpine huts, along with nearby trees, signposts, rocks, and fences, with swastika drawings. Austrian chapters Linz and Radstadt affixed swastikas to their huts. These swastikas were not the result of vandalism; the sturdy placards suggested deliberate planning and construction. Vacationers wondered if the swastika was now the Alpine Association's new insignia. Pichl himself argued that the swastika represented a pure German disposition and culture. But the image of the swastika on an Alpine lodge was too striking to be anything other than a "sign of bigotry." In an open letter to the German chapters, Pichl attempted to dispel suspicion. "German politics should always be *völkisch*," he wrote, "but *völkisch* thought and activities are not linked to politics."[71] No one was fooled. Critics saw Pichl and his lackeys for what they were: "storm troops for political objectives" who sought to turn an organization of "earnest German mountain climbers" into a "toy for political parties."[72]

The battle culminated in 1924. Section Klagenfurt authored a proposal to dissolve Section Donauland outright. Klagenfurt delegates promised that Austrian chapters would secede if the resolution failed to pass. To pacify the Austrians and forgo debate over the Klagenfurt resolution, the executive board proposed the so-called Rosenheimer Compromise. "Surrender" would have been a more accurate epithet. The board yielded, agreeing to expel Donauland if Pichl disbanded the Deutschvölkische Bund and ceased his agitation. In addition, the Austrians would have to wait eight years before they could introduce legislation to have the "Aryan paragraph" inserted as a condition of membership in the club as a whole. And they could propose such legislation only if a third of the German sections, which also had to represent at least a third of the German votes, supported the move. The executives intended the resolution to be a stopgap measure, preventing Pichl and his supporters from introducing petitions to ban Jews from the entire club. But by now supporting Donauland's removal, the executive board became Pichl's accomplice. The Rosenheimer Compromise passed with an overwhelming majority, as then did the Klagenfurt resolution.[73] Democracy proved Donauland's undoing.

When Donauland members voted nonetheless to remain in the club, executives scheduled a special meeting in Munich on December 1924 to decide the chapter's fate. In a vote of twenty-six to one, the board sent the resolution to expel Donauland before the assembly. Philip Reuter was the one holdout, and his frustration with the situation was tangible. Despite the tremendous pressure from his fellow executives, Reuter refused to compromise his principles, even after receiving anonymous death threats. Given the number of political assassinations in the early 1920s, such threats were not idle. Yet he had no intention of being party to what he saw as "political terror" and the miscarriage of justice. He sharply criticized the board for its lack of fortitude and its failure to take a moral stand. Instead of the so-called compromise, he favored splitting from the Austrians. Reuter even hired lawyers to determine the legality of the club's actions.[74]

To make its decision appear lawful and not capricious, the executive board accused Donauland of underhanded dealings and fraudulent transactions. According to the trumped-up charges, the chapter had misrepresented itself to the executive committee regarding the purchase of the Mainzer hut (Section Mainz supported Donauland). In addition, Donauland had supposedly infringed upon the work regions of other Austrian chapters. The chapter had also attempted to lease land from Section Austria through an agent who refused to reveal his affiliation with Donauland. The accusations were flimsy at best. The charges were intended to prejudice German members against Donauland, many of whom had appeared disinterested in the debates. Few German climbers understood why such extreme measures were being taken. A number of chapters, like Bremen and Breslau, requested clarification, hence the charges.[75]

Donauland supporters conducted their own public relations campaign. Karl Arnold lobbied hard for Donauland among chapters in the club's Northwest German Group. He and several elders like Stüdl promised to cancel their membership if the agitators destroyed the club's "old tendencies."[76] Bayerland pledged to support Donauland, as did Mannheim, Nuremberg, Mainz, Essen, Frankfurt, and several Hamburg members. Sympathetic newspapers across Germany and Austria publicized the chapter's story. Their portrayal of the Alpine Association was not

FIGURE 13 "So, now it is just us."
Source: Der Götz von Berlichingen 51 (1924).

flattering. Several editorials asserted that "the stampede of anti-Semitic elements" and "racial anti-Semitic dogma" have turned the club into a "refuge for *Unkultur.*" Filled with "malicious fools," "alpine halfwits," "brawlers," and "cretins," the association had become "an absurd caricature of what it originally was and should have remained." A highly circulated cartoon illustrated this point. Titled "The Cleansed of Jews Alpine Association," it portrays a group of men and women inside a hut as a bunch of braying asses. The notice "Dogs and non-Aryans are not allowed" hangs above the door. Swastikas and Nazi trappings litter the windows, walls, and meager furniture, as well as the hiking equipment. A particularly fierce-looking donkey wears a paramilitary uniform with edelweiss and swastika badges. As the group heads out for a hike, they all cheer: "So, now it is just us."[77]

The message was unmistakable. But the shock value of such caricatures returned low dividends. German members found the editorials and cartoons more insulting than convincing. Donauland's media exposure seemed to do more harm than good. During the December meeting, supporters gave a valiant effort for a lost cause. Some derided the obvious politic motives behind the eviction proposal. In a clear reference to the Nazis, speakers accused the thuggish group of "short-sighted fanatics" of reshaping parts of Germany and now making their presence felt in the Alpine Association.[78] Berlin representatives criticized the Austrians' anti-Semitic stance and the club's blind acquiescence to right-wing politics. One delegate addressed the association's hypocrisy, sneering that the Alpine Association could stand as a model of racial purity. Not only could it expel Donauland, but it should also, in the name of racial purity, ban anyone with a venereal disease. He chided that even "chronic alcoholics" should not be members in this "racially pure" association. His last comment caused such outrage that he could not finish his speech. Others reminded the assembly that members of Donauland had sent care packages and financial aid to Germans in the Ruhr valley and that Donauland's board members were distinguished veterans who had earned more war medals than had those on Section Austria's executive board. Lastly, Oskar Marmorek, Donauland's representative, appealed to the members' sense of justice and the association's identity as a "community of law." As such, the association's utmost interest should be upholding minority rights and civil liberties. The issue extended beyond the decision of a civic organization to expel one of its chapters. The assembly's decision dictated the future development of the association and could undermine the German and Austrian republics; to set aside civil liberties and disregard minority rights paved the way for despotism.[79]

In the end, members valued the association's unity above Donauland's inclusion in the club. The announcement by the greater Munich area chapters was typical. These chapters (with the exceptions of Bayerland and Isartal, which refused to sign the announcement) stated that their vote for the expulsions had nothing to do with confession or politics but only with the well-being of the association: "In some instances in human and social life, the special interests of the few must stand back for the sake of the greater whole." The statement reflected an important change in mountaineering, an activity that trumpeted individual liberty in the nineteenth century. There was no denying that Donauland's Jewish membership was the critical factor. Few had the courage to defend the rights of the oppressed. The decision to oust Donauland displayed the association's general acceptance of Pichl's racial anti-Semitism. Nearly all delegates voted for the chapter's dissolution. Of the 1,853 ballots, only 190 voted against the proposal.[80]

Once again, newspapers carried the Donauland story across both countries. A few supported the Austrians; most did not. "Pure air in the mountains," announced one right-wing paper. For other dailies, their headlines said it all: "Terror Has Won," "A Cultural Shame," and "The Decay of the Alpine Association Begins!" were just a few. In many quarters, public opinion of the association soured. Observers indicted the club for failing to take a stand against the Austrian "swastika-wearers" and "racist fanatics." One editorial found it strange that the club sided with those disturbing the peace in order to reestablish peace. Others called the "swastika decision" a "mockery of manly courage." Anyone who "did not recognize Herr Hitler as the Savior of the German people" should have voted against Donauland's expulsion. The Alpine Association had once been the "model of apolitical neutrality," but now recent events told a different story. "With the entrance of anti-Semitism," an article related, "it fell swiftly, madly down to the dark depths of *völkisch* demagoguery." Speeches sounded like "excerpts from a *völkisch* catechism." Editors wondered how "even a single republican of character could bear such an organization."[81]

· · · · · · · · · · · · ·

Donauland did not disappear. It continued to exist as an independent and successful Alpine organization. Some chapters in Germany, like the Academic Dresden section, adopted anti-Semitic statutes. But most, like the little Berchtesgaden chapter that voted down a proposal to restrict membership based on race or religion, did not. Still, several alpinists felt that they were no longer part of a mountaineering club but rather of an anti-Semitic one.[82] Some Jewish members remained unclear as to how the decision to ban Donauland affected their status. Two Munich members wrote to the executive board for clarification on membership requirements. In its reply, the executive committee explained that each chapter retained its autonomy in its membership requirements.[83] Yet the events of 1924 poisoned the association's atmosphere and set a dangerous precedent. Reverberations from Donauland's expulsion continued to shape the club, as well as Alpine tourism, throughout the decade.

With the situation in Vienna settled, agitation shifted to Berlin. By 1924, some Berlin executives worried that their chapter was becoming "too Jewish."[84] A February 1925 memorandum from Berlin's chairman, Rudolf Hauptner, voiced concern over the rising number of Jewish members in the chapter. If the trend continued, he worried that Christian members would leave and Berlin would become a predominantly Jewish chapter. To appreciate the consequences of such a development, Hauptner pointed to Donauland's doom. He proposed closing membership to Jews to preserve the chapter.[85] The memorandum provoked outrage. In a sequence of events reminiscent of Vienna in 1921, the two sides faced off in the executive board elections. Hauptner won.[86] Frustrated, several members left the chapter and established the German Alpine Association Berlin (Deutscher Alpenverein Berlin, AV-Berlin) in April 1925. Hans Kaufmann, a Berlin lawyer and a Jew, served as the first chairman.

AV-Berlin's program was simple: "Pure Alpinism with disengagement from all politics."[87] The club did not discriminate on religion, gender, or political leaning, as other chapters in Berlin did. It sought to overcome the quarrels that had been carried into the mountains. Like Donauland, it intended to pursue the original goals of the Alpine Association. Indeed, the two clubs cooperated and published a joint newsletter. Similar to Section Austria's reaction to the creation of Donauland, the Berlin chapter called the establishment of AV-Berlin "dirty rivalry." But the founders of AV-Berlin did not see themselves in competition with the German and Austrian Alpine Association, since they sought only to provide fellowship and opportunities for friends of the Alps.[88] Like Donauland, they claimed to not be an opposition chapter.

Unlike what happened in Vienna, AV-Berlin encouraged its members to remain in the Berlin chapter and lobby for change. In response, the Berlin chapter expelled them. Questions arose over the legality of such actions. Seven former members of Section Berlin filed a lawsuit with the district court for readmittance into the chapter. In a lengthy legal battle, the plaintiffs brought their case before the district court, the court of appeals, and Germany's supreme court. The courts denied the plaintiffs' lawsuit and settled the case in favor of the defendant, Section Berlin.[89] As with the association's vote to dissolve Donauland, the legal decision set precedent for future membership restrictions.

Following AV-Berlin's lead, several members among the Munich chapters left in 1927 to establish the South German Alpine Association Munich. It, too, presented itself as a "purely alpinist apolitical club." This group worked in conjunction with AV-Berlin and Donauland and followed similar aims. It hosted weeklong mountain tours, opened a library, and offered various training courses every weekend in Munich.[90] The three major cities, which had witnessed the development of anti-Semitic tendencies within the Alpine Association, also supported the growth of nondiscriminatory organizations.

As the establishment of these new groups demonstrated, anti-Semitic feelings in the association thrived after Donauland's expulsion. Section Mark Brandenburg ridiculed what it called the "Actually Jewish Alpine Association Berlin." A business owner in Munich complained that the Alpine Association's newsletter advertised Jewish companies. "As you well know," he wrote to the executive board, "the Alpine Association did not emerge from Jewish stores, rather from the good middle class, whose highest duty has always been to fight such enterprises." There were plenty of other struggling "German" businesses that could use the recognition. Others continued to affirm that "mountaineering is a German sport and the Alps are of German nature." An article in the *Frankfurter Zeitung*, "Racially Pure Mountains," reaffirmed that Jews should be kept out of the Alps. As for the accomplished Jewish mountaineers, they were "troublemakers" who "offended poor alpinists."[91] The typical chauvinistic drivel remained.

The merger of the Austrian Tourist Club and the Austrian Mountain Association with the Alpine Association in 1930 reinforced those trends. Both clubs banned Jews. Some members hoped that the addition of the former rivals would create an economic windfall for the club. Many more saw greater significance. In a narcissistic stupor, the clubs congratulated themselves for laying the foundation for the future unification of Germany and Austria. Every speech oozed with self-importance. One deputy claimed that the merger would rectify the injustices of the "dictated" peace settlements. Another recited verses from Ernst Moritz Arndt's song "The German Fatherland," just like during the club's Walhalla ceremony in 1913. Loud cheers greeted the president of the Austrian Tourist Club when he declared that the merger represented the completion of a *völkisch* aim and announced that Germany and Austria had the "same great *Volk*-destiny of unification."[92] With Donauland banned, the departure of progressives from the club, and the merger with the Austrian Tourist Club and the Austrian Mountain Association, the fusion of anti-Semitism to the Alpine Association was all but complete.

· · · · · · · · · · · · ·

As tensions heightened during the interwar years, hiking groups, tourist clubs, and outdoor organizations from across the political spectrum found themselves at odds with each other. The Donauland debacle soured relations between the Alpine Association and the Friends of Nature organization. Both clubs grew rapidly during the 1920s, but the Naturfreunde soon outpaced the Alpenverein. By 1923 the socialist club had more members in over a thousand chapters across central Europe. It, too, spoke in terms of solidarity, but in a very different sense from the Alpine Association. The Friends of Nature had also built over 150 of its own huts, though few were located in the high Alps. Cost was one factor that limited Friends of Nature activities in the mountains; respect for the Alpine Association's work regions was another. Prior to the war, the two clubs had a somewhat collegial relationship. After defeat in 1918, they synchronized their language about Alpinism. Both saw it as a means to rebirth and renewal. The Alpine Association emphasized national wellness and recovering from the psychological damages of war; the Friends of Nature focused on physical health, particularly curing workers' bodies of tuberculosis and other illnesses exacerbated by the conflict. Although they had divergent aims, the two groups shared hundreds of members in common.[93]

Trouble once more began in Vienna. Class antagonisms had been simmering for some time in the capital. During the 1920s they boiled over into violence. Austrian Social Democrats organized the Republikanischer Schutzbund (Republican Defense League) in 1923, ostensibly to protect the party from right-wing radicals. Soon it counted around eighty thousand armed members. Meanwhile, demobilized soldiers had returned home and formed local, loosely organized militias called the Heimwehr, which mirrored the German Freikorps. Heimwehr groups were anti-Marxist and generally opposed parliamentary democracy, although beyond that they shared no single ideology. This did not stop Ignaz Seipel, the Christian Social chancellor during the 1920s, from using the militia for his political gain. His policies stirred anger among the Left. Seipel worked to establish cooperation among the Catholic Church, industrialists, and his party while assailing those on the Left as enemies of the state. The private armies spilled blood in street brawls and sporadically fought during political marches. Leftist agitation in Austria mounted with the 1927 July Revolt, during which over eighty protesters were killed and hundreds wounded. Passions were so inflamed that when the Austrian Tourist Club and the Austrian Mountain Association announced their merger with the Alpine Association, socialist newspapers denounced the "bourgeois front" for its "boundless hatred of the working class." "The leadership of the Alpine Association marches with the radical right," declared one editorial. One contributor to *The Mountaineer*, the newsletter for a Friends of Nature chapter in southern Bavaria, urged members to resign from the Alpine Association.[94]

Another editorial hit close to the mark when it called Pichl a "general for the Heimwehr." His gang participated in discriminating against the Left, just as they did against Jews. The correlation was easy for his supporters to make. In the nineteenth century, the Christian Social Party employed anti-Semitism in its campaigns against the liberals. When the socialists rose to prominence, anti-Semitism remained the opposition's tool. The political Right now pointed to Jews as Bolshevik saboteurs. How "capitalistic Jews" became Soviet agents in this fantasy was unclear, but reality mattered little to people like Pichl, who worked to limit the Naturfreunde's influence in the Alps. Activists conspired with clerics and innkeepers to hound socialist tourists out of Alpine villages. Local newspapers turned on the Friends of Nature. Pichl and other Austrians raised hut fees for nonmembers, placing the cost of travel outside a working-class budget. The era of cooperation had ended. "Section Austria was once the gathering place of scholars, earnest actual mountaineers, businessmen and intellectuals," remarked one Friends of Nature member, "but that has since changed. . . . Some people in its current management use the chapter for their own dark aims and have made it into the most vulgar sort of political fighting organization."[95]

Opponents had long accused the Friends of Nature of bringing politics into the Alps. But as discussed in chapter 2, political storms surged around the Alps before the Friends of Nature even existed. The Alpine Association's buildings had served as lightning rods during those tempests. When Section Austria ejected the lower classes from it lodges, the huts once again attracted fury. With some justification, socialists viewed the huts as preserves of privilege.[96] Pichl's actions convinced Friends of Nature members that they needed their own huts, especially in the more popular regions of the Alps. As part of the fund-raising campaign, the club sold "Defiance Donation" medallions. Members could purchase the badge, which signified that they "condemn and despise the National Socialist spirit of Section Austria."[97] Pichl's gang retaliated with vandalism. During the construction project of the Friends of Nature hut on Dachstein, the club encouraged visitors to carry up building supplies.

In a batch of materials, one compulsive Nazi had scrawled on every shingle, "Aryan workers! Don't build huts for Jews!"[98]

Their common enemy drew Donauland and the Friends of Nature closer together. After Donauland's expulsion, the two clubs reached an agreement concerning their respective huts; members of both organizations received the same rights and access.[99] The Friends of Nature also experienced a boost in membership after 1924 when a number of mountaineers canceled their membership out of anger with the Alpine Association's actions. This was the case in Hamburg, where members publicly announced their displeasure with the association's direction, although in effect the departure of progressively minded members further concentrated the association's anti-Semitism.

・・・・・・・・・・・・・

The Alpine Association's racist leanings and reactionary turn drew the attention of government officials in both the Austrian and Weimar republics. The Vienna City Council's finance committee, which was heavily Social Democratic, awarded lucrative grants in the early 1920s to develop tourism. Most of those went to the Friends of Nature. During the committee's discussions, officials noted with disappointment that various tourist clubs were restricting access to lodges based on a person's race or party affiliation, unlike the Friends of Nature, whose huts welcomed all Alpine enthusiasts. Since many of the club's members were city workers and employees, council members felt that they had a responsibility to support these projects. But not all favored such spending. One Christian Social representative defended the Alpine Association, explaining that the club needed to reserve beds for its own members. Moreover, he remarked that Naturfreunde members had a rather poor reputation as guests in the huts, which elicited sharp protests from his colleagues.[100] And even the most ardent Christian Socialist could not deny Pichl's Nazi leanings. Social Democrats referred to the prevalence of swastikas in the huts and expulsion of Friends of Nature members as proof enough of the Alpine Association's political allegiance. One official labeled the club in no uncertain terms: it was the "vanguard of the *Hakenkreuzler* [Nazis]."[101]

Likewise, the Weimar government looked upon the Alpine Association with growing concern. When in 1929 the club moved its headquarters from Munich to Innsbruck (as per its statutes), it lost its *Rechtsfähigkeit* (legal license) as a domestic corporation under German law. In years past, when the club's headquarters were located in Austria, state ministries in

Berlin had rubber-stamped the organization's "legal standing of a foreign person or corporation" to cover its German chapters. This time, however, some officials voiced concern regarding the club's orientation. Testimony before the Ministry of the Interior accused the association of widespread anti-Semitic practices. Officials believed that the executive board had failed to stem the racist tide. They found it unsurprising that rumors continued to surface regarding the harassment of Jewish tourists in the Alps and believed that the trends pointed to a clear "Aryanization" of the club. The recent merger with the Austrian clubs confirmed these suspicions. Once more, perceptions mattered. To the general public, the association appeared as a haven for anti-Semitic fanatics. Several Germans and Austrians remarked that the association was not supportive of the republics. A number of chapters still hoisted imperial colors above their huts, those flags that, according to detractors, had "brought death and ruin over the entire world."[102] The evidence seemed overwhelming. Officials concluded that the German and Austrian Alpine Association was following anti-Semitic tendencies and that these endeavors stood in stark contradiction to Weimar's constitution. In response to assassinations and putsches in the 1920s, Social Democrats remained deeply wary of right-wing extremism. As the largest party in the German Reichstag, they saw no reason to confer legal standing to the club.[103]

Although loss of its license represented a setback for the Alpine Association, it continued to operate as before. But some things had changed. Following Donauland's dissolution, the club experienced a sharp drop in membership. The stabilization of Germany's currency might partially explain the downturn. But then the number of tourists in the Alps reached record highs during those years, as did membership in the Friends of Nature. "The Alpine Association must adjust itself to the new era," asserted one member soon after the end of the war, "and must break with some aspects of the past."[104] Yet in many ways, the association found itself trapped by its own history. The club's dedicated adherence to its nineteenth-century Greater German identity gave Pichl the leverage to force through his Pan-German agenda. The loss of South Tyrol and the ban on *Anschluss* left the members searching for a sense of wholeness that wholly warped their sense of community. During the Donauland debates, one executive rationalized that the decision to ban the chapter was not an injustice, rather a necessity.[105] To preserve the association and maintain order, Donauland had to be expelled. In their desperate search for unity, members were willing to uphold the greater good at the expense of civil liberties.[106] All of this took place against the backdrop of the mountains and informed the image of these high places as contested political space. The political reorganization of central Europe had reshaped perceptions of the Alps among the defeated. German and Austrian hikers now planned their expedition itineraries according to which hut they intended to visit and which huts should be avoided. Lodges became ideological markers in the mountains. When one executive foretold that the interwar turmoil could not leave the Alpine Association "untouched," he was right.[107] The actions of a few and the complacency of the many had changed Alpinism. What emerged from the 1920s was a more racist, right-wing, yet still influential Alpine Association whose longing for lost mountains threatened the foundations of civil society in Germany and Austria.

6

Mechanical Mountains
Movies and Motors Remake the Alps

Every change in our earth's surface is caused by a pair of forces. . . . So that means in our case: the inner forces build up the mountains; the external forces destroy them.

—Franz Heritsch, *Die Entstehung der Hochgebirgsformen* (1927)

Mountains were in vogue during the interwar years. Being an Alpine adventurer of any sort was immensely fashionable. Savvy advertisers used the rugged landscape to sell everything from clothes and sporting goods to chocolates and magazines. Images of towering peaks suffused popular culture. Dime store novels told tales of harrowing climbs, lost love, and heroic death in the Alps. Serious writers invoked the mountains as well, most famously Thomas Mann. Mountain movies—*Bergfilme*—were perhaps the most popular form of mass media.[1] Some critics remarked that people shattered by the war found outlet in the Alpine films. Maybe moviegoers just enjoyed watching films that were shot outdoors and not in a studio. Whatever the reason, the movies certainly encouraged people to seek out the dramatic landscape that they saw on the silver screen. Urged on by melodramatic novellas, cinematic fantasies, fast skis, and sleek cars, people toppled the heights. The Alps, once a means to escape from the masses, had become a sanctuary for the masses.

If the mountains appeared crowded before the war to contemporaries, they seemed positively packed in the 1920s and 1930s. Just as political and social dislocation funneled people desperate for escape to the mountains during the 1860s and 1870s, the turmoil of the interwar years multiplied anxieties by orders of magnitude. Visitors to the Eastern Alps increased by upward of 250 percent. The number of Alpine lodges likewise grew, while membership enrollments in major Alpine clubs hit record numbers.[2] To meet demand, municipalities subsidized road and cog-rail construction, often completing developments that had begun before the war. Metal girded the mountains. This was the heyday of cable car construction. Steel lines streamed down from all the popular mountaintops and many minor ones while engineering marvels, most notably the Grossglockner High Alpine Road, etched new contours on the landscape.

Such mass consumerism disgusted most die-hard climbers. Reactions varied, but nearly every response attempted to somehow change consumption patterns and scale back tourism in the mountains. In most cases, these efforts followed prewar trends. Yet the context of postwar recovery made the stakes higher. Alpine enthusiasts sought to bring a disconsolate *Volk* to the mountains, believing that the mountain environment could somehow heal the wounds of war. The more Germans and Austrians climbing the peaks, the better. But if desecrated by blundering masses and rampant technology, then how would the Alps provide the necessary "physical and spiritual conditioning" needed to secure the future?[3] Few could find a way out of this quandary. For their part, hardcore alpinists became increasingly reactionary and, like Eduard Pichl's Alpine anti-Semitism, sought extremist solutions to the dilemmas of mass tourism.

·············

In the desperate days following defeat, the allure of the mountains lay in their appeal to heroic individualism and the promise of epic adventure. No other medium better publicized this vision of the Alps than the mountain films. Movies in Germany first made their appearance in the 1890s and steadily gained in popularity. The film industry witnessed impressive growth during the early twentieth century. Around a thousand theaters screened movies in 1910. By the start of the First World War, that number had more than doubled. During the Weimar Republic, cinemas could seat over a million people, and German-made films dominated the marketplace. Indeed, Germany rivaled the United States in movie production and film quality. German directors and movie stars, including Fritz Lang and Marlene Dietrich, garnered international fame. German expressionism and the classic detective film genre influenced the development of film noir in Hollywood. Critics praised the films, like Robert Wiene's *The Cabinet of Dr. Caligari* (1920), for their artistic daring and vision.

The silver screen did not enthrall everyone. Some conservative social commentators decried movies for warping German culture, stunting intellects, or threatening authority. Perhaps the naysayers had a point. The more famous films, like Fritz Lang's *Metropolis* (1927) and *M* (1931), F. W. Murnau's *The Last Laugh* (1924), and Josef von Sternberg's *The Blue Angel* (1930), along with Wiene's production, did convey messages of social insecurity and political turmoil, with underlying storylines that hinted to impending crises. Some scholars have since seen in these movies an explanation for Hitler's success. Film critic Siegfried Kracauer points to mountain films specifically as clear indicators of the sort of antimodernism that played into Nazi hands. He views the so-called promethean promptings of the mountains films, with their "idolatry of glaciers and rocks," epic struggles against insurmountable odds, and the fascination with heroic death, as symptomatic of an antirationalism on which the Nazis later capitalized.[4]

Dark though some were, Weimar films did not pave the way for totalitarianism. Nazi magnetism required much more than movie attraction. National Socialists certainly took their cues from the mass appeal of motion pictures and later turned film into a propaganda juggernaut, but enjoying a few hours of escapist entertainment did not transform moviegoers into passive political stooges. Besides, though cinema connoisseurs often dismissed them as pulp, the mountain films appealed to Germans and Austrians across the political spectrum. Both radical and reactionary journals praised the *Bergfilme* for their stunning visual effects. The *Völkischer Beobachter*, a Nazi mouthpiece, proclaimed that attending the screening of *The White Hell of Piz Palü* (1929) was "a tremendous film experience." The communist newsletter *Die Rote Fahne* declared that it was "undoubtedly one of the best German films."[5]

Whereas most movies in the 1920s had relied on artificial studio scenery, the *Bergfilme* were especially remarkable for their outdoor locations and daredevil stunts. Arnold Fanck directed the majority of these movies with respected mountaineer Luis Trenker as his leading actor. Sepp Allgeier led the film crew and defied movie-making convention. His assistants strapped cameras on their skis, dangled from ropes over cliffs, and wedged themselves in crevasses at all angles to shoot the action sequences. The actors, typically experienced climbers or expert skiers, took acrobatic risks on the peaks as well in this era before stunt doubles and safety wires. Fanck spared no expense and hauled the most advanced film equipment up the heights.[6] The results were breathtaking.

Even seasoned alpinists found images of the mountain to be stirring.[7] Cinemas like the Ufa-Palast in Berlin screened the mountain films to packed audiences. Modern machinery brought mountain magic to urban viewers.

The movies presented the Alps as the edges of civilization, the landscape itself starring as both a magnificent setting and as a lead character. Emptiness and space defined the high frontier. The mountain movies were akin to contemporary American westerns. Fanck's mountains served as the transcendental landscape, the very iconography of romanticism. High-altitude epiphanies, where enlightenment came only after tempting death, were one of his common motifs. Hollywood movies likewise stressed the harshness of the wilderness with its wide skies and arid lands. In both genres, the land nurtured a particular breed of people. Women were sturdy and self-reliant but typically played supporting roles while the action centered on men. Men were taciturn, tough, and true, not afraid to match their mettle against an unforgiving environment. Cowboys and gunslingers came from the same stock as mountaineers, lonesome men with shared codes of honor, men to emulate.

Serious climbers, however, held misgivings about the films and generally condemned the entire *Bergfilme* genre as kitsch. In their minds, the movies gave a false impression of mountaineering. The films encouraged dilettantes to search for the symbolic, dramatic landscape that they saw on the silver screen. Often they climbed without tour guides and lacked proper equipment. The realities of the Alpine environment left many gravely injured or dead. Concerned about the increasing number of accidents in the Alps, mountaineers directed their ire toward the movie directors. "Our movement has nothing against those sensation-seeking city-dwellers," one climber wrote. But if directors invoked the phrase "mountain climbing is destiny," they had to strive to tell a realistic story.[8] One angry critic fumed about those films "teeming with alpine-athletic impossibilities," which he found to be somehow "technically and morally" damaging to Alpinism.[9] Many felt that the *Bergfilme* should be more educational and less entertaining.

Instead, mountain movie storylines often leaned toward the melodramatic, with emotional and typically tragic endings. "Fanck grew more and more keen on combining precipices with passions," Siegfried Kracauer observes, "inaccessible steeps and insoluble human conflicts."[10] *The Holy Mountain* (1926) epitomized the overwrought histrionics. Leni Riefenstahl made her debut in this film, the young starlet who later gained notoriety as Hitler's chief film producer. The script reads like a sappy soap opera. Riefenstahl plays Diotima, a vibrant dancer with a "stormy soul" who lived by the sea. She becomes entangled in a love triangle with two ruggedly handsome mountaineers, Vigo and "the Friend," played by Ernst Petersen and Luis Trenker, respectively. Vigo is young and athletic and spends his time winning ski competitions. Trenker's character, a "magnificent man," often wanders alone among the mountains where he can contemplate life in peaceful solitude. Unbeknownst to the other, both men have fallen in love with Diotima. When Trenker's character sees her embrace another man, he seeks to escape the pain by climbing the deadly north face of a nearby mountain. As a loyal comrade, Vigo accompanies him, despite the heightened peril of winter melt and seasonal change. The higher they climb, the deeper Trenker's character sinks into madness. Reflecting the men's psychological turmoil, avalanches and snowstorms engulf them. While hunkered in a cave, Vigo confesses his love for Diotima. Seized by rage, the Friend throws Vigo over the brink but then snaps to his senses as the rope connecting the two men catches hold. Suspended above the void, the young climber cannot scramble to safety, and the Friend lacks the strength to pull him up. Rather than cut the rope and save himself, Trenker's character holds steady through the night, slowly freezing to death. At the break of dawn, a rescue team arrives, only to witness the two frozen climbers topple over the precipice. Devastated, Diotima retreats back to the sea.

Critics panned the screenplay but praised the scenery. The mise-en-scène set the emotional tone throughout the movie. Soaring peaks, billowing clouds, and cascading waterfalls gave the audience a sense of majesty and power. Rarely were scenes shot indoors. When Diotima imagines the man of her dreams, he stands alone, high on a summit, silhouetted against the bright sky. The intertitles helped give meaning to nature. Intoxicated by Diotima's dance, Trenker's character rushes to the mountains where he can "savor his overwhelming experience." The scene segues to snowy slopes that are empty of people but for the solitary wanderer. Fanck juxtaposed the Friend's trek across ice and stone with Diotima frolicking in fields of flowers. The contrast designated the cold gray-scale world above as a male domain and the fertile and colorful realm below as female. During a fateful moment on the Friend's descent, he crosses paths with Diotima as she explores the countryside. "It must be beautiful up there," she remarks. "Beautiful, difficult, dangerous," he replies. Other annotations during the film carry the same message. One note card describes the mountains as "wild and fantastic, like a gothic cathedral." Another states, "The mountainside reveals Nature's ferocious power." Seeing the Föhn wind wreak havoc, the Friend cries, "And let storm and avalanche roar the wild songs with it."[11] When asked what one searched for on the heights, Trenker's character pauses and then answers simply, "One's self." The script was romanticism writ large on the silver screen. Fanck had simply tapped into the wistful desire for premodern mountains. This was nothing new.

Fanck's juxtaposition of solemnity and joy, however, was something rather novel. While the solitary Friend trudges up the hills, Vigo and his pals speed down the slopes. Vigo's easy smile and flippant approach to the mountains contrast sharply with the Friend's stern countenance and serious purpose. Vigo revels in wintry fun; covered in snow he skis gleefully across the landscape. Slalom races and cross-country ski meets had become immensely popular during the interwar years, especially among young people, and Fanck tapped into that as well. In one long sequence, a gaggle of skiers engage in a wild chase at a fast and frantic pace. They jump, slide, and dig their way to the finish, ignoring the "fairy tale beauty" of the snow-dappled fir trees and sparkling white fields. With Vigo, nature does not so much expand the mind as exercise the body. The sensibilities nearly reverse what Trenker's character displays, though they are no less engaging. Fanck was filming at his best, following right behind the skiers as they swooped down the mountain and glided across the fields. The exhilarating race scenes mesmerized outdoor enthusiasts across Germany and Austria. Likewise, the Friend's final dilemma and the film's climax riveted moviegoers to their seats. Fanck had found the right recipe of beautiful and tragic.

The most successful mountain film was *The White Hell of Piz Palü*. It premiered in Vienna (the male lead was Austrian), and during the 1929–30 season it was the second biggest box-office hit in Germany.[12] Fanck based the film on a short newspaper story. Five climbers, including a young woman, found themselves trapped on a mountain near Innsbruck, and their tour guide had broken his leg. Snowstorms delayed rescue efforts. Unable to reach them from below, a few intrepid rescuers climbed the adjacent face and rappelled down the peak. The effort took four days. By the time they reached the trapped climbers, only the woman and the youngest of the others were alive. The tour guide had sacrificed himself for them; he had given them his winter coat and then frozen to death.[13]

In Fanck's version, Dr. Johannes Krafft and his young wife, Maria, are enthusiastic alpinists. But during one winter climb, an avalanche sweeps her away into an icy crevasse, a consequence of Krafft's blatant arrogance in the face of the mountain's might. He spends the next decade wandering the mountainside, lost in grief, until he crosses paths with a pair of young lovers, Hans and Maria (once more Petersen and Riefenstahl paired together), who have traveled to the Alps to celebrate their recent engagement. They join Krafft in an ascent of Piz Palü's treacherous north face. During the climb, Hans falls and injures his head. Krafft breaks his leg while saving him. An avalanche blocks their return route and buries a group of students climbing below. Krafft, Hans, and Maria sit stranded on a ledge for three days before an airplane discovers them. Seeing that the young couple might not survive, Krafft gives them his jacket. The rescue party saves Hans and Maria, but Krafft finally finds peace in his mountain tomb.

In *Piz Palü*, the environment plays the lead. Subtlety was not Fanck's strength. Foreboding music with a looming massif, along with such intertitles as "the mountain rages" or "the mountain holds her captive in its icy grave," frame the natural feature as a malevolent force. As in *The Holy Mountain*, the mysterious Föhn wind signals peril. Its warm desert airs unleash chaos on the frozen heights. When Krafft mocks the stormy gusts and rushing torrents of snowmelt, the mountain kills his wife. A furious avalanche dashes five young climbers down to an icy demise when they dare the north face. The same wrath routs and breaks Hans and Krafft. The natural world, more than the mediocre acting, conveys the melodrama. During times of dread, danger, or death, the mountain makes a sudden appearance. Its bulk dominates the screen. Fearsome clouds swirl about the summit like vapors or spirits, and avalanches thunder down the slopes. Humans appear tiny and insignificant against the vast landscape. Yet however unforgiving and cruel the mountain is, it simultaneously offers a sense of romance and delight. Violence and horror are inseparable from peace and pleasure. The young couple pick the snowy peaks to celebrate their love, as had Krafft and his wife. Playing in the snow and exploring hidden couloirs convert the mountain's emotional charge. Fanck constantly cut to extended shots of the Janus-like mountain to heighten anticipation. Doing so also allowed him to compensate for a thin script and stretch a brief newspaper notice into a movie marathon.

Even tetchy mountaineers found aspects of *The White Hell of Piz Palü* praiseworthy, though with some reservation. A reviewer for the *Alpine*

Newspaper declared that of all the Alpine films, this one made the strongest impression. He especially liked the portrayal of human affairs in the struggle with the mountain.[14] Another critic recommended the film for its daring photography and technical merits, but he, like many other mountaineers, found the screenplay absurd. No real climber would attempt such a difficult ascent with strangers, much less with a young inexperienced woman. Some hoped that the "sensation-hungry masses" might learn a lesson: people who took risks in the Alps died.[15] Still, the film caused concern among some climbing circles because it presented only the "dark side" of Alpinism. "Difficulties, arduousness, horrible dangers, and their tragic effects" were the hallmarks of the film "without the slightest reference to the light side of Alpinism with its soul-edifying and ethical meaning."[16]

Mountaineering circles criticized the *Bergfilme* so severely precisely because the Alps had become so value-laden and politicized. The fiercest objections echoed voices past; rampant consumerism corrupted the Alpine aesthetic. Movie reviews disguised a deeper malaise. Some commentators felt the capitalistic greed ruined the artistic value of the mountain films. Several blamed avaricious producers, although regional rivalry may have influenced opinions. Industry fat cats in Berlin—not Fanck's Freiburg-based company—cheapened productions by focusing entirely on ticket sales. A few had keener eyes and saw the films as a visual expression of a "capitalist mentality," part of a larger venture that encompassed the Alpine landscape. As the popular movies demonstrated, the mountains were nothing more than another means to get rich.[17] Alpinism was a business, not a pastime. As a lure for large earnings, the films shaped consumption patterns, promoted mass tourism, and thereby indirectly funded extensive railroad and highway programs. Therein lay the insolvable dilemma for Alpine enthusiasts. The mountains offered redemption for a defeated *Volk*, but altering the Alps to accommodate the masses threatened the very pillars of the nation.

· · · · · · · · · · · ·

"People come and go," Luis Trenker concluded after the war, "but mountains endure forever."[18] The Alps endured but were no longer the same mountains that climbers had conquered in the nineteenth century. Massive capital investment projects further mechanized the heights during the interwar years. Such enterprises followed trends that had begun before 1914. Now mountain mania demanded more. Two projects in particular represented the broader technological and environmental changes in the mountains: the Zugspitzbahn and the Grossglockner High Alpine Road. Both launched in the late 1920s, and both ventures marked milestones. The Zugspitzbahn, the cogwheel train that clambered up from Garmisch to the Zugspitzplatt, the limestone plateau just below Germany's highest summit, was the last of its kind. Cable cars and gondolas soon eclipsed cogwheel trains in the 1920s as the preferred mode of public transportation up the Alps. Automobiles also set new trends. More motorists than ever before raced along Alpine highways, exhilarating in the sharp curves, steep ascents, and splendid vistas. Yet the cost of road construction at high altitudes was exorbitant. Other than demonstrating engineering triumphs and entertaining thrill-seekers, the highways provided needless infrastructure. Nevertheless, the Austrian government threw its weight behind the Grossglockner High Alpine Road project, more to establish the republic's legitimacy than anything else. Both projects greatly diversified Alpine tourism and deepened the "democratization of the mountains."[19] But emasculated mountains no longer menaced would-be conquerors with threats of danger or death. In correlation, trains and highways radicalized certain mountaineering circles, deepening both their doubts of mass tourism and their disillusionment with the republics.

Protest, war, and then hyperinflation had delayed the Zugspitzbahn project until the pressures of mass tourism pushed it forward, though not without howls from mountaineers. Alpinists were no more ready to accept the train in 1925 than they had been a quarter century earlier. Opponents regurgitated the same tired arguments. Clubs like the Alpine Association claimed that trains corrupted the character of the mountain and further disconnected people from nature. Members could not decide whether the Zugspitzbahn would reduce the number of overnight guests in the club's huts or turn its properties into gaudy hotels. Either case spelled ruin. Some feared a domino effect: the train would bring even more development on the summits; soon other mountains would fall. Satisfying the "modern travel urge of the masses" meant making the Alps "general and mechanical," the exact converse of traditional mountaineering ideals. One youth organizer predicted that this would prevent adolescents from experiencing "untouched" mountains, something tantamount to a national catastrophe. Articles in Alpine journals pressed "real" mountaineers to battle the Zugspitzbahn.[20]

Advocates maintained that trains benefited mountain sports and tourism as well as the local communities. A few hopeful train enthusiasts speculated that the Zugspitzbahn would advance economic unity between Bavaria and Tyrol, despite political division. Journalists noted that during the 1800s, detractors had voiced similar doubts about steam locomotives, which were now a normal part of modern life. To refute charges that any sort of transport ruined the mountain, the Bavarian Ministry for Trade, Industry, and Commerce conducted extensive studies on Switzerland's Jungfrau train. The commission paid particular attention to how the Swiss funded, built, and maintained the line, concluding that the benefits of cogwheel trains outweighed the costs.[21] Promoters likewise rejected objections from elitists. Members of the Alpine Association opposed transport up the mountains, but several million other Germans did not. Non-alpinists had rights to the heights, too. Thousands already went on pilgrimages to the Zugspitze. Installing a train to the famous peak changed nothing. Or, as one glum mountaineer later observed, "On the Zugspitze there is not very much left to spoil."[22]

While Germans debated, Austrians took the initiative. Tyrolean officials quickly approved plans for a cable car up their side of the Zugspitze in 1924.[23] The little republic moved faster than its larger neighbor to invest in Alpine tourism. Limited funds made the choice easier: a cable car was the only affordable option. In record time, Bleichert and Company, the same Leipzig firm that had been so busy before the war, erected the then-highest aerial tram in the Alps. Engineers bolted massive metal towers to the rock face, giving the mountain's silhouette a thorny look. When operations began in July 1926, Austrian commentators praised the Zugspitze cable car as a technological marvel and tremendous national achievement, although the cable car stopped at 2,805 meters, 160 meters short of the peak. Apparently the additional hike over rocky terrain disappointed most visitors, especially with the poor weather that summer. Nevertheless, within a month between four hundred and five hundred people used the tram daily.[24] The Austrian government later commemorated the occasion with a five-schilling postage stamp. On it, a giant pylon with steel girders and taut cables supported an ascending passenger car while an airplane soared overhead. Snow-capped mountains squatted low in the background, diminished by machines and human progress. The image's message was unmistakable.

Tyrolean ingenuity galvanized the Bavarians. After construction on the cable car began in early 1925, Munich mountain climbers and conservationists hosted numerous protests, together with several hiking clubs, nature societies, and youth organizations. The hope was to halt train construction on the Zugspitze's German side. During an April event, alpinists packed the Löwenbräukeller (some four thousand people by one count) and discussed cures for the "mountain train fever" that gripped the Alps. "Money, luxury, and convenience," they declared, "are not the medicines that people in Germany need"; rather, they were the drugs of addiction.[25] The meeting soon turned into a catchall gathering of discontent. Predictably, participants griped about industry and insensitive tourists desecrating the landscape. Many worried that after trains breached the mountains, other iniquitous aspects of modern life were sure to follow. Speakers imagined the Zugspitze with bars, clubs, and casinos, a veritable Monte Carlo. A few Luddites entertained thoughts of attacking machinery. Optimists placed their hope in the democratic process. Through a referendum, the Swiss had rejected plans for a Matterhorn train and a proposal to extend lines up to the Jungfrau peak. Germans could do the same. "Our Matterhorn is our Zugspitze," one speaker exclaimed. Pessimists asserted that comparisons with Switzerland were meaningless. The Alps covered almost the entire country; what difference did a few trains make? For Germany's narrow mountain range, though, even one or two cogwheel lines connoted disaster. Activists could at least all agree that "mechanization, materialization, capitalization, and industrialization" destroyed the Alpine landscape. But the assertion was broad, vague, and practically meaningless. The day generated little substance. Several months later, Munich conservationists organized the First German Nature Protection Day. Supporters gathered in the city on the eve of Oktoberfest and mostly repeated sentiments from April. They protested mountain trains in general and construction on the Zugspitze, "the towering landmark of German soil," specifically. The event's closing speech, "Nature Protection and Industry," warned against the industrial exploitation of natural resources. Audience members reiterated that they opposed the industrialization of mass tourism, not the time-honored methods of conquering mountains. Their problem was not with enjoying the Alps but with how people went about doing it.[26]

Participants at these protests displayed an ironic lack of self-awareness. Members of the Alpine Association in particular voiced such hypocrisy that their remarks would be almost comical were they not so ominous. Mountaineers directed their bile against materialism, the "disgusting plunder of civilization." They were not the only ones to attack materialistic attitudes during the interwar years. Other groups, many on the far right but also some on the extreme left, condemned materialism as the bane of German idealism or "true" German culture. Few bothered to clarify what that actually meant. Die-hard climbers, themselves products of bourgeois culture, reviled the changes in the Alps with the same language. Once again, mountaineers denounced the cost of technology even as they reaped the benefits. Bringing "modern civilization's achievements" to the mountains somehow deprived humanity, unless that meant blazing trails or constructing huts. Unlike cable cars or luxury ski lodges, rugged trails and rustic huts apparently elevated the human condition. Contradictions abounded. For the Alpine Association, machines and mass tourism did more than shatter the stillness above. "A mountain with a train station and a hotel on the peak," as one member fumed, "is no longer a mountain."[27] Yet the club had celebrated when it completed the Münchner Haus and installed an advanced weather station on top of the Zugspitze years earlier. No one explained how a metal-capped summit differed from a cable car stop. In the previous century, the association had often portrayed itself as the harbinger of progress; its huts civilized the heights and brought wealth to impoverished vales. Its modernizing efforts opened the Alps to popular tourism. The club readied the mountains for mass consumption. Members criticized the supposed materialism now taking hold on the heights but deflected responsibility for making that possible in the first place. During the Munich demonstrations, climbers failed to grasp the paradox of their protests.

On the other side of town, government officials fretted away. The demonstrations received much press but had little political repercussion. Rather, ministers faced a mounting trade deficit. The Bavarian highlands seriously lagged in commercial development when compared to Tyrol or Vorarlberg. Austria's Alpine provinces had acted quicker to subsidize aerial trams. Cable cars "exerted an extraordinary power of attraction on tourism," noted one Bavarian minister, and provided lucrative revenue streams. But instead of realizing that mountain trains generated money, opponents in Germany believed that construction raised taxes. Delay had effectively given Austria the competitive edge in the tourism industry. The rub was that several German firms provided the Austrians with working capital. German vacationers took their money to Tyrol rather than spent it in the Bavarian mountains. As a result, Austria built more cable cars and attracted more tourists, all at Germany's expense.[28]

Eager to turn a profit from Alpine tourism, the Bavarian government finally awarded the Zugspitzbahn concession to a consortium of Munich and Berlin firms in 1928.²⁹ Construction lasted from 1928 until 1930. During the first two phases, men laid tracks from Garmisch to Eibsee, the lake near the foot of the Zugspitze. Trains started running along this line in late 1929. This was easy terrain where workers and civil engineers faced few obstacles; the grueling part lay ahead. In the third phase, the tracks climbed from Eibsee up to the peak, almost eight kilometers. The last half tunneled through the mountain before emerging at the Schneefernerhaus station, located just below the summit. Workers had to first chisel out temporary tracks to lug up the heavy equipment, food, and other necessary supplies. The men also had to build their own barracks. Distances from the lowlands required some eight hundred employees to live on-site. During tunnel excavations, the construction workers fared little better than coal miners. Initially they had to drill by hand until equipment lorries hauled up the gas-powered generators. Even with power tools and dynamite, the work was exhausting. From this point on, the mountain's geology dictated the timetable. The consortium had consulted several noted geologists and mountaineering experts before settling on the tunnel's location. Developers weighed several factors. They needed a spot with low occurrences of avalanches and rockslides, which could block the tunnel's entrance or damage the summit station. Tunneling required stable limestone deposits to avoid cave-ins. Engineers also had to account for water seepage and calculate the best spots for ventilation shafts. Besides geological factors, topography and wind currents determined where planners could erect the cable car for the final ascent from summit station to the mountaintop. But all things considered, the mountain's geology proved mostly favorable for engineering.

Once construction began, furious protests simmered down to sullen grumbles. Demonstrations ended, but not disapproval. An indignant Garmisch official sneered that the train was just another Prussian ploy to keep Bavaria down, referring to the consortium's Berlin partners. He scorned the Swiss and Tyrolean demolition engineers, calling them the "gravediggers" of the Zugspitze. One journalist exposed the plight of the contract workers, supposed slaves to big business and capitalism no matter the risk of lightning strikes, avalanches, blizzards, or rockslides.³⁰ Yet what continued to draw attention to the Zugspitzbahn was not political blustering or human exploitation but rather the environmental degradation. Even though developers had received a certificate of approval from the State Committee for Nature Conservation as part of their bid, nature lovers remained skeptical. The massive dig only raised their doubts. Conservationists inferred environmental damage from the assault on the senses. Thunderous detonations, whining power drills, and loud generators deafened passing hikers. The bangs and clangs of machinery created an awful racket inside the mountain. Smells changed. Instead of fragrant scents from wildflowers, pine trees, and dewy grass, diesel fumes choked the morning air. The "invasion" of electric lines, utility poles, and steel pylons altered the Zugspitze's visual profile. Dust and smoke from the blasts obscured views. Rubble from the excavations littered the trails, especially along the popular Höllental route. Paths turned into bouldering problems. People now had to squeeze and scramble their way around the debris. Developers attempted to appease nature preservationists through compromise. To protect the Alpine tundra, tunneling stopped short of the peak. Sometimes large monetary settlements soothed matters, like when dynamiting caused structural damage to the Münchner Haus and the weather observatory.[31]

Although conservationists railed against pollution from construction sites, cable cars reduced the human footprint on the mountainside in the long term. Sightseers by the thousands sailed to the summits without trampling the delicate Alpine ecology. Besides, the ride up was fun, as was the journey through the Zugspitze tunnel. For most people, the trip was far more enjoyable than trudging up the steep slopes, maybe even for committed alpinists. As one mountaineer teased his fellows, they had campaigned against the mountain trains but were the first aboard when the trams started running.[32] The first passengers chugged up the Zugspitze in July 1930. A year later a hotel opened at the Schneefernerhaus, and the aerial tram began carrying people to the summit. Despite the worsening economy in 1931, nearly forty-six thousand people rode the train, and over 80 percent of them continued on with the cable car.[33]

Perhaps alpinists were too exhausted from their fight over Germany's highest peak to battle on Austria's. More likely they were too distracted. Franz Wallack's plans for the Grossglockner High Alpine Road project had taken shape in the mid-1920s, and construction lasted for most of the 1930s. German mountaineers were either too busy confronting the Zugspitzbahn consortium or weathering their country's political and economic tempests of the 1930s. Maybe members of the Alpine Association remembered that one of their own chapters, Klagenfurt, had already built a private road on the Grossglockner. That road had won the heights yet lost the club its moral high ground to oppose future state-funded highways in the mountains. The executive board decided to not issue any resolution against the Grossglockner project. Since Wallack had the government's full backing, protest would have been futile. In fact, the club had inadvertently assisted Wallack; he used its maps to design the road. Moreover, because of the highway's anticipated financial benefits, it had strong popular support.[34]

Austria's economy was in need of a boost. The rough-hewn rump of a chopped-up empire, the new republic had lost its Adriatic seaports, Dolomite highways, and most productive agricultural lands, once key components of Habsburg commerce. Little was left now except Vienna's decaying splendor and the country's lovely mountains. The Alpine provinces faced financial dilemmas of their own. The commodities market for the region's timber and dairy products went bust after the war. But tourist attractions, such as popular ski resorts, boomed. Astute financial planners encouraged government spending on tourism infrastructure, including cable cars and highways. They hoped to direct the flow of business from Italy to Germany through Austria, as well as to attract wealthy vacationers, especially Americans and their dollars. "Rich Americans are looking for thrills," remarked one newspaper editorial. "They journey to London just to experience the famous fog[;] they will travel to Austria to drive on the Alpine highways." "Build the roads," another journalist exclaimed, "and the wealth will come."[35]

Driving the Alps was all the rage. With over 150 major roads running across the mountains, motorists could now explore the Alpine Arc from end to end. This was not easily done before 1914. Swiss cantons once barred road access to most privately owned motor vehicles. But by 1920, the federal post office had retired its horsed carriages for delivery trucks, which led to improved roads and opened the way for touring cars. Revised customs regulations also made travel less difficult. After the war, roads along the Austro-Italian frontier frequently crisscrossed the border. Rather than produce their triptyque and suffer delays at the numerous guard posts and customhouses, drivers now had to submit their papers only once in each direction. Newly formed automobile clubs also helped facilitate travel. They published road atlases and driving manuals, giving practical advice on everything from handling hairpin turns to preventing cars from overheating on the inclines. With guidebooks and maps on the dashboard, more motorists than ever before revved up their engines and headed for the mountains.

The Dolomites in particular were a popular travel destination. By all accounts, this "motorist paradise" contained excellent highways and uniquely impressive scenery. The main drag from Bolzano to Cortina was just the start. Following the outbreak of war, Austrian and Italian construction battalions built so many roadways that they transformed the entire district. The Alps may have "lost their terror for modern motorists," yet the mountains retained their magic.[36] Travelers could survey "inspiring panoramas of snow-capped peaks and glistening glaciers" in the height of summer, pull over for a picnic amidst a "riot of flowers," and then continue on to the next stunning natural feature. This was the charm of driving in the Alps. Cable cars pulled people to a given point along a single line, but motorists could visit several lookouts and take in a variety of scenes. The roads' design, with their dips and serpentine curves, were visually pleasing, especially when compared with those in the flatlands, and drew attention to the mountains' splendor. Sharp turns and steep climbs enforced slower speeds, allowing passengers time to enjoy the view. Machines bestowed an aesthetic appreciation of the Alps in ways that scaling the actual peaks could not.[37]

Zigzagging along high altitude roads with breathtaking views exhilarated drivers (though maybe not passengers prone to car sickness), but the terrain frustrated highway surveyors and civil engineers. Overcoming the natural landscape resulted in some of the most scientifically engineered and well-built roads of the day, as was the case on the Grossglockner. These highways, enlightenment projects in a way, brought rationality and order to a jumbled landscape. Yet the contours of the slopes gave the roads a twisting, seemingly organic shape that defied straight, symmetrical lines and thus still satisfied romantic preconceptions of the Alps. Engineers designed these tracks to last. Generally, the higher one drove, the better the road. Unlike mean city streets, Alpine highways did not so badly suffer the wear and tear of heavy congestion. Even with the growing preponderance of motoring tourists, gridlock on the heights was uncommon.[38] With every ascending mile, the roads improved and traffic receded.

Just as mountaineers spoke of finding freedom in the Alps, so too did motorists. Similar to nineteenth-century hiking guidebooks, travel manuals from the 1920s encouraged drivers to "hasten to the highest mountain roads for the mere sake of escaping from the turmoil of the plains." With no stoplights, few patrolmen, and even fewer rules, other than to avoid hurtling off a cliff, auto enthusiasts could race around lofty peaks with a wonderful sense of liberty. Perhaps climbers and car drivers had more in common than they thought. Both found joy in reaching new horizons. They shared an attraction to danger, sometimes deadly. They wandered the wide world with the same romantic outlook. As one commentator explained, there were no mountaineers or motorists, only wanderers. Although some assumed a necessary antagonism between traditional climbing customs and modern "motor mountaineering," others replied, "There is nothing . . . in Alpine road travel by car that is essentially inimical to pre-existing institutions."[39]

Yet there was. Motorists may have asserted similarities between themselves and mountaineers, but snooty alpinists did not. Even if buses did shuttle eager vacationers more quickly to the trailheads from the rail stations, passengers missed the point. A person was supposed to hike up the valley, across pastures, and through pine forests to mentally prepare for the struggle ahead. To leave enough daylight for lingering on the summit and for the descent, climbers needed to depart during the predawn darkness, which added to the mystical aspect of the mountain experience. As for those who drove up to the peak, they too missed the point. Climbs required intense physical exertion and focus. Muscle exhaustion calmed the mind to a meditative state, allowing a person to forget everyday woes. Motor vehicles robbed the entire outing of meaning. They were also a menace. Sputtering engines coughed clouds of exhaust smoke, ruining the peaceful ambience and polluting the air. Grinding gears could be heard up and down the slopes. Dairy farmers were not very keen on new roads cutting across their pastures and disturbing their herds. For hard-core mountaineers, cars represented the most revolting aspects of city life. Motor vehicles not only urbanized the Alpine landscape but also presented the real threat of collisions or getting run over. Drag racing up the mountain became a dangerous pastime for thrill seekers. A simple fender-bender might turn deadly if drivers swerved over the brink. Rusting corpses of crashes, too heavy to tow out of the canyons, became permanent features. Once again elitist climbers lost. Their old-fashioned attitudes were no match for sleek cars whose drivers had money to spend, especially after the markets crashed.

Economic meltdown in the 1930s changed attitudes toward the marriage of nature and technology. Protesting the union was a luxury of bull markets. The battle against the Zugspitzbahn raged when the German economy had rebounded. Developers who submitted draft plans for a major highway over Austria's main Alpine crest in 1924 were castigated as fools. But after calamity hit, preserving mountains in the face of

FIGURE 14 Molding mountains. Source: Salzburg Landesarchiv, Nachlass Wallack II, Fotoalbum 14, 1935, p. 26.

pervasive financial ruin struck the destitute as wildly irresponsible. Proponents now framed the Grossglockner High Alpine Road as the country's largest public work relief project. Attuned to the tenor of penury, government officials played the Grossglockner High Alpine Road project to the melody of prosperity. Similar to President Franklin Roosevelt's New Deal and its Civilian Conservation Corps, Austrian officials hoped constructing scenic roads would reduce unemployment and generate wealth. Salzburg's governor and president of the Grossglockner High Alpine Road Corporation, Franz Rehrl, repeatedly claimed that the project would cure the country's economic and political ills. The highway represented a new, resurgent Austria, a country capable of tremendous engineering feats. State conservationists toed the line and described the highway as the place where "nature and technology come together peacefully." Crewmen broke ground in 1930, just a couple of months after the Zugspitzbahn started running and right when European economies began to collapse. Various firms simultaneously managed different stretches of the highway, each with hundreds on the payroll.[40] Over the course of five years, thousands worked on the route.

Engelbert Dollfuss, Austria's chancellor from 1932 until his assassination by Nazi terrorists two years later, saw the project as a means to modernize the Alps and reverse the region's fiscal misfortunes. So did his successor, Kurt Schuschnigg, who wrote the foreword in the project's marketing brochure. "The groans and pounding of machines mingled with the mountain's stillness," he began, "and thousands of hands struggled with Nature's wild and barren land." He was careful, though, to couch the Grossglockner project not in terms of demolishing mountains but rather as the opportunity for gainful employment.[41]

When politicians stressed the highway's supposed economic benefits, they downplayed its environmental and human costs. Those "thousands of hands" wielded jackhammers, steam shovels, and road rollers. For years, workers lacerated the mountainside and carted away loads of rocks and dirt, sometimes snow and ice. Photographs showed battalions of crewmen, armed with simple shovels, excavating all along the planned route. Wallack described the whole experience as a "relentless fight against forces of nature."[42] As part of the battle, engineers leveled uneven slopes into terraced gradients, giving the ridgelines a corkscrew appearance. Work could be dangerous. The men labored almost entirely outside in the elements. A few died from exposure or in avalanches and rockslides. With so many people concentrated on-site, garbage and human waste quickly accumulated. Tranquil Alpine dells turned into dirty cauldrons of construction activity. But once completed, the highway was a sight to behold. The long, looping road garlanded the mountain and glittered as sunshine flashed on windshields. At dusk the green fir trees, some dusted with snow, glowed in the headlamps. With the lights, scents, and tinsel-like highway, the mountain almost felt like Christmas.

FIGURE 15 Construction on the Grossglockner High Alpine Road.
Source: Salzburg Landesarchiv, Nachlass Wallack I, Baubericht 1934, nrs. 298 and 561 (top and center); Nachlass Wallack II, Fotoalbum 15, 1936, p. 29 (bottom).

In September 1934, Wallack and Rehrl climbed aboard a Steyr 100 and tested the nearly completed highway. The road slithered up to Kaiser-Franz-Josefs-Höhe, where tourists could park at the welcome center and look out over the Pasterze, Austria's longest glacier. Just above towered Grossglockner's distinctive pyramid-shaped peak. A few days later, over eight thousand people attended the opening ceremony. Dignitaries included Chancellor Schuschnigg, President Wilhelm Miklas, and several other high-ranking officials. Members of the foreign press reported on the event, describing the road as the greatest engineering feat in the Alps. Radio Wien broadcasted the festivities.[43] Road crews finished the last stretch of highway the following summer. The First International Grossglockner Grand Prix marked the occasion; drivers from across Europe raced their cars and motorcycles over the mountain. The road's popularity proved the naysayers wrong. By the start of summer vacation in 1939, nearly a million toll-paying visitors had driven on the road.[44] The completion of the Grossglockner High Alpine Road cemented changes in the Alps and ushered in the era of automobile Alpine tours.

Only when plans to construct parking lots and a large visitors' center near Grossglockner's peak became public did the Alpine Association take action. The club now joined forces with a vast array of Austrian civic and academic organizations, including the Academy of Science, the Geographical Society, the Geological Society, the Mineralogical Society, the Zoological-Botanical Society, and the Austrian Society for Nature Protection, and lobbied the Austrian government to halt construction. In telling language, alpinists claimed that the project "castrated" the mountain and allowed its summit to be "taken without a struggle."[45] In internal memoranda, the association condemned as "egotistical" and "short-sighted" those in the Austrian government who supported the construction. After a lawsuit to halt the construction failed, the club's language of nature protection became increasingly militaristic. Members refused to "lay down their arms" or "abandon their posts." Despite their lost battle, they "held their pure shields high" and castigated Schuschnigg's government for turning the Grossglockner into a "woeful monument of ignorance and ingratitude."[46]

In response to mass tourism, mountaineers tried to turn back time. Nostalgia for an earlier, supposedly simpler age had beckoned pioneer climbers to the Alps in the first place. Wistful for mountains without machines, some alpinists fled to distant peaks in the Andes or Himalayas, far away from the crowds, cable cars, and modern highways.

FIGURE 16 Sleek machines and rugged mountains.
Source: Steyr Brochure 1935. Courtesy of Dr. Gerhard Troyer and
Renate Troyer-Berann.

FIGURE 17 Grossglockner Visitor Center on Kaiser-Franz-Josefs-Höhe.
Source: Salzburg Landesarchiv, Nachlass Wallack II,
Fotoalbum 7, 1933, p. 7.

Others sought to minimize the human touch on the heights. As the self-appointed warden of the Eastern Alps, the Alpine Association had reacted most forcefully to the mechanization of the heights. Impotent to stop the Zugspitzbahn or Grossglockner High Alpine Road projects, the club instead instituted its own outdoor educational programs and internal reform. With each course of action, the club faced the future by looking backward.

Impetus for most reforms came from the recently established "mountaineering group," which comprised some sixty German and Austrian sections located chiefly along the club's "Alpine backbone." These chapters assembled serious mountain climbers, all men, who advanced old-fashioned nineteenth-century mountaineering. Members of the group claimed that they did not want to keep the mountains for themselves. But they did. When the hard core watched hordes of tourists clamber up the peaks, they fought to preserve the heights for "true mountaineers." Mediocre men (never mind women), "inferior climbers," did not deserve a mountaineering mystique. A die-hard alpinist stressed that "the high mountains are there primarily for the mountain climber, and it should never be the task of an Alpine club to impair a mountain climber from his entitled claim." Such impairment included ruining climbing walls with paths for the masses, building grandiose huts on the summits, or even maintaining an open membership. These men were shamelessly egotistical. What concerned them was the withering of (their) individualism under the weight of blundering masses. More open-minded alpinists considered the mountaineering group a collection of extremists, to which its members protested, "We are not fanatics."[47]

They were. Like others before the war, the mountaineering group argued that paved trails and hotel-like cabins ruined the Alpine ambience. But the "fanatics" also demanded a ban on alcohol, the return to itchy hay mattresses, and keeping renovations to a simple, old-fashioned style. Lodges with soft feather beds, comfy private rooms, warm meals, copious alcohol, loud music, fresh-baked goods, and a waitstaff degraded mountaineering's traditional Spartan ethos. These extreme climbers believed that "luxury" huts attracted a certain undesirable type of person, a "snob" who knew nothing of climbing and even less about Alpine etiquette.[48] Snobs who were accomplished alpinists, however, were admitted gladly.

The mountaineering group's rhetoric laid bare its bigotry. During the inflation of the 1920s, the cost of Alpine tours became affordable to a wider social constituency. Membership in the Alpine Association peaked at more than two hundred thousand in 1923. Serious climbers spurned the so-called inflation members as "un-Alpine" individuals who had joined the club for materialistic reasons.[49] "For little more than the cost of a glass of beer," one bitter alpinist complained, "these 'inflation-members' receive so many benefits [of membership]." Elitists feared that the association's imprudent expansion threatened the club with "proletarianization," which might even lead some to characterize the club as "a guild of Alpine proles."[50] Using the association's financial straits as a cover, the group proposed several dues increases, although everyone recognized these proposals for what they were—attempts to restrict membership. The hard-core members also proposed increasing hut fees with the aim to close the mountains to the less fortunate. Failing at that, they did their best to make the lower classes feel unwelcome in the lodges.

The association's politics made for strange bedfellows. For Eduard Pichl, these actions went too far. He was among the most vocal critics of any attempt to restrict membership based on class, mostly because serious climbers wanted to oust the very rabble from the club's ranks that he had recruited in his crusade against Section Donauland. Incensed, Pichl called this class-based agenda "selfish and *unvölkisch*." He claimed that the mountains should be within the reach of all ordinary Germans and Austrians. The Alps served the greater good. Access to the heights elevated the Aryan race, which for Pichl and his ilk meant keeping the peaks free of Jews but not of the lower classes (unless, of course, they were socialist agitators).[51] In this fight, Pichl's detractors grudgingly found themselves on his side, though for very different motives. They adhered to what they believed were the founders' intentions: open membership to anyone interested in the Alps.

Although the mountaineering group made up a small percentage of the club's membership, it had enough pull to dictate policy. A new series of rules, the "Tölzer guidelines" issued in 1923, catered to hard-core climbers. New huts and trails could be built only if they contributed to "mountaineering needs." Such huts were to be simple in construction and have no full-time proprietor. Chapters were to refrain from clearing new trails and to reduce the number of trail markers. Paths deemed unnecessary would not receive financial support. The guidelines discouraged advertising huts in train stations and newspapers. Huts that did have a proprietor were to be maintained in the simplest way possible, including a reduction in alcohol sales and baked specialty goods. Climbers received priority over day-hikers in the huts. The guidelines also denied hut access to film companies. Lodges could have mattresses and wool blankets, but feather beds were banned, as were any mechanical instruments such as gramophones. The guidelines stipulated that lights-out began at ten o'clock sharp and that unmarried men and women must sleep separately. Visitors had to obey the rules or else suffer their names on the association's published "black list."[52]

No wonder membership in the Alpine Association dropped. Currency stabilization in the mid-1920s only partly explains the decline. Many, especially those distant from the Alps, found the guidelines heavy-handed. People from northern and central Germany could not travel to the Alps every Sunday; for extended stays in the mountains, it was imperative to have nicer facilities. Moreover, northerners had fewer opportunities to adequately train for the Alpine environment. The more strenuous physical prerequisites made membership seem less appealing.[53] Those chapters that had lost huts and their "work region" in the war also raised concerns that the new guidelines prevented them from building new huts for their members. Others found the restrictions to be utter nonsense. One easygoing hiker even suggested chiseling steps in the upper reaches of the mountains; far from detrimental, such relief, however small, might be welcomed by an exhausted climber during a challenging ascent. Many felt that the guidelines made the overall Alpine experience too costly. But the fact that stricter regulations weeded out the membership thrilled the mountaineering group.[54]

The mountaineering group's bravado attracted male chauvinists. A more exclusive male-oriented club delighted those who disliked the growing number of female alpinists. With its hardened approach to mountain climbing, the mountaineering group had little tolerance for physically weaker women. Its members made it clear that real mountain climbing was a man's undertaking.[55] These climbers typified the overbearing masculinity of mountaineering. Misogynistic alpha males stereotyped the sport and filled the ranks of climbing clubs the world over. The British Alpine Club had never allowed female members. The Swiss Alpine Club had accepted women until 1907, when it revised its membership qualifications. But Swiss female climbers were no shrinking violets; they formed their own club in 1918, the Schweizer Frauen-Alpenclub (Swiss Women's Alpine Club).

The German and Austrian Alpine Association did not ban women, but its constituent chapters could. Even though Sections Berlin and Mark Brandenburg, among others, prohibited female members, women secured themselves in associational life. They attended the annual convention in significant numbers, most as wives but some as delegates. A few women contributed to the monthly newsletter. Women participated in mountain excursions, right alongside men.[56] During the club's first fifty years, executives rarely needed to address gender relations. Except for some grumblers in the corner, this loose arrangement seemed to keep tempers cool.

The war upset the status quo. By 1919, both the Austrian and German republics had enfranchised women, granting them full rights as voting citizens. New fashions, including women with short hair wearing long pants, and greater public presence blurred gender lines and added to male insecurities. Male chauvinists seethed as more female adventurers than ever before scaled the Alps. Yet seeing women on the heights was hardly new. Women had played key roles in local Alpine economies for generations and most recently had proven instrumental to the war effort. Alfred Steinitzer, a veteran and vocal member of the Alpine Association, pushed for the greater inclusion of women. He had witnessed the critical role women had played on the Alpine front. Mothers of the nation's next generation deserved exposure to Alpinism as much as men did. He even suggested that women sit on the association's board of directors.[57] Here was the difference: chauvinists had deemed as acceptable women in bulky dresses hiking alongside their husbands in the 1870s, but seeing single girls in loose-fitting pants scale the steeps in the 1920s, or facing a woman executive, was something else entirely. The Tölzer guidelines attempted to mitigate male anxieties and restore balance. While not explicitly aimed against women, the guidelines certainly provided for gender discrimination. But Steinitzer's ideas gradually took hold. In 1936, the *Deutsche Alpenzeitung* dedicated a special issue to "The Woman in the Mountains," with several articles covering well-known female climbers.

Female alpinists did not suddenly become visible during the interwar years. Plucky ladies had long participated in Alpinism, going back to the early nineteenth century. But linking women and machines was something new. Male chauvinists saw a direct connection between the mechanization of the mountain and the feminization of mountaineering. They spoke of machines castrating mountains, robbing the peaks (and the men who climb them) of their vigor. Blaming women for the gelded Alps came easily. Trains, cars, and aerial trams arrived loaded with female tourists. Outdoor stores now catered to female customers, with tailor-made clothing and custom-designed equipment for female bodies. More women taking risks in the Alps made men apprehensive. Leni Riefenstahl's movies did not help matters. Her female characters, whether a fickle-hearted dancer or a well-meaning fiancée, corrupted, endangered, or killed the male leads. Impotent to halt intrusions by machines and women left insecure men in a state of enraged emasculation.

Male rancor stewed in Berlin. Unlike Munich or Vienna, Berlin maintained its all-male tradition right until 1919, when the chairman proposed to allow women members—and unleashed a firestorm of fury. His supporters spoke of social equality, the need for more dues-paying members to bolster the chapter's financial position, and the unspoken rivalry with Munich and Austria. One traditionalist reminded his colleagues of the benefits of having female members. Who better to cook and clean in the huts and keep the lodges in order?

Opponents tried scare tactics. They warned that women members would receive the same rights and benefits as the men, so women could be elected to the board. Some predicted that women of different social groups would not mix well during chapter gatherings. Even those who did would do nothing but gossip during meetings. Many felt that women simply had no business climbing mountains. "There are those women who want to be members of the chapter," one member spat, "who have not once even climbed the Berliner Kreuzberg," a small hill in the city. Women did not belong. Men had opened the Alps, and they could do without any "feminine influence on our endeavors."[58] For these male chauvinists, only in the mountains could they reaffirm what being a man meant. Following defeat in war, the Alps were their last resort.

So bitter was male vitriol that a group of Berlin women tried to copy their Swiss sisters and create an all-female chapter in 1924. But club executives refused to splinter the membership further and rejected the proposal. Women outside Berlin agreed. They wanted female members to be integrated within the chapters, not ghettoized and tempting Section Donauland's fate.[59]

Misogynistic fury evolved into moral outrage. Although public opinion forced the Berlin men to relent, it also raised concerns about loose sexual behavior in the mountains. Sleeping arrangements in the huts could be intimate. Climbers often piled on a hay-covered loft, usually relying on shared body heat to stay warm. Men and women sleeping in such close quarters shocked the straitlaced. Prudes imagined the worst. Maybe they were right. Even the club's elderly chairman admitted that wandering freely in the Alps in the fresh air and romantic vistas might encourage "lax morals" among some. Enough people were apparently enjoying sex on the summits to cause a backlash. The Tölzer guidelines explicitly required that unmarried men and women sleep apart in the huts. One moralistic climber declared it was "high time" to purify the mountains of "the revolting phenomenon of Alpinism *sexualis*." He never clarified whether that meant open homosexuality or simply unmarried men and women having sex. In any case, such "indecency" provoked violent reactions. To combat this "dreadful state of affairs," his chapter refused "those people" access to its huts. "And when they do enter," he added, "we throw them out head-first."[60]

Women faced an uphill battle. Climbing mountains was easy compared to handling male chauvinists or moralistic crusaders. But women had the Alpine Association's own patriotic rhetoric on their side. If the club intended to help heal the nation by bringing people to the mountains, then it needed to include both men and women. Along this vein, one female contributor to the newsletter dismissed stereotypes and instead discussed values. She argued that the rights of membership and access to the mountains should not be based on physical prowess. Moreover, defining Alpinism as a set of ethics gave women equal rights to participate. She claimed that male and female members shared the same system of values, and in a time of social instability, German women as well as German men required courage and self-confidence. Bolstering women's sense of responsibility made female participation in the club vital for the nation. Women, like men, learned through Alpinism that "the individual is there not only for herself but also for others and for the whole."[61] For those who believed in the club's mission, her position was unassailable. Men had to either reject the language of national recovery or accept the growing prominence of female mountaineers.

· · · · · · · · · · · · · ·

Machines had changed the iconic mountain; they had altered "not only its fabric but also its architecture."[62] The mountain's sights, sounds, and smells revealed structural alterations to its profile with protruding pylons, streaming cables, serpentine highways, humming generators, groaning engines, and diesel fumes. Mechanized mountains invited the masses. In addition to the clanks and bangs of machinery, thousands of clamoring voices filled the air. Being a climber required a close connection with the natural world. A person had to physically grapple with stone and ice to reach the summit, with death but a misstep away. With every inch upward, fingers carefully felt the rock edges, searching for just the right hold. Perhaps in no other human-nature relationship did the finest details matter so much. This was an intimate embrace. Scraped hands, sunburned faces, frostbitten toes, muscular bodies, and steely eyes still squinting from snow blindness were once the telltale signs of hard-core mountaineers. Now machines allowed tourists with flabby bodies to zip around the Alps, gazing across gorgeous vistas through their windshields, apparently with only a coarse connection to the land. It seemed that with machines anyone could be a mountaineer, whether a "young, prospective climber, a veteran of the mountains, a harmless saunterer, an ice- and winter-tested extreme-alpinist, a mountain dweller, or a city resident from the distant lowlands."[63]

Social commentators extrapolated grave consequences from the changes in mountaineering and the Alps. Mass tourism carried troubling implications. Most disturbing was the diminishing role of the individual. What climbers had sought on the heights in the nineteenth century had become increasingly difficult to find. The rise of the machine-driven consumer society overwhelmed individuality, and not only that of mountaineers. One critic called this mass society the "empire of automatons." He described the dark industrial nightmare: "The life of the individual person will become a reliable and ascertainable sub-function of a fully mechanical world," he predicted, "those dreams of being a component part, never failing, the always reliable society-mechanism, the mass-man."[64] The heights had been the last holdout against a mechanized world. But now it appeared that machines had vanquished the mountains.

Alpinism had evolved from a personal experience to a mass phenomenon, and the Alps now sheltered and revitalized the modern "mass-man."[65] Despite protests from extreme alpinists and conservative social commentators, these were not necessarily negative developments. Mass tourism did lead to the "democratization" of mountaineering, and many hoped that such a change would alleviate the "class hatred" that plagued the republics. That bigots crushed their hopes makes such efforts no less commendable. The nineteenth-century rhetoric of finding joy, peace, and inspiration on the peaks, climbing out of darkness to reach enlightenment, and making hardy men (and some strong women) in the mountains applied equally well to the interwar years. Climbing enthusiasts saw the Alps as "beacons of light" for those lost in the "shadows of existence."[66] The interplay of light and darkness carried over from the early days of industrialization. But instead of personal edification, many mountaineers now spoke in terms of national salvation. Individualism, once admired, now ran contrary to the new Alpine ethos. As one writer stated, "whoever does not think egotistically" must recognize the importance of "mass pursuits in the mountains."[67]

But accomplished mountaineers could be an egotistical lot. Although influential Alpine clubs now advanced mountaineering as a collective mindset, many individuals did not. As before the war, proponents of open mountains continued to clash with elitist climbers. The Alpine Association attached a particular national agenda to Alpine tourism, yet independently minded alpinists (a sizable number) often ignored the program. And hard-core alpinists held sway in the club. During the Alpine Association's 1932 annual meeting, a delegate from Innsbruck responded to what he viewed as a disturbing trend in Alpine tourism over the past decade: the preferential treatment of serious mountain climbers. "We are not an Alpine club, which pursues ultimate-tourist [*hochturistische*] goals, rather our aims are to enable as many people as possible to get to know the Alps." "We recognize only members," he clarified, "not just hard-core alpinists [*Hochalpinisten*]."[68]

In the face of such criticism, extreme climbers became increasingly reactionary. They fought to retain the elements of heroic struggle and death-defying feats that were once so intrinsic to the Alpine experience. And they denigrated anyone they deemed unworthy to claim the title of mountaineer. Their actions filtered out the more open-minded, progressive, and cosmopolitan climbers from the Alpine Association, leaving behind a concentration of populist anti-Semites like Pichl and elitist mountaineers who shunned the weak. The two groups made a poisonous combination. With their venom they assailed the German and Austrian republics. They held the limp socialist democracies responsible for ruining the peaks with machines and rampant consumerism. But one splinter group in Bavaria, led by Adolf Hitler, vowed to protect the Alps and began to draw disillusioned mountaineers into its fold.

7

Fascist Landscapes
Nature Lovers and Nazi Desperadoes on the Alpine Frontier

> Even though the Reich-German Alpine area is rather small, it still grants instructive insights into the blueprint of young mountains, especially right here where the particular circumstances of the mountain border cede special problems.
> —Max Richter, *Die deutschen Alpen und ihre Entstehung* (1937)

Like a good number of nature conservationists and outdoor enthusiasts, many alpinists did praise Hitler's apparent desire to protect the Alpine wilderness. The National Socialist vision of a Greater Germany anchored by the Alps endeared the party to climbing clubs, including the Alpine Association, whose members had long proclaimed the unbreakable Alpine bonds between Germany and Austria. Even the old mountaineering language of struggle and conquest resonated with Nazi rhetoric. Hitler's rants against materialism and the failings of parliamentary government drew in like-minded mountaineers, who blamed the German and Austrian republics for defiling the rugged frontier with rampant consumerism. Right-wing rabble-rousers, like Eduard Pichl, were already disparaging the governments and decorating Alpine lodges with swastikas in the early 1920s. For Nazi sympathizers, the adoption of the Aryan paragraph in many chapter statutes and Section Donauland's dissolution in 1924 stirred hopes. Meanwhile, as mass tourism opened the Alps into a far more cosmopolitan landscape during the interwar years, intransigent climbing clubs simultaneously closed ranks and turned increasingly intolerant.

Nazi propagandists saw opportunity. Mountaineering still held its allure in the 1930s. The daring albeit doomed attempts by German expeditions to conquer distant summits, most notably Nanga Parbat in the Himalayas, captured national attention. Hitler greeted the men who had first climbed the Eiger's north face in 1938 as heroes. Alpine tourism appealed to Nazi officials, who presented mountain climbers as archetypal Germans. Mountaineers were "hardened people" whose courage and strength Germany needed.[1] They harkened back to a "glorious past" and transferred the strength of the "German earth" to the *Volk*. The mountaineering community developed comradeship, while difficulty, danger, and death served as its proving ground. Mountain climbing made "men of action" who did not question motives or goals. The Alps became instruments of political indoctrination and mountaineering a means to militarize the national body. This vast Alpine realm of national might suggested a certain sense of hubris on the part of both those who defeated the mountains and those who sought to conquer Europe.

Yet not all alpinists had cordial relations with the Nazis. The construction of the German Alpine Road across the Bavarian highlands and Hitler's support of automobile tourism in the Alps horrified most mountaineers. Conservation-minded climbers felt immense frustration with Nazi officials whose aims were only to strengthen the German body, not to preserve nature. The party's green rhetoric proved nothing more than empty promises. The same was true for the language of unity. Despite lofty talk that the Alps united Germans and Austrians, the uneasy relationship between the Nazi regime and the Austrian government remained a special source of problems for Alpine enthusiasts. Adhering to regulations in one country meant breaking the law in the other. Climbers had to act with caution. Political antagonisms and border closures added to the growing hostility between the two countries. Animosity pervaded the Alps. Until the *Anschluss* in 1938, the tall peaks exposed the barriers between Germany and Austria and the fissures within Nazi society.

・・・・・・・・・・・・・

Perilous landscapes counteracted political instability—or so it seemed with the Alps. Paradoxically, the mountains at once threatened mortal danger while providing a sense of security. Massive rocks could both menace and soothe. In the modern era, the Alps had increasingly become a "point of pilgrimage," particularly during times of upheaval. With their "unchanging nature," "elemental power," "eternal presence," and "almighty strength," the Alps held a peculiar "force of attraction."[2] Amateur psychiatrists during the 1920s diagnosed the fascination with deadly places as a longing for stability and wholeness. One layperson related the appeal of mountain climbing to the disconnect that Germans and

Austrians felt with the external world in the interwar years. Still others speculated that the era's focus on material success appeared superficial and empty; wealth offered little solace. But with each step toward the summit, the mountains fortified climbers to face the modern world.[3] Reaching the peak nourished the soul in ways that financial gain never could.

Such justifications for putting one's life in jeopardy extended back to the nineteenth century but carried different implications after the First World War. In 1922, Gustav Müller applied this pseudo-psychoanalysis in his article on the Alps and Germany's future. This was the same Gustav Müller who served on the Alpine Association's executive board, chaired the Bavarian Section Hochland, and had repeatedly and quite vocally supported the dissolution of the predominantly Jewish chapter, Donauland. His political sympathies became even more apparent in his article. In his view, the German people suffered from defeat in war as well as from the despair of modernity. The key to reviving the Volk lay in the Alps. But what made these mountains so therapeutic? To understand the attraction to the heights, he asked mountaineers why they climbed. Most gave the typical answers. Some stated they did so out of pleasure; others remarked on nature's majesty, the struggle to the top, and the search for freedom, peace, and beauty. Many believed that Alpinism elevated the spirit, comforted the soul, invigorated the body, and reconciled man with nature.[4] Had Müller interviewed the pioneer generation of alpinists, he would have heard similar responses.

Yet Müller remained unconvinced. Echoing hack psychologists, he turned to the problem of modern man. Egotistical, "over-intelligent," and "soulless," this product of the "civilized world" shunned tradition, religion, and communal bonds. Modern man desired only materialistic success, accolades for cold intellectualism, or rewards for naked ambition. Attachment to superficial achievement apparently left a hole in the soul, and this inner emptiness supposedly caused the urgings to the heights. Not the love of nature or the joy of exercise but the revulsion to the "hollowness, wasteland, and void of civilization" drove modern man to the mountains. Only on the heights could these hollow men break free from their "chains of egoism and materialism" and find fulfillment.[5]

Flight from modernity, however, was not how the Alps would save the Volk. Instead, national salvation lay in collective struggle. Mountaineering required strenuous and continuous physical and mental exertion. Struggle was the quintessential characteristic of the Alpine experience and, in Müller's opinion, was something that was also innately German. More than anyone else, German mountaineers understood that the will to struggle was a natural imperative; they carried the "struggle-principle" with them in their daily lives. Those who lacked this drive, whether people or nations, faced ruin. Thus these towering heights were a reservoir whose wells provided "Alldeutschland" with the "will, courage, and strength to struggle for existence." Only up above could the *Volk*, especially young people, recognize struggle as the "iron world order." In this way, the next generation could fulfill its duties through "struggle, toil and danger" and make the nation once more "great" and "invincible."[6] Müller's approach marked a departure from nineteenth-century mountaineering sensibilities. In the prewar years, struggle had meant that an individual matched his or her mettle against the mountains; following defeat, it implied collective action toward a nationalistic agenda.

Müller was not the only one who found the future in the Alps. His contemporary Hermann Czánt, a colonel in the Austrian army, had become obsessed with preparing for the next war. His books contained illustrated maps of an ever-expanding Slavic menace that threatened Europe with darkness. Since he viewed "modern war" as a total war of race against race, civilian populations required military training, and what better way than through Alpinism? Skiing, climbing, and hiking could play an essential role in readying Germans and Austrians for battle. Training in the Alps cultivated perseverance, determination, confidence, calmness (what Czánt called "cold-bloodedness"), courage, and the ability to deal with panic—all the traits of a good soldier. Hardship in the mountains prepared a person for the privations of war. Besides, the magnificent landscape fostered a profound love for the Fatherland, which Czánt felt was vital for a soldier. Even more important, engagement in the Alps overcame the divides between Germany and Austria. It generated a fighting spirit based not on "Prussian militarism" but rather on "national sport" and the shared natural landscape.

Throughout the 1920s, the colonel relentlessly pursued his agenda, which overlapped with Müller's call to action in nearly every respect. In addition to publishing books on the topic, Czánt lobbied the German and Austrian governments to provide subsidies to tourist and ski clubs and to fund military training programs in the Alps. He also wanted greater centralization and a governmental department to administer these clubs, something that the Nazis later implemented. He petitioned both the German and Austrian army High Commands to establish a mountain warfare department and a liaison office for civilian Alpine clubs.[7] Like Müller, Czánt emphasized adolescent conditioning in the Alps. Based on his own experience, the colonel was confident that such instruction would "win youth over" and instill in them the intrinsic desire to defend Deutschtum. Always with an eye toward a future war, he encouraged civilian alpinists, whom he felt embodied the "highest manly virtues," to design and teach the ski and mountain survival courses for teenagers. Through a militaristic Alpine education, Czánt predicted that a sense of pride and self-respect would spread across Germany and Austria, encouraging a "new spirit of initiative" and a "spirit of attack" while preparing an "elite troop of brave, self-sacrificing, combat-ready and fighting-fit men for the Fatherland."[8]

Czánt's and Müller's right-wing sympathies were unmistakable and seemingly played into Hitler's hands. Müller's cultural criticisms resonated among Nazi supporters. His term "Alldeutschland," along with the emphasis on combative struggle and invincibility, indicated certain political leanings. So too did Czánt's warmongering and racist worldview. Their blatant antimaterialism and antimodernism hinted at the growing trends in German and Austrian society toward the same rejection of liberal values that had underlain the expulsion of Donauland from the Alpine Association. That Hitler's Beer Hall Putsch coincided with these developments was no mere accident. Müller and Czánt had touched a nerve. Allusions to future greatness, calls to struggle, and charges to do one's duty energized Nazi sympathizers. The discussion of hollow men finding fulfillment and preparing for the next war through collective "unselfish struggle" in the Alps neatly wrapped fascist ideology in the neo-romanticism of nature lovers. For the disillusioned or embittered, this message struck home. Combined with Germany's and Austria's instability in the 1930s, this new approach to Alpinism fed into National Socialist dreams of unity, triumph, and domination.

Some historians have argued that the antimaterialism, irrationalism, and now militarism of mountaineering, as expressed by the likes of Müller and Czánt, paved the way for Hitler's seizure of power.[9] On the face of it, the club seemed more predisposed than any other outdoor organization to embrace fascism. To a significant degree, the trends within the association during the first three decades of the twentieth century—the shift from Greater German to Pan-German nationalism, the emphasis on collective struggle, militarism, and anti-Semitism—suggested sympathies that would make Gleichschaltung (synchronization) with the Nazi state an easy transition. Members professed an apolitical stance, but Donauland's fate spoke otherwise. By the time Hitler took power in 1933, the association had already initiated a "self-synchronization," aligning itself within his political and social order. Loyal mountaineers wore their edelweiss pin, a "unifying symbol of all German peoples," not only as a token of membership in the Alpine Association but also as a badge of allegiance to the regime.[10]

Yet symbolism only went so far. A closer look reveals that mountaineering's alignment with the Nazi state was hardly seamless. The supposed strong affinities between Alpinism and Nazism weaken under closer scrutiny. Other historians have recently noted that conservation organizations were not simply pawns in the Nazi scheme. Both Thomas Lekan and John Alexander Williams have shown that the Nazi regime's incorporation of conservation and hiking clubs was uneven and incomplete, largely because those clubs held such intractable definitions of nature and Heimat.[11] Typically, these groups were regional organizations. The Alpine Association, on the other hand, presented a host of unique challenges to the Nazis because of its transnational structure. The association's presence in Austria as well as in Germany made Gleichschaltung with the Nazi state challenging. The club's joint legal status in Austria and Germany frustrated Nazi party officials, but it afforded the association room to maneuver through the labyrinth of overlapping party and state authorities. Compared with other regionally based hiking clubs and nature conservation groups, the Alpine Association retained a significant degree of relative autonomy during the peace years of the Third Reich.

・・・・・・・・・・・・・

Soon after the Nazis assumed power in January 1933, they took a particular interest in conservation and hiking clubs, viewing outdoor recreation as another instrument of political indoctrination. In keeping with fascist ideals of beauty, body image, and athleticism, the party faithful did encourage a respectable level of physical fitness. As with nearly every aspect of civic life, the Nazis established elaborate new hierarchies of control for sport clubs, outdoor organizations, and nature groups. Hiking and mountaineering clubs fell under the purview of the newly named director of the Reich Sports Office, SA (Sturmabteilung, the Nazi Party's paramilitary wing) colonel Hans von Tschammer und Osten, who oversaw the governing body of all sports in Nazi Germany, the Deutsche Reichbund für Leibesübungen (Sports League of the German Reich,

DRL). The DRL regulated all clubs and organizations that involved any sort of sport or physical exercise. An avid sports fan, von Tschammer took tremendous pleasure in organizing most major sporting events in the country, such as the annual Football-Federation Cup and the 1936 Berlin Olympics, but mostly he managed the Gleichschaltung process for regional and local outdoor organizations. Those that did not fall in line, including all social democratic and communist sport clubs, were dissolved. The independent Berlin Alpine Association and the Friends of Nature, both labeled socialist organs, were among the disbanded.

Mountaineering clubs garnered special attention. Von Tschammer believed mountain climbing to be essential for Germany's progress for the same reasons that Müller and Czánt articulated. Accordingly, von Tschammer established yet another regulatory body under the DRL, the Deutscher Bergsteiger- und Wanderverband (German Mountaineering and Hiking Club Federation, DBW). He appointed Paul Bauer, a well-known alpinist, Nazi, and member of the Alpine Association, as its head. This body coordinated all the hiking, camping, and nudist groups in Germany, as well as mountaineering clubs. But with its more than two hundred thousand members spread across two countries in 311 German chapters and 108 Austrian chapters, complete oversight of the Alpenverein was impossible. Recognizing the structural limits of synchronization, in July 1933 von Tschammer decided that the Alpine Association would not be merged with other regional hiking organizations and that local sport commissioners and party officers would have no authority over the individual chapters.[12] This was a landmark decision and set the club apart from other civic organizations.

The DBW did not take direct control of the Alpine Association, did not deal exclusively with the Alps, and did not care about making mountains accessible to scientific research. Bauer's job was instead to ensure that civic associations conformed to Nazi ideology. Like his superiors, Bauer believed that every "joyful mountain trip" served national purposes. "We focus on people and not on dead things," he once remarked.[13] His statement revealed an important change in attitudes toward the mountains from those alpinists who earlier in the century viewed the mountains as alive. Moreover, Bauer cared little for the Alps themselves; his interests really lay with distant Himalayan peaks.

Bauer and other like-minded mountaineers extended Nazism's obsession with the East to the upper reaches of the world in Asia. The lure of the East, the so-called Drang nach Osten, had become the party's driving focus with grandiose plans to colonize and remake lands, most of which were currently part of Poland. German geographers, for example, envisioned ways of draining and damming the Pripet Marshes along the Polish and Soviet border, with ominous plans that brought together National Socialist ideas of race and place with visions of "civilizing" landscapes. So enthralled were party followers with ideas of racially and environmentally engineering the East European space that many used the term *Ostrausch* to describe the mania.[14] Such feelings applied equally well to toppling the Himalayas. Despite its Bavarian and Austrian roots, the Nazi Party focused on foreign peaks far more than on the modest (and already defeated) ones back home. Climbing the Alps had become routine; conquering the highest mountains on earth, on the other hand, brought world renown. One mountain in particular, Nanga Parbat, the world's ninth-tallest summit, dominated Nazi visions. German expeditions attempted to conquer it five times during the 1930s; all failed. In the course of those sieges, eleven mountaineers died. In the wake of the tragedies, contemporaries soon referred to Nanga Parbat as Germany's "Mountain of Destiny."[15]

Fixated on conquering the tallest mountains in the world, Bauer left *Gleichschaltung* efforts to the Alpine Association's executives. Soon after Hitler took power, Paul Dinkelacker, head of the association's administrative committee, mailed a circular to the German chapters urging local chairmen to change their titles to "führer" and to restrict membership to Aryan Germans.[16] Others focused on the club's so-called Jewish problem. In the spring of 1933, Section Rostock sent a confidential memorandum to the German chapters that explained the significance of Hitler's victory for mountaineers. Echoing Müller's warning, Rostock foretold a future that held only two possibilities: "struggle to victory or linger to downfall." Part of the struggle required eliminating the internal enemy. "Now it is high time," the Rostock group concluded, "to ground the Association on a pure German foundation" and rid the club of Jews. Not one to miss an opportunity, Eduard Pichl also sent out circulars to Austrian and German chapters. Encouraged by the Rostock memorandum, he believed that German chapters might now be more inclined to support his own agenda. He reminded the German chapters of their duty to the Fatherland; they were "valuable champions of German purity, German unity, greatness and freedom" and thus now obligated to completely remove Jews from the club.[17]

A few German chapters responded. Hamburg, Hanover, Freiburg, and Munich implemented the "Aryan clause" and their chairmen adopted the führer title that summer. Freiburg declared that all members must be Aryan Germans, with the exception of Jews who had joined the chapter before August 1914, those who had fought in the war, or those who had lost a father or son in the war. But those exceptions applied only to current members.[18] Hanover and Hamburg stated simply that members could be only "persons of Aryan lineage." "Indeed, in its inner character," Hamburg's chairman explained, "the Alpine Association was always national, social, and *völkisch*."[19] As the largest German chapter, with over eight thousand members, Munich attracted the media's attention. In July, city newspapers reported on the decision to designate the chapter's chairman, Georg Leuchs, as führer and to add the "Aryan clause" to the bylaws. "For the well-informed there can be no doubt," the editors wrote, "that the service of the Alpine Association not only lies in the field of mountain-tourism but also in the national sphere." Confirming the Hamburg chairman's impression, journalists observed, "In the Alpine Association the prevailing spirit had always a national-socialist element."[20]

Maybe the reporters were correct. Many members of the executive board and chapter representatives took pride in their self-synchronization efforts. They too proclaimed that the club had always been sympathetic to the Nazi cause, although that may well have been an act of self-preservation. After a rival publicly questioned his "national reliability" in the *Völkischer Beobachter*, the Nazi Party's newspaper, Georg Leuchs responded that his "national mentality" dated back long before March 1933, and he reminded readers that the chapter's executives had greeted the Nazi assumption of power with jubilation, as proprietors hoisted Nazi banners over Munich's Alpine huts.[21] Eager to demonstrate a clear devotion to Hitler, the club's 1933 annual report declared that the German chapters were "unanimous" in their support of the "regime of national reconstruction and its Führer." The report maintained that as a sign of their allegiance, most German chapters had adopted the führer principle.[22]

The report was an enormous exaggeration. Many German chapters hardly bothered to institute *Gleichschaltung*. Only a minority had adopted the "Aryan clause." Rostock and Pichl's bellicose clamoring fell largely on deaf ears. Even after the passage of the Nuremburg Laws in 1935, some chapters like Rhineland-Cologne sidestepped the explicit "Aryan clause" by stating that prospective members had to be citizens and have at least two sponsors to be considered for membership.[23] As late as

1938, the Austrian Gymnastics Group called on the German chapters to remove all non-Aryans without exception, indicating that a good number of chapters still allowed Jewish members.[24] After a closer reading of the DBW statutes revealed that using the term "führer" was optional, the Berlin chapter changed the title of its head back to "chairman."[25] Members voted down Pichl's resolution to change the club's name to the "German Alpine Association," restrict membership to German-Aryans, and rename the chapters as the more German-sounding *Zweige* (branches) rather than *Sektionen*. The *Zweige* designation had implied greater centralization, as "branches" connoted less autonomy.[26]

Autonomy, however, often depended on the whims of local officials, despite von Tschammer's decree. The Freiburg chapter chafed under the heavy hand of a resident Nazi official. In the fall of 1934, its chairman complained that the district Nazi indoctrination officer had canceled the chapter's annual lecture mere hours prior to the event. The lecture had been advertised in the university and across the city, and its cancellation caused a great deal of embarrassment for the chapter. The local official not only had ignored proper procedures but also had acted with callousness, and in any case he lacked the authority to oversee the chapter's internal matters. The chairman feared that the official might make more capricious decisions in the future. He forwarded the letter to Bauer and asked for clarification.[27] Whatever answer Bauer provided, von Tschammer's decree amounted to window dressing at the local level.

Even as the Nazi regime extended control over Alpine clubs, its lines of authority became increasingly muddled. Attempting to clarify matters, Bauer further divided the DBW into smaller units, such as the German Mountaineering Group, which administered the Alpine Association. But then in 1934 he established the Reichsverband Deutsche Bergsteiger (National Association of German Mountaineers), which also became an affiliate group within the DRL. Whereas the DBW had managed groups, the National Association of German Mountaineers dealt with individuals. It remained unclear to many whether the latter succeeded the former or if the two groups competed for authority. Although clubs belonged to Bauer's DBW, some alpinists were members in the National Association of German Mountaineers. To add to the confusion, in 1936, as Berlin prepared to host the Olympics, Hitler moved the Reich Sport Office to the Ministry of the Interior. Von Tschammer, who continued to run the DRL, now reported directly to Wilhelm Frick, the Third Reich's minister of the Interior.[28]

Institutional chaos and the dizzying array of new regulations gave even the most devoted Nazi mountaineer pause. In the attempt to sort out the problems of Gleichschaltung, the German chapters set up a central Reich-German Section Forum in 1936, headed by Fritz Rigele, a longtime member of the association, accomplished mountain climber, Nazi ideologue, and gifted bureaucrat. Frick and Franz von Papen, Germany's ambassador to Austria, also attended the club's annual meeting in 1936 to clarify the association's status. Frick himself had belonged to the Alpine Association since 1904. Von Papen was also a favorite given his recent efforts to ease tensions with Austria. At the meeting, Frick reaffirmed the importance of the Alpine Association to the Nazi cause and promised to improve relations with Austria, as did von Papen. Their presence thrilled the delegates, but their speeches did little to alleviate the administrative confusion. And before the talented Rigele could work out a viable solution, he suffered a traumatic head injury while climbing in the Alps and died in 1937.[29]

Had Rigele lived, though, he would have stood powerless before the institutional chaos and political infighting that defined the Third Reich. Lines of overlapping authority created bitter rivalries. Frick's efforts to consolidate control over Germany's police forces infuriated Heinrich Himmler, Hitler's chief paladin, and resulted in Frick's eventual banishment to Prague. Nazi higher-ups treated von Papen as expendable. Serving Hitler from the margins, first in Vienna and later in Istanbul, was the best he would do. Fierce, often unresolved disputes were a systemic part of the Nazi state's structural anarchy. The Alpine Association's situation showcased the Third Reich's polycentric nature. The club's relative independence stemmed from both its transnational organization and the regime's structural chaos. Dual-state status afforded the association a degree of latitude for a time because even Nazi officials became disoriented in the Third Reich's labyrinthine hallways of power—although, as we will see in the next section, Nazi Germany's tense relationship with Austria allowed mountaineers very little leeway in the Alps.

. . . .

The fulcrum of enmity between Austria and Germany rested on the Alps. Troubles began in 1933. Austrian patriots claimed the National Socialist regime was engaged in a "brutal fight" with Austria and that its "work of blind destruction" threatened their country.[30] They, along with Chancellor Engelbert Dollfuss, a decorated veteran of the Alpine front, opposed any union with Germany. To correct what he saw as the failings of the First Republic, Dollfuss introduced what historians now call Austrofascism in the spring of 1933, a hybrid of Italian corporate fascism and Austrian Catholicism. He curtailed civil liberties, formed the Vaterländische Front (Fatherland Front) organization with its crutch cross banner and "Austria Awake!" slogan, and moved against his two major opponents, the Social Democrats and the National Socialists. The Austrian Nazi Party had flirted with obscurity for most of the 1920s. In 1928 its membership roll barely exceeded forty-four hundred names. By the 1930s, however, the party's numbers had increased nearly tenfold to over forty-three thousand and now exerted tremendous pressure on Dollfuss to reverse his stance against *Anschluss*. Austrian Nazis expressed open resentment toward their government. They accused it of being "anti-German" and "the enemy of Greater Germany."[31] When the Austrian government rebuffed Nazi envoys in May 1933, Hitler imposed a thousand-mark tax on German visitors to Austria. The levy effectively closed the border and crippled Austria's tourist industry, which was already limping from the Great Depression. Over fourteen hundred mountain guides, ski instructors, and porters lost their jobs. Tourism declined by 58 percent.[32] In retaliation, Dollfuss outlawed the Nazi Party a month later. Austrian Nazis who escaped imprisonment fled to the Alps along the German border, from which they engaged in acts of terrorism against the state. The mountains regained their valence of terror but with a charge entirely different from the dread of yore. The exploits of these "terror bands of hired desperadoes" (as the Friends of Nature had described Austrian Nazis years earlier) poisoned German-Austrian relations.[33] The situation turned lethal after the failed National Socialist coup in Austria and Dollfuss's assassination in 1934. Meanwhile, mountaineers found themselves caught in the delicate balance between Germany and Austria, where the slightest misstep could tip the scales for greater violence.

The Alpine Association had to be especially mindful of its actions. To many Austrians, the club looked like a cover for Nazi activities, and for good reason: nearly all the association's Austrian chapters backed Hitler's regime. Detractors called the Alpine Association "anti-Austrian" and opposed to Austrian interests. Several critics sent letters to the government charging that association officials "expressed a subversive position in greetings and words."[34] In a newsletter titled *Storm over Austria*, journalists accused the Alpine Association of harboring fugitive Austrian

Nazis and allowing these fanatics use of its lodges to hold meetings and plan terrorist actions against the government.[35] One editor called the Alpine huts "agitation-central for the Hitlerei in Austria." He reminded his readers that these lodges on Austrian soil had been built with German money. The denunciations recalled Austrian hostility toward the association during the Kulturkampf years in the 1870s. Given that the insular places had sheltered the Austrian chapters' vile anti-Semitism and that many had all but declared their open devotion to the Nazi regime, it was no surprise that many Austrians viewed the association's edelweiss badge as a substitute for the outlawed swastika.[36]

Any appearance of political activity would jeopardize the club's legal standing in Austria. So when Raimond von Klebelsberg (the same University of Innsbruck professor who had replaced Josef Donabaum in 1922 and was now chairman of the association) sat down to peruse his morning newspaper on 23 October 1933 and came across the article titled "Alpine Association Organizes Mountain Troops for Hitler!," he reacted with understandable alarm. By the next day, newspapers in Tyrol and Vienna had picked up on the story. The original article in the *Tiroler Anzeiger*, Klebelsberg's paper, had reprinted a circular from the Munich chapter, in which Georg Leuchs stated that a mountain troop was being organized and any Munich mountaineer was welcome to join. Apparently a number of members had already expressed interest, and Leuchs was convinced that many more would want to be involved in this "national front."[37] The editors cynically remarked that this topic should be of great interest to Austrians, given the unlikelihood that the troop was being organized to clear the Alps of communist enclaves, as the Germans had suggested. With each rendition of the story, the association's position appeared increasingly insidious. The Viennese *Volks-Zeitung* insisted that this Alpine militia was being mustered to fight against Austria. It also claimed that the "Austrian Legion"—exiled Austrian Nazis—were being trained in Bavaria for an offensive against Austria. The article speculated that the "brown circles" in Bavaria did not place much faith in this "Austrian Legion" and thus entrusted the Alpine Association to put together a mountain troop.[38]

Klebelsberg was outraged. The danger was that the Austrian government could now classify the German chapters as political clubs as a result of Leuchs's circular. This move not only would put the Austrian chapters in a risky position but also meant that the Austrian government could seize control of the association's huts and assets.[39] In his defense, Leuchs responded that the newspapers had misrepresented his circular. The local SA unit, not the Munich chapter, was organizing a militia and had asked Leuchs to inform his constituents. The militia would be a subdivision of the local SA group, not part of the Munich chapter. Besides, Leuchs reasoned that the creation of a mountain troop was an internal matter for Germany and had nothing to do with Austria. As for the accusation that he had violated the club's regulations, he rationalized that announcing the formation of an Alpine militia was a "national," not a political, enterprise.[40] In its press release to the Austrian media, the club explained that local SA personnel had pursued this matter without approval from their superiors, who had no intention of establishing any sort of Alpine brigade.[41] The strategy worked. Within a matter of months, the whole affair was largely forgotten.

Still, distress lingered. So long as tensions ran high, the Alpine border remained closed. Sensationalist media roused anger on both sides with its all-out propaganda campaign. The situation was a nightmare for mountaineers. Most German Alpine lodges stood on Austrian soil, so most were forced to close. Since hut fees contributed significant funds to chapters' operating budgets, the local boards faced a fiscal crisis, compounded by a drop in membership, as thousands of alpinists now saw little reason to renew their dues. Some Austrian chapters even suggested splitting the association. Calls to create a purely Austrian club were also reminiscent of the bitterness expressed by Austrian patriots in the mid-1800s.[42] The irony was that the association had planned its 1933 annual meeting in Bludenz to be particularly significant; it was in this town sixty years earlier that the Austrian and German Alpine Associations had voted to merge. Frick's Ministry of the Interior denied requests for special permission for the German board members and chapter delegates to enter Austria. The club lobbied the German chancellery to waive the thousand-mark fee but to no avail. At the last minute mountaineers found a location in Liechtenstein to which both Germans and Austrians could travel.[43]

It took Ambassador von Papen years to work out a compromise. Austrian Nazis had vacillated between an armed seizure of government and a more moderate approach of working within the cabinet to gain control. Violent tactics had failed in 1934. Having learned his lesson from the Beer Hall Putsch, Hitler ordered the Austrian branch to follow legal avenues with the aid of von Papen. Negotiations concluded in July 1936. Hitler recognized Austria's sovereignty and lifted the travel tax, but only after Kurt Schuschnigg, Dollfuss's successor, granted amnesty to imprisoned Nazis, promised the "national opposition" seats in his government, and acknowledged Austria as a "German State."[44] On paper the country's domestic affairs were Schuschnigg's to manage, although the Austrian chancellor followed a deliberate policy of appeasement with his larger, stronger neighbor.

The settlement, however, did not reconcile all Austrians to Germans. Some Austrian mountaineers disliked German Nazi climbers for their rude and arrogant behavior in the Alps. One old Viennese alpinist sent an open letter titled "Our Mountains!" to his local newspaper. He traveled to the mountains to forget about work, politics, and the city but claimed that this was no longer possible. Now he encountered younger Germans in the lodges who did nothing but boast loudly about their regime. This was not patriotism, the old climber declared; it was shameless propaganda, and true alpinists did not act in such a fashion. He recounted an ugly incident. When in the mountains, ahead of him climbed a young German couple. When they passed a group of descending Germans, they greeted each with "Heil Hitler" and raised their arms in salute. When the old climber passed this group, he hailed them with the "provocative 'Heil Österreich.'" The Germans jeered at him as they passed and continued to mock him on their way down. The aged Austrian spat that not even the Italians acted so badly.[45]

Despite the old climber's insistent title, events over the past three years raised the question: Whose mountains? The crux of the issue was control. In retaliation to Austria's firm self-determination, Hitler denied Germans access to the Alps and further weakened the country's ailing economy. Alpinists had suffered the trauma of losing beloved mountains in 1918 and now experienced the ordeal all over again. But given the rhetoric of Alpine brotherhood and the incessant talk of deep, geological bonds between Austrians and Germans, pain from this trial separation felt far worse. If German mountaineers could no longer claim the landscape, neither could most Austrians. Nazi outlaws hid away in the jagged landscape, whose synclines and crests provided natural cover for sinister plots. To some it seemed as if the Alps themselves abetted the desperadoes. The Alpine Association, once the self-styled warden over the heights, now found itself powerless and uncomfortably pinched between two mutually hostile governments. The club's very existence came into question. Any false move in the mountains threatened dismantlement. Attempts to control the Alps in the 1930s imbued the landscape with new political meaning. Contested peaks threw into sharp relief the terrain's gaping chasms and deep canyons, fitting metaphors for the rifts between Hitler's regime and the Austrian republic.

....

As with geopolitics, domestic infighting within Nazi Germany shaped the Alps. A month before the border opened, the German army's Mountain Brigade made plans for a new training center in Bavaria's Berchtesgadener Land. Renowned for its majestic natural beauty, the district housed some of Germany's tallest mountains, including the Watzmann and Hochkalter, the picturesque Alpine lake Königsee, and the northernmost glacier in the Alps, the Blaueis (Blue Ice) Glacier, what many considered the country's only glacier. Like a tiny peninsula, the province poked into Austria due south of Salzburg. The army's decision to establish a mountain combat school complete with exercise grounds and shooting ranges across the Kühroint meadows and near the Blaueis Glacier unleashed furious protests from the recently reorganized Forestry Administration. The fields belonged to a nature conservation zone and the glacier was a certified Naturdenkmal (natural monument), a legally protected piece of the natural landscape.

Foresters mounted a vigorous albeit trite defense. Military exercises would ruin the peace and "essence" of the mountain. This would be especially tragic since the Berchtesgadener highlands supposedly retained their "original character" and contained the last vestiges of Alpine wilderness. Whether the area's primeval state actually remained intact given its immense popularity among climbers and skiers was beside the point. The Forestry Administration employed whatever argument it could, regardless of inconsistencies. Weapons training would disturb protected nature and disrupt tourism. Invasive construction of barracks and supply sheds would spoil the natural scenery. Never mind that the Alpine Association had built the nearby Blaueis Hut just in 1922. Caretakers drew a distinction between mountaineering and the military. They certainly did not want soldiers clambering over the only glacier that sat completely within Germany's borders. But it would be a shame to restrict the general public's access to one of Germany's nicest nature protection areas. Army officers suggested that a shooting range would aid nature conservation by greatly reducing tourism's impact, but foresters replied that firearms and artillery practice would only drive tourists into previously untouched territory. Others observed that military blueprints called for construction in a very volatile avalanche zone. They suggested different locations for the training grounds.[46]

The army refused to compromise. It had been trying for years to conduct maneuvers in the region. Back in 1924, the local commander had planned a two-month-long military exercise for the upcoming summer. His timing could not have been worse. At that moment, Bavarian state agencies were already considering legislation to convert the area into a nature protection zone.[47] Having lost that round, the army anticipated a favorable outcome the next time under the new regime. Conditions that made for a good nature reserve were precisely what attracted the military. The vicinity was sparsely inhabited. Few roads meant restricting access was easy. The remoteness of the place kept most people away. Only deft mountaineers and nimble skiers ventured to the Blaueis Glacier. The region's unique terrain perfectly suited military purposes. The rocky cirque with its amphitheater shape formed the ideal backstop for a firing range. Precipitous ravines provided excellent training sites for the troops. Moreover, the Kühroint meadows were conveniently near the military depot in Bad Reichenhall. The location was just too good.

Conservationists placed their faith in the law. In 1935, the Third Reich introduced the most comprehensive environmental legislation in Europe, the Reichsnaturschutzgesetz (Reich Nature Protection Law). Hans Klose, a leading conservationist, drafted the legislation, and on paper the law's reach was impressive. It replaced the patchwork of state and municipal laws within a centralized administration that oversaw nature protection for the entire country. It, too, was a form of *Gleichschaltung*. In the past, Germany's federalist structure had stymied efforts to create a uniform approach to nature conservation. The law expanded the number of protected areas and defined new land-use guidelines. Government agencies could now designate entire landscapes as protected. Within a few years, the legislation had established thousands of natural monuments and hundreds of conservation areas. Although much of the legwork for the legislation was done during the Weimar Republic, the Nazis got the credit. Encouraged by these efforts to protect the natural world, one jubilant alpinist declared Nazi Germany to be "the most modern of all culture-states."[48] The law was indeed progressive, but in practice its implementation was inconsistent and incomplete. The legislation lacked the funding and manpower to make it truly effective. Local law enforcement ignored its statutes when it suited them, as did the military.[49]

For their part, Bavarian foresters had hoped Hermann Göring would protect Berchtesgadener Land from the army's incursion. He styled himself as an outdoor enthusiast and often spent his free time hiking or hunting. He belonged to the Alpine Association and in his fitter days had been an avid climber. Conservationists counted him in their corner. Göring had recruited Klose to draft the Reich Nature Protection Law and shuffled the legislation past the Nazi Reichstag for quick approval. The law organized the Reich Nature Protection Office under the new Reich Forest Office, which Göring grabbed. In a bid to increase his influence, Göring placed himself as the Reich's chief forester and Germany's chief conservationist. His play for this position reflected his love for hunting more than a concern for Germany's nature, besides being another way to outdo Wilhelm Frick. After 1936 Göring also headed the Four-Year Plan, the economic strategy hell-bent on preparing the country for war. His obligations contradicted each other. Other than expanding game parks to satisfy his hunting urge, he paid little attention to nature conservationism. When foresters in Berchtesgaden wrote to him requesting support in 1936, he ignored their letters and ordered the Mountain Brigade's commander to begin work immediately. As was usually the case in Nazi Germany with nature conservation, military goals and economic interests took higher priority. In typical fashion, Göring's attitude exacerbated the ill will that had developed between local forestry officials and low-ranking officers in the brigade. His dismissive remark that the army was taking the interests of hunting and nature conservation into account provided little consolation.[50]

Bavarian foresters were not the only ones to see their hopes dashed. Conservationists across Germany had wanted to believe in the new regime. They interpreted the Nazi rhetoric of *Blut und Boden* (blood and soil) as a clear commitment to safeguarding Germany's natural environment, although that ideology really had little to do with nature protection. National Socialism addressed environmental concerns more as a way to gain legitimacy with middle-class voters. Nevertheless, nature lovers became some of Hitler's most committed followers in large part because they felt frustrated with the ineptitude of Weimar democracy and its pervasive consumerism. Mass consumption of the Alps so alarmed mountaineers that they added a nature conservation clause to the Alpine Association's revised statutes in 1927. The more nationalistic argued that the mountains needed to be free of cars and trains to preserve their "Germanness." They pressured Weimar officials to defend the Alpine wilderness from "modern industry" with the exhortation "You are German!"[51] Believing that Nazis would secure a "nature-protection mentality," one member warned agents of industry, "Hands off our peaks, which are as sacred to us as the German *Volk* itself!"[52] But on the Blaueis Glacier, the Nazi regime's economic and military priorities were calculated to disappoint.

Alpinists did not despair at first. Thinking that the Alps had a special place in Hitler's heart, mountaineers pressed forward with their nature protection agenda. They couched their approach in Nazi ideology. The Alps were great wells of German strength and sources of spiritual renewal. Mountain climbing also reaffirmed the connection between the nation and nature. In their proposals, Alpine conservationists cited Hitler. "The German landscape must in all events survive," one such petition quoted from the Führer, "for it is and always was the fountainhead of power and strength of the *Volk*."[53] The parallels between Hitler's statements and the program of the Alpine Association struck many members and cemented their enthusiasm for his regime. Especially uplifting were his disparaging remarks about technology's role in corrupting man's relationship with nature. Alpinists, too, blamed "the age of machines" and "over-civilization" for man's (and the mountains') "inner flattening" and the "mechanization of and disengagement from every tradition."[54]

If mountaineers deemed Hitler a Luddite in the service of nature, then they were badly mistaken. He willingly employed technology to mold the German landscape and demonstrate Nazi mastery over the natural world. Perhaps no other undertaking demonstrated this point better than the regime's Alpine Road project. It would cut across the Alps, beginning in Lindau on Lake Constance and skirting along the bottom of Bavaria all the way to Berchtesgaden. Blueprints for a cross-Alpine route that followed the chain's east-west axis rather than the usual north-south direction took shape in the late 1920s. Planners designed the stretch specifically for tourism. It would connect popular vacation destinations and lead drivers up the country's most impressive heights. Not only did engineers intend for the panoramic views to be awe-inspiring, but the road's grandiose construction would match the landscape. With the Alps as massive abutments, the highway would arch across the mountains. Wherever possible, masons would use native stone instead of concrete, and preferably rocks with lichen or other vegetation to give the road an organic feel. Similar to the Autobahn, surveyors included a green strip for indigenous flora between the parapet and the roadway. The project blended together nature, technology, and mass consumption in ways that deflated serious alpinists but elated Nazi technocrats.[55]

The highway served multiple interests. The Bavarian government saw the project as a means to bolster tourism and create much-needed jobs. Its ministers took their cues from Austria and Italy. The Grossglockner High Alpine Road and Italy's expanding highway infrastructure provided useful models. Franz Wallack's labor-intensive undertaking had put thousands to work, and the Italian Dolomites now attracted more sightseers than the Swiss Alps, mostly because South Tyrol had better roads (thanks largely to the First World War). Besides, a German Alpine highway would be a wonderful way to showcase Bavaria's natural beauty and convince tourists that they need not cross the border to see stunning mountains. Others believed that the road held high strategic value. In the interests of national defense, border areas should be accessible to military vehicles. Nazi officials voiced all these sentiments as well but added the tenor of international rivalry. Neighboring countries—Italy, Switzerland, Austria, and France—had all embarked on Alpine highway construction. To stay competitive, Germany must catch up.

Rivalry with Austria was especially fierce. Although Austrian officials claimed that the Grossglockner High Alpine Road would build peace in Europe by bringing people closer together, German Nazis viewed the project as a direct challenge. After the border closed, the Austrian government changed its tune. Now the highway celebrated Austrian initiative and know-how. It symbolized Austria's independence and asserted the country's strength vis-à-vis Hitler's Germany. Schuschnigg described Wallack's engineering feat as a source of national pride. Not ones to be outdone, the Nazis bragged about the "longest and most beautiful work" of the Führer and how Germany's "mightiest road" was the "envy of the world." Using the most modern equipment, workers molded the Alps in the regime's image. The "sonorous song" of iron scraping stone echoed down the range. To Nazi ears, this music of "work, honor, and peace" signaled the arrival of a "new Germany."[56]

Not everyone found the melody uplifting. Others heard only the harsh din of construction. Rather than ushering in the sound of tranquility, building the highway was ruining the peace. Many feared that quaint Alpine villages would soon be sites of traffic jams. One doctor expressed concern that blaring horns and exhaust fumes would upset his sanatorium patients.[57] Before Hitler outlawed other political parties, some remaining Social Democrats in the Bavarian state parliament suspected the Nazis of ulterior motives. After all, the National Socialists had plenty of opportunities to support previous job creation initiatives and road improvement projects before coming to power but had refused to do so on political grounds. Backing the legislation would have meant aligning with the Left. Committed socialists believed that the road's economic stimulus would benefit only crony capitalists. As for attracting investment, one critic snapped, "Foreign millionaires are not coming here because of beautiful roads in the Bavarian Alps." "Maybe the National Socialists promote Alpine highways," speculated another detractor, "to have a better way to Mussolini in Rome."[58]

The Nazis ignored complaints, particularly those from nature conservationists, and championed technology. The Bavarian State Committee for the Care of Nature warned that automobile traffic would ruin the "mood" in the mountains and greatly diminish the joys of wandering.[59] But many others welcomed the dawning of a new era: *Autowandern*. Contrary to the accusations of antimodernism, the Nazis enthusiastically embraced "auto wandering" in the Alps. One contributor to the party's newsletter, *Völkischer Beobachter*, declared that the Führer had dismissed "medieval antagonisms" toward cars and drivers and sought to expand road networks ever higher. Modern-minded Nazis viewed motor vehicles as essential to the German desire to wander; automobiles simply allowed more Germans to wander farther and more efficiently.[60] Auto enthusiasts failed to see any contradiction in traveling by car to connect with nature. Indeed, they viewed "auto wandering" as a "kind of return to nature."[61] Making automobiles affordable also provided the Nazis plenty of support to ignore conservationist grievances. Besides, the Nazis could legitimately claim that they were continuing the work of the Alpine Association by opening previously impassable regions in the Alps.[62] Proponents repeatedly asserted that auto tourism would benefit Alpine villages in the long run: health resorts could now remain open in winter, skiers could reach virgin slopes, and construction would reinvigorate Germany's economy. But in the end, what really counted was that Hitler supported the project.

The project, however, ran into problems almost immediately. Construction was painstakingly slow and exorbitantly expensive. Since the Autobahn project took higher priority, the Alpine highway received limited state funding. Within months it had run out of money. Environmental conditions, notably heavy snowfall during the 1935 season, delayed progress. So too did the herculean efforts to bring thousands of men and tons of equipment high up remote mountains. More than twenty-five thousand workers labored to build over a hundred bridges, along with several tunnels and viaducts across the rugged landscape. Surveyors frequently changed the route, which stretched anywhere from three hundred to over four hundred kilometers. But much of the work was an exercise in futility. After years of labor, only a portion of the road opened to traffic.[63] Soon thereafter, Hitler launched his war and lost all interest in the project.

The highway never reached its terminus in Berchtesgadener Land, but other forces converged on this tiny Bavarian county. It seemed that nearly everyone had a stake in this lovely corner of Germany. Mountaineers and skiers prized the county's slopes; the military valued the land's ruggedness; conservationists fought to preserve the mountains from the hordes. The small market township Berchtesgaden had recorded close to thirty thousand visitors in 1913.[64] The numbers skyrocketed twenty years later, in part because Hitler and a few other prominent Nazis had purchased villas in Obersalzberg, the Alpine retreat just above the town. With the Führer spending more time at his chalet, tourism in the region swelled. The nearby Watzmann peak, Germany's third-highest mountain and a popular destination spot ever since Caspar David Friedrich first exhibited his painting of the mountain in 1825, became utterly overrun.[65]

Hitler's Berghof headquarters turned the little county into an unlikely nexus of geopolitics and the staging area for the *Anschluss*. It was to Berchtesgaden where Hitler summoned Schuschnigg in February 1938, brutally berated the chancellor for not honoring their 1936 agreement, threatened military action, and bullied him into an accord that strengthened the Austrian Nazi Party's position. And a few weeks later, it was there in the Berchtesgadener salient that Hitler positioned his infantry and armored divisions, poised on the Alpine frontier to take Austria.

. . . .

Relations deteriorated rapidly. A month after the Berchtesgaden summit, events culminated in military action. As mandated by the February agreement, Schuschnigg appointed Arthur Seyss-Inquart as minister of the Interior and Public Security. A lawyer by training, Seyss-Inquart had aligned himself with the so-called national opposition during the 1930s, although he did not formally join the Nazi Party until 1938. Now with someone sympathetic to their cause controlling the country's police forces, Austrian Nazis became increasingly bolder and bellicose with their public displays. For his part, Schuschnigg adopted a less passive, more defiant stance. He organized a plebiscite, "for a free and German, independent and social, for a Christian and united Austria, for peace and work and the equality of all who declare themselves for Nation and Fatherland," to be held on 13 March.[66] The fix was in. No one under the age of twenty-four (suspected Nazi sympathizers) could participate; no list of those eligible was distributed; and people who could vote received only "yes" ballots. But the rigged plebiscite guaranteed German intervention. Under heavy pressure from Hitler and after garnering no support from Mussolini or the British, Schuschnigg cancelled the vote on 11 March. Hours later he and his entire government, with the exception of Seyss-Inquart, resigned. A radio announcement relayed events, and Austrian Nazis responded, taking over local governments around the country. The next day, the German troops crossed the Salzach River and advanced without incident toward Vienna. Seyss-Inquart, now the head of state, signed the Anschluss into law the day after that. Hitler's entourage soon followed. Euphoric thousands in Linz and Vienna wildly cheered his arrival.

Mountaineers rejoiced. At least that was what Nazi media outlets proclaimed. One incident in particular was an advertising executive's dream. According to initial accounts, days after the Anschluss, Hannes Schneeberger, a twenty-seven-year-old photographer and chauffeur from Matrei in East Tyrol, along with two companions, climbed Grossglockner and planted a large swastika banner atop the mountain's summit cross, supposedly the first Nazi flag on Greater Germany's now highest mountain. Schneeberger's feat earned him the chance to meet Hitler. A picture of the two appeared in newspapers across the country. Schneeberger wore his finest Tyrolean Tracht, complete with lederhosen, loden coat, richly embroidered leather belt and suspenders, knee-high knitted wool socks, and a felt hat with an incredible feather. He gazed admiringly at the Führer. In front of the men sat a large photo of the famous summit cross with its swastika banner waving in the wind.[67] Standing there in his traditional garb, with his golden locks and rugged good looks, Schneeberger embodied the picture-perfect Nazi. The story was almost too good to be true.

As it turned out, Schneeberger was too good to be true. Those who knew him doubted the story from the start. "Schneeberger is not normal," one climber confided; "he lives in delusions of grandeur and wants to use any opportunity to become famous." He seemed more like a lost soul, having roamed around the world from Africa to India, China, Japan, and the United States for much of his adult life.[68] He had tried to secure a mountain guide license with the Alpine Association but was denied because of his ongoing unauthorized and rather irresponsible guide work. At the time of his climb up Grossglockner, he was no longer even a member of the club.

He was also not the first to hoist the swastika up Grossglockner. That deed belonged to Sepp Bacher, an unemployed and infirmed trek guide from Kaprun. Truth proved better than fiction in this Grossglockner fiasco. On the evening of 15 March, the day after Hitler entered Vienna, Bacher dug up his hidden stash of Nazi paraphernalia from his garden, kissed his wife goodnight, and then departed for the mountain with a swastika flag tucked in his backpack. Still suffering from a long sickness, he climbed alone through the night, guided only by moonlight across the treacherous Karlinger Glacier, and reached the peak in the early morning hours. The spring thaw was still months away; temperatures during the ascent must have been freezing. Bacher risked hypothermia and debilitating frostbite, besides the high likelihood of plummeting to his death in the darkness. His midnight climb to the summit was a daring effort, if not foolhardy. After unfurling the flag and catching his breath, he simply turned around and headed back home.

Writers for the *Völkischer Beobachter* had a public relations field day with the modest Bacher. "An indomitable fighting spirit, as only a National Socialist has," extolled a typical retelling, "born of unspeakable love and enthusiasm for the liberation movement [a Nazi euphemism for the *Anschluss*] and his Führer, gave him the strength to struggle on. . . . Though his weakened body would no longer respond, the iron will left all adversity and nausea behind." Schneeberger, on the other hand, had hiked up the much easier south face in sunny conditions with support from friends, "a rather risk-free performance."[69]

Politics as theater played out on Grossglockner's stage. Schneeberger and Bacher's drama opened the show. The following acts presented the iconic mountain as "German-to-the-core," a realm of freedom, and a site of liberation. One confused alpinist exclaimed, "Adolf Hitler—you have not only liberated the German *Volk* in Austria, you have also preserved our dearly loved mountains from further desecration! Our mountains are free and free shall they remain for all time!"[70] Few seemed to consider the utter nonsense of such a statement. If anything, the Nazis had demonstrated a complete willingness to exploit nature, not to mention their utter disregard for civil rights and personal liberties. But the audience seemed mesmerized with the mountain; no one looked behind the curtain. When Seyss-Inquart announced at the Alpine Association's annual meeting that the Third Reich had greater environmental awareness than the bygone Austrian republic and that "all plans to despoil nature" on Grossglockner had been put on hold, audience members leapt from their seats and cheered.[71] The mountain's props and set decorations—"green valleys, shimmering heights, brilliant glaciers, rushing, roaring waters, still lakes, dark grottos filled with polished ice"—drew eyes toward the regime's apparent concern for nature but away from its brutalization of people and actual disregard for the environment. Likewise, when the Nazis merged the many nature reserve areas in Hohe Tauern into a single large preservation, the largest in the Eastern Alps, they placated conservationists.[72] The peak had now acquired dual meanings as the pinnacle of the Third Reich. The mountain symbol was both uplifting and crushing. "Unrivaled and alone," Grossglockner symbolized greatness, power, and an everlasting empire, yet it also connoted domination, terror, and ruin.

For the time being, however, most members of the Alpine Association could hardly contain their joy. "Austria is ours and its mountains are once again ours," one alpinist in Dresden cried, echoing the sentiments of nearly every chapter in Germany. "Raise your hearts," he exclaimed; "raise your hands [in Nazi salute]."[73] Anschluss made the club's compound title irrelevant. On 14 March 1938, two days after German troops marched into Vienna, the German and Austrian Alpine Association formally changed its name to the Deutscher Alpenverein (German Alpine Association, DAV). While secretaries crossed out "and Austria" on the club's letterhead, members congratulated themselves for their decades-long work of promoting German and Austrian unity. Austrian mountaineers could now openly express their loyalty to the Nazi regime while their chapters argued over who got to name a hut after Hitler.

The Anschluss completed the transformation of the Alpine Association from a semi-autonomous civil organization into an organ of the National Socialist state. When Klebelsberg introduced Seyss-Inquart before the 1938 general assembly, he asked, "What could better exemplify this new age than the participation of Austria's first man in our annual meeting?" The outgoing chair was certainly correct; Seyss-Inquart's presence signaled the club's takeover by the National Socialists. Von Tschammer did not parse words: "Love for the mountains must now be a militant National Socialist position," he declared, and the club must become a "tight National Socialist organization." *Gleichschaltung* proceeded swiftly. Most previous board members were forced out. Seyss-Inquart immediately demoted Klebelsberg and Dinkelacker. Reinhold von Sydow, Robert Rehlen, and Eduard Pichl stayed on as honorary members of the board but had little say. Executives had to be members of the Nazi Party. In addition, the club's editor-in-chief was required to belong to the Reich Press Chamber. The Nazis restructured the organizational apparatus, dividing the club's upper-level management into a mountaineering division and an administrative division.[74] Innsbruck now housed the association's permanent headquarters. The chairman was now called the club führer. All chapters were now formally called branches and were required to file annual compliance forms with the Innsbruck office. Seyss-Inquart also issued a new charter in 1938; its first clause now read, "The aim of the Association is the corporal and spiritual development of its members through well-planned, active physical exercise and fostering the *Volksbewußtsein* [national consciousness] in the spirit of the National Socialist State." The revised statutes concluded the club's synchronization with the Nazi state. Conforming to the führer principle, Seyss-Inquart unilaterally made every decision; all parliamentary practices ended. As one Nazi ideologue explained, "Political relationships based on statutes, parliamentarianism, and so forth, which many Nationalist-Socialists had viewed as blemishes of the old DÖAV, were no longer necessary."[75]

The return of Sudetenland chapters into the club quelled most opposition. Some of the association's oldest chapters had existed in Warnsdorf, Teplitz, Carlsbad, Prague, and other cities in Bohemia. The dismemberment of the Habsburg Empire in 1919 had involved amputating those chapters from the Alpine Association. Transplanted to Czechoslovakia, the severed members never took to their new host. Instead, they became cancerous tumors whose malignant German irredentism metastasized in the 1930s. As with the Austrian chapters before the *Anschluss*, there was no mistaking the political orientation of the Sudeten German Alpine clubs. These alpinists embraced the new order. After Hitler annexed the Sudetenland in October 1938, the incorporation of those chapters into the DAV further solidified Nazi control over the club.[76]

Yet not all mountaineers readily accepted *Gleichschaltung*. A few days after German troops entered Austria, the Alpine Association's Graz chapter chairman organized a meeting for the city's several mountaineering clubs. He proposed consolidating all the groups into a single large chapter. Several independently minded alpinists proposed instead a loose gang of fellow climbers rather than a licensed club. When DAV forbade such a move, the situation turned tense. Complaining that many of the merged "Alpine" clubs had in fact little to do with mountaineering and denouncing the maneuver as "un-German," these climbers refused consolidation.[77] Others protested the loss of chapter autonomy. The club's constituent parts had lost their independence, what had been a defining feature of the organization and the source of its dynamism since the nineteenth century. As one dissenter remarked, the association's strength and appeal stemmed from individual and self-regulating chapters. Turning them into dependent organs "would entail the end of the Alpine Association."[78]

Arbitrary arrests and fear enforced conformity. The fate of Alois Scheiber served as a cautionary tale to those who resisted. Scheiber was a highly decorated first responder for Tyrolean Mountain Rescue and a "true mountain comrade" but too outspoken with his anti-Nazi views. Not long after the *Anschluss*, the Gestapo arrested him and then whisked him off to stand trial in Berlin. The regime accused him of breaking statute #90 of the Reich Penal Code, but none of his Austrian colleagues knew what that meant. Only later did they learn that the Gestapo had used Scheiber's supposed associations with communists, "enemies of the state," as pretext to silence a vocal critic. Desperate friends pleaded with the DAV to use its influence to help a respected alpinist, but to protect its interests the club refused to get involved. Seyss-Inquart reminded mountaineers that they were now "the representatives of the Führer." "Mountain climbing and hiking," he announced, "are no longer private affairs of individuals." Abandoning Scheiber was a poignant indication of the club's values and new political orientation.[79]

Images and articles in the Alpine Association's 1939 journal confirmed dissident fears. A full-page ink drawing set the tone. Two climbers pause on the summit of a rugged mountain. From its muscular peak the men gaze out toward the horizon and take stock of the world. A vast Alpine landscape opens up before them. In the distance, a swastika crest peeks from behind the hills as if it were the morning sun heralding the dawn. A mighty eagle perches atop the Nazi emblem. Higher than the heights, its massive body fills the sky, dominating the view and diminishing all else. It was an epic picture, simple but powerful.

Essays reiterated the importance of Alpinism and the Alps. The heights forged the "total, harmonious, National-Socialist German man," a "type of warrior," and a "hero in a realistic sense." His purpose

FIGURE 18 The Nazi eagle rising over the Alps.
Source: Zeitschrift des Deutschen Alpenvereins 70 (1939).

was not to be "good" but to be "hard." Mountain climbing made men for Hitler's Germany. "The German *Volk* will be like a *Volk* of mountaineers," with help from a massive landscape that instilled a "particular attitude and hardness." The mission of the DAV was to now carry the values of mountaineering to the entire *Volk* and thereby to strengthen the nation. This exhortation might have jogged the memories of older alpinists. They had once urged the club to the same task, some at the turn of the century and many more after the lost war. But the emphasis had shifted from the spiritual to the physical, from rebuilding to destruction.

Instead of helping souls recover from defeat, the Alps hardened bodies for conquest. Mountaineering became the country's "present and future warlike face." Through its "total mobilization" and "comprehensive arming," Alpinism readied the "new Germany" and the "new war-like Volk" for a new war.[80]

. . . .

"The image of new Alpinism," one troubled alpinist wrote as he watched with apprehension Nazism's growing might, "is the depiction of our modern age."[81] Few heeded his warning. For those fixated on uniting Germany and Austria, Hitler's triumph brought glad tidings. To Eduard Pichl and his racist climbing cronies in Austria, the rise of the Third Reich confirmed the righteousness of their actions. They saw themselves on the side of history. Developments during the interwar years had tilted the entire club to the Right. While some German mountaineers tried to set the balance straight, most others slid willingly over. Some saw no choice in the matter; if they wanted to uphold German-Austrian Alpine unity as the club's defining feature, then they had to comply. This meant that bringing the Alpine Association into Hitler's fold after 1933 required little force, even if some alpinists held reservations and despite the club's long-standing democratic practices and official nonpartisan stance.

That mountaineers so passively surrendered their personal liberty and individual autonomy to dictatorship that opposed both should surprise us. After all, freedom and independence were the hallmarks of Alpinism, stretching back to its pioneer days. Part of the attraction for braving the heights, a compelling reason to put one's life at risk, was to escape the very rules, laws, and state oversight that defined civilization. Perhaps mountaineering's mystique and ostensible rejection of modernity made climbers susceptible to right-wing demagoguery. Or maybe the Nazi Party's values of discipline, strength, and superiority wooed stalwart Alpine adventurers. Some claimed that Nazi "dreamers, idealists, and illusionists" had conjured hopes.[82] In their spells they wed "Eternal Mountain" visions to "Eternal Germany" fantasies, casting a heady charm. Too many mountaineers supposedly allowed themselves to be mesmerized. Yet many alpinists turned to Hitler out of profound frustration or maybe naive desperation, not blind seduction. They had grown discouraged with the limits of parliamentary democracy to protect the Alps against industry and consumerism. Disheartened and bitter, many bourgeois mountaineers placed their faith in the only palatable alternative: the National Socialist Party with its holistic vision of nation, race, and nature and the promise of a better future. But in the end, hopes were dashed and the Nazis' edifice crumbled. The center could not hold, not even with the Alps as its foundation.

Conclusion
The Retreat of Nations

"We Swiss—yes and the English and French and Americans too—we climb mountains for sport," observes Andreas Benner, the stalwart Swiss Alpine guide in James Ramsey Ullman's 1945 best seller, The White Tower. "But the Germans, no. What it is they climb for I do not know. Only it is not for sport."[1] A dime novel loaded with wartime propaganda and filled with the usual mountaineering clichés, Ullman's book nevertheless addresses similar themes of mountains and nationhood that Arnold Zweig had discussed. The story follows the adventures of a motley crew of climbers attempting to conquer the fictional eponymous peak, the Weissturm, in the midst of the Second World War. The main protagonist, Martin Ordway, a captain in the American Army Air Corps, flies bombing runs over Germany. On one fateful mission his plane is hit, his crew killed, but he manages to fly the damaged bomber as far as Switzerland before bailing out. Miraculously, he parachutes into the very same valley, Kandermatt, where he had spent the summers of his youth.

When Ordway crash-lands in the valley, he finds that a particular malaise has afflicted the peaceful Swiss pastoral. Isolated from Europe's conflict, the inhabitants languish. Nicholas Radcliffe, an aging English geologist and former member of various Himalayan expeditions who now makes the valley his home, had considered stealing back to Britain and aiding the war effort but finds that he lacks the courage to do so. Siegfried Hein, a German infantry officer on convalescent leave and the novel's principal antagonist, suffers battle fatigue. Carla Alton, a Viennese exile and Ordway's childhood sweetheart, has disappeared to the valley. After learning that her husband has become an ardent Nazi, she has aborted her pregnancy and fled Austria. Paul Delambre, a wealthy Frenchman, and his half-Dutch, half-Swedish wife have escaped occupied France to find refuge in the Alps. Delambre is a broken man, a would-be writer battling alcoholism, "sterile, impotent, lost," while his wife appears numb to the world; their love is spent. Even Benner lives under a dark cloud. The looming mountain haunts him. Having worked as a guide his whole life, he struggles to find a purpose now that the war has all but ended his profession. Feelings of aimlessness and stagnation fester. In a phrase reminiscent of Gustav Müller's criticism of modernity, Benner simply states, "There is an emptiness."[2]

To fill the holes in their hearts, the refugees seek to conquer the White Tower. The thought of taking the mountain revitalizes the "six lost, impotent human fragments" and spurs them to action. Ullman rehashes the typical Alpine motifs of escape and rejuvenation together with national stereotypes. The American is the "doer" whose rugged individualism inspires the "broken-down" Europeans. Benner plays the role of the stalwart Swiss guide. Radcliffe personifies the eminently proper British gentleman-scholar, while Delambre portrays a forlorn French intellectual. Carla is the good Austrian who had denounced the *Anschluss* and resisted Nazi tyranny. Siegfried Hein, with his "hairless and strongly muscled" body and resolute willpower, represents the Germans. Ullman is hardly subtle with his stock descriptions of supposed national characteristics: "Do you know why it is I who am going alone to the top of the Weissturm, while the rest of you drop off one by one for this excuse or the other?" Hein asks. "It is for exactly that reason: because I am German. Because I am climbing for Germany."[3]

Hein's simplistic assertion ties to the complexity of values that had shaped Alpinism and the mountains themselves since the mid-nineteenth century and leading up to the Second World War. Mountaineering illustrated the dichotomy of individuality and collective identity that informed views of nature and nationhood in Germany and Austria. The context of conflict mattered in the evolution of mass tourism. During the First World War, soldiers had looked to the Alps as natural fortresses protecting the nation. The high mountains came to symbolize both individual vigor and collective strength. These ideas had circulated before 1914, when the trauma of war welded them to the landscape. After 1918, the Alps stood as the national bastion for both Germany and Austria. But they still remained a means of personal transcendence. Together, these two attributes defined the Alps as both a sanctuary and a sanatorium for a defeated nation. More German and Austrian mountaineering "apostles" now promoted Alpinism as a collective ethos contributing to the "care and cultivation of national convictions and patriotic morale."[4] Through its activities, the Alpine Association hoped to spread this revised mountaineering ethos among those unfamiliar with the Alps. Convinced that the search for danger and difficulties displayed the "vitality of the

German *Volk*," the club emphasized individual development and the strengthening of the collective will through struggle.⁵ Perhaps Ullman had a point when he asserted that in the early twentieth century, Germans climbed for reasons more serious than sport. Siegfried Hein certainly reinforces this view when he asks, "A mountain is climbed by raising one foot above the other; but what makes the foot rise?"⁶ Nazi warmongers easily appropriated this mountaineering ethos of collective struggle as their own. They stormed and blustered endlessly on the Alps. For them, the Alpine redoubt provided the perfect environment to prepare the *Volk* for the next war.

Strangely enough, after 1939 Nazi hawks hardly gave the mountains a second thought. They had turned their attention to the conquest of Europe and the destruction of the Soviet Union. The Alpine landscape's valences of war and peace had reversed themselves. In times of peace, conquering mountains provided a substitute for war. In the midst of war, the Alps now offered a haven of peace. With most of Europe under German occupation, the mountains were indeed insulated from the fighting, and the Nazi state made a point of keeping them that way. The Alpine Association received instructions from the Ministry of the Interior to maintain appearances and by all means possible to preserve the status quo in the mountains. Work in the Alps was to continue as before. "Uncertainty and anxiety may not prevail in the *Heimat*," went the orders, "while our soldiers engage in the hard, heroic struggle." The regime offered discount railway tickets and the Alpine Association reduced hut fees for men in uniform, including the Waffen-SS.⁷ The Alps went from readying the *Volk* for battle to soothing war-weary soldiers home on leave. Even Hitler started to spend more time at his Alpine retreat.

Motifs of escape, rejuvenation, and security resonated so strongly because the mountains appeared unchanging and everlasting. The peaks were where many believed they could find "eternal solace for the tragedy of life."⁸ The Alps had become a repository for the hopes, fears, and longings held by many Germans and Austrians. Spending time there meant withdrawing into a more perfect past. Ullman's characters express this nostalgia. For all the havoc wrought by war, the mountains stand above the fray. "Day and night come; sun and rain and snow and fog and wind come; and with each of them it's [the mountain] different," Radcliffe explains to Ordway. "It's different and yet it doesn't change. The years and the centuries come, and it doesn't change."⁹ Mountaineers spoke in similar terms. According to author and alpinist Josef Ittlinger, time itself yielded to the Alps. "For millennia," he wrote in his 1924 book, *Eternal Mountains*, "the high stone structures of the mountains have remained unspoiled across the span of time and have changed neither their essence nor their appearance."[10]

Yet the Alps had changed. Alpinism had transformed the peaks both structurally and symbolically. Over the long course of the nineteenth and twentieth centuries, mountaineering clubs recast the heights from forbidding to inviting places. First lodges, blazed trails, and climbing routes equipped with fixed cables, pitons, stemples, ladders, and bridges (called *via ferrata*, "road of iron," in Italian and *Klettersteig*, "climbing path," in German), then cogwheel trains, cable cars, and highways altered the landscape. Together war and mass tourism quickened the pace of environmental change in the mountains. The First World War was central to these developments. German and Austrian alpinists recognized its transformations as fundamental: "The mountains on the battlefields, especially the much sought-after ones, have lost their true countenance." Wanderers now encountered "old barracks[,] . . . abandoned turrets," and the graves of soldiers "whose bodies protect the *Heimat* from danger."[11] Likewise, the Alpine Association's efforts had altered the land when its members opened the mountains to the masses. Latticed with paths, rail lines, and roads, teeming with people, trains, and cars, by the start of the Second World War the Alpine frontier looked and felt different from the pioneering days of the mid-nineteenth century.

Climbing purists greeted these transformations with trepidation. For them, the shrill train whistles and blaring car horns in the Alps sounded the "death knell" of mountaineering's golden age, the time before the hordes crowded the heights.[12] These men thought of the Alpine frontier in ways that reflected Frederick Jackson Turner's views of the American West. Turner claimed that the frontier, "the meeting point between savagery and civilization," was the distinguishing feature of American development. Life on the outer edge produced the rugged individualism and exceptional ingenuity that defined the American character. Later generations of historians have rightly called into question Turner's thesis, noting that he ignored gender, race, and the victims of this westward expansion and critiquing his assertion that the frontier was "free land."[13] But his viewpoints resonated with contemporary German and Austrian mountaineers. Grappling with the Alps and prevailing over them likewise made for a particular national identity based on the mountains. Even though humans had long populated the region, many urban adventurers saw the Alpine frontier as empty, unproductive land ready for the taking. Just as Turner looked to the vanished frontier with nostalgia, serious alpinists believed that something had been lost with modernized mountains.

But not all tourists despaired at the sight of more lodges, trails, and roads in the Alps. Many saw these modifications of the land as material improvements. As the mountains changed over this long time span, so too did the meaning of Alpinism. During the 1860s, liberal notions of independence and personal freedom were the hallmarks of mountaineering. By 1939, climbing mountains for many Germans and Austrians now meant more than searching for the personal sublime; it connoted collective solidarity and racial superiority. Once again the Great War played a pivotal role in this transformation. So too did the Alpine Association. As the largest mountaineering organization in the world, the club was the flag bearer of Alpinism. Yet with chapters flung across two countries, the club itself housed a variety of interests that were often at odds with each other. Its members attached an array of conflicting cultural, social, political, and environmental values to their actions in the Alps. Factionalism within the mountaineering community gave Alpinism its verve. This dynamism also meant that the meaning of Alpinism evolved as tensions in the highlands increased. The extension of technology in the Alps, the focus on adolescent outdoor education, and the efforts of nature conservationists all contributed to a new understanding of Alpine engagement. Militarism became a larger facet of Alpinism during the interwar years, as did anti-Semitism.

Alpinism's evolving meaning reflected the various notions of nationhood that converged on the peaks at different times. The emphasis on personal autonomy and individual development was an extension of liberalism's prevalence in the urban bourgeois milieu during the late nineteenth century. Then the First World War and its pressures of patriotism shifted focus from private lives to the public sphere; Alpinism became a tool for national defense and the common good. Social dislocation, economic turmoil, and heightened cultural anxieties following defeat in 1918 politicized civic Alpinism to an unprecedented degree, which resulted in a decided shift to the right. But as we saw, the path from Section Donauland's dissolution to the Third Reich was not a linear trajectory. Membership in the Alpine Association fell noticeably in reaction to Donauland's ejection. After 1933, independent-minded mountaineers still clashed with Nazi officials. In a telling move, the Nazis had waited

FIGURE 19 "Over the Alps." B-17 Flying Fortresses of the U.S. Eighth Air Force on a bombing mission to Munich. 25 February between 1942 and 1945. Source: Library of Congress.

until they had taken control of Austria in 1938 and unfurled their banner atop Grossglockner before they claimed the Alps as their emblems. Even then the Eastern Alps remained rife with tension, revealing that fundamental conflict in Alpinism was not about coming to terms with politically divided mountains; otherwise the *Anschluss* would have assuaged that grief. Rather, tensions in Alpinism distilled down to an ideological conflict between the individual and the collective, what some mountaineers called the contradiction between "personality and mass-man."[14] Quarrels over accessibility versus nature protection, the back-and-forth of populist hiking and elitist mountaineering debates, and the troubled relationships among religion, race, and recreation all signaled this deep-seated ideological division in both German and Austrian society. Even defeat in 1945 did not fully alleviate these tensions.

· · · · · · · · · · · · ·

Near the end of the Second World War, Heinrich Himmler and Joseph Goebbels actually entertained ideas and propagated plans for an

Alpenfestung (Alpine fortress). But when Allied bombers breached the peaks and turned the Third Reich to rubble, the *Alpenfestung* proved to be just a ploy. With the collapse of Hitler's reign, however, new dilemmas arose out of the ruins. For some, Nazi shadows still darkened the mountains. As historian David Blackbourn has pointed out, landscapes are far from neutral in Germany, where National Socialism contaminated the meaning of the physical environment as it polluted Germany's political atmosphere.[15] Austrian writer Elfriede Jelinek views the Alps as reminders of Austria's complicity in the Third Reich's terror. Several of her stories and plays use the mountain setting to assail her fellow citizens' selective memory and to attack their complacency.[16] She has good reason to do so. The Austrian and the German Alpine Associations, now separate clubs and formally reconstituted in 1951 and 1952 respectively, were slow to publicly apologize for the Donauland affair, their treatment of Jewish alpinists, and their collaboration with the Nazis. Only in 2001 did the German Alpine Association erect a tiny memorial stone outside the Alpine Museum in Munich and read aloud a proclamation, "Against Intolerance and Hate." In 2009 the club revised its statutes, making explicit its political neutrality and commitment to religious, ideological, and ethnic tolerance, as well as to gender equality. Other than this added clause, the statutes repeated nearly verbatim the prewar language. Austrians seemed more reluctant to come to terms with the past. To his dying day, Eduard Pichl remained steadfastly unapologetic for his anti-Semitic actions. "If I stood at the beginning of life," he mused in his final letter, "I would want to live it again exactly so." His 1955 obituary in the Austrian Alpine Association's newsletter made no mention of Donauland, remembering simply that his tenure as chairman of Section Austria included several hut and trail construction projects.[17] The club finally renamed the Eduard-Pichl-Hut the Wolayersee Hut in 2002. The Austrian bylaws, however, were also almost identical to the 1927 version and did not include a "tolerance clause," unlike the German statutes.

If the affiliation of Alpinism and anti-Semitism seemingly dissolved after the Second World War, other older contradictions resurfaced. Alpine tourism's quandary of consumption versus conservation remained unresolved. Both the German and Austrian clubs promoted mountaineering and Alpine sports as their principal aim yet also sought to "preserve the beauty and naturalness of the mountain world."[18] Opposing objectives were a systemic part of the clubs' programs, an inherent and irreconcilable tension of tourism. Meanwhile, in recent years, visitors to the Alps have increased exponentially. In 1999, a United Nations Commission on Sustainable Development report qualified tourism as the world's leading industry and estimated the Alpine share of global tourism around 10 percent. Millions now visit the mountains every year.[19] High-profile extreme sporting events, such as transalpine adventure races, are advertised across social media and have brought even greater attention to the mountains. During the ride up in the Zugspitzbahn, a short audio commentary informs passengers that "over the course of the years one thing has never changed—the fascination with the Zugspitze." The daily long queue of people waiting to stand for a moment on its peak drives the point home. Nor is Germany's highest mountain alone. The entire Alpine region is supersaturated with tourists.

In a way, postwar tourism helped decouple the mountains from a nationalistic past. Prior to 1945, Europeans characterized the Alps as a national retreat. After the Second World War, the thinking changed. Climate change, fears that unabated tourism would destroy the fragile Alpine ecosystem, and the development of the European Union now prompted international cooperation. Warming patterns over the past century have reduced Europe's glacial area by up to 40 percent. Underground temperatures have risen, heating up mountain rock and soil. The Alps are becoming more arid. Suitable habitat for rare Alpine flora and fauna is shrinking. Since many of them have developed special adaptations in their physical structure, physiology, and behavior, they face extinction if warming trends continue. Heightened ecological concerns propelled the creation of national nature reserves in the Alps. Bavaria established the Berchtesgaden National Park in 1978, which incorporated areas around the Königsee that had been protected since 1910. Three years later, Carinthia, Salzburg, and Tyrol signed a three-province agreement that led to the formation of the largest nature reserve of the Alps, National Park Hohe Tauern. Both parks are a mix of "primeval Alpine landscapes" and "carefully and painstakingly cultivated" pastures.[20] Humans are prohibited from the most ecologically vulnerable areas but are otherwise free to use the land. The same holds true for many mountain parks in France, Italy, and Switzerland. Nature reserves protect approximately 10 percent of the Alpine region, but people are actually excluded from less than 1 percent. The sheer volume of tourists crisscrossing increasingly open borders convinced environmentalists and government officials that only an international framework could reconcile ecological concerns with economic interests.

Just as Europe moved toward an ever-closer union, so too did national parks in the Alps. In 1991, the Alpine countries and the European Union ratified the Convention on the Protection of the Alps that coordinated management efforts and linked the reserves into a single network. This level of interstate cooperation was unprecedented. Recognizing the region as a "single space in a global context" that requires "supernational protection," the convention signaled the retreat of nations from the Alps.

Yet the new century has also witnessed a return of the old. Modern-day mountaineers echo sentiments of nineteenth-century Alpine pioneers, who had often climbed the Alps out of a longing for a simpler age. In 2001 a group of British and Swiss climbers embarked on a ten-day expedition up routes made famous during the golden age of Alpinism, doing so dressed up like gentlemen alpinists from the 1800s. Complete with tweed jackets, trilbies, braces, bowties, and hobnailed boots, the explorers intended to publicize the changes in mountaineering as well as ecological transformations in the Alps since the previous century. The lone female alpinist suffered a full-length tweed skirt, several layers of underwear, a heavy canvas poncho, and a wide-brimmed felt hat. A sense of nostalgia hung over their journey. In some instances, retracing original routes proved impossible because retreating glaciers had changed the environment so much.[21]

Other visitors have gravitated away from corporate hotels and crowded ski resorts. People living high on the slopes have found that tourists will pay top dollar to stay in outbuildings on family farms. Old hay sheds, former granaries, and weather-beaten huts that may have once housed cattle or goats have been converted into "luxury" chalets. In a sense, Alpine tourism has come full circle. "People want to be closer to nature," one Austrian proprietor observed, "and go back to simple, honest things." Yet it also seems that people prefer nineteenth-century charm with twenty-first-century comfort. Renovated chalets often include private saunas and five-star service, in addition to wood-burning ovens and antique furniture. Wealthy vacationers seek to escape modern life up to a point. They do not stay in these chalets to churn their own butter, gather eggs for their breakfast, or labor in the fields. Paradox remains fully part of the Alpine landscape. Perhaps that is part of the attraction. Whatever the reason, the urge to visit high places has hardly diminished. As one mountain resident remarked, "Life is more beautiful and much grander when you're looking over the whole world."[22]

If the attraction of the Alps is as alluring as ever in the new millennium, their ambiguities are still equally confounding, particularly concerning the relationship between tourism and nationhood on the Alpine frontier. In 2001, the director of the Alpine Archive in Munich, Johannes Merck, reflected on this quandary after receiving an inquiry about Germany's highest mountain: "When did the Zugspitze become German?" The old Bavarian, once an intrepid climber who still believed that every German should hike up the Zugspitze, read aloud the letter during a staff meeting and gave an exasperated snort. The other volunteer archivists around the table, ancient mountaineers all, shook their heads and scowled. They grumbled some vague answers. One suggested that the peak had become German during Napoleon's invasions in the early 1800s. Another wondered if the mountain had not always been German. A third interjected that the Zugspitze was Bavarian long before it was German. Merck pondered what becoming German even meant. They soon set the letter aside and returned to the business of sorting old documents.[23] Their impatience with the query was telling. But as the discussion revealed, the Alps remain both realities in the present and ruins from the past.

Notes

ABBREVIATIONS

BHA		Bayerisches Hauptstaatsarchiv, Munich, Germany
	KA	Kriegsarchiv
	MF	Ministerium der Finanzen
	MK	Ministerium für Unterricht, Kultus, Wissenschaft und Kunst
	MWi	Ministerium für Wirtschaft, Infrastruktur, Verkehr und Technologie
	StK	Staatskanzlei
HAA DAV		Historisches Alpenarchiv Deutscher Alpenverein, Munich, Germany
	BGS	Bundesgeschäftsstelle
HAA OeAV		Historisches Alpenarchiv Österreichischer Alpenverein, Innsbruck, Austria
	FV	Fremde Vereine
	HÜW	Hütten- und Wegebau
	SE	Sektionen
	ZV	Zentral Verein
ÖSA		Österreichisches Staatsarchiv, Vienna, Austria
	AdR	Archiv der Republik
	AVA	Allgemeines Verwaltungsarchiv
	KA	Kriegsarchiv
SAG		Staatsarchiv Graubünden, Chur, Switzerland
SBA		Schweizerisches Bundesarchiv, Bern, Switzerland
SLA		Salzburg Landesarchiv, Salzburg, Austria

INTRODUCTION

1. Zweig, Dialektik der Alpen, 375.
2. Ibid., 384.
3. Fitzsimmons and Veit, "Geology and Geomorphology of the European Alps"; Dal Piaz, "History of Tectonic Interpretations of the Alps"; Collet, Structure of the Alps. See Price, Mountains and Man.
4. The literature on these topics is too extensive to be cited here. For a good overview, see H. Smith, Continuities of German History.
5. Emmer, "Geschichte des Deutschen und Österreichischen Alpenvereins," 198; Blackbourn, History of Germany, 210.
6. Burnet, Sacred Theory of the Earth, 112.
7. M. Weber, "Wissenschaft als Beruf," 524–55.
8. Berlepsch, Alps, 2. For more on the changing views of mountains, see Nicolson's classic study Mountain Gloom and Mountain Glory; for the German context, see Ireton and Schaumann, Heights of Reflection. See also Macfarlane, Mountains of the Minds; Beattie, Alps; Schama, Landscape and Memory; Short, Imagined Country; and Rudwick, Bursting the Limits of Time.
9. Hofmann, "Unsere Pflichten," 277; Schmidkunz, Der Kampf über den Gletschern, 18; "Der neue Feind"; Deye, "Kriegsbilder aus den Hochalpen," 162.
10. See Confino, Nation as Local Metaphor.
11. Zeller, "Das Hochkaltergebirge," 180–81.
12. Maier, "Aus Karwendel und Wetterstein," 165.
13. The single best study on the German idea of Heimat remains Applegate's Nation of Provincials.
14. The assertion is that Germany followed a special path (Sonderweg) of development that culminated in the Third Reich. Because of supposed peculiarities—most prominently a profound distrust of modernity and inherently illiberal leanings—Germans (and Austrians) were naturally drawn to authoritarian and later fascist ideology. Supporters of the Sonderweg thesis have contended that the bourgeois rejection of modernity crippled Germany's democratic development. The literature on this topic is massive. The most pertinent studies include K. Bergmann, Agraromantik und Großstadtfeindschaft; and Sieferle, Fortschrittsfeinde? See also Stern, Politics of Cultural Despair; Mosse, Crisis of German Ideology; Stern, Failure of Illiberalism; and Craig, Politics of the Unpolitical.
15. Amstädter, Der Alpinismus; see also Müller, "Geschichte des Deutschen und Österreichischen Alpenvereins."
16. Stephen, Playground of Europe, 49, 65. For an excellent synopsis of these developments, see Williams, "Chords of the German Soul"; see also his monograph Turning to Nature in Germany. Recent years have witnessed a boom in the literature on conservation and modernity; for general overviews, see Mauch, Nature in German History; and Lekan and Zeller, Germany's Nature. See especially Günther, Alpine Quergänge; and Lekan, Imagining the Nation in Nature; Rohkrämer, Eine andere Moderne; Rollins, Greener Vision of Home; Brüggemeier, Cioc, and Zeller, How Green Were the Nazis?; and Uekoetter, Green and the Brown.

17. See Maier's remarks at http://h-net.msu.edu/cgi-bin/logbrowse.pl?trx=vx&list=H-German&month=1102&week=b&msg=wSiNPf2FLYSpdAgcTzlz3w&user=&pw.

18. Applegate, "Europe of Regions," 1169, 1182. For more on subnational places, see Blackbourn and Retallack, *Localism, Landscape, and the Ambiguities of Place*; and M. Anderson, *Frontiers*.

19. Ploch and Schilling, "Region als Handlungslandschaft," 122–57, cited in Applegate, "Europe of Regions," 1182.

20. See Bailey, "Identifying Ecoregion Boundaries"; and Loveland and Merchant, "Ecoregions and Ecoregionalization."

21. Sheehan, "What Is German History?"; Zahra, "Looking East," 7; Liulevicius, *German Myth of the East*; Turner, "Significance of the Frontier in American History," 210. The literature on Turner's frontier thesis is extensive. Of the more recent discussions, see Faragher, *Rereading Frederick Jackson Turner*; and Limerick, *Legacy of Conquest*.

22. See Scott, *Seeing Like a State*; Koshar, *German Travel Cultures*, 4–5; Baranowski and Furlough, *Being Elsewhere*, 3–4; Murdock, "Tourist Landscapes and Regional Identities"; and Judson, "Every German Visitor." See also Moranda, *The People's Own Landscape*.

23. Withey, *Grand Tours and Cook's Tours*, 159; Lekan, "'Noble Prospect,'" 839. See also P. Smith, *History of Tourism*; and Veblen, *Theory of the Leisure Class*.

24. Koshar, "What Ought to Be Seen." See also Mendelson, "Baedeker's Universe."

25. Leopold, *A Sand County Almanac*, 129–33; Urry, *Tourist Gaze*. The classical text on tourism's environmental impact is Rothman, *Devil's Bargains*.

26. Ring's popular history *How the English Made the Alps* typifies the unbalance in the scholarship. See also Colley, *Victorians in the Mountains*; Hansen, *Summits of Modern Man*; Fleming, *Killing Dragons*; Braham, *When the Alps Cast Their Spell*; and Schama, *Landscape and Memory*.

27. Stephen, *Playground of Europe*, 67; Schama, *Landscape and Memory*, 502.

28. Kirchner, "Mind, Mountain, and History." See also Ellis, *Vertical Margins*.

29. Aurada, "Die Alpenvereinskartographie," 117. See also Zimmer, "In Search of Natural Identity."

30. Kirchner, "Mind, Mountain, and History," 442.

31. Trautwein, "Zum Anfang," 2.

32. Buzard, *Beaten Track*, 2; for an excellent discussion on this topic, see Lekan, "'Noble Prospect.'"

33. Alden, "Mountains and History," 519–30.

34. Ibid., 526.

35. For more on development in the Alps, see Mathieu, *History of the Alps*; and Bätzing, *Die Alpen*.

CHAPTER ONE

1. HAA OeAV, *Verhandlungsschrift des Österreichischen Alpenvereins* (1864), 49. Leslie Stephen made a similar remark a few years later: "Mountaineering—like so many other things—has become a fashion with many who don't really care about it." Stephen, *Playground of Europe*, 318.

2. Frank, "Air Cure Town," 191–93, 198.
3. Fowler, *Iceman*.
4. Johann, "Impact of Industry."
5. Mathieu, *History of the Alps*, 50; Viazzo, *Upland Communities*, 20. See also Frödin, *Zentraleuropas Alpwirtschaft*.
6. Wessinger, "Zur Alpenwirthschaft."
7. See Netting, *Balancing on an Alp*.
8. Berlepsch, *Alps*, 308; Coolidge, *Alps in Nature and History*, 8–14. He notes that such Alpine pastures were mentioned as early as the 700s.
9. Tschudi, *Sketches of Nature in the Alps*, 184.
10. Economic historians have disagreed over Austria's economy development and the extent to which the stock market crash in 1873 hampered growth. See M. Schulze, "Machine-Building Industry"; Gross, "Economic Growth and the Consumption of Coal"; Komlos, *Habsburg Monarchy as a Customs Union*; Rudolf, *Banking and Industrialization in Austria-Hungary*; and Good, *Economic Rise of the Habsburg Empire*.
11. M. Schulze, "Machine-Building Industry," 288.
12. Arnold, "Die Eisenbahnverbindung"; see also König, *Bahnen und Berge*.
13. "Jahresbericht des Österreichischen Alpen-Vereins"; Emmer, "Geschichte des Deutschen und Österreichischen Alpenvereins," 198; Kreuter, "Über Eisenbahnen im Gebirge"; Torpey, *Invention of the Passport*, 76–80.
14. Reulecke, *Geschichte der Urbanisierung in Deutschland*, 203; Fremdling, *Eisenbahnen und deutsches Wirtschaftswachstum*.
15. For an excellent discussion of the commodification of the Alps, see Frank, "Air Cure Town."
16. HAA OeAV, *Verhandlungsschrift des Österreichischen Alpenvereins* (1864), 13.
17. See Kocka, "Bildungsbürgertum"; and Hettling and Hoffmann, "Der Bürgerliche Wertehimmel," 346.
18. See Blackbourn, *Populists and Patricians*; Koshar, *Social Life, Local Politics, and Nazism*; Judson, *Exclusive Revolutionaries*; and Urbanitsch, "Bürgertum und Politik."
19. See Evans and Lee, *German Peasantry*.
20. Coolidge, *Alps in Nature and History*, 3; Kariel and Kariel, "Socio-cultural Impacts of Tourism," 3. For more on Franz Senn, see Oberwalder, *Franz Senn*.
21. Sueß, "Ein Betrag zur Gründungsgeschichte des Alpenvereins," 304; ÖSA-AVA, Unterricht KB Dt.-Öst, Alpenverein 1, Korrespondenz Eduard Mojsisovics.
22. "Petermann's Mittheilungen der Geographie," 270, cited in Gidl, *Alpenverein*, 26.
23. HAA OeAV, *Verhandlungsschrift des Österreichischen Alpenvereins* (1864), 48–50.
24. Ibid., 14.
25. Ibid., 68–71; Emmer, "Geschichte des Deutschen und Österreichischen Alpenvereins," 179–80.
26. ÖSA-AVA, Unterricht KB Dt.-Öst, Alpenverein 1, "Aufruf an alle Alpenfreunde!," June 1869; see also Dreyer, *Der Alpinismus*.
27. Aurada, "Die Alpenvereinskartographie," 117; Emmer, "Geschichte des Deutschen und Österreichischen Alpenvereins," 372.
28. Hofmann, "Bericht über das erste Vereinsjahr," 25.
29. Trautwein, "Zum Anfang," 2.

30. Emmer, "Geschichte des Deutschen und Österreichischen Alpenvereins," 198.
31. "Jahresbericht 1873," 34.
32. Arauda, "Die Alpenvereinskartographie," 117.
33. Emmer, "Geschichte des Deutschen und Österreichischen Alpenvereins," 372.
34. For more on the composition of the clubs, see Amstädter, *Der Alpinismus*; and Gidl, *Alpenverein*.
35. See Dominick, *Environmental Movement in Germany*, 58–61; and Rollins, *Greener Vision of Home*, 103–12.
36. For more on the prevalence of democratic practices in Germany, see M. L. Anderson, *Practicing Democracy*; Sperber, *Kaiser's Voters*; Suval, *Electoral Politics in Wilhelmine Germany*; and Fairbairn, *Democracy in the Undemocratic State*.
37. See Judson, *Exclusive Revolutionaries*; and Boyer, *Culture and Political Crisis in Vienna*.
38. "Sectionsberichte," 30–37.
39. HAA DAV, Berlin carton, *Kostüm-Ordnung für das Winterfest der Sektion Berlin des D.u.Oe. Alpenvereins*, 2–3.
40. Berlepsch, *Alps*, 2.
41. "Anlagen zur Vereinsgeschichte."
42. HAA OeAV, Hütten Grundbuch, "Überlassungsvertrag zwischen der Gemeinde Pitztal und akademischen Section Graz," 1901.
43. HAA OeAV HÜW 5.1, "Weg- und Hütten-Bauordnung," 1879.
44. See HAA OeAV HÜW 10.3, "Votum der Section München" and "Motivenbericht," 1890.
45. "Vereins-Angelegenheiten," MDÖAV 11 (1909): 148.
46. HAA DAV, Verhanglungsschrift der 41. (1910) Hauptversammlung, 10.
47. Emmer, "Beiträge zur Geschichte," 349.
48. HAA OeAV HÜW 10.7, "Zusammenstellung der Subventions-Gesuche für die General-Versammlung Passau," 1899.
49. "Ausgaben der Vereinskasse," ZDÖAV 50 (1919): 211.
50. See Berghahn, *Imperial Germany*.
51. HAA OeAV, Hütten Grundbuch, "Villacher-Häuser," number 6. The gulden was the standard unit currency used in the Habsburg Empire and was set on the silver standard. When the empire adopted the gold standard in 1892, the krone became the official currency. One gulden purchased two kronen. Prior to unification in 1871, several German states used the *Vereinsthaler*, which was introduced in 1857. After unification, Germany went on the gold mark. At the turn of the century, one krone equaled approximately 0.80 German marks.
52. HAA OeAV, Hütten Grundbuch, "Nürnberger-Hütte," number 68.
53. "Verschiedenes," MDÖAV 14 (1910): 174. Its success may be the result of a certain flair for business. That preceding year, the chapter sold over eighteen thousand postcards.
54. HAA OeAV SE/81/401B, Innsbruck: Franz-Senn-Hütte. See also HAA OeAV HÜW 6.1, "Pläne von Schutzhütten des Deutschen und Oesterreichischen Alpenvereins," 1877.

55. Emmer, "Beiträge zur Geschichte," 340, 351.
56. "Die feierliche Eröffnung der 'Freiburger Hütte' auf der Alpe Formarin."
57. HAA DAV, Berlin carton, *Die Berliner Hütte*.
58. Klebelsberg, "Die Eiszeitliche Vergletscherung der Alpen," 26; " Die XL. (XXXVI.) Hauptversammlung des D.u.Ö. Alpenvereins zu Wien," MDÖAV 18 (1909): 222.
59. HAA OeAV, Beirat 1896/23/1, "Berichte über die wissenschaftlichen Unternehmungen des D.u.Oe.A.V., Neue Gletschermarkierung 1895"; HAA OeAV, Gletschervermessung 23.4, Koch and Klocke, "Über die Bewegung der Gletscher," *Separat-Abdruck aus den Annalen der Physik und Chemie* (1879); "Zur Gletscher-Frage"; HAA OeAV Gletscher Berichte.
60. HAA OeAV, Commission/23/1, *Presse*, 9 June 1891. For more on climatology, see Coen, "Climate and Circulation in Imperial Austria."
61. HAA OeAV, Beirat/23/1, "Einrichtung einer meteorologischen Station erster Ordnung auf dem Brocken," 1892. The second highest was the Säntis Station, located in the Swiss Appenzell Alps.
62. HAA OeAV, Zugspitze/23/3, *Verhandlungen der bayerischen Kammer der Abgeordneten*, 20 April 1898, 148–49.
63. *Das Bayerische Vaterland*, 23 November 1898.
64. Erk, "Ein meteorologische Obervatorium auf der Zugspitze."
65. HAA OeAV, Zugspitze/23/3, "Übereinkommen über ein Thurm für die meteorologische Hochstation auf der Zugspitze." See also HAA DAV DOK 2 SG/60/1, "50 Jahre Observatorium Zugspitze (1900–1950)."
66. *Innsbrucker Tagblatt*, 7 September 1876.
67. Baedeker, *Eastern Alps*, xxii.
68. Tschudi, *Sketches of Nature in the Alps*, 158; Stephen, *Playground of Europe*, 48.
69. Despite the stir, no one repeated Schmitt and Saunter's accomplishment for several months until a Dutch woman, Madame Immink, reached the peak in 1891. Davis, *Dolomite Strongholds*, 110–11.

CHAPTER TWO

1. Kordon, "Bergwandern in der Ankogelgruppe," 249, 252; Meyer, "Zwischen Sixt und Barberine," 88.
2. Mann, *Magic Mountain*, 4.
3. Hettling and Hoffmann, "Der Bürgerliche Wertehimmel," 346. See also Blackbourn and Evans, *German Bourgeoisie*.
4. Emmer, "Geschichte des Deutschen und Österreichischen Alpenvereins," 198; Blackbourn, *History of Germany*, 210.
5. Oertel, "Sport, Alpinismus und Schilauf," 6.
6. Meyer, "Zur Entwicklung des Bergsteigers," 259.
7. HAA OeAV ZV/1/1, *Protokolle der 40. (1909) Generalversammlung*, 5; Dreyer, *Der Alpinismus*, 141.
8. Kiene, "Die Puezgruppe" (1914), 342.
9. HAA OeAV ZV/1/1, *Verhandlungsschrift der 43. (1912) Hauptversammlung*, 5–6.
10. "Hygiene des Sports"; Baumgärten and Sandtner, "Schneeschufahrten," 222.

11. For more on sanatoriums in Switzerland, see Barton, *Healthy Living in the Alps*; for disease and society, see also Evans, *Death in Hamburg*.

12. O. Maier, "Aus Karwendel und Wetterstein," 176.

13. Lammer, "Die Grenzen des Bergsports," 244.

14. Kiene, "Die Puezgruppe" (1914), 342; O. Maier, "Aus Karwendel und Wetterstein," 159.

15. Lidtke, *Alternative Culture*; Lekan, *Imagining the Nation in Nature*, 69; see also Williams, *Turning to Nature in Germany*.

16. HAA OeAV, Sitzung des Hauptausschusses des D. u. Ö. A.-V. (13 May 1910): 4.

17. *Der Naturfreund* (1901): 112.

18. Ibid. (1913): 228.

19. Ibid. (1911): 24.

20. Oertel, "Sport, Alpinismus und Schilauf," 9.

21. Aichinger, "Die Julischen Alpen," 297.

22. Preuß, "Neues zum Turenprogramm der Saarbrücker Hütte," 121; O. Maier, "Aus Karwendel und Wetterstein," 174.

23. Oertel, "Sport, Alpinismus und Schilauf," 9; Kees, "Im Reiche des Ortlers," 77.

24. Kiene, "Die Puezgruppe" (1914), 343.

25. Dreyer, *Der Alpinismus*, 135.

26. HAA OeAV ZV/1/1, Verhandlungsschrift der 41. (1910) Hauptversammlung, 22; "Vereins-Angelegenheiten," MDÖAV 1 (1912): 12.

27. "Das Alpine Museum in München," 15; see also Sheehan, *Museums in the German Art World*.

28. "Vereins-Angelegenheiten," MDÖAV 7 (1912): 100; HAA OeAV ZV/1/1, Verhandlungsschrift der 43. (1912) Hauptversammlung, 45; Verhandlungsschrift der 44. (1913) Hauptversammlung, 54–55.

29. Dreyer, *Der Alpinismus*, 153.

30. "Von unserem Alpinen Museums," 153.

31. Dreyer, *Der Alpinismus*, 155.

32. "Die Feier des fünfzigjährigen Bestandes der Sektion Austria," 307.

33. Cited in Whiteside, *Socialism of Fools*, 10.

34. Trautwein, "Zum Anfang," 2.

35. "Literature," MDÖAV 8 (1913): 129; "Literature," MDÖAV 4 (1909): 56. Kutzen's book is not too dissimilar from Wilhelm Riehl's work. See Riehl, *Naturgeschichte des Volkes*.

36. "Bericht über die zeite General-Versammlung," ZDAV 2 Abth. II (1870/1871): 570.

37. Ibid., 576.

38. Cited in Amstädter, *Der Alpinismus*, 26.

39. Dreyer, *Der Alpinismus*, 152.

40. *Neue Tiroler Stimmen*, 3 August 1876.

41. Ibid., 22 August 1876; 9 September 1876.

42. "Nachtrag zur Alpenvereins-Affaire," ibid., 27 September 1876; for more on the discussion of Alpinism and religion, see Blaubeuren, "Der Alpensport."

43. *Preußen und der Alpenverein*, 1–16.

44. Judson, "Tourists and Modernizers."

45. ÖSA AVA, Unterricht KB Dt.-Öst 1, 3; "Interne Angelegenheit des Alpen-Club Österreich," *Österreichische Alpenzeitung* (1882): 10; and HAA OeAV, Fremde Vereine, Alpenclub Austria.

46. *Österreichische Touristenzeitung* (1893), 13–16.

47. "Angeblicher und wirklicher Patriotismus," *Innsbrucker Tagblatt*, 25 August 1876.

48. "Der Alpenverein als Hochverräther," ibid., 7 September 1876.

49. "Die Feier des fünfzigjährigen Bestandes der Sektion Austria," 308.

50. "Die XLII. (XXXVIII.) Hauptversammlung des D.u.Ö. Alpenvereins zu Coblenz," 168.

51. "Die 44. (40.) Hauptversammlung des D.u.Ö. Alpenvereins zu Regensburg," 200.

52. Ibid.

53. HAA OeAV ZV/1/1, *Verhandlungsschrift der 44. (1913) Hauptversammlung*, 29–30.

54. Hermann Göring was a member of this chapter.

55. HAA DAV BGS 1 SG/189/1–4, S. Mark Brandenburg.

56. Ibid., SG/8/1, Akad. S. München.

57. HAA OeAV, Sitzung des Hauptausschusses des D. u. Ö. A-V., 18 July 1910.

58. See Wistrich, *Antisemitism*.

59. For more on Pan-Germanism, see Chickering, *We Men Who Feel Most German*; Whiteside, *Socialism of Fools*; and Schorske's essay "Politics in a New Key: An Austrian Trio" in *Fin-de-Siècle Vienna*. See also Oxaal, Pollak, and Botz, *Jews, Antisemitism and Culture in Vienna*; and Beller, *Vienna and the Jews*.

60. ÖSA AVA, Nachlass Pichl, carton 56, "Aus meinem Lebenslauf," undated.

61. HAA OeAV Fremde Vereine, Österreichischer Gebirgsverein.

62. *Preußen und der Alpenverein*, 9.

63. Mailänder, "Jüdische Beiträge zum Alpinismus," 241–42; Rudovsky, *Festschrift*, 173; ÖSA AVA, Nachlass Pichl, carton 61, "Verehrliche Schwestersektion!," 1 August 1921.

64. "Die XL. (XXXVI.) Hauptversammlung des D.u.Ö. Alpenvereins zu Wien," 223.

65. Preuß, "Der Gosaukamm," 219.

66. Semple, *Influences of Geographic Environment*, 521.

CHAPTER THREE

1. "Verschiedenes," *MDÖAV* 9 (1912): 126.

2. Emmer, "Beiträge zur Geschichte," 350; "Verschiedenes," *MDÖAV* 9 (1912): 126; "Vereins-Angelegenheiten," *MDÖAV* 10 (1909): 136.

3. Lekan, "'Noble Prospect,'" 824–31.

4. Emmer, "Beiträge zur Geschichte," 340.

5. Lieberich, "Neuer Alpinismus," 307.

6. Plank, "Zur Zukunft des Alpinismus," 7.

7. HAA OeAV SE/81/503B, Innsbruck: Wege letter to Section Bayerland dated 1 May 1909.

8. "Nochmals Höhenwege," 112.

9. Ibid.

10. "Ibid., 111.

11. HAA OeAV ZV/1/1, *Verhandlungsschrift der 42. (1911) Hauptversammlung*, 6.

12. Ibid., *Protokoll der XXXVII. (XXXIII.) Generalversammlung des Deutschen und Österreichischen Alpenvereins* (1906): 243–46.
13. HAA OeAV SE/81/503B, Innsbruck: Wege letter to Section Bayerland dated 1 May 1909.
14. Emmer, "Beiträge zur Geschichte," 340.
15. Weitzenböck, "Zur ferneren Zukunft des Alpinismus," 268.
16. "Nochmals Höhenwege," 111.
17. Zoeppritz, "Über die Bedürnissfrage bei Weg- und Hüttenbauten."
18. HAA OeAV ZV/1/1, *Protokoll der XXVII. (XXIII.) Generalversammlung des Deutschen und Österreichischen Alpenvereins* (1896): 14.
19. Ibid., *Protokoll der XXVIII. (XXIV.) Generalversammlung des Deutschen und Österreichischen Alpenvereins* (1897): 17–18.
20. Ibid., *Verhandlungsschrift der 42. (1911) Hauptversammlung*, 14.
21. Ibid., 6, 16.
22. Ibid., *Protokoll der XXV. (XXI.) Generalversammlung des Deutschen und Österreichischen Alpenvereins* (1894): 13.
23. Ibid., *Verhandlungsschrift der 42. (1911) Hauptversammlung*, 5.
24. Allen, *Culture and Sport of Skiing*, 2. For an excellent analysis of skiing's cultural and environmental history in the Alps, see Denning, *Skiing into Modernity*.
25. Zdarsky, *Lilienfelder Schilauftechnik*; he described the ski bindings in his brief article "Der Alpen- (Lilienfelder-) Ski."
26. See Allen, *Culture and Sport of Skiing*, 129, 133.
27. Paulcke, "Auf Skiern im Hochgebirge"; Hoek, "Skifahrt auf das Blindenhorn"; Löwenbach, "Ueber Lilienfelder Skitechnik"; Madlener, "Einiges über alpinen Skilauf."
28. Hoek, "Zehn Winter mit Schiern in den Bergen," 52.
29. HAA OeAV ZV/1/1, *Verhandlungsschrift der 43. (1912) Hauptversammlung*, 33–34.
30. Oertel, "Sport, Alpinismus und Schilauf," 6.
31. Lammer, "Ist der Sport kulturschädlich?," 111–12.
32. HAA OeAV ZV/1/1, *Verhandlungsschrift der 43. (1912) Hauptversammlung*, 31.
33. Aichinger, "Die Stellung des Alpenvereins zum alpinen Schilauf," 37.
34. "Ausschuss zur Förderung der Schituristik im D.u.Ö. Alpenverein."
35. P. Schulze, "Die Alpenvereinshütten im Winter," 91.
36. HAA OeAV ZV/1/1, *Protokoll der 40. (1909) Generalversammlung*, 40.
37. Reuther, "Unsere Schutzhütten im Winter," 308.
38. Oertel, "Die Frage der Schutzhütten in Winter," 255.
39. A. Steinitzer, "Die Schituristik und der D. u. Ö. Alpenverein," 8.
40. Barker, "Traditional Landscape."
41. "Bergbahnen und alpiner Naturschutz."
42. A. Steinitzer, "Über Höhenwege," 281.
43. Menger, "Die turistische Bedeutung der Karwendelbahn."
44. BHA MWi 10783, Die Fern-Ortler-Bahn.
45. Ibid. 8581, Zugspitzbahn.
46. Ibid. 8584, Wolfgang Adolf Müller, "Vorwort," Zugspitzbahn.
47. Ibid. 8582, Zugspitzbahn.

48. Ibid. 8577, Bergbahnen: Wendelsteinbahn.
49. Freeston, *Alps for the Motorist*, 35.
50. HAA OeAV SE/94/503, Klagenfurt: Wege, memorandum dated 20 January 1902.
51. Ibid., Klagenfurt: Wege, *Kärntner Nachrichten*, 17 May 1900.
52. Reinthaler, "Neben und über der Dolomitenstrasse." See also "Automobilfahrten in Tirol"; "Automobilverkeh."
53. HAA OeAV ZV/1/1, *Verhandlungsschrift der 43. (1912) Hauptversammlung*, 8. The Hanover delegate, Professor Arnold, was referring to Schaubach, author of *Die Deutschen Alpen*. This work comprised several volumes published in 1845, 1846, 1847, and 1850, with the last edition issued in 1867.
54. H. Steinitzer, "Zur Umfrage betreffend die Gestaltung unserer Vereinsschriften."
55. HAA OeAV ZV/1/1, *Verhandlungsschrift der 44. (1913) Hauptversammlung*, 5.
56. Ibid., *Verhandlungsschrift der 42. (1911) Hauptversammlung*, 6.
57. Ibid., *Verhandlungsschrift der 44 (1913) Hauptversammlung*, 37.
58. Williams, "Ecstasies of the Young," 166, 177. Several works discuss youth in Imperial Germany. See Stachura, *German Youth Movement*.
59. Haserrodt, "Die Grenzen des Bergsports," 283; see also Hoek, "Zehn Winter mit Schiern in den Bergen," 96.
60. Enzensperger, *Alpenfahrten der Jugend: Im Wetterstein* and *Alpenfahrten der Jugend: Im Allgäu*.
61. HAA OeAV ZV/1/1, *Protokoll der 40. (1909) Generalversammlung*, 25–26. The 1911 Annual Report stated that in the first year of coverage, the association compensated forty-one cases with 10,061.34 marks. See HAA DAV, *Verhandlungsschrift der 43. (1912) Hauptversammlung*, 49.
62. Enzensperger, "Alpenfahrten der Jugend," 21, 40.
63. HAA OeAV ZV/1/1, *Verhandlungsschrift der 44 (1913) Hauptversammlung*, 35–40.
64. Lieberich, "Die Jugendbergfahrten," 321–22.
65. "Alpines Jugendwandern in Innsbruck."
66. HAA OeAV ZV/1/1, *Verhandlungsschrift der 42. (1911) Hauptversammlung*, 5.
67. Ibid., 57.
68. Dominick, "Nascent Environmental Protection," 259–60.
69. See Dominick, *Environmental Movement in Germany*; and Lekan, *Imagining the Nation in Nature*.
70. Rollins, *Greener Vision of Home*, 271–72.
71. Dominick, "Nascent Environmental Protection," 264, 271.
72. "Verein zum Schutz und zur Pflege der Alpenpflanzen," *MDÖAV* (1901): 252.
73. SBA E16 40 348, Nationalpark im Unterengadin; SBA E16 40 368, Schweizerischer Nationalpark im Engadin; SBA E9500.25 1967/47 37, Nationalpark Gründung Akten; SBA E16 41 365, Schweizerischer Nationalpark im Unterengadin Jahresbericht 1915; SBA E16 40 358, Schweizerischer Nationalpark im Unterengadin, Jagd und Fischerei-Verbot; Kupper, "Science and the National Parks." See also Sautter, "Der künftige 'Nationalpark' der Schweiz."
74. "Verschiedenes," *MDÖAV* 21 (1909): 267.
75. Guttenberg, "Naturschutz und Naturschutzgebiete," 59; *Deutsche Alpenzeitung* II (October 1913–March 1914): 3.

76. Witlaczil, "Einiges über Naturschutz in den Alpen."

77. "Der neue Alpennaturschutzpark im Pinzgau"; Draxler, "Der neue Alpennaturschutzpark in den Hohen Tauern." Draxler's article contained some inaccuracies. At the time of publication, negotiations over the lease were still ongoing. See Guttenberg's letter, MDÖAV 21 (1913): 312. Years later the property became incorporated in the much larger Hohe Tauern National Park, which was established in the 1980s.

78. A. Steinitzer, "Über Höhenwege," 281.

79. HAA OeAV ZV/1/1, Verhandlungsschrift der 44. (1913) Hauptversammlung, 40–42.

80. Jugoviz, "Über Natur- und Heimatschutz," 127. See also Giannoni, "Bergbahnen und Alpiner Naturschutz," 107; Halbfass, "Naturschutz in den Alpenländern."

81. Emmer, "Beiträge zur Geschichte," 321.

CHAPTER FOUR

1. F. Weber, Alpenkrieg, 51–52.

2. The nomenclature in the literature can be confusing. Sometimes South Tyrol is used to refer to the entire region. Often times Italians refer to the area only as the Trentino. Today, South Tyrol is the autonomous Province of Bolzano–Alto Adige, or simply Alto Adige, in northern Italy, where the majority of the population speak German. Trentino is the autonomous province directly south of Bolzano and is dominated by Italian speakers. Together, the two are known as the Trentino–Alto Adige region. Both were part of the Tyrol Crownland until 1919. For more on ethnicity in Tyrol, see Cole and Wolf, Hidden Frontier. I thank Wilko Graf von Hardenberg for his illuminating discussion on these matters.

3. Baedeker, Eastern Alps, xiv; Deutsche Alpenzeitung II (October 1913–March 1914): 17.

4. Krebs, Das österreichisch-italienische Grenzgebiet, 1.

5. "An unsere Mitglieder!"

6. "Unseren Kämpfern!" 230; see also Renker, "Bergsteiger im Kriege," 55; A. Steinitzer, "Alpinisum, der Deutsche und Österreichische Alpenverein und der Krieg," 102; and Barth, "Bergfahrten und Wanderungen," 146. See also Pfannl, "Der Alpinismus und der Krieg."

7. Pircher, Militär, Verwaltung und Politik, 45. See also Schindler, Isonzo.

8. Marinelli, "Regions of Mixed Populations in Northern Italy"; Freshfield, "Southern Frontiers of Austria." Both cited in Minghi, "Boundary Studies and National Prejudices."

9. Penck, Die österreichische Alpengrenze, 6–7, 75.

10. "Alpines," Deutsche Alpenzeitung (1913): 43; "Der Streit um das Bremer Haus an der Bocca di Brenta," 137–38; HAA OeAV, Hauptausschuss Sitzung, 29 May 1914.

11. Why Italy Must Have Her Boundary on the Oriental Border of the Julian Alps, 3–7.

12. HAA OeAV ZV/6/101, Münchner Neueste Nachrichten, 5 March 1915.

13. Ibid., letter for Hauptausschuss, 2 April 1915.

14. Ibid., letter from Innsbruck to the Hauptausschuss, 18 March 1915.

15. SBA E27 13233, Akten des Grenzdetachement Graubünden, 23 January 1915. For a good synopsis of the Schlieffen Plan, see Chickering, Imperial Germany and the Great War, 20–23.

16. Steinitzer, "Alpinismus," 99–100.

17. Ibid., 102–3.

18. See Czánt, Militärgebirgsdienst in Winter; and Menger, "Alpenverein und Weltkrieg," 171.

19. SBA E72 1000/721 13555, Sitzung des schweizerischen Bundesrats, 24 April 1915; memorandum to the General, 7 March 1915; memorandum from Armeestab, 7 March 1917, "Massnahmen an der Südgrenze anlässlich des Kriegseintritts Italiens im Mai 1915."

20. Köll, Der Krieg auf den südlichen Ortler-Bergen, 5; Cassar, Forgotten Front, 2. Different authors give significantly different numbers. In his semi-autobiographical book on the war in the Alps, actor and movie director Luis Trenker wrote that Italy sent two armies, twelve infantry divisions, and 180 battalions with just as many batteries against the South Tyrol line. Trenker, Kampf in den Bergen, 85. For the most recent literature on the war in the Alps, see Thompson, White War; Root, Battles in the Alps; and Armiero, "Nationalizing the Mountains."

21. Schindler, Isonzo, xii. See also Czánt, Alpinismus, 182–84.

22. HAA OeAV Bearbeiten/83/2, Gipfelbücher: Kreigsnotizen; Kabisch, Helden in Fels und Eis, 26–27. See also Mittermaier, Der Schrecken des Krieges; and Hartungen, "Die Tiroler und Vorarlberger Standschützen."

23. Langes, Die Front in Fels und Eis, 10.

24. Schalek, Tirol in Waffen, 55.

25. Reich, Unser deutsches Alpenkorps in Tirol, 14; BHA KA Alpenkorps 441, "Kriegserfahrungen: Wochenberichte und Erfahrungen im Gebirgskrieg 1915–1918," 19 June 1915.

26. ÖSA KA Austrian High Command KPQ 26, memo, 21 February 1917.

27. Böhm, "Mobililierung in Tirol."

28. See Eisterer and Steininger, Tirol und der Erste Weltkrieg; Ompteda, Bergkrieg, 199; and Schmidkunz, Der Kampf über den Gletschern, 10.

29. Renker, Als Bergsteiger gegen Italien, 11; Schalek, Tirol in Waffen, 17–18.

30. HAA OeAV ZV/1/1, Hauptversammlung Protokolle, 8 November 1914.

31. "Zwei Jahre Kriegsfürsorge des D. u. Ö. Alpenvereins."

32. Arnold, "Vorträge über den österreich-italienischen Kriegsschauplatz."

33. Menger, "Alpenverein und Weltkrieg," 186.

34. "Sektionsberichte," MDÖAV 5/6 (1915): 57.

35. Handl, "Von der Marmolata-Front II," 161.

36. BHA KA Alpenkorps 441, "Kriegserfahrungen: Wochenberichte und Erfahrungen im Gebirgskrieg 1915–1918."

37. ÖSA AVA, Nachlass Pichl, carton 56, "Aus meinem Lebenslauf," undated.

38. Renker, Als Bergsteiger gegen Italien, 80.

39. Czánt, Alpinismus, 14.

40. Reich, Dolomiten Wacht, 9.

41. Ompteda, Bergkrieg, 15.

42. Das Plöckengebiet im Weltkrieg, 74. For more on German armies on the eastern front, see Liulevicius, War Land on the Eastern Front; and Stone, Eastern Front.

43. HAA OeAV, Bearbeiten/83/2, Gipfelbücher: Marmolata.

44. Renker, "Der Krieg in den Bergen," 230.

45. SBA E72 17862, "Feldbefestigung im Graubünden 1914–1917."
46. "Die Kriegsereignisse in unseren Alpen," MDÖAV 9/10(1916): 77.
47. Schmidkunz, *Der Kampf über den Gletschern*, 15; Gatti, "Das Marmolata-Gipfelbuch."
48. BHA KA Alpenkorps 445, Italienische Armee.
49. Ibid. 441, "Kriegserfahrungen: Wochenberichte und Erfahrungen im Gebirgskrieg 1915–1918."
50. A. Steinitzer, *Der Alpinismus in Bildern*, 363.
51. Renker, *Als Bergsteiger gegen Italien*, 9.
52. SBA E27 13950, letter to Third Armeekorps, 30 July 1915, Kontrolle der Urlaubgänger Fremder Heer, 1915–1919.
53. BHA KA Alpenkorps 445, Italienische Armee.
54. SBA E27 13551, Süd-Südostgrenze, 12 July 1915; see also SBA E27 13233, Akten des Grenzdetachement Graubünden.
55. Ibid., letter from Kommando Sixth Division to Kommando des Third Armeekorps, 20 September 1915.
56. SBA E27 13551, Süd-Südostgrenze, letter to Sixth Division, 5 September 1916, and letter from Batallion Command, 11 October 1916.
57. BHA KA Alpenkorps 445, Italienische Armee.
58. SBA E27 13232, Grenzdetachement Engadin.
59. Ibid. 13233, Grenzdetachement Graubunden Monatsbericht pro Juli 1917, 31 July 1917; Grenzdetachement Graubunden Operativ-Bericht, Akten des Grenzdetachement Graubünden, 28 February 1918.
60. SBA E27 13190, Armeestab, 15 March 1916, Kontrolle des Grenzverkehrs mit Italien 1914–1919. See also SAG XI 20, b1, WWI intern.
61. Renker, "Bergtage im Felde," 180.
62. Rungen, *Brennende Südfront*, 135.
63. Schalek, *Tirol in Waffen*, 82.
64. Renker, *Als Bergsteiger gegen Italien*, 10.
65. BHA KA Alpenkorps 1283, Befehle des K. u. K. Landesverteidigungskommandanten in Tirol.
66. See Müller, *An Der Kampffront in Südtirol*, 29–30; Schmidkunz, *Der Kampf über den Gletschern*, 69; and Kabisch, *Helden in Fels und Eis*, 34.
67. Clausewitz, *The Essential Clausewitz*, 34.
68. Schalek, *Tirol in Waffen*, 110; Röck, *Die Festung im Gletscher*, 77; F. Weber, *Alpenkrieg*, 174; Schemfil, *Die Pasubio-Kämpfe*, 282.
69. Deye, "Kriegsbilder aus den Hochalpen," 162.
70. Schmidkunz, *Der Kampf über den Gletschern*, 11.
71. Jugoviz, "Über Natur- und Heimatschutz," 127.
72. BHA KA Alpenkorps 1335, Einsatz in Tirol: Akt Reuter—Barackenbau; BHA KA Alpenkorps 148, Deutsch-Österreichische Lagenkarten der Subrayone IV und V vom 8. Juni mit 2. Oktober 1915; Müller, "Von den Wundern der Südfront," 150–51.
73. Schmidkunz, "Von den Schutzhütten," 62.
74. HAA OeAV, Hauptausschuss, 19 September 1915.
75. Czánt, *Alpinismus, Massenwintersport und Weltkrieg*, 224.

76. Trenker, Berge in Flammen, 5. For recent German scholarship on the memory of the war in the Alps, see Kuprian and Überegger, Der Erste Weltkrieg im Alpenraum; Mazohl-Wallnig, Kuprian, and Barth-Scalmani, Ein Krieg, zwei Schützengräben; and Wachtler, First World War in the Alps.

77. Ompteda, Bergkrieg, 175, 196–97.

78. ÖSA KA AdTK, 1931 Detusche Grp. and Kps, 28 August 1915; Zöhnle, "Der Krieg und der Alpinismus"; Schmidkunz, "Von den Schutzhütten," 62.

79. BHA KA Alpenkorps 445, Italienische Armee.

80. Renker, Als Bergsteiger gegen Italien, 84.

81. Rungen, Brennende Südfront, 329.

82. BHA KA Alpenkorps 438, Vorbereitungen für den Winter; F. Weber, Alpenkrieg, 265.

83. Renker, Als Bergsteiger gegen Italien, 24.

84. Schmidkunz, Der Kampf über den Gletschern, 228.

85. F. Weber, Alpenkrieg, 97.

86. Handl, "Von der Marmolata-Front II," 149; Krug, Alpenkrieg, 46.

87. Schmidkunz, Der Kampf über den Gletschern, 66. Schmidkunz revised the popular expression "Der Berg ruf" (the mountain calls) to "Der Berg brüllt."

88. Hess, "Die Kriegsereignisse in unserem Alpen," 45.

89. Benesch, "Kriegssommertage im Hochköniggebiet," 122.

90. Renker quoted in Kabisch, Helden in Fels und Eis, 76–77.

91. F. Weber, Alpenkrieg, 266–67; Schmidkunz, Der Kampf über den Gletschern, 250. Weber wrote that close to ten thousand soldiers died that day. Schmidkunz's date of Thursday, 13 December 1916, contradicts Weber. They are both wrong. The destructive avalanches occurred on either Thursday the fourteenth or Friday the fifteenth in December 1916.

92. Langes, Die Front in Fels und Eis, 32.

93. Ginzkey, Die Front in Tirol, 50–51. The italics are the author's. Krug, Alpenkrieg, 79; Schmidkunz, Der Kampf über den Gletschern, 66; Handl, "Von der Marmolata-Front II," 149.

94. Skofizh and Tursky, "Schneeschuhfahrten in den Hohen Tauern," 216.

95. Cassar, Forgotten Front, 209.

96. Cornwall, Undermining of Austria-Hungary, 406–7. See also Healy, Vienna and the Fall of the Habsburg Empire.

97. Ginzkey, Die Front in Tirol, 112. See also Wiltschegg, Österreich—der "Zweite Deutsche Staat?," 137.

98. Renker, "Bergtage im Felde," 185.

99. Zöhnle, "Der Krieg und der Alpinismus"; see also Rothberg, "Auf Kriegsspuren im Ortlergebiet."

100. HAA DAV, Hans Lukas, Nach 14 Jahren an der Alpenfront (Graz: Steiermärkischen Landesdruckerei, 1932).

101. Ompteda, Bergkrieg, 228.

CHAPTER FIVE

1. Menger, "Alpenverein und Weltkrieg," 168.

2. ÖSA AdR, BKA-I SL ZGK Zentralgrenzkommission files.

3. "Eingabe an das deutschösterreichische Staatsamt des Äussern."
4. Boltelini, "Die Deutschen und die Ladiner in Südtirol."
5. "Alpenvereinsfundgebung für Deutsch-Südtirol."
6. HAA OeAV ZV/6/103, Südtirolfrage 1919.
7. "Aus dem Vereinsleben," *Mitteilungen der Sektion Berlin* 173 (1919): 3–4.
8. HAA OeAV ZV/6/102, Schutzhütten 1918/19.
9. See ibid. ZV/6/103, Südtirolfrage 1919; ZV/6/106, Schutzhütten 1922; ZV/6/107, Schutzhütten 1923–1925.
10. Ibid. ZV/6/113, Grenzverkehr Österreich-Italien.
11. Ibid. ZV/6/103, Schutzhütten 1921.
12. Ibid. ZV/6/106, Schutzhütten 1922.
13. Ibid. ZV/6/107, Schutzhütten 1923–1925, "Südtirols Not under der Herrschaft Italiens," undated; Bater, "Der Faschismus und Südtirol." For the *Auslandsdeutschtums* remark, see HAA OeAV ZV/6/109, Südtirol Aktion 1.
14. HAA OeAV ZV/6/108, Südtirolfrage 1926.
15. Ibid. ZV/6/110, Südtirol Aktion; ZV/6/119, Vortragreise Hans Kiene.
16. Ibid., ZV/6/107, Schutzhütten 1923–1925; ZV/6/301, Politik: Nationales.
17. Ibid., ZV/6/129, Südtirol: Reiseführer und Denkschriften.
18. HAA DAV, Dresden carton, "Ski Heil!" *Mitteilungen der Jugendgruppe* 3 (1923): 5–6; "In Nordböhmen," *Mitteilungen der Jugendgruppe* 3 (1924): 6; "Das Land meiner Wünsche, Südtirol und die Berge meiner Sehnsucht, die Dolomiten!," *Mitteilungen der Jugendgruppe* 10 (1927): 4.
19. Ibid., "Zehn Gebote für den Südlandsfahrer," *Mitteilungen der Jugendgruppe* 2 (1925): 5.
20. HAA OeAV ZV/6/109, Südtirol Aktion 1.
21. "Das 'Alpenvereins-Edelweiss' verboten!"; HAA OeAV ZV/6/109, Südtirol Aktion 1; ZV/6/111, Südtirol Aktion; ZV/6/115, Unterstützung für Südtirol.
22. HAA OeAV ZV/6/129, Südtirol: Reiseführer und Denkschriften.
23. Ibid. ZV/6/114, Touristenabkommen Österreich-Italien.
24. Ibid. ZV/6/107, Schutzhütten 1923–1925.
25. Ibid. ZV/1/1, *Verhandlungsschrift der 58. (1932) Hauptversammlung*, 6; *Verhandlungsschrift der 52. (1926) Hauptversammlung*, 6.
26. "Aus dem Vereinsleben," *Mitteilungen der Sektion Berlin* 173 (1919): 4.
27. Boyer, *Culture and Political Crisis in Vienna*, 438.
28. Gould, "Austrian Attitudes toward Anschluss," 220.
29. Boyer, "Silent War and Bitter Peace," 25; see also Gould, "Austrian Attitudes toward Anschluss," 229–30; and Macartney, *Social Revolution in Austria*, 258.
30. Gould, "Austrian Attitudes toward Anschluss," 226.
31. Kleinwaechter, *Self-Determination for Austria*, 12–14, 25.
32. HAA OeAV ZV/1/1, *Verhandlungsschrift der 46. (1920) Hauptversammlung*, 45–46.
33. Gould, "Austrian Attitudes toward Anschluss," 228.
34. HAA OeAV ZV/1/1, *Verhandlungsschrift der 46. (1920) Hauptversammlung*, 47.
35. Ibid., *Verhandlungsschrift der 50. (1924) Hauptversammlung*, 8.
36. Hofmann, "Unsere Pflichten," 278.
37. "Von der 50. Jahreshauptversammlung des D. u. Ö. A.-V.," 254.

38. HAA DAV, Dresden carton, "Unseren Alpenfahrern ins Tagebuch," *Mitteilungen der Jugendgruppe—Dresden* 3 (1925): 7.

39. Rudovsky, *Festschrift*, 184.

40. Paschinger, "Die Einbussen der deutschen alpinen Vereine."

41. "Zur Überfremdung im S.A.C."; Gurtner, "Überfremdung." See also G. Müller, "Der S.A.C. und die Überfremdung," 85–86; H. Müller, "Der S.A.C. und die Überfremdung," 102.

42. Brüggemeier, Cioc, and Zeller, *How Green Were the Nazis?*, 6; Allen, *Culture and Sport of Skiing*, 245.

43. HAA OeAV ZV/6/202, Donauland: Protest.

44. Pauley, "Political Antisemitism in Interwar Vienna," 153.

45. ÖSA AVA, *Nachlass Pichl*, carton 61, Eduard Pichl, "Verehrliche Schwestersektion! Denkschrift der österreichischen Sektionen des Deutschen und Österreichischen Alpenvereins in der Angelegenheit Donauland," 1 August 1921.

46. Berkley, *Vienna and Its Jews*, 153.

47. Healy, *Vienna and the Fall of the Habsburg Empire*, 312; Pauley, "Political Antisemitism in Interwar Vienna," 154.

48. HAA OeAV ZV/6/205, Donauland: Beschwerden; see also Rudovsky, *Festschrift*, 153.

49. "In eigener Sache," *Nachrichten der Sektion Donauland* 1 (1921); HAA OeAV ZV/6/201, Donauland: Gründung und Kämpfe.

50. HAA DAV, Berlin carton, letter to the *Hauptleitung des Deutsch-Österreichischen Alpenvereins*, 17 September 1921.

51. Ruduvsky, *Festschrift*, 149.

52. HAA OeAV ZV/6/201, Donauland: Gründung und Kämpfe.

53. ÖSA AVA, *Nachlass Pichl*, carton 56, "Aus meinem Lebenslauf"; Pichl, "Alpenverein und reines Deutschtum," 55; HAA OeAV ZV/6/202, Donauland: Protest. For an excellent overview of these developments, see Achrainer, "'So, jetzt sind wir ganz unter uns!'"

54. Kaufmann, "Die Gründung des Deutschen Alpenvereins Berlin," 159; "50. Hauptversammlung des Deutschen und Österreichischen Alpenvereins zu Rosenheim," 111; HAA OeAV ZV/1/1, *Verhandlungsschrift der 49. (1923) Hauptversammlung*, 18.

55. HAA OeAV ZV/1/1, HA Protokolle 24. Sitzung May 1921.

56. Ibid. ZV/6/203, Donauland: Mißtrauensvotum; ÖSA AVA, *Nachlass Pichl*, carton 61, Pichl, "Der Deutschvölkische Bund im Deutschen und Österreichischen Alpenverein," 1922. He had wanted to call the group the Arierbund (Aryan League) but decided that the name Deutschvölkische Bund sounded more appealing.

57. HAA OeAV ZV/1/1, HA Protokolle 26. Sitzung April 1922; ibid., *Verhandlungsschrift der 48. (1922) Hauptversammlung*, 26–27; ÖSA AVA, *Nachlass Pichl*, carton 61, Pichl, "An unsere Stammesbrüder im Deutschen Reich!," 1922; HAA OeAV ZV/1/1, *Verhandlungsschrift der 49. (1923) Hauptversammlung*, 11.

58. HAA OeAV ZV/6/206, Donauland: Anträge; Kees, "Alpenvereine und Politik," 170.

59. HAA OeAV ZV/1/1, *Verhandlungsschrift der 50. (1924) Hauptversammlung*, 35.

60. Ibid., HA Protokolle 28th Sitzung May 1923.

61. Ibid., *Verhandlungsschrift der 49. (1923) Hauptversammlung*, 19.

62. Ibid. ZV/6/223, Donauland: Arbeitsgebiet; ZV/6/212, Donauland: Verschiedenes.

63. Ibid. ZV/6/204, Donauland: Antrage an die HV.

64. Ibid. ZV/6/205, Donauland: Beschwerden; ZV/1/1, HA Protokolle 30 Sitzung April 1924.

65. ÖSA AVA, *Nachlass Pichl*, carton 61, Pichl, "Verehrliche Schwestersektion!"

66. "Verhandlungsschrrift der außerordentlichen Hauptversammlung des D. u. Oe. Alpenvereins zu München am 14. Dezember 1924," 14.

67. HAA OeAV ZV/6/213, Donauland: Ausschluss.

68. "Die Judenfrage in Alpenland."

69. HAA OeAV ZV/6/231, AV Donauland: Verschiedenes, "Die Muskete" (1922).

70. "Das Hüttenplakat," 116; "Zur Frage des Arierparagraphen," 113.

71. ÖSA AVA, *Nachlass Pichl*, carton 61, Pichl, "An unsere Stammesbrüder im Deutschen Reich!"

72. "Das Hakenkreuz," *Der Naturfreund* (1923): 63–64; "Die Politik in den Bergen," 105, 131, 159–60; "Augsburg," *Nachrichten der Sektion Donauland* 2 (1921); ÖSA AVA, *Nachlass Pichl*, carton 61, Pichl, "Verehrliche Schwestersektion!"

73. HAA OeAV ZV/1/1, *Verhandlungsschrift der 50. (1924) Hauptversammlung*, 27–29, 37–38. The Rosenheimer Compromise passed by a vote of 1,660 to 70. The Klagenfurt resolution passed by 1,547 votes to 110.

74. Ibid. ZV/6/210, Donauland: Zustimmung der HA; ZV/6/213, Donauland: Ausschluss; ZV/6/209, Donauland: ao Hauptversammlung; ZV/1/1, HA Protokolle 32 Sitzung December 1924.

75. Ibid. ZV/6/209, Donauland: ao Hauptversammlung.

76. Ibid.

77. See *Neues Wiener Tagblatt, Neue Leipziger Zeitung, Berliner Börsen Zeitung, Freiburger Tagespost, Wiener Stimmen,* and *Wiener Allgemeinen Zeitung,* among others in HAA OeAV ZV/6/209, Donauland: ao Hauptversammlung and ZV/6/211, Donauland: Zeitungsausschnitte; see also ÖSA AVA, *Nachlass Pichl*, carton 61, Sonderabdruck aus *Der Bergsteiger* 49 (1924).

78. "Die Außerordentliche Hauptversammlung des Deutschen und Österreichischen Alpenvereins," 12.

79. "Verhandlungsschrrift der außerordentlichen Hauptversammlung des D. u. Oe. Alpenvereins zu München am 14. Dezember 1924," 18; "Die Außerordentliche Hauptversammlung des Deutschen und Österreichischen Alpenvereins," 9.

80. "Zur außerordentlichen Alpenverein-Hauptversammlung," *Der Bergsteiger* 50 (1924): 405; "Die außerordentlichen Alpenverein-Hauptversammlung," 415.

81. For various newspaper clippings, see HAA OeAV ZV/6/213, Donauland: Ausschluss; see also "Alpenverein = Filiale des Stahlhelms," *Welt am Montag*, 26 February 1925.

82. "Verschiedenes," MDÖAV 17 (1924): 230; Martin, "Alpinismus und Antisemitimus."

83. HAA DAV, Munich carton, letter to the executive committee from Dr. W. Levinger and Dr. Julius Heilbronner, 19 December 1924; response from the executive committee, 5 January 1925.

84. "Die Krisis in der Sektion Berlin," *Mitteilungen der Sektion Berlin*, December 1924; see also "Sektion Berlin für Donauland," *Vossische Zeitung*, 28 November 1924.

85. HAA DAV, Berlin carton, Rudolf Hauptner, "Und die Herren Mitgleider der Sektion Berlin!," 14 February 1925.

86. Ibid., letter from Berlin to the executive committee, 14 March 1925.
87. "Gründung eines unpolitischen Alpenvereins in Berlin."
88. "Vereinsnachrichten des Deutschen Alpenvereins Berlin," *Nachrichten der Sektion Donauland* 58 (1926): 59; ibid., 65 (1926): 164.
89. "Der Kampf im Alpenverein"; HAA DAV, Berlin carton, "Sonderdruck aus den Mitteilungen der Sektion Berlin," March 1931; *Münchner Neueste Nachrichten*, 31 January 1926, nr. 30, p. 26; "Vereinsnachrichten des Deutschen Alpenvereins Berlin," *Nachrichten der Sektion Donauland* 80 (1928): 29.
90. "Gründung des Süddeutsche Alpenvereins München"; see also HAA OeAV ZV/6/231, AV Donauland: Verschiedenes.
91. HAA OeAV ZV/6/303, Politik: Arierparagraph; see "Rassenreine Berge?," *Frankfurter Zeitung*, 25 February 1931.
92. ÖSA AVA, Unterricht KB Dt.-Öst., Alpenverein 2; HAA OeAV ZV/1/1, *Verhandlungsschrift der 56. (1930) Hauptversammlung*, 19, 25–27.
93. See Ansmann, *Jugend und Natur*; HAA OeAV, Fremde Vereine; and Pils, *Berg Frei!*, 76.
94. HAA OeAV ZV/6/304, Politik: Alpenverein als politischen Verein, "Bürgerliche einheitsfront in der Touristik," *Arbeiter-Zeitung*, 17 December 1930; *Der Bergwanderer* (1923): 4–5.
95. *Nachrichten der Sektion Austria* (1923): 7.
96. Hartwig, "Die politische Auswirkung unserer unpolitischen Tätigkeit."
97. *Nachrichten der Sektion Austria* (1923): 7.
98. "Der Ingrimm unserer Feinde," 159.
99. HAA OeAV ZV/6/213, Donauland: Ausschluss, "Hüttenbegünstigungen für Sektion Donauland," *Arbeiter-Zeitung*, 24 December 1924.
100. HAA OeAV, FV, undated newspaper article, 1923.
101. "Ist der Alpenverein ein politischer Verein?"; *Neues Wiener Tagblatt*, 19 January 1929; "Politik und Bergsteigen"; HAA OeAV ZV/6/304, Politik: Alpenverein als politischen Verein, Finanz Ausschuss Sitzung, 4 January 1929.
102. "Die Politik in den Bergen."
103. HAA OeAV, History Varia, "Bermerkungen Preußens zu der Reichsratsvorlage über die Rechtsfähigkeit des Deutschen und Österreichischen Alpenvereins," Reichsministers des Innern I B 7031/23.6, 26 June 1930; see also Zebhauser, *Alpinismus im Hitlerstaat*, 88–89.
104. Menger, "Alpenverein und Weltkrieg," 194.
105. HAA OeAV ZV/1/1, *Verhandlungsschrift der 50. (1924) Hauptversammlung*, 37; ÖSA AVA, Nachlass Pichl, carton 61, Pichl, "An unsere Stammesbrüder im Deutschen Reich!"
106. "Recht – Notrecht – Faustrecht," 153. Members of Donauland called the Alpine Association a *Wehralpenverein*. See also "Rosenheim," 128.
107. HAA OeAV ZV/1/1, *Verhandlungsschrift der 48. (1922) Hauptversammlung*, 3.

CHAPTER SIX

1. For a detailed analysis of the many themes in these films, see Rentschler, "Mountains and Modernity"; and Rapp, *Höhenrausch*. Numerous mountain films were also produced in Austria and Switzerland.

2. Moriggl, "Zehn Jahre Vereinsgeschichte," 319.

3. HAA OeAV ZV/1/1, *Verhandlungsschrift der 57. (1931) Hauptversammlung*, 6; "Was will Austria?"

4. Brockmann, *Critical History of German Film*, 24–25, 43–47; Kracauer, *From Caligari to Hitler*, 111–12. For more on Weimar films, see Isenberg, *Weimar Cinema*; and Kaes, *Shell Shock Cinema*.

5. *Völkischer Beobachter* 297 (1929); *Die Rote Fahne* 235 (1929), cited in both Rapp, *Höhenrausch*, 128, and Rentschler, "Mountains and Modernity," 143.

6. See Rentschler, "Mountains and Modernity," 146, 150

7. Lörner, "Bemerkungen zum Film 'Die weiße Hölle vom Piz Palü.'"

8. Ibid., 389.

9. "Nützen oder schaden alpine Filme uns Bergsteigern?" 5; see also Barth, "Die Berge im Film," 71.

10. Kracauer, *From Caligari to Hitler*, 110.

11. Bonney explained that "the Föhn is a wind from the south, hot, stifling, and dry, supposed to come from the deserts of North Africa. The air becomes close and stifling; the sky thickens to a muddy, murky condition; animals become restless and mankind is conscious of a sense of lassitude and disquiet"; see his book *Building of the Alps*, 247.

12. Rentschler, "Mountains and Modernity," 150n. *The White Hell of Piz Palü* was second behind Fritz Lang's *The Girl in the Moon*. Rapp, *Höhenrausch*, 10–11, 128.

13. Rapp, *Höhenrausch*, 119. Fanck also based some of his stories loosely on Gustav Renker's Alpine adventure stories.

14. Lörner, "Bemerkungen zum Film 'Die weiße Hölle vom Piz Palü,'" 388.

15. Gatti, "Zum Film," 344; "Noch einmal 'Der Kampf ums Matterhorn,'" 1025.

16. "Einmal ein guter Bergfilm."

17. "Alpinismus und Film."

18. Trenker, *Berge in Flammen*, 267; see also Mosse, *Fallen Soldiers*, 117.

19. Lammer, "Massenbesuch der Berge"; HAA OeAV ZV/1/1, *Verhandlungsschrift der 49. (1923) Hauptversammlung*, 6; Bergmann, "Hochmut zwischen zwei Welten," 114; Moriggl, "Was ist und was bietet des Gesamtverein?," 18.

20. "Zur Frage der Bergbahnen"; "Der Kampf um die Zugspitzbahn"; "Die Zugspitzbahn."

21. BHA MWi 8592, *Prospekt für die elektrische Zugspitz-Zahnradbahn*, Bayr. Zugspitzbahn 1926; see also MWi 8585, Zugspitzbahn.

22. BHA MWi 8580, Zugspitzbahn, letter from Dr. Friedrich Mader, Direktor der Tiroler Hauptbank, to Kommerzienrat Josef Böhn, Direktor der bayr. Filialen der Deutsche Bank in Munich, 2 August 1924; MWi 8554, Alpenbahnen: Obersalzberg, letter to bayr. Staatsministerium für Handel, Industrie, Gewerbe, 22 July 1926; MWi 8551, Bergbahnen, newspaper article, undated; Klette, "Die bayerische Zugspitzbahn."

23. "Von der Zugspitzbahn."

24. BHA MWi 8591, Zugspitzbahn, *Die Bayerische Zugspitzbahn Denkschrift*, 1927.

25. HAA OeAV ZV/1/1, *Verhandlungsschrift der 53. (1927) Hauptversammlung*, 55–56.

26. "Bergbahnen"; "Gegen Bergbahnen—gegen die Zugspitzbahn"; BHA MWi 8546, Alpenbahnen: verschiedenes, letter from LfN to bayr. Staatsministerium für Handel, Industrie, Gewerbe, 25 September 1925.

27. "Gegen Bergbahnen—gegen die Zugspitzbahn," 107.

28. BHA MWi 8546, Alpenbahnen: verschiedenes, letter from Bayer. Staatsministerium für Handel, Industrie u. Gewerbe to the Staatministeriums für Finanzen, 29 November 1926.

29. Ibid. 8592, Bayr. Zugspitzbahn, Niederschrift, 9 June 1927; ibid. 8593, Bayr. Zugspitzbahn, letter from Staatsministerium des Innern to SM für Handel, Industrie u. Gewerbe, 1 March 1928.

30. Ibid. 8594, Bergbahnen: Bayr. Zugspitzbahn, letter from Berzirksamt Garmisch to Staatsministerium des Aussern, 15 September 1929; "Arbeiterdrama auf der Zugspitze," *Frankfurter Zeitung*, no. 17, 7 January 1929.

31. "Zur Frage der Bergbahnen," 131; BHA MWi 8584, Bergbahnen: Bayr. Zugspitzbahn, letter from the Alpine Association to the Bayerische Zugspitzbahn, 7 November 1929; BHA MWi 9594, Bergbahnen: Bayr. Zugspitzbahn, Report of the Bavarian State Committee for the Care of Nature and the Bavarian State Association for Homeland Protection regarding the Bavarian Zugspitzbahn Project.

32. Schraud, "Der Bergsteiger, das Werkzeug und die Maschine"; Kaiser, "Der Alpinismus und unsere Zeit"; "Zur Frage der Bergbahnen," 129, 132.

33. BHA MWi 8591, Zugspitzbahn, Technische Erläuterungsberichte zum ausführlichen Projekt der Bayer. Zugspitzbahn, undated; ibid. 8597, Bayr. Zugspitzbahn, Bayerische Zugspitzbahn AG Aufsichtsratssitzung am 22 April 1932; ibid. 8595, Bergbahnen: Bayr. Zugspitzbahn. For more on the train's blueprints, see ibid. 8591, Bayr. Zugspitzbahn Konsortium, and ibid. 8602, Berg-Zugspitz Pläne.

34. HAA OeAV, HA Protokoll, 44. Sitzung 1930. For a detailed history of the highway, see Rigele, *Die Grossglockner-Hochalpenstrasse*.

35. SLA, Zeitungen Bände, Großglockner-Hochalpen Strasse, *Kärntner Tageblatt* (1931–32), 18; *Tageblatt*, 17 March 1925; *Tageblatt*, 15 April 1930. See also SLA, Nachlass Wallack II, *Das Projeckt der Grossglockner-Hochalpenstrasse* (1925).

36. *Allgemeine Automobil-Zeitung* 1.8 (1900): 4.

37. Freeston, *Alps for the Motorist*, 3, 8–9; Massinger, "Alpenstrasse," 104–6.

38. Freeston, *Alps for the Motorist*, 5–6, 10, 68–69.

39. Ibid., 3, 10, 17; "Auto oder nicht"; Graber, "Mit dem Auto auf Schweizer Hochstrassen"; SLA, Nachlass Wallack II, Emil Meletzki, "Der Bedeutung der Glocknerstrasse für den Bergsteiger."

40. SLA, Nachlass Wallack I, Großglockner Hochalpenstrasse A. G. Baubericht, 30 November 1933.

41. Ibid., II, Franz Rehrl, "Fünf Jahre Arbeit zum Wohl unseres Vaterlandes Österreich"; ibid., Rehrl-Akten, carton 114.

42. Wallack, *Die Grossglockner-Hochalpenstrasse*, 204.

43. SLA, Nachlass Wallack I, Großglockner Hochalpenstrasse A. G. Baubericht, 30 September 1934.

44. Wallack, *Die Grossglockner-Hochalpenstrasse*, 211.

45. "Aufruf zum Gamsgruben-Projekt der Großglockner-Hochalpenstraße"; "Der Alpenverein mit Naturschutz betraut!" 166; "Denkschrift gegen die beabsichtigte Zerstörung des Naturschutzgebietes," 114–15.

46. Tisch, "Freie Berge," 111; HAA OeAV ZV/1/1, *Verhandlungsschrift der 62. (1936) Hauptversammlung*, 31; *Verhandlungsschrift der 63. (1937) Hauptversammlung*, 26.

47. HAA OeAV ZV/1/1, Verhandlungsschrift der 45. (1919) Hauptversammlung, 22; Verhandlungsschrift der 51. (1925) Hauptversammlung, 48; "Die Ziele der Bergsteigergruppe im DÖAV," 1; Flaig, "Der Zerfall des Alpinismus," 53.

48. Flaig, "Der Zerfall des Alpinismus," 55.

49. See remarks made by Rehlen during the 1923 annual meeting, HAA OeAV ZV/1/1, Verhandlungsschrift der 49. (1923) Hauptversammlung, 4; Lammer, "Massenbesuch der Berge," 1; Bing, "Der Alpinismus als Zeitbild," 73.

50. See remarks made by Müller during the 1924 annual meeting, HAA OeAV ZV/1/1, Verhandlungsschrift der 50. (1924) Hauptversammlung, 6.

51. Ibid., Verhandlungsschrift der 51. (1925) Hauptversammlung, 46.

52. Ibid., Verhandlungsschrift der 49. (1923) Hauptversammlung, "Richtlinien für Alpenvereinshütten und Wege," 32–34.

53. Kees, "Zu den neuen Richtlinien für Alpenvereinhütte und Wege," 52.

54. HAA OeAV ZV/1/1, Verhandlungsschrift der 52. (1926) Hauptversammlung, 45; Verhandlungsschrift der 54. (1928) Hauptversammlung, 34; Verhandlungsschrift der 55. (1929) Hauptversammlung, 53–54.

55. Oertel, "Ewigkeitswerte im Alpinismus," 157.

56. For more on gender and the Alpine Association, see Günther, Alpine Quergänge. For an American perspective, see Schrepfer, Nature's Altars.

57. A. Steinitzer, "Alpinismus, der Deutsche und Österreichische Alpenverein und der Krieg," 104.

58. "Die Mitgliedschaft der Frauen," Mitteilungen der Sektion Berlin 177 (1919): 8–9; ibid., 178 (1919): 6; "Aus dem Vereinsleben," Mitteilungen der Sektion Berlin 176 (1919): 4–5.

59. HAA OeAV ZV/1/1, Verhandlungsschrift der 50. (1924) Hauptversammlung, 5; Große, "Sollen wir deutschen Bergsteigerinnen," 79–80.

60. HAA OeAV ZV/1/1, Verhandlungsschrift der 50. (1924) Hauptversammlung, 10.

61. Große, "Die Frau in den Bergen," 77.

62. Bing, "Der Alpinismus als Zeitbild," 73.

63. HAA OeAV ZV/1/1, Verhandlungsschrift der 51. (1925) Hauptversammlung, 54.

64. Rudovsky, "Bergwandern und Bergsteigen," 4.

65. Praxmarer, "Vom Sinn des Bergsteigertums," 10; Bing, "Der Alpinismus als Zeitbild," 74.

66. J. Mayr, "Vorwart," 4; Deutsch, Aus Österreichs Revolution, 25.

67. Moriggl, "Zehn Jahre Vereinsgeschichte," 334.

68. HAA OeAV ZV/1/1, Verhandlungsschrift der 58. (1932) Hauptversammlung, 56.

CHAPTER SEVEN

1. HAA OeAV ZV/1/1, Verhandlungsschrift der 63. (1937) Hauptversammlung, 14.
2. Gustav Müller, "Die Berge und ihre Bedeutung," 1–2.
3. Kaiser, "Zur Psychologie des Alpinismus," 285–86.
4. Gustav Müller, "Die Berge und ihre Bedeutung," 2.
5. Ibid., 3–6.
6. Ibid., 8.
7. Czánt, Alpinismus, Massenwintersport und Weltkrieg, 11, 63–64, 98.

8. Czánt, Alpinismus, 305; Czánt, Alpinismus, Massenwintersport und Weltkrieg, 62–63; HAA OeAV ZV/1/1, Verhandlungsschrift der 50. (1924) Hauptversammlung, 9.

9. See Amstädter, Alpinismus.

10. HAA DAV, Freiburg carton, "Rundschreiben des Führers der reichsdeutschen Sektionen des D. u. Ö. Alpenvereins," Nachrichten der Sektion Freiburg 3 (1933): 2; "Hauptversammlung des des D. u. Ö. Alpenvereins," Nachrichten der Sektion Freiburg 4 (1933): 3.

11. Lekan, Imagining the Nation in Nature; Williams, Turning to Nature in Germany.

12. HAA DAV, Freiburg carton, Nachrichten der Sektion Freiburg 3 (1933): 1–2.

13. Mitteilungen des Fachamtes Bergsteigen im Deutschen Reichsbund für Leibesübungen, cited in Zebhauser, Alpinismus im Hitlerstaat, 159, 194–95.

14. Blackbourn, Conquest of Nature, 251–63; more generally, see Liulevicius, German Myth of the East.

15. Isserman and Weaver, Fallen Giants, 171–82; Höbusch, "Narrating Nanga Parbat."

16. HAA OeAV ZV/1/1, Verhandlungsschrift der 59. (1933) Hauptversammlung, 46.

17. ÖSA AVA, Nachlass Pichl, carton 61, "An die reichsdeutschen Sektionen des Deutschen und Österreichischen Alpenvereins," undated.

18. HAA DAV, Freiburg carton, letter for Sektion Freiburg to the Executive Committee, 26 June 1933.

19. "Sektionsnachrichten," MDÖAV 3 (1933): 65; HAA DAV, Hamburg carton, Jahresbericht 1933 Sektion Hamburg.

20. Münchner Zeitung, 20 July 1933.

21. HAA DAV, Munich carton, letter from Munich to the administrative board, 27 December 1933.

22. HAA OeAV ZV/1/1, Verhandlungsschrift der 59. (1933) Hauptversammlung, Jahresbericht 1932/33, 51.

23. HAA DAV, Rhineland-Cologne carton.

24. "Vereinsangelegenheiten," MDAV 4 (1938): 93.

25. HAA DAV, Berlin carton, letter from Sektion Berlin to the administrative board, 16 February 1934.

26. Schulenburg, "Deutscher und Österreichischer Alpenverein," 5.

27. HAA DAV, Freiburg carton, letter to Gauführer Witzemann from Sektion Freiburg, 28 October 1934.

28. Zebhauser, Alpinismus im Hitlerstaat, 138–40.

29. Schulenburg, "Deutscher und Österreichischer Alpenverein," 5.

30. ÖSA AVA, Nachlass Pichl, carton 61, "Reichssport," 15 July 1934, no. 193.

31. Ibid., "An die reichsdeutschen Sektion des DÖAV," Sektion Rostock; Schulenburg, "Deutscher und Österreichischer Alpenverein," 4.

32. HAA OeAV ZV/1/1, Verhandlungsschrift der 62. (1936) Hauptversammlung, 25. See also Verhandlungsschrift der 61. (1935) Hauptversammlung, Jahresbericht 1934/35, 65.

33. "Die Politik in den Bergen," 160.

34. ÖSA AVA, Nachlass Pichl, carton 61, letter dated 5 June 1934.

35. Ibid., Die Innsbrucker Zeitung, 23 June 1934, no. 141.

36. Ibid., "Der Österreicher," series 21, May 1934; HAA DAV, Munich carton, Die Heimatschützer, 11 November 1933.

37. "Der Alpenverein organisiert Gebirgstruppen für Hitler!," *Tiroler Anzeiger*, 23 October 1933.

38. "Der Alpenverein organisiert Gebirgstruppen für Hitler!," *Volks-Zeitung*, 24 October 1933.

39. HAA DAV, Munich carton, letter dated 24 October 1933.

40. Ibid., letter dated 27 October 1933.

41. Ibid., press release issued by administrative board, 1933.

42. HAA OeAV ZV/6/305, "Gründung eines österreichischen Alpenvereins?," *Innsbrucker Nachrichten*, 18 May 1934; "Bergfreunde sollen getrennt werden," *Stuttgarter Tagblatt*, 23 May 1934.

43. ÖSA AVA, *Nachlass Pichl*, carton 61, "Die 1000-Mark-Grenzsperre und der Deutsche und Oesterreichische Alpenverein," *Reichspost*, 4 June 1933, no. 154.

44. Carsten, *First Austrian Republic*, 230; Jelavich, *Modern Austria*, 212.

45. "Unsere Berge!," *Wiener Stadt Stimmen*, 23 September 1937.

46. BHA MF 83984, Staatsministeriums der Finanzen: Landesforstverwaltung Stützpunkte Kühroint und Blaueis.

47. BHA MK 51195, Naturschutz in den Alpen, letter from Landesschuss für Naturpflege to Staatsministerium des Innern, 21 November 1924; letter from Staatsministerium des Innern to Reichswehrkreiskommando VII, 13 November 1924; letter from Staatsminister des Innern to Wehrkommando, 25 July 1925.

48. Tisch, "Freie Berge," 111.

49. For more on this, see Lekan, *Imagining the Nation in Nature*, 176; and Closmann, "Legalizing a Volksgemeinschaft," 18–42. See also Lekan, "Regionalism and the Politics of Landscape Preservation"; and Radkau and Uekötter, *Naturschutz und Nationalsozialismus*.

50. BHA MF 83986, Staatsministeriums der Finanzen: Landesforstverwaltung Überlassung von Staatswaldgrund für militärische Zwecke in Oberbayern.

51. "Wer soll und will der Verein Naturschutzpark"; see also Williams, "Protecting Nature between Democracy and Dictatorship," 183–206.

52. Tisch, "Freie Berge," 111.

53. BHA MK 51195.

54. Roßmanith, "Der Naturschutzpark in den Hohen Tauern Salzburgs," 152.

55. BHA StK 6950, Die Deutsche Alpenstrasse, 1935; "Das Wunderwert Deutsche Alpenstrasse."

56. "Das Wunderwert Deutsche Alpenstrasse."

57. Schwink, "Deutsche Alpenstraße"; Siemer, "Die Alpenstraße als Mittel zur Hebung des Fremdenverkehrs"; BHA MWi 2747, Alpenstraße, letter to Staatsminister Ess from Dr. Wigger in Partenkirchen, 16 March 1934.

58. BHA Landtag 14613, Bau der Alpenstrasse u. Förderung des Fremdenverkehrs im Alpengebiet, Antrag, 19 January 1933.

59. BHA MWi 2747, Alpenstraße, letter from Landesausschuss für Naturpflege to Staatsministerium des Innern, 8 August 1933.

60. *Völkischer Beobachter*, 19 June 1935.

61. Mair, "Die Kunst des Alpenfahrens"; Rockenfeller, "Autowandern in den Bergen"; "Mit dem Auto zurück zur Natur." See also Koshar, "Organic Machines," 111–39; and Zeller, *Straße, Bahn, Panorama*.

62. BHA MWi 2747, Knorz, "Die Bayerische Alpenstrasse," 1.

63. *Münchner Neueste Nachrichten*, 15 December 1934; ibid., 8 January 1935; *Völkischer Beobachter*, 9 July 1938.

64. BHA MK 51195, Naturschutz in den Alpen: Georg Wenig, "Berchtesgaden als Fremdenort und die Bergbahnen im Staatl. Naturschutzpark der Berchtesgadener Alpen" (1927).

65. Ibid., letter from Bayr. Landesausschuss für Naturpflege and Bayr. Landesverein für Heimatschutz to Staatsministerium für Wirtschaft, 4 February 1935; BHA MWi 8561, Bergbahnen: Watzmannbahn, letter from Bayr. Landesausschuss für Naturpflege and Bayr. Landesverein für Heimatschutz to Staatsministerium für Wirtschaft, 22 November 1935; *Völkischer Beobachter*, 4 June 1935.

66. Jelavich, *Modern Austria*, 221.

67. *Münchner Neueste Nachrichten*, 14/15 April 1938.

68. HAA OeAV ZV/4/20, DAV 1938 bis 1945, Auszug aus dem Schreiben, 19 May 1938.

69. *Völkischer Beobachter*, 20 April 1938; HAA OeAV ZV/4/20, DAV 1938 bis 1945, letter from DAV to Reichssportamt, 29 April 1938.

70. Tisch, "Freie Berge."

71. HAA OeAV ZV/1/1, *Verhandlungsschrift der 64. (1938) Hauptversammlung*, 14.

72. "Das Feld der deutschen Bergsteiger," 17; see also press clippings in HAA OeAV ZV/4/15, DAV 1938 bis 1945: Presse 1938; HAA OeAV ZV/1/1, *Verhandlungsschrift der 64. (1938) Hauptversammlung*, 92–93.

73. "Im Deutschen Alpenverein," *Münchner Neueste Nachrichten*, 18 March 1938, 17; HAA OeAV ZV/1/1, *Verhandlungsschrift der 64. (1938) Hauptversammlung*, 84; "Ein Volk—Ein Reich—Ein Führer!" *Monats-Blätter der Sektion Saarbrücken* 15, no. 4 (1938): 38; *Nachrichten der Sektion Dresden* 4 (1938): title page.

74. HAA OeAV ZV/1/1, *Verhandlungsschrift der 64. (1938) Hauptversammlung*, 4, 49–50.

75. Schulenburg, "Deutscher und Österreichischer Alpenverein," 5.

76. HAA OeAV ZV/4/23, DAV 1938 bis 1945: Sudetendeutschen Alpenverein, letter from Sektion Reichenberg to the DAV, 26 October 1938. For more on liquidations, see ZV/4/10, DAV 1938 bis 1945: Julius Gallian; ZV/4/8, DAV 1938 bis 1945: Anschluss von Vereinen; and ZV/6/232, AV Donauland: Liquidiesung.

77. Ibid. ZV/4/11, DAV 1938 bis 1945: Anschluss alpiner Vereine in Graz, letter from Ludwig Obersteiner to the DAV, 21 September 1938.

78. Ibid. ZV/4/25, DAV 1948 bis 1945: Neue Satzung; ZV/4/29, DAV 1938 bis 1945: Entwürfe Zweigvereine u. Gruppen—Mustersatzunge, letter from Hermann Cuhorst, 12 July 1938.

79. HAA OeAV ZV 4.20 DAV 1938 bis 1945, letter to DAV, 2 May 1938; HAA DAV *Verhandlungsschrift der 64. (1938) Hauptversammlung*, 81.

80. Seyß-Inquart, "Der Auftrag," 1–2; see also his remarks in HAA OeAV ZV/1/1, *Verhandlungsschrift der 64. (1938) Hauptversammlung*, 56. Sild, "Der Neue Weg"; HAA DAV, Munich carton, "70. Jahresbericht, Vereinsjahr 1939," *Zweig München*.

81. Bing, "Der Alpinismus als Zeitbild," 74.

82. Dobiasch, "Zeitfragen, Zeitaufgaben des Alpinismus von Heute," 6.

CONCLUSION

1. Ullman, White Tower, 72. Ullman's books helped popularize mountaineering among his American readers in the late 1940s. See Isserman and Weaver, Fallen Giants, 232–34, 340–41.
2. Ullman, White Tower, 59, 86, 231.
3. Ibid., 407.
4. HAA OeAV ZV/1/1, Verhandlungsschrift der 50. (1924) Hauptversammlung, 24.
5. Others like Karl Prusik contended that this search for death and danger revealed the German will to self-annihilation. See Dromowicz, "Triebfedern und Verantwortlichkeit im Alpinismus," 134.
6. Ullman, White Tower, 400.
7. "Krieg und Alpenverein"; HAA OeAV ZV/4/121, DAV 1938–1945 Wehrmacht: Benützung der Schutzhütten durch Wehrmachtsangehörige.
8. Meyer, "Zur Entwicklung des Bergsteigers," 260.
9. Ullman, White Tower, 62.
10. Ittlinger, Ewige Berge, 6.
11. Renker, "Bergtage im Felde," 185.
12. Weitzenböck, "Zur ferneren Zukunft des Alpinismus."
13. Turner, "Significance of the Frontier in American History," 199–227.
14. Dobiasch, "Zeitfragen," 4.
15. Blackbourn, Conquest of Nature, 18.
16. Jelinek, Die Kinder der Toten; Jelinek, In den Alpen; Jelinek, Totenauberg.
17. "Eduard Pichl," Mitteilungen des Österreichischen Alpenvereins, 10 (1955): 41.
18. DAV statutes, 2009.
19. "Tourists' Heavy Alpine Toll," BBC News, 30 August 2001.
20. See the Nationalpark Hohe Tauern website, http://www.hohetauern.at, and the Nationalpark Berchtesgaden website, http://www.nationalpark-berchtesgaden.de/index.htm.
21. "Alpinism: Then and Now," BBC News, 26 August 2001.
22. Bradly, "In Austria, a Chalet for the Night."
23. Johannes Merck, interviewed by author, 25 October 2001, Munich, Historical Alpine Archive, German Alpine Association, Munich.

Bibliography

ARCHIVAL COLLECTIONS

Berlin, Germany
    Bundesarchiv Deutsches Reich–Lichterfelde
    Preussisches Geheimes Staatsarchiv
Bern, Switzerland
    Schweizerisches Bundesarchiv
Bolzano, Italy
    Historisches Alpenarchiv Alpenverein Südtirol
    Südtiroler Landesarchiv
Chur, Switzerland
    Staatsarchiv Graubünden
Innsbruck, Austria
    Historisches Alpenarchiv Österreichischer Alpenverein
    Tiroler Landesarchiv
Klagenfurt, Austria
    Kärtner Landesarchiv
Ludwigsburg, Germany
    Staatsarchiv Ludwigsburg
Munich, Germany
    Bayerisches Hauptstaatsarchiv
    Historisches Alpenarchiv Deutscher Alpenverein
    München Stadtsarchiv
Salzburg, Austria
    Salzburg Landesarchiv
Stuttgart, Germany
    Hauptstaatsarchiv Stuttgart
Vienna, Austria
    Österreichisches Staatsarchiv

PERIODICALS

Allgemeine Automobil-Zeitung
Die Alpen
Der Alpenfreund
Alpenländische Monatshefte
Alpina
Bergland: Illustrierte alpenländische Monatschrift
Der Bergsteiger
Der Bergwanderer
Deutsche Alpenzeitung

Frankfurter Zeitung
Der Gebirgsfreund
Innsbrucker Tagesblatt
Jahresbericht des Deutschen und
 Österreichischen Alpenvereins
Jahresbericht Sektion Berlin
Jahresbericht Sektion München
Mitteilungen der Jugendgruppe-Dresden
Mitteilungen der Sektion Berlin
Mitteilungen des Deutschen Alpenvereins
 (MDAV)
Mitteilungen des Deutschen und
 Österreichischen Alpenvereins (MDÖAV)
Mitteilungen des Österreichischen Alpenvereins
Monats-Blätter der Sektion Saarbrücken

Münchner Neueste Nachrichten
Münchner Zeitung
Nachrichten der Sektion Austria
Nachrichten der Sektion Donauland
Nachrichten der Sektion Dresden
Nachrichten der Sektion Freiburg
Der Naturfreund
Neue Tiroler Stimmen
Österreichische Alpenpost
Österreichische Alpenzeitung
Österreichische Touristenzeitung
Vossische Zeitung
Zeitschrift des Deutschen Alpenvereins (ZDAV)
Zeitschrift des Deutschen und Österreichischen
 Alpenvereins (ZDÖAV)

PUBLISHED PRIMARY SOURCES

Aichinger, J. "Die Julischen Alpen." ZDÖAV 40 (1909): 291–318.
———. "Die Stellung des Alpenvereins zum alpinen Schilauf." MDÖAV 3 and 4 (1914): 35–37.
Alden, Edmund K. "Mountains and History." Annual Report of the American Historical Association (1894): 519–30.
"Das 'Alpenvereins-Edelweiss' verboten!" Der Bergsteiger 7 (1929): 1142.
"Der Alpenverein mit Naturschutz betraut!" MDAV 7 (1938): 166–67.
"Der Alpenverein organisiert Gebirgstruppen für Hitler!" Tiroler Anzeiger, 23 October 1933.
"Der Alpenverein organisiert Gebirgstruppen für Hitler!" Volks-Zeitung, 24 October 1933.
"Alpenvereinsfundgebung für Deutsch-Südtirol." MDÖAV 7 and 8 (1919): 48–50.
"Alpenverein und Heimatschutz." MDÖAV 10 (1936): 255–56.
"Alpenverein und reines Deutschtum." Der Bergsteiger 1 (1923): 55.
"Das Alpine Museum in München." MDÖAV 2 (1912): 15–18.
Alpines Handbuch. 2 vols. Leipzig: F. A. Brockhaus, 1931.
"Alpines Jugendwandern in Innsbruck." MDÖAV 1 and 2 (1914): 20.
"Alpinismus und Film." Deutsche Alpenzeitung 22 (1927): 427–29.
"Alpenverein = Filiale des Stahlhelms." Welt am Montag, 26 February 1925.
"An unsere Mitglieder!" MDÖAV 15 (1914): 201.
"Anlagen zur Vereinsgeschichte." ZDÖAV 50 (1919): 199–204.
Ansmann, Alb. Jugend und Natur. Vienna: Verlag des Touristen-Vereins die Naturfreunde, 1923.
Arnold, Carl. "Die Eisenbahnverbindung zwischen Norddeutschland und den Alpen." MDÖAV 4 (1885): 45–46.
Arnold, Karl. "Vorträge über den österreich-italienischen Kriegsschauplatz." MDÖAV 13 and 14 (1916): 116–17.

"Aufruf zum Gamsgruben-Projekt der Großglockner-Hochalpenstraße." MDÖAV 5 (1936): 113.
"Aus der Tätigkeit unserer Jugendgruppe." MDÖAV 11 (1936): 279–84.
"Ausschuss zur Förderung der Schituristik im D.u.Ö. Alpenverein." MDÖAV 8 (1914): 117–19.
"Die Außerordentlichen Alpenverein-Hauptversammlung." Der Bergsteiger 2 (1924): 414–15.
"Die Außerordentliche Hauptversammlung des Deutschen und Österreichischen Alpenvereins." Nachrichten der Sektion Donauland 42 (1925): 7–16.
"Automobilfahrten in Tirol." MDÖAV 16 (1900): 193.
"Automobilverkehr." MDÖAV 15 (1908): 194.
"Auto oder nicht." Deutsche Alpenzeitung 21 (1926): 488.
Baedeker, Karl. The Eastern Alps: Handbook for Travelers. Leipzig: K. Baedeker, 1911.
Barth, Hans. "Die Berge im Film." MDÖAV 7 (1923): 70–71.
———. "Bergfahrten und Wanderungen im Adamello-Bereich." ZDÖAV 48 (1917): 125–48.
Bater, Hans. "Der Fascismus und Südtirol." Alpenländische Monatshefte (1924): 243–46.
Baumgärten, J., and Karl Sandtner. "Schneeschuhfahrten in den Niederen Tauern." ZDÖAV 42 (1911): 203–25.
Benesch, Fritz. "Kriegssommertage im Hochköniggebiet." ZDÖAV 48 (1917): 102–24.
"Bergbahnen." Deutsche Alpenzeitung 20 (1925): 450–51.
"Bergbahnen und Alpiner Naturschutz." MDÖAV 7 (1913): 107.
"Bergfreunde sollen getrennt werden." Stuttgarter Tagblatt, 23 May 1934.
Bergmann, Georg Franz. "Hochmut zwischen zwei Welten." Nachrichten der Sektion Donauland 74 (1927): 114–15.
"Bergsteigen als inneres Erlebnis." Deutsche Alpenzeitung 33 (1938): 197–200.
"Bericht über die zeite General-Versammlung des deutschen Alpenvereins." ZDAV 2. II Abtheilung (1870/1871): 569–84.
Berlepsch, H. The Alps: Of Sketches of Life and Nature in the Mountains. London: Longman, Green, Longman, and Roberts, 1861.
Bing, Walter. "Der Alpinismus als Zeitbild." Deutsche Alpenzeitung 26 (1931): 70–75.
———. "Der Mut im Bergkrieg: Ein Beitrag zur Psychologie des Krieges an der Südfront." Nachrichten der Sektion Donauland 107 (1930): 58–60.
Blab, Georg. Alpines Handbuch. Leipzig: F. A. Brockhaus, 1931.
Blaubeuren, P. Fischer von. "Der Alpensport vom moralischen und religiösen Gesichtspunkte aus beurteilt." Deutsch-evangelische Blätter 23 (1898): 573–85.
Böhm, Alois Robert. "Mobililierung in Tirol." Deutsche Alpenzeitung 14.2 (October 1914–March 1915): 327.
Boltelini, Hans von. "Die Deutschen und die Ladiner in Südtirol." MDÖAV 3 and 4 (1919): 17–20.
Bonney, T. G. The Building of the Alps. London: T. Fischer Unwin, 1912.
Bücherei-Verzeichnis der Sektion Breslau des Deutschen und Österreichischen Alpenvereins. Breslau: Brehmer and Minuth, 1930.

Bücherverzeichnis der Zentral-Bibliothek des Deutschen und Oesterreichischen Alpenvereins in München. Munich: Lindauer, 1902.

Bühler, Hermann. *Die Alpenvereinsbücherei*. Munich: F. Bruckmann, 1934.

Büttner, Rudolf. "Alpines Jugendwandern mit politischen Hindernissen." *Deutsche Alpenzeitung* 33 (1938): 201–2.

Burnet, Thomas. *The Sacred Theory of the Earth*. London: R. Norton, 1691.

Clar, E. "Naturschutz im Glocknergebiet." *MDÖAV* 6 (1936): 141–42.

Clausewitz, Carl von. *The Essential Clausewitz: Selections from On War*. Edited by Joseph Greene. Mineola, NY: Dover Publications, 2003.

Collet, Léon. *The Structure of the Alps*. London: Edward Arnold and Co., 1927.

Conrad, Walter. *Die kaufmännische Bedeutung der österreichischen Alpenwasserkräfte*. Vienna: Lehmann and Wentzel, 1910.

Coolidge, W. A. B. *Alpine Studies*. New York: Longmans, Green, 1912.

———. *The Alps in Nature and History*. London: Methuen, 1908.

Cysarz, Herbert. *Berge über Uns*. Munich: Langen Müller, 1935.

Czánt, Hermann. *Alpinismus: Massentouristik, Massenskilauf, Wintersport, Militäralpinistik*. Berlin: Verlag für Kulturpolitik, 1926.

———. *Alpinismus, Massenwintersport und Weltkrieg*. Munich: Bergverlag Rudolf Rother, 1900.

———. *Militärgebirgsdienst in Winter: Beherrschung des hohen Schnees*. Vienna: C. W. Stern, 1907.

Davis, J. Sanger. *Dolomite Strongholds: The Last Untrodden Alpine Peaks*. London: George Bell and Sons, 1896.

"Denkschrift gegen die beabsichtigte Zerstörung des Naturschutzgebietes der Pasterze in der Bauperiode 1936 der Großglockner-Hochalpenstraße." *MDÖAV* 5 (1936): 114–15.

Deutsch, Julius. *Aus Österreichs Revolution: Militärpolitisch Erinnerungen*. Vienna: Verlag der Wiener Volksbuchhandlung, 1930.

"Der Deutsche Alpenverein erstattet drahtlich Meldung." *MDAV* 4 (1938): 82.

"Deutscher Alpenverein." *MDAV* 4 (1938): 81.

Deye, Adolf. "Kriegsbilder aus den Hochalpen." *ZDÖAV* 48 (1917): 162–76.

Dinkelacker, Paul. "Zeitenwende." *MDÖAV* 1 (1935): 1–2.

Dobiasch, Sepp. "KdF und die Berge." *Deutsche Alpenzeitung* 33 (1938): 129–32.

———. "Zeitfragen, Zeitaufgaben des Alpinismus von Heute." *MDÖAV* 1 (1933): 4–7.

Draxler, J. "Der neue Alpennaturschutzpark in den Hohen Tauern." *MDÖAV* 20 (1913): 292–95.

Dreyer, Aloys. *Der Alpinismus und der Deutsch-Österreichische Alpenverein*. Berlin: Marquardt, 1909.

———. *Bücherverzeichnis der Zentral-Bibliothek des Deutschen und Österreichischen Alpenvereins*. Munich: In Kommission bei der J. Lindauerschen Buchhandlung, 1906.

Dromowicz, Wilhelm. "Triebfedern und Verantwortlichkeit im Alpinismus." *Der Bergsteiger* 2 (1924): 134–35.

Durig, A. "Turistisch-Medizinische Studien." *ZDÖAV* 43 (1912): 25–51.

Eckschlager, Karl. "Aus den Karwanken." *ZDÖAV* 40 (1909): 271–90.

"Eingabe an das deutschösterreichische Staatsamt des Äussern." MDÖAV 3 and 4 (1919): 15–16.
"Einmal ein guter Bergfilm." Nachrichten der Sektion Donauland 101 (1929): 129–30.
Emmer, Johannes. "Beiträge zur Geschichte des Deutschen und Österreichischen Alpenvereins in den Jahren 1895–1909." ZDÖAV 40 (1909): 319–68.
———. "Geschichte des Deutschen und Österreichischen Alpenvereins." ZDÖAV 25 (1894): 177–393.
Enzensperger, Ernst. *Alpenfahrten der Jugend: Im Allgäu.* Munich: J. Lindauersche Buchhandlung, 1912.
———. *Alpenfahrten der Jugend: Im Wetterstein.* Munich: J. Lindauersche Buchhandlung, 1911.
———. "Alpenfahrten der Jugend: Nach einem Vortrag in der Alpenvereinssektion München." MDÖAV 2 and 3 (1913): 21–23, 39–40.
———. *Die Alpine Jugendwanderbewegung und der Deutsche und Oesterreichische Alpenverein.* Munich: Pössenbacher, 1931.
———. *Wie soll unsere Jugend die Alpen Bereisen: Technische Anleitungen und wissenschaftliche Anregungen.* Munich: J. J. Meyer, 1925.
Erk, F. "Ein meteorologische Obervatorium auf der Zugspitze." MDÖAV 10 and 11 (1898): 121–23, 133–36.
"Die Eröffnung des Alpinen Museums in München." MDÖAV 24 (1911): 292–93.
"Ertüchtigung unserer Jugend." *Der Bergsteiger* 5 (1927): 521–22.
Falger, F. "Zur Frage des Jugendwanderns in den Alpen." MDÖAV 12 (1927): 131–32.
"Die Feier des fünfzigjährigen Bestandes der Sektion Austria des D. u. Ö. Alpenvereins." MDÖAV 24 (1912): 307–9.
"Die feierliche Eröffnung der 'Freiburger Hütte' auf der Alpe Formarin." *Feldkircher Zeitung*, 18 August 1894.
"Das Feld der deutschen Bergsteiger." *Münchner Neueste Nachrichten*, 18 March 1938.
Filek, Egid. "Ethische Werte des Bergsteigens." *Der Bergsteiger* 4 (1926): 157–58.
Finkelstein, H. "Jugendherbergen und Volksgesundheit." Nachrichten der Sektion Donauland 61 (1926): 103–4.
Fischer, Hans. "Jugend und Wandern." *Deutsche Alpenzeitung* 24 (1929): 11–15.
Flaig, Walther. "Der Zerfall des Alpinismus und die Wege zum Wiederaufstieg." MDÖAV 6 (1923): 53–56.
Flex, Walter. *Der Wanderer zwischen beiden Welten.* Munich: C. H. Beck, 1938.
"Die XL. (XXXVI.) Hauptversammlung des D.u.Ö. Alpenvereins zu Wien." MDÖAV 18 (1909): 217–26.
"Die XLII. (XXXVIII.) Hauptversammlung des D.u.Ö. Alpenvereins zu Coblenz." MDÖAV 15 (1911): 165–69.
"Die 43. (39.) Hauptversammlung des D.u.Ö. Alpenvereins zu Graz." MDÖAV 18 (1912): 223–27.
"Die 44. (40.) Hauptversammlung des D.u.Ö. Alpenvereins zu Regensburg." MDÖAV 14 (1913): 199–203.
"Die 50. Hauptversammlung des Deutschen und Österreichischen Alpenvereins zu Rosenheim." Nachrichten der Sektion Donauland 36 (1924): 109–12.
Freeston, Charles L. *The Alps for the Motorist.* London: Cassell and Company, 1926.

Freshfield, Douglas W. "The Southern Frontiers of Austria." *Geographic Journal* 46 (1915): 413–35.
Frey, Georg. "Was bedeuten uns die Berge Heute? Ein Beitrag zum Naturschutz in den Alpen." *MDÖAV* 11 (1937): 283–85.
Freytag-Loringhoven, Frhr. v. *Gebirgskämpfe*. Berlin: Ernst Siegfried Mittler und Sohn, 1912.
Frödin, John. *Zentraleuropas Alpwirtschaft*. Oslo: H. Ascheoug and Co., 1940.
"Fünf Jahre Austria-Jungmannschaft." *Nachrichten der Sektion Austria* 4 (1927): 7–8.
Gallian, Otto. *Monte Asolone: Kampf um einen Berg*. Leipzig: Koehler and Amelang, 1935.
Gatti, Norbert. "Das Marmolata-Gipfelbuch." *MDÖAV* 21 and 22 (1917): 140–45.
———. "Zum Film: 'Der Berg des Schicksals.'" *Der Bergsteiger* 2 (1924): 343–45.
"Gegen Bergbahnen—gegen die Zugspitzbahn." *MDÖAV* 9 (1925): 101–8.
German Mountain Warfare. Washington, D.C.: Military Intelligence Division, War Department, 1944.
Geschichte der Alpenvereinssection München. Munich: Alpenvereinssection München, 1900.
Giannoni, E. "Bergbahnen und alpiner Naturschutz." *MDÖAV* 7 (1913): 107.
Ginzkey, Franz Karl. *Die Front in Tirol*. Berlin: S. Fischer Verlag, 1916.
Graber, Alfred. "Mit dem Auto auf Schweizer Hochstrassen." *Deutsche Alpenzeitung* 24 (1929): 115–23.
Große, Margarete. "Die Frau in den Bergen." *MDÖAV* 7 (1924): 76–78.
———. "Sollen wir deutschen Bergsteigerinnen einen eigenen Verein oder wenigstens eine eigene Alpenvereinssektion anstreben?" *MDÖAV* 7 (1925): 79–80.
"Gründung des Süddeutsche Alpenvereins München." *Nachrichten der Sektion Donauland* 73 (1927): 103.
"Gründung eines unpolitischen Alpenvereins in Berlin." *Nachrichten der Sektion Donauland* 46 (1925): 83.
Gurtner, Othmar. "Überfremdung, Entwürdigung und andere Laster." *Alpina* 27 (1919): 128–29.
Guttenberg, A. von. "Naturschutz und Naturschutzgebiete." *ZDÖAV* 44 (1913): 54–61.
"Das Hakenkreuz." *Der Naturfreund* 27 (1923): 63–64.
"Das Hakenkreuz auf dem Großglockner." *MDAV* 4 (1938): 93.
Halbfass, W. "Naturschutz in den Alpenländern." *MDÖAV* 16 (1914): 220–21.
Hamza, Ernst. "Folkloristische Studien aus dem niederösterreichischen Wechselgebiete." *ZDÖAV* 44 (1913): 81–127.
Handl, Leo. "Von der Marmolata-Front." *ZDÖAV* 47 (1916): 212–18.
———. "Von der Marmolata-Front II." *ZDÖAV* 48 (1917): 149–61.
Handl, Leo, and Hermann Wopfner. "Die Samnaungruppe." *ZDÖAV* 45 (1914): 264–87.
Hartwich, Emma. "Die Frau in den Bergen." *MDÖAV* 3 (1924): 26–28.
Hartwig, Th. "Die politische Auswirkung unserer unpolitischen Tätigkeit." *Der Naturfreund* 33 (1929): 35.
Haserrodt, H. "Die Grenzen des Bergsports." *MDÖAV* 23 (1910): 282–83.

Hemingway, Ernest. *A Farewell to Arms*. New York: Scribner, 1929.
Hess, Heinrich. "Die Kriegsereignisse in unserem Alpen." MDÖAV 1 through 16 (1917): 8–9, 32–33, 45–47, 75–77, 108–10.
Hoek, Henry. "Skifahrt auf das Blindenhorn." ZDÖAV 35 (1904): 166–71.
———. "Zehn Winter mit Schiern in den Bergen." ZDÖAV 40 (1909): 51–96.
Hofmann, Egon. "Unsere Pflichten." *Der Bergsteiger* 2 (1924): 277–78.
Hofmann, Karl. "Bericht über das erste Vereinsjahr des Deutschen Alpenvereins." ZDAV 1. II Abtheilung (1869/1870): 25–29.
"Das Hüttenplakat." *Nachrichten der Sektion Donauland* 26 (1923): 116–17.
Hyde, Walter Woodburn. "Alps in History." *Proceedings of the American Philosophical Society* 75 (1935): 431–42.
"Hygiene des Sports." MDÖAV 22 (1910): 267–69.
"Der Ingrimm unserer Feinde." *Der Naturfreund* 28 (1924): 159.
"Ist der Alpenverein ein politischer Verein?" *Tiroler Sonntags-Blatt*, 20 January 1929.
Ittlinger, Josef. *Ewige Berge: Erlebnisse und Gesichte*. Munich: Rösl and Cie., 1924.
"Jahresbericht des Österreichischen Alpen-Vereins." ZDÖAV 3 (1872): 94–96.
"Jahresbericht 1873." ZDAV 4. II Abtheilung (1873): 32–39.
"Die Judenfrage in Alpenland." *Der Naturfreund* 26 (1922): 88.
"Jugendwandern der Sektion Donauland." *Nachrichten der Sektion Donauland* 6 (1922): 34.
Jugoviz, Rudolf. "Über Natur- und Heimatschutz." MDÖAV 9 (1914): 126–28.
Kabisch, Ernst. *Helden in Fels und Eis: Bergkrieg in Tirol und Kärnten*. Stuttgart: Loewes Verlag Ferdinand Carl, 1941.
Kaiser, Hans. "Der Alpinismus und unsere Zeit." *Deutsche Alpenzeitung* 21 (1926): 1–5.
———. "Zur Psychologie des Alpinismus." MDÖAV 22 (1924): 285–88.
Kalender des Deutschen und Österreichischen Alpenvereins. Munich: Deutscher und Österreichischer Alpenverein, 1903.
"Der Kampf im Alpenverein: Die Klage der Ausgeschlossenen gegen die Sektion Berlin." *Berliner Tageblatt—Abend-Ausgabe*, 31 May 1927.
"Der Kampf um die Zugspitzbahn." MDÖAV 7 (1924): 79.
Kaufmann, Hans. "Die Gründung des Deutschen Alpenvereins Berlin und seine Ziele." *Nachrichten der Sektion Donauland* 52 (1925): 159–61.
Kees, Hermann. "Alpenverein und Politik." *Der Bergsteiger* 1 (1923): 170–72.
———. "Aufgaben der Zeit." *Der Bergsteiger* 2 (1924): 397–98.
———. "Im Reiche des Ortlers." MDÖAV 6 (1909): 75–77.
———. "Zu den neuen Richtlinien für Alpenvereinhütte und Wege." *Der Bergsteiger* 1 (1923): 52–53.
Kiene, Hans Paul. "Die Puezgruppe." ZDÖAV 43 (1912): 247–72.
———. "Die Puezgruppe." ZDÖAV 45 (1914): 315–43.
Klebelsberg, Raimond von. "Die Eiszeitliche Vergletscherung der Alpen: Unter besonderer Berücksichtigung der Ostalpen." ZDÖAV 44 (1913): 26–39.
Kleinhans, F. "Grenzen und Ziele Alpiner Erschließungsarbeit." MDÖAV 12 (1926): 136–38.
Kleinhans, W. "Jugend und Alpinismus." MDÖAV 14 (1924): 174.
Kleinwaechter, Friedrich F. G. *Self-Determination for Austria*. London: George Allen and Unwin, 1929.

Klette, Werner. "Die bayerische Zugspitzbahn." *Deutsche Alpenzeitung* 24 (1929): 381.

Kordon, Frido. "Bergwandern in der Ankogelgruppe: Der neuen Alpenvereinskarte zum Geleite." ZDÖAV 40 (1909): 238–70.

Krebs, Norbert. *Das österreichisch-italienische Grenzgebiet*. Berlin: Teubner, 1918.

Kreuter, Franz. "Über Eisenbahnen im Gebirge." ZDÖAV 15 (1884): 228–61.

"Krieg und Alpenverein." *Deutsche Alpenzeitung* 34 (1939).

Krug, Franz Joseph. *Alpenkrieg: Felderlebnisse von Österreichs Südwestfront*. Graz: Deutsche Vereins-Druckerei, 1918.

Kugy, Julius. *Alpine Pilgrimage*. London: Murray, 1934.

Kurz, Fritz. "Bergfahrten zwischen Kaiserjoch und Flexenpass." ZDÖAV 44 (1913): 161–81.

Lammer, Eugen Guido. *Bergsteigertypen und Bergsteigerziele*. Vienna: Deutscher und Österreichischer Alpenverein, 1924.

———. "Die Grenzen des Bergsports." MDÖAV 20 (1910): 243–45.

———. "Ist der Sport kulturschädlich? (eine Auseinandersetzung mit H. Steinitzer)." MDÖAV 9 (1910): 111–14.

———. "Massenbesuch der Berge." MDÖAV 1 (1923): 1–3.

Lieberich, H. "Die Jugendbergfahrten in der A.V.S. Hochland 1913." MDÖAV 22 (1913): 319–22.

———. "Neuer Alpinismus." MDÖAV 21 (1913): 305–7.

Lörner, Hermann. "Bermerkungen zum Film 'Die weiße Hölle vom Piz Palü.'" *Deutsche Alpenzeitung* 25 (1930): 388–91.

Löwenbach, Georg. "Ueber Lilienfelder Skitechnik." MDÖAV 1 (1901): 6–7.

Lukas, Hans. *Nach 14 Jahren an der Alpenfront: Eindrücke und Erinnerungen eines ehemaligen Frontsoldaten während einer Reise ins einstige Kriegsgebiet*. Graz: Druck der steiermärkischen Landesdruckerei, 1930.

Lunn, Arnold. *The Alps*. London: Williams and Norgate, 1914.

———. *The Mountains of Youth*. Oxford: Oxford University Press, 1925.

———. *The Swiss and Their Mountains: A Study of the Influence of Mountains on Man*. London: George Allen and Unwin, 1963.

Macartney, C. A. *The Social Revolution in Austria*. New York: Cambridge University Press, 1926.

Madlener, Max. "Einiges über alpinen Skilauf." MDÖAV 23 (1901): 277–80.

Maier, O. P. "Aus Karwendel und Wetterstein: Altmodische Fahrten." ZDÖAV 45 (1914): 159–76.

Mair, Kurt. "Die Kunst des Alpenfahrens." *Deutsche Alpenzeitung* 30 (1935): 201–8.

Mann, Thomas. *Betrachtungen eines Unpolitischen*. Frankfurt: S. Fischer Verlag, 1983.

———. *The Magic Mountain*. New York: A. Knopf, 1995.

Manz, Hugo. *Bewaffnete Alpenheimat: Ein Buch von Ersatzheer im Alpenraum*. Innsbruck: Gauverlag Tirol, 1941.

Marinelli, Olinto. "The Regions of Mixed Populations in Northern Italy." *Geographic Review* 7 (1919): 129–48.

Martin, Alfred von. "Alpinismus and Antisemitismus." *Die Alpen* 1 (1925): 51–52, 140–42.

Massinger, Carl. "Alpenstrasse." *Deutsche Alpenzeitung* 24 (1929): 104–6.
Mayr, Julius. "Vorwart: Ein Halbjahrhundert Alpenverein." ZDÖAV 50 (1919): 1–4.
Mayr, Michael. "Die Entwicklung der nationalen Verhältnisse in Welschtirol." ZDÖAV 48 (1917): 59–83.
Menger, Heinrich. "Alpenverein und Weltkrieg." ZDÖAV 50 (1919): 168–94.
———. "Die turistische Bedeutung der Karwendelbahn." MDÖAV 16 (1912): 197–98.
Menschen im Hochgebirge: Festgabe für Hans Pfann. Munich: Eigenverlag, 1933.
Merkl, Adolf. "Die Staatliche Betreuung der großdeutschen Landschaft." MDAV 5 (1938): 115–16.
Meyer, Oskar Erich. *Tat und Traum: Ein Buch Alpinen Erlebens*. Munich: Bergverlag, 1920.
———. "Zur Entwicklung des Bergsteigers." MDÖAV 18 (1913): 258–60.
———. "Zwischen Sixt und Barberine (Die Berge vom Mont Buet bis zur Tour Salliere)." ZDÖAV 41 (1910): 85–136.
"Mit dem Auto zurück zur Natur." *Deutsche Alpenzeitung* 31 (1936): 432.
Moriggl, Josef. "Was ist und was bietet der Gesamtverein?" MDÖAV 2 (1924): 18–19.
———. "Zehn Jahre Vereinsgeschichte, 1919–1929." ZDÖAV 60 (1929): 301–55.
Müller, G. "Der S.A.C. und die Überfremdung." *Alpina* 27 (1919): 85–86.
Müller, Gustav. "Die Berge und ihre Bedeutung für den Wiederaufbau des Deutschen Volkes." ZDÖAV 53 (1922): 1–9.
Müller, Hans. "Der S.A.C. und die Überfremdung." *Alpina* 27 (1919): 102.
Müller, Karl. *An der Kampffront in Südtirol: Kriegsbriefe eines Neutralen Offiziers*. Leipzig: Velhagen und Klafing, 1916.
———. "Von den Wundern der Südfront," MDÖAV 21 and 22 (1917): 150–56.
"Die Münchner Bergsteiger gegen den Bau von Bergbahnen." *Der Bergsteiger* 3 (1925): 118–19.
"Naturschutz im Glocknergebiet." MDÖAV 1 (1936): 5–6.
"Der neue Alpennaturschutzpark im Pinzgau, Salzburg." *Deutsche Alpenzeitung* 13.2 (October 1913–March 1914): 45.
"Der neue Feind." MDÖAV 11 and 12 (1915): 109.
"Noch einmal 'Der Kampf ums Matterhorn.'" *Der Bergsteiger* 7 (1929): 1025–29.
"Nochmals Höhenwege und andere alpine Entwicklungserscheinungen." MDÖAV 8 (1912): 111–12.
"Nützen oder schaden alpine Filme uns Bergsteigern?" *Der Bergsteiger* 8 (1930): 2–8.
Oertel, Eugen. "Ewigkeitswerte im Alpinismus." MDÖAV 9 (1928): 155–59.
———. "Die Frage der Schutzhütten in Winter auf der Hauptversammlung in Regensburg." MDÖAV 18 (1913): 255–58.
———. "Sport, Alpinismus und Schilauf." MDÖAV 1 (1909): 6–9.
———. "Unsere Schutzhütten im Winter: Eine Erwiderung." MDÖAV 1 and 2 (1914): 6–7.
Ompteda, Georg. *Bergkrieg*. Berlin: Wilhelm Kolk, 1932.
Paschinger, Viktor. "Die Einbussen der deutschen alpinen Vereine durch den Frieden von St. Germain." *Alpenländische Monatshefte* (1924): 764.
Patéra, Lothar. "Die Cavallogruppe." ZDÖAV 42 (1911): 298–328.
Paulcke, W. "Auf Skiern im Hochgebirge." ZDÖAV 33 (1902): 170–86.

Penck, Albrecht. *Die österreichische Alpengrenze*. Stuttgart: J. Engelhorns, 1916.
Pfannl, Heinrich. "Der Alpinismus und der Krieg—dieser eine wahrhaftige Krieg!" *Österreichische Alpenzeitung*, 5 December 1914.
Pichl, Eduard. "Alpenverein und reines Deutschtum." *Der Bergsteiger* 1 (1923): 53–55.
———. "Das Heldische im Bergsteigen." MDÖAV 4 (1934): 77–78.
Plank, Karl. "Zur Zukunft des Alpinismus." MDÖAV 1 (1912): 6–7.
Landeskameradschaftbund Kärnten, ed. *Das Plöckengebiet im Weltkrieg*. Selbstverlage, 1932.
"Die Politik in den Bergen." *Der Naturfreund* 28 (1924): 105–6, 131–32, 159–60.
"Politik und Bergsteigen." *Neuste-Zeitung*, 25 January 1929.
Praxmarer, Konrad. "Vom Sinn des Bergsteigertums: Der Alpinismus—eine Politische Bewegung." MDÖAV 1 (1931): 9–11.
Preuß, Paul. "Der Gosaukamm." ZDÖAV 45 (1914): 219–63.
———. "Neues zum Turenprogramm der Saarbrücker Hütte." MDÖAV 9 (1912): 119–22.
Preußen und der Alpenverein: Ein Wink für die hohe Regierung. Vienna: F. Eipeldauer and Comp., 1876.
"Recht – Notrecht – Faustrecht." *Nachrichten der Sektion Donauland* 39 (1924): 152–53.
Register zu den Vereinsschriften des Deutschen und Österreichischen Alpenvereins. Graz: Deutscher und Österreichischer Alpenverein, 1896.
Reich, Albert. *Dolomiten Wacht*. Munich: Josef Huber, 1917.
———. *Unser deutsches Alpenkorps in Tirol: Ein Erinnerungswerk*. Munich: Joseph Huber, 1917.
Reinthaler, Marie. "Neben und über der Dolomitenstrasse." MDÖAV 14 (1912): 172.
Renker, Gustav. *Als Bergsteiger gegen Italien*. Munich: Verlag Walter Schmidkunz, 1918.
———. "Bergsteiger im Kriege." MDÖAV 9 and 10 (1917): 55–57.
———. "Bergtage im Felde: Tagebuchblätter von Dr. Gustav Renker." ZDÖAV 48 (1917): 177–200.
———. *Heilige Berge*. Erfuhrt: C. Bertelsmann Verlag, 1938.
———. "Der Krieg in den Bergen." ZDÖAV 47 (1916): 219–36.
———. *Schicksal in der Nordwand*. Berlin: Keil Verlag, 1938.
Reuther, O. "Unsere Schutzhütten im Winter: Ein Beitrag zur Benutzungsfrage." MDÖAV 21 (1913): 307–8.
Richter, Eduard. *Die Erschliessung der Ostalpen*. Berlin: Verlag des Deutschen und Oesterreichischen Alpenvereins, in Commission der J. Lindauer Buchhandlung in München, 1893.
Rickmer-Rickmers, W. "Vorläufiger Bericht über die Pamir-Expedition des Deutschen und Österreichischen Alpenvereins." ZDÖAV 45 (1914): 1–51.
Riefenstahl, Leni. *Kampf in Schnee und Eis*. Leipzig: Hesse and Becker Verlag, 1933.
Rieger, Ernst. "Naturschutz und Alpenverein." MDÖAV 4 (1934): 78–80.
Riehl, Wilhelm. *Die bürgerliche Gesellschaft*. Frankfurt: Ullstein, 1976.
———. *Naturgeschichte des Volkes als Grundlages einer deutschen Sozialpolitik*. Edited by David J. Diephouse. Lewiston, N.Y.: Edwin Mellen Press, 1990.
Röck, Christian. *Die Festung im Gletscher: Vom Heldentum im Alpenkrieg*. Berlin: Ullstein, 1935.

Rockenfeller, Theo. "Autowandern in den Bergen." *Deutsche Alpenzeitung* 31 (1936): 218–21.

"Rosenheim." *Nachrichten der Sektion Donauland* 37 (1924): 128–29.

Rosenheim: Sein Alpenvorland und seine Berge. Rosenheim: Bensegger Verlag, 1886.

Roßmanith, Gebhard. "Der Naturschutzpark in den Hohen Tauern Salzburgs." ZDÖAV 68 (1937): 152–56.

Rothberg, E. von. "Auf Kriegsspuren im Ortlergebiet." *Deutsche Alpenzeitung* 23 (1928): 140–44.

Rudovsky, Franz. "Bergwandern und Bergsteigen." In *Alpines Handbook*, vol 2. Leipzig: F. A. Brockhaus, 1931.

———. *Festschrift zum 70 Jährigen Bestand des Zweiges Austria, D.U.Ö.A.V., 1862–1932*. Vienna: Verlag des Zweiges Austria, D.u.Ö.A.V., 1932.

Rungen, Rolf. *Brennende Südfront: Ein Österreichischer Kriegsroman*. Berlin: Paul Aretz Verlag, 1933.

Sandtner, Karl. "Die Fanes- (Heiligenkreuzkofel-) Gruppe." ZDÖAV 44 (1913): 221–43.

Sautter, Guido. "Der künftige 'Nationalpark' der Schweiz, ein Vorbild für die übrigen Alpenländer." MDÖAV 7 (1910): 85–88.

Schalek, Alice. *Am Isonzo: März bis Juli 1916*. Vienna: L. W. Seidel and Sohn Verlag, 1916.

———. *Tirol in Waffen: Kriegsberichte von der Tiroler Front*. Munich: Hugo Schmidt Verlag, 1915.

Schätz, Jos. Jul. "Der Alpenteil des Deutschen Reiches." ZDÖAV 67 (1936): 1–14.

Schaubach, Adolf. *Die deutschen Alpen: Ein Handbuch für Reisende durch Tyrol, Österreich, Steyermark, Oberbayern und die anstoßenden Gebiete*. Jena: Fr. Frommann, 1871.

Schemfil, Viktor. *Die Pasubio-Kämpfe, 1916–1918*. Bregenz: Teutsch, 1937.

Schmid, Anton. "Die alpinen Vereine und die Übererschließung der Ostalpen." *Der Bergsteiger* 5 (1927): 335.

———. "Das Bergsteigen als eine künstlerische Bildungsmöglichkeit und ein Mittel zur Weltanschauung." MDÖAV 9 (1931): 197–98.

Schmidkunz, Walter. "Bergsteigergebote." MDÖAV 13 (1926): 148–49.

———. *Der Kampf über den Gletschern: Ein Buch von der Alpenfront*. Erfurt: Gebr. Richters Verlagsanstalt, 1934.

———. "Von den Schutzhütten an und hinter der Alpenfront." MDÖAV 9 and 10 (1918): 62–65.

Schmitt, Fritz. "Berge und Bergsteiger in Großdeutschland." *Deutsche Alpenzeitung* 33 (1938): 429–31.

Schraud, Ludwig. "Der Bergsteiger, das Werkzeug und die Maschine: Eine Erwiderung." *Deutsche Alpenzeitung* 20 (1925): 401–3.

Schulenburg, Friedrich Werner von. "Deutscher und Österreichischer Alpenverein—Deutscher Bergsteigerverband—Deutscher Alpenverein." ZDAV 70 (1939): 4–6.

Schulze, P. "Die Alpenvereinshütten im Winter." MDÖAV 7 (1912): 91–93.

Schwink, Lothar. "Deutsche Alpenstraße." *Deutsche Alpenzeitung* 28 (1933): 226.

"Sectionsberichte und Mitglieder-Verzeichnis." ZDAV 1. II Abtheilung (1869/1870): 30–60.

Semple, Ellen Churchill. *Influences of Geographic Environment on the Basis of Ratzel's System of Anthropo-Geography*. New York: Henry Holt and Company, 1911.
Seyß-Inquart, Arthur. "Der Auftrag." ZDAV 70 (1939): 1–3.
Siber, Rudolf. "Sind Wir ein Verkehrsverein?" *Der Bergsteiger* 3 (1925): 238–39.
Siemer, Ludwig. "Die Alpenstraße als Mittel zur Hebung des Fremdenverkehrs im deutschen Alpengebiet." *Deutsche Alpenzeitung* 28 (1933): 237.
Sild, Meinhart. "Der neue Weg." ZDAV 70 (1939): 7–9.
Simmel, Georg. "Die Alpen." *Qualitative Sociology* 16 (1993): 179–84.
Skofizh, Hans, and Franz Tursky. "Schneeschuhfahrten in den Hohen Tauern." ZDÖAV 44 (1913): 195–220.
"Statistisches vom D.u.Ö. Alpenverein." MDÖAV 8 (1934): 182–84.
Steininger, Karl. "Aus den Lechtaler Bergen: Ein Begleitwort zur Karte." ZDÖAV 42 (1911): 174–202.
Steinitzer, Alfred. "Alpinismus, der Deutsche und Österreichische Alpenverein und der Krieg." MDÖAV 15 and 16 (1917): 99–104.
———. *Der Alpinismus in Bildern*. Munich: R. Piper and Company Verlag, 1924.
———. "Die Schituristik und der D. u. Ö. Alpenverein." MDÖAV 1 and 2 (1914): 7–8.
———. "Über Höhenwege und andere alpine Entwicklungserscheinungen." MDÖAV 23 (1911): 281–82.
Steinitzer, Heinrich. "Menschen und Berge (in China)." ZDÖAV 40 (1909): 21–50.
———. "Zur Umfrage betreffend die Gestaltung unserer Vereinsschriften: Das Alpenvereinshandbuch der Zukunft." MDÖAV 17 (1912): 207–9.
Stephen, Leslie. *The Playground of Europe*. London: Longmans, Green, and Co., 1871.
Stolz, Otto. "Deutsche Alpen." MDAV 7 (1938): 167–68.
———. "Tirols Stellung in der deutschen Geschichte." ZDÖAV 44 (1913): 62–80.
"Der Streit um das Bremer Haus an der Bocca di Brenta." MDÖAV 9 (1913): 137–38.
Sueß, Edward. "Ein Betrag zur Gründungsgeschichte des Alpenvereins." MDÖAV 24 (1912): 304–5.
Tisch, Fritz. "Freie Berge." MDAV 5 (1938): 111–12.
Toth-Sonns, Werner. "Bergsteigerfreiheit—Bergsteigerwille." *Deutsche Alpenzeitung* 30 (1935): 225–26.
Trautwein, Theodor. "Zum Anfang." ZDÖAV 1 (1869/1870): 1–3.
Trenker, Luis. *Berge in Flammen*. Berlin: Neufeld and Henius, 1931.
———. "Gedanken zum Deutschen Film." *Deutsche Alpenzeitung* 30 (1935): 143–45.
———. *Kampf in den Bergen: Das unvergängliche Denkmal der Alpenfront*. Berlin: Neufeld and Henius, 1931.
Trumpp, Julius. "Neue Aufgaben, neue Ziele im Deutschen Alpenverein." *Deutsche Alpenzeitung* 33 (1938): 193–95.
Tschudi, Friedrich von. *Sketches of Nature in the Alps*. London: Longman, Brown, Green, and Longmans, 1856.
Turner, Frederick Jackson. "The Significance of the Frontier in American History." *Annual Report of the American Historical Association* (1893): 199–227.
Ullman, James Ramsey. *The White Tower*. New York: J. B. Lippincottt Company, 1945.
"Unsere Berge!" *Wiener Stadt Stimmen*, 23 September 1937.

Unsere Jungmannschaft. Vienna: Verlag des Zweiges Austria des Deutschen und Österreichischen Alpenvereins, 1928.
"Unseren Kämpfern!" MDÖAV 17 and 18 (1914): 230–31.
Veblen, Thorstein. *The Theory of the Leisure Class: An Economic Study in the Evolution of Institutions*. New York: Macmillan, 1899.
"Verhandlungsschrrift der außerordentlichen Hauptversammlung des D. u. Oe. Alpenvereins zu München am 14. Dezember 1924." MDÖAV 2 (1925): 14–20.
"Von der 50. Jahreshauptversammlung des D. u. Ö. A.-V." *Der Bergsteiger* 2 (1924): 254–57.
"Von der Zugspitzbahn." *Der Bergsteiger* 2 (1924): 385.
"Von unserem Alpinen Museums." MDÖAV 12 (1912): 153–56.
Wagener, Siegfried. "Alpine Jugendbewegung." *Nachrichten der Sektion Donauland* 54 (1925): 190–91.
Wallack, Franz. *Die Grossglockner-Hochalpenstrasse: Die Geschichte ihres Baues*. Vienna: Springer Verlag, 1949.
Walland, Heinrich. "Die Erziehung unserer Jugend zum Alpinismus." MDÖAV 11 (1914): 152–53.
"Was geht im Naturschutzgebiet am Großglockner Vor?" MDÖAV 1 (1937): 1–5.
"Was will Austria?" *Nachrichten Sektion Austria* 1 (1927): 6.
Weber, Fritz. *Alpenkrieg*. Klagenfurt: Artur-Kollitsch Verlag, 1935.
Weber, Max. *Politik als Beruf*. Berlin: Duncker and Humblot, 1968.
———. "Wissenschaft als Beruf." In *Gesammelte Aufsätze zur Wissenschaftslehre*, 524–55. Tubigen: Verlag von J. C. B. Mohr, 1922.
Weitzenböck, Richard. "Zur ferneren Zukunft des Alpinismus." MDÖAV 22 (1911): 267–68.
"Wer soll und will der Verein Naturschutzpark." *Monats-Blätter der Sektion Saarbrücken* 9.8 (1932): 63–65.
Wessinger, A. "Zur Alpenwirthschaft." MDÖAV 1 (1888): 5–7.
Why Italy Must Have Her Boundary on the Oriental Border of the Julian Alps. [Rome?], 1918.
Whymper, Edward. *Scrambles amongst the Alps in the Years 1860–1869*. London: John Murray, 1900.
Widder, W. "Naturschutz im Glocknergebiet." MDÖAV 8 (1935): 187–88.
Witlaczil, Emanuel. "Einiges über Naturschutz in den Alpen." MDÖAV 19 (1913): 273–74.
Wolter, Oscar. "Über die Wege des Alpinismus." *Deutsche Alpenzeitung* 26 (1931): 225–26.
"Das Wunderwert Deutsche Alpenstrasse." *Völkischer Beobachter*, 31 August 1935.
Zdarsky, Mathias. "Der Alpen- (Lilienfelder-) Ski." MDÖAV 23 (1903): 282–83.
———. *Lilienfelder Schilauftechnik*. Hamburg: Richter, 1896.
Zeck, Hans. *Österreich im Großdeutschen Volksreich*. Berlin: Edwin Runge Verlag, 1938.
Zeller, Max. "Das Hochkaltergebirge (Westliche und Südliche Wimbachkette)." ZDÖAV 45 (1914): 177–218.
"Die Ziele der Bergsteigergruppe im DÖAV." MDÖAV 1 (1925): 1–2.
Zoeppritz, Victor. "Über die Bedürnissfrage bei Weg- und Hüttenbauten." MDÖAV 22 (1896): 274–75.

Zöhnle, Adalbert. "Der Krieg und der Alpinismus." MDÖAV 1 (1917): 1.
"Die Zugspitzbahn." MDÖAV 18 (1924): 236–37.
"Zur Außerordentlichen Alpenverein-Hauptversammlung." *Der Bergsteiger* 2 (1924): 405–6.
"Zur Frage der Bergbahnen." *Deutsche Alpenzeitung* 22 (1927): 129–36.
"Zur Frage des Arierparagraphen." *Nachrichten der Sektion Donauland* 36 (1924): 112–13.
"Zur Gletscher-Frage: Ein Wort an alle Freunde alpiner Wissenschaft." *Separat-Abdruck aus Nr. 11 u. 12 des I. Bandes der Neuen Folge der Deutschen Alpen-Zeitung*, 9 April 1881.
"Zur Überfremdung im S.A.C." *Alpina* 27 (1919): 174.
"Zwei Jahre Kriegsfürsorge des D. u. Ö. Alpenvereins." MDÖAV 13 and 14 (1916): 115–16.
Zweig, Arnold. *Dialektik der Alpen*. Berlin: Aufbau-Verlag, 1997.
Zwiedineck-Südenhorst, Otto von. "Einige Betrachtungen über die kosten der Turistik Einst und Jetzt." ZDÖAV 41 (1910): 18–29.

SECONDARY SOURCES

75 Jahre Sektion Mittelfranken des Deutschen Alpenvereins 1902–1977: Festschrift. Nuremberg: Die Sektion, 1977.
80 Jahre Akademische Sektion Wien. Vienna: Österreichischer Alpenverein, 1968.
100 Jahre Sektion Nürnberg des Deutschen Alphenvereins. 1869–1969. Nuremberg: Deutscher Alpenverein, Sekt. Nürnberg e. V., 1969.
100 Jahre Sektion Steinnelke, 1898–1998: Festschrift. Vienna: Österreichischer Alpenverein, 1998.
1874–1974: 100 Jahre Sektion Linz, Österreichischer Alpenverein. Linz: Sektion Linz des Österreichischer Alpenvereins, 1974.
Achrainer, Martin. "'So, jetzt sind wir ganz unter uns!' Antisemitismus im Alpenverein." In *Hast du meine Alpen gesehen? Eine jüdische Beziehungsgeschichte*, edited by Hanno Loewy and Gerhard Milchram, 288–317. Hohenems, Austria: Jüdisches Museum Hohenems, 2009.
Agnew, John A. *Place and Politics: The Geographical Mediation of State and Society*. Boston: Allen and Unwin, 1987.
———, ed. *Political Geography: A Reader*. New York: Arnold, 1997.
Agnew, John A., and James Duncan, eds. *The Power of Place: Bringing Together Geographical and Sociological Imaginations*. Boston: Unwin Hyman, 1989.
Allen, E. John B. *The Culture and Sport of Skiing: From Antiquity to World War II*. Amherst: University of Massachusetts Press, 2007.
Der Alpine Gedanke in Deutschland. Munich: F. Bruckmann, 1950.
"Alpinism: Then and Now." *BBC News*, 26 August 2001.
Amstädter, Rainer. *Der Alpinismus: Kultur, Organisation, Politik*. Vienna: WUV-Universitäts Verlag, 1996.
Anderson, Benedict. *Imagined Communities: Reflections on the Origin and Spread of Nationalism*. New York: Verso, 1996.

Anderson, Malcolm. *Frontiers: Territory and State Formation in the Modern World.* Cambridge: Polity Press, 1996.

Anderson, Margaret Lavinia. *Practicing Democracy: Elections and Political Culture in Imperial Germany.* Princeton: Princeton University Press, 2000.

Applegate, Celia. "Among the Bourgeoisie: Recent Writings on the German Middle Classes and Their Milieu." *European History Quarterly* 21 (1991): 383–87.

———. "A Europe of Regions: Reflections on the Historiography of Sub-national Places in Modern Times." *American Historical Review* 104 (1999): 1157–82.

———. *A Nation of Provincials: The German Idea of Heimat.* Berkeley: University of California Press, 1990.

Armiero, Marco. "Nationalizing the Mountains: Natural and Political Landscapes in World War I." In *Nature and History in Modern Italy*, edited by Marco Armiero and Marcus Hall, 231–50. Athens: Ohio University Press, 2010.

———. *A Rugged Nation: Mountains and the Making of Modern Italy.* Cambridge: White Horse Press, 2011.

Aron, Stephen. "Do Borderlands Still Have Borders?" *Journal of the West* 47 (2008): 3–7.

Aspetsberger, Friedbert, ed. *Der Bergfilm 1920–1940.* Innsbruck: StudienVerlag, 2002.

Aurada, Fritz. "Die Alpenvereinskartographie—ein bedeutender Faktor in der alpinen Erschließung und Erforschung Südtirols." *Österreich in Geschichte und Literatur* 31, no. 2 (1987): 116–31.

———. *100 Jahre Alpenvereinskartographie: Die Alpenvereinskarte und ihre Entwicklung.* Vienna: ÖAV Sektion Edelweiß, 1962.

Bahm, Karl. "Beyond the Bourgeoisie: Rethinking Nation, Culture, and Modernity in Nineteenth-Century Central Europe." *Austrian History Yearbook* 29 (1998): 19–35.

Bailey, Robert. "Identifying Ecoboundaries." *Environmental Management* 34 (2005): 14–26.

Baranowski, Shelley. *Strength through Joy: Consumerism and Mass Tourism in the Third Reich.* New York: Cambridge University Press, 2004.

Baranowski, Shelley, and Ellen Furlough, eds. *Being Elsewhere: Tourism, Consumer Culture, and Identity in Modern Europe and North America.* Ann Arbor: University of Michigan Press, 2001.

Barendse, Rene. *Borderlands: A Theoretical Survey.* Occasional Paper 4. Rotterdam: Centre of Border Studies, 1994.

Barker, Mary. "Traditional Landscape and Mass Tourism in the Alps." *Geographical Review* 72 (1982): 397.

Barton, Susan. *Healthy Living in the Alps: The Origins of Winter Tourism in Switzerland 1860–1914.* Manchester: University of Manchester Press, 2009.

Bätzing, Werner. *Die Alpen: Geschichte und Zukunft einer europäischen Kulturlandschaft.* Munich: C. H. Beck, 2003.

Baud, Michiel, and Willem Van Schendel. "Toward a Comparative History of Borderlands." *Journal of World History* 8 (1997): 211–42.

Beattie, Andrew. *The Alps: A Cultural History.* New York: Oxford University Press, 2006.

Behrenbeck, Sabine. *Der Kult um die Toten Helden: Nationalsozialistische Mythen, Riten und Symbole 1923 bis 1945.* Vierow: SH-Verlag, 1996.

Beller, Steven. *Vienna and the Jews, 1867–1938*. New York: Cambridge University Press, 1989.

Berghahn, Volker. *Imperial Germany, 1871–1918: Economy, Society, Culture, and Politics*. New York: Berghahn Books, 2004.

Bergier, Jean-François. "Histoire des Alpes: Perspectives Nouvelles." *Schweizerische Zeitschrift für Geschichte* 29 (1979): 3–10.

Bergmann, Klaus. *Agraromantik und Großstadtfeindschaft*. Meisenheim am Glan: Anton Hain, 1970.

Bergsteigen und Wandern in der Steiermark. Schutzhüttenverzeichnis. 1870–1970. 100 Jahre Sektion Graz-St. G. V. des Oeav. Graz: Österreichischer Alpenverein, Sektion Graz, 1970.

Berkley, George E. *Vienna and Its Jews: The Tragedy of Success, 1880s–1980s*. Cambridge, Mass.: Abt Books, 1988.

Bessel, Richard. *Germany after the First World War*. Oxford: Clarendon Press, 1993.

Blackbourn, David. *The Conquest of Nature: Water, Landscape, and the Making of Modern Germany*. New York: W. W. Norton, 2006.

———. *History of Germany, 1780–1918: The Long Nineteenth Century*. Hoboken, N.J.: Wiley Blackwell, 2003.

———. *Populists and Patricians: Essays in Modern German History*. Boston: Allen and Unwin, 1987.

Blackbourn, David, and Geoff Eley. *The Peculiarities of German History: Bourgeois Society and Politics of Nineteenth-Century Germany*. Oxford: Oxford University Press, 1984.

Blackbourn, David, and Richard Evans, eds. *The German Bourgeoisie: Essays on the Social History of the German Middle Class from the Late Eighteenth to the Early Twentieth Century*. New York: Routledge, 1991.

Blackbourn, David, and James Retallack, eds. *Localism, Landscape, and the Ambiguities of Place: German-Speaking Central Europe, 1860–1930*. Toronto: University of Toronto Press, 2007.

Boa, Elizabeth, and Rachel Palfreyman. *Heimat—a German Dream: Regional Loyalties and National Identity in German Culture, 1890–1990*. Oxford: Oxford University Press, 2000.

Botz, Gerhard. *Gewalt in der Politik: Attentate, Zusammenstösse, Putschversuche, Unruhen in Österreich 1918 Bis 1938*. Munich: Wilhelm Fink Verlag, 1983.

Bourdieu, Pierre. "Identity and Representation: Elements for a Critical Reflection on the Idea of Region." In *Language and Symbolic Power*, edited by John B. Thompson, 220–28. Cambridge, Mass.: Harvard University Press, 1991.

Boyer, John W. *Culture and Political Crisis in Vienna: Christian Socialism in Power, 1897–1918*. Chicago: University of Chicago Press, 1995.

———. *Political Radicalism in Late Imperial Vienna: Origins of the Christian Social Movement, 1848–1897*. Chicago: University of Chicago Press, 1981.

———. "Silent War and Bitter Peace: The Revolution of 1918 in Austria." *Austrian History Yearbook* 34 (2003): 1–56.

Bradly, Kimberly. "In Austria, a Chalet for the Night." *New York Times*, 31 January 2010.

Braham, Trevor. *When the Alps Cast Their Spell: Mountaineers of the Alpine Golden Age*. London: The In Pinn, 2004.

Brandli, P. "Warum Steigt der Mensch Auf Hohe Berge?" *Les Alpes: Revue du Club Alpin Suisse* 51 (1975): 80–83.
Brockmann, Stephen. *A Critical History of German Film*. Rochester: Camden House, 2010.
Bruckmüller, Ernst. *Nation Österreich: Kulturelles Bewußtsein und Gesellschaftlich-Politische Prozesse*. Vienna: Böhlau, 1996.
———. *Sozialgeschichte Österreichs*. Vienna: Herold, 1985.
Bruckmüller, Ernst, Hannes Stekl, Péter Hanák, and Ilona Sármány-Parsons, eds. *Bürgertum in der Habsburgermonarchie*. Vienna: Böhlau, 1990.
Brüggemeier, Franz-Josef, Mark Cioc, and Thomas Zeller, eds. *How Green Were the Nazis? Nature, Environment, and Nation in the Third Reich*. Athens: Ohio University Press, 2005.
Buzard, James. *The Beaten Track: European Tourism, Literature, and the Ways to "Culture," 1800–1918*. New York: Clarendon Press, 1993.
Carey, Mark. "Mountaineers and Engineers: The Politics of International Science, Recreation, and Environmental Change in Twentieth-Century Peru." *Hispanic American Historical Review* 92 (2012): 107–41.
Carsten, F. L. *The First Austrian Republic: A Study Based on British and Austrian Documents*. Brookfield, Vt.: Gower, 1986.
Cassar, George H. *The Forgotten Front: The British Campaign in Italy, 1917–1918*. London: Hambledon Press, 1998.
Chickering, Roger. *Imperial Germany and the Great War, 1914–1918*. Cambridge: Cambridge University Press, 1998.
———. *We Men Who Feel Most German: A Cultural Study of the Pan-German League, 1886–1914*. Boston: Allen and Unwin, 1984.
Cioc, Mark. *The Rhine: An Eco-Biography, 1815–2000*. Seattle: University of Washington Press, 2002.
Closmann, Charles. "Legalizing a Volksgemeinschaft: Nazi Germany's Reich Nature Protection Law of 1935." In *How Green Were the Nazis? Nature, Environment, and Nation in the Third Reich*, edited by Franz-Josef Brüggemeier, Mark Cioc, and Thomas Zeller, 18–42. Athens: Ohio University Press, 2005.
Coen, Deborah R. "Climate and Circulation in Imperial Austria." *Journal of Modern History* 82 (2010): 839–75.
Cole, John W., and Eric R. Wolf. *The Hidden Frontier: Ecology and Ethnicity in an Alpine Valley*. New York: Academic Press, 1974.
Coleman, Annie Gilbert. *Ski Style: Sport and Culture in the Rockies*. Lawrence: University of Kansas Press, 2004.
Colley, Ann C. *Victorians in the Mountains: Sinking the Sublime*. Burlington, Vt.: Ashgate, 2010.
Confino, Alon. *The Nation as Local Metaphor: Württemberg, Imperial Germany, and National Memory, 1871–1918*. Chapel Hill: University of North Carolina Press, 1997.
Cornwall, Mark. *The Undermining of Austria-Hungary: The Battle for Hearts and Minds*. New York: St. Martin's Press, 2000.
Cosgrove, Denis E. *Social Formation and Symbolic Landscape*. 2nd ed. Madison: University of Wisconsin Press, 1998.

Cosgrove, Denis E., and Stephen Daniels, eds. *The Iconography of Landscape: Essays on the Symbolic Representation, Design and Use of Past Environments*. Cambridge: Cambridge University Press, 1988.

Craig, Gordon. *The Politics of the Unpolitical: German Writers and the Problem of Power, 1770–1871*. New York: Oxford University Press, 1995.

Culver, Lawrence. *The Frontier of Leisure: Southern California and the Shaping of Modern America*. New York: Oxford University Press, 2010.

Dabrowski, Patrice. "'Discovering' the Galician Borderlands: The Case of the Eastern Carpathians." *Slavic Review* 64 (2005): 380–402.

Dal Piaz, Giorgio V. "History of Tectonic Interpretations of the Alps." *Journal of Geodynamics* 32 (2001): 99–114.

Denning, Andrew. *Skiing into Modernity: A Cultural and Environmental History*. Oakland: University of California Press, 2015.

Deutscher Alpenverein Sektion Mittelfranken. *75 Jahre Sektion Mittelfranken des Deutschen Alpenvereins 1902–1977: Festschrift*. Nuremberg: Die Sektion, 1977.

Di Stefano, Diana. *Encounters in Avalanche Country: A History of Survival in the Mountain West, 1820–1920*. Seattle: University of Washington Press, 2013.

Ditt, Karl. "The Perspective and Conservation of Nature in the Third Reich." *Planning Perspectives* 15 (2000): 161–87.

Dominick, Raymond. *The Environmental Movement in Germany: Prophets and Pioneers, 1871–1917*. Bloomington: Indiana University Press, 1992.

———. "Nascent Environmental Protection in the Second Empire." *German Studies Review* 9, no. 2 (1986): 257–91.

Dyck, Cameron, Ingrid Schnieder, Marilyn Thompson, and Randy Virden. "Specialization among Mountaineers and Its Relationship to Environmental Attitudes." *Journal of Park and Recreation Administration* 21 (2003): 44–62.

Eidson, John R. "German Local History as Metaphor and Sanction." *Anthropological Quarterly* 66 (1993): 134–48.

Eisenberg, Christiane. "Sportgeschichte: Eine Dimension der Modernen Kulturgeschichte." *Geschichte und Gesellschaft* 23 (1997): 295–310.

Eisterer, Klaus, and Rolf Steininger, eds. *Tirol und der Erste Weltkrieg*. Vienna: Österreichischer Studien Verlag, 1995.

Ellis, Reuben. *Vertical Margins: Mountaineering and the Landscapes of Neoimperialism*. Madison: University of Wisconsin Press, 2001.

Engel, Claire Eliane. *A History of Mountaineering in the Alps*. New York: Charles Scribner's Sons, 1950.

Ester, Hans, Hans Hecker, and Erika Poettgens, eds. *Deutschland, aber wo liegt es? Deutschland und Mitteleuropa*. Atlanta: Rodopi B. V., 1993.

Evans, Richard. *Death in Hamburg: Society and Politics in the Cholera Years, 1830–1910*. New York: Penguin, 2005.

Evans, Richard, and W. R. Lee, eds. *The German Peasantry: Conflict and Community in Rural Society from the Eighteenth to the Twentieth Centuries*. London: Croom Helm, 1986.

Fairbairn, Brett. *Democracy in the Undemocratic State: The German Reichstag Elections of 1898 and 1903*. Toronto: University of Toronto Press, 1997.

Falls, Cyril. *Caporetto 1917*. London: Weidenfeld and Nicolson, 1965.

Faragher, John Mack. *Rereading Frederick Jackson Turner: The Significance of the Frontier in American History, and Other Essays*. New York: H. Holt, 1994.

Febvre, Lucien. *A Geographic Introduction to History*. New York: Alfred A. Knopf, 1932.

Festschrift Zur Hauptversammlung des Österreichischen Alpenvereines in Kufstein. Innsbruck: Süd-West-Presseverlag, 1967.

Festschrift Zur Hundertjahrfeier der Sektion Frankfurt des Deutschen Alpenvereins. Frankfurt am Main: Sektion Frankfurt a. M. e. V., 1969.

Finsterwalder, R. *Die Alpenvereinskarte und ihr Gebrauch*. Munich: der Verein, 1984.

Fitzsimmons, Sean, and Heinz Veit. "Geology and Geomorphology of the European Alps and the Southern Alps of New Zealand: A Comparison." *Mountain Research and Development* 21 (2001): 340–49.

Fleming, Fergus. *Killing Dragons: The Conquest of the Alps*. New York: Atlantic Monthly Press, 2002.

Fowler, Brenda. *Iceman: Uncovering the Life and Times of a Prehistoric Man Found in an Alpine Glacier*. Chicago: University of Chicago Press, 2001.

Frank, Alison. "The Air Cure Town: Commodifying Air in Alpine Central Europe." *Central European History* 45 (2012): 185–207.

Frei, Norbert. *National Socialist Rule in Germany: The Führer State, 1933–1945*. Oxford: Blackwell, 1993.

Fremdling, Rainer. *Eisenbahnen und deutsches Wirtschaftswachstum, 1840–1879*. Dortmund: Gesellschaft für Westfälische Wirtschaftsgeschichte, 1975.

Gay, Peter. *Weimar Culture: The Outsider as Insider*. New York: Harper Torchbooks, 1968.

Gidl, Anneliese. *Alpenverein: Die Städter entdecken die Alpen: Der Deutsche und Österreichische Alpenverein von der Gründung bis zum Ende des Ersten Weltkrieges*. Vienna: Böhlau, 2007.

Gillis, John, ed. *Commemorations: The Politics of National Identity*. Princeton: Princeton University Press, 1994.

Good, David. *The Economic Rise of the Habsburg Empire, 1750–1914*. Berkeley: University of California Press, 1984.

Gordon, Sarah. *Hitler, Germans, and the "Jewish Question."* Princeton: Princeton University Press, 1984.

Gould, S. W. "Austrian Attitudes toward Anschluss: October 1918–September 1919." *Journal of Modern History* 22(1950): 220–31.

Grandner, Margarete. "Staatsbürger und Ausländer: Zum Umgang Österreichs mit den jüdischen Flüchtlingen nach 1918." In *Asylland wider Willen: Flüchtlinge in Österreich im europäischen Kontext seit 1914*, edited by Gernot and Oliver Rathkolb Heiss, 60–85. Vienna: Ludwig-Boltzmann-Institut, 1995.

Green, Abigail. *Fatherlands: State-Building and Nationhood in Nineteenth-Century Germany*. New York: Cambridge University Press, 2004.

Green, D. Brooks, ed. *Historical Geography: A Methodological Portrayal*. Savage, Md.: Rowman and Littlefield, 1991.

Gross, Nachum T. "Economic Growth and the Consumption of Coal in Austria and Hungary, 1831–1913." *Journal of Economic History* 31 (1971): 898–916.

Guelke, Leonard. *Historical Understanding in Geography*. New York: Cambridge University Press, 1982.

Günther, Dagmar. *Alpine Quergänge: Kulturgeschichte des bürgerlichen Alpinismus, 1870–1930*. Frankfurt: Campus Verlag, 1998.

Hanke, Hans. *100 Jahre Österreichischer Alpenverein, 1862–1962*. Vienna: Österreichischer Alpenverein, 1962.

Hansen, Peter. *The Summits of Modern Man: Mountaineering after the Enlightenment*. Cambridge, Mass.: Harvard University Press, 2013.

Hardtwig, Wolfgang. "Bürgertum, Staatssymbolik und Staatsbewußtsein, 1871–1914." *Geschichte und Gesellschaft* 16 (1990): 269–95.

Hartungen, Christoph von. "Die Tiroler und Vorarlberger Standschützen—Mythos und Realität." In *Tirol und der Erste Weltkrieg*, edited by Klaus Eisterer and Rolf Steininger, 61–104. Vienna: Österreichischer Studien Verlag, 1995.

Healy, Maureen. *Vienna and the Fall of the Habsburg Empire: Total War and Everyday Life in World War I*. New York: Cambridge University Press, 2004.

Hebert, Günther. *Das Alpenkorps: Aufbau, Organisation und Einsatz einer Gebirgstruppe im Ersten Weltkrieg*. Boppard am Rhein: Harald Boldt Verlag, 1988.

Hermand, Jost. *Grüne Utopien in Deutschland: Zur Geschichte des ökologischen Bewußtseins*. Frankfurt: Fischer, 1991.

Hettling, Manfred, and Stefan-Ludwig Hoffmann. "Der bürgerliche Wertehimmel: Zum Problem individueller Lebensführung im 19. Jahrhundert." *Geschichte und Gesellschaft* 23 (1997): 333–59.

Höbusch, Harald. "Narrating Nanga Parbat: German Himalaya Expeditions and the Fictional (Re-)Construction of National Identity." *Sporting Traditions* 20 (2003): 17–42.

Holzner, Johann. "Der Dolomitenkrieg im 'Tiroler' Film." In *Tirol und der Erste Weltkrieg*, edited by Klaus Eisterer and Rolf Steininger, 227–54. Vienna: Österreichischer Studien Verlag, 1995.

Hooson, David. *Geography and National Identity*. Cambridge: Blackwell, 1994.

"Im Deutschen Alpenverein." *Münchner Neueste Nachrichten*, 18 March 1938.

Ireton, Sean, and Caroline Schaumann, eds. *Heights of Reflection: Mountains in the German Imagination from the Middle Ages to the Twenty-First Century*. Rochester, N.Y.: Camden House, 2012.

Isenberg, Noah. *Weimar Cinema: An Essential Guide to Classic Films of the Era*. New York: Columbia University Press, 2008.

Isserman, Maurice, and Stewart Weaver. *Fallen Giants: A History of Himalayan Mountaineering from the Age of Empire to the Age of Extremes*. New Haven: Yale University Press, 2008.

Jelavich, Barbara. *Modern Austria: Empire and Republic, 1800–1986*. New York: Cambridge University Press, 1987.

Jelinek, Elfriede. *In den Alpen*. Berlin: Berlin Verlag, 2002.

———. *Die Kinder der Toten*. Reinbek: Rowohlt, 1995.

———. *Totenauberg*. Reinbek: Rowohlt, 1991.

Johann, Elisabeth. "The Impact of Industry on the Landscape and Environment of Austria Prior to the First World War." *Forest and Conservation History* 34, no. 3 (1990): 122–24.

Jones, Larry Eugene. *German Liberalism and the Dissolution of the Weimar Party System, 1918–1933*. Chapel Hill: University of North Carolina Press, 1988.

Judson, Pieter. "Every German Visitor Has a Völkisch Obligation He Must Fulfill: Nationalist Tourism in the Austrian Empire, 1880–1918." In *Histories of Leisure*, edited by Rudy Koshar, 147–68. New York: Berg, 2002.

———. *Exclusive Revolutionaries: Liberal Politics, Social Experience, and National Identity in the Austrian Empire, 1848–1914*. Ann Arbor: University of Michigan Press, 1996.

———. *Guardians of the Nation: Activists on the Language Frontiers of Imperial Austria*. Cambridge, Mass.: Harvard University Press, 2007.

———. "Tourists and Modernizers: Nationalizing Rural Central Europe around 1900." In *Moderne als Konstruktion II*, edited by Werner Suppanz et al., 19–21. Vienna: Passagen Verlag, 2006.

Kaes, Anton. *Shell Shock Cinema: Weimar Culture and the Wounds of War*. Princeton: Princeton University Press, 2009.

Kaltenegger, Roland. *Das Deutsche Alpenkorps im Ersten Weltkrieg*. Stuttgart: Leopold Stocker Verlag, 1995.

———. *Die Geschichte der Deutschen Gebirgstruppe 1915 bis Heute*. Stuttgart: Motorbuch Verlag, 1980.

Kariel, Herbert G., and Patricia E. Kariel. "Socio-cultural Impacts of Tourism: An Example of the Austrian Alps." *Geografiska Annaler: Series B, Human Geography* 64 (1982): 1–16.

King, Jeremy. *Budweisers into Czechs and Germans: A Local History of Bohemian Politics, 1848–1948*. Princeton: Princeton University Press, 2002.

Kinser, Samuel. "Annaliste Paradigm? The Geo-historical Structuralism of Fernand Braudel." *American Historical Review* 86 (1981): 63–105.

Kirchner, Walther. "Mind, Mountain, and History." *Journal of the History of Ideas* 11 (1950): 435–39.

Klecatsky, Hans R., and Beate Lutz. "Chronik einer transnationalen europäischen Alpenregion." In *Federalisme, Regionalisme, et Droit des Groupes Ethniques en Europe*, edited by Theodor Veiter, 202–13. Vienna: Wilhelm Braumüller, 1989.

Klein, Kerwin. "A Vertical World: The Eastern Alps and Modern Mountaineering." *Journal of Historical Sociology* 24 (2011): 519–48.

Klueting, Edeltraud, ed. *Antimodernismus und Reform: Zur Geschichte der deutschen Heimatbewegung*. Darmstadt: Wissenschaftliche Buchgesellschaft, 1991.

Kocka, Jürgen. "Bildungsbürgertum—Gesellschaftliche Formation oder Historikerkonstrukt?" In *Bildungsbürgertum im 19. Jahrhundert, Teil IV: Politischer Einfluß und gesellschaftliche Formation*, edited by Jürgen Kocka, 9–20. Stuttgart: Ernst Klett, 1989.

———. *Bürger und Bürgerlichkeit im 19. Jahrhundert*. Göttingen: Vandenhoeck and Ruprecht, 1987.

———. *Facing Total War: Germany Society, 1914–1918*. Leamington Spa, Warwickshire: Berg Publishers, 1984.

———, ed. *Max Weber, der Historiker*. Göttingen: Vandenhoeck and Ruprecht, 1986.

Koerner, Joseph Leo. *Caspar David Friedrich and the Subject of Landscape*. New Haven: Yale University Press, 1990.

Köll, Lois. *Der Krieg auf den südlichen Ortler-Bergen, 1915–1918*. Innsbruck: Universitätsverlag Wagner, 1957.

Komlos, John. *The Habsburg Monarchy as a Customs Union: Economic Development in Austria-Hungary in the Nineteenth Century*. Princeton: Princeton University Press, 1983.

König, Stefan, Hans-Jürgen Panitz, and Michael Wachtler. *Bergfilm: Dramen, Trick und Abenteuer*. Munich: F. A. Herbig Verlagsbuchhandlung, 2001.

König, Wolfgang. *Bahnen und Berge: Verkehrstechnik, Tourismus und Naturschutz in den Schweizer Alpen, 1870–1939*. Frankfurt: Campus Verlag, 2000.

Koselleck, Reinhart. "Volk, Nation, Nationalismus, Masse." In *Geschichtliche Grundbegriffe: Historisches Lexikon zur politisch-sozialen Sprache in Deutschland*, vol. 7, edited by Otto Brunner, Werner Conze, and Reinhart Koselleck, 141–432. Stuttgart: Klett-Cotta, 1992.

Koshar, Rudy. *German Travel Cultures*. Oxford: Berg, 2000.

———. *Germany's Transient Pasts: Preservation and National Memory in the Twentieth Century*. Chapel Hill: University of North Carolina Press, 1998.

———. "Organic Machines: Cars, Drivers, and Nature from Imperial to Nazi Germany." In *Germany's Nature: Cultural Landscapes and Environmental History*, edited by Thomas Lekan and Thomas Zeller, 111–39. New Brunswick, N.J.: Rutgers University Press, 2005.

———. *Social Life, Local Politics, and Nazism: Marburg, 1880–1935*. Chapel Hill: University of North Carolina Press, 1986.

———. "What Ought to Be Seen." *Journal of Contemporary History* 33 (1998): 330–31.

Kracauer, Siegfried. *From Caligari to Hitler: A Psychological History of the German Film*. Revised and expanded ed. Princeton: Princeton University Press, 2004.

Kupper, Patrick. "Science and the National Parks: A Transatlantic Perspective on the Interwar Years." *Environmental History* 14 (2009): 60–63.

Kuprian, Hermann J. W., and Oswald Überegger, eds. *Der Erste Weltkrieg im Alpenraum: Erfahrung, Deutung, Erinnerung/La Grande Guerra nell'arco alpino: Esperienze e memoria*. Innsbruck: Wagner, 2006.

Lahner, Alfred. *1874–1974: 100 Jahre Sektion Linz, Österreichischer Alpenverein*. Linz: Sektion Linz des Österreichischer Alpenvereins, 1974.

Landry, Marc. "Europe's Battery: The Making of the Alpine Energy Landscape, 1870–1955." Ph.D. diss., Georgetown University, 2013.

Langes, Gunther. *Die Front in Fels und Eis: Der Weltkrieg 1914–1918 im Hochgebirge*. Bozen: Verlagsanstalt Athesia, 1972.

Laven, David, and Timothy Baycroft. "Border Regions and Identity." *European Review of History* 15 (2008): 255–75.

Lekan, Thomas. *Imagining the Nation in Nature: Landscape Preservation and German Identity, 1885–1945*. Cambridge, Mass.: Harvard University Press, 2004.

———. "A 'Noble Prospect': Tourism, Heimat, and Conservation on the Rhine." *Journal of Modern History* 81 (2009): 824–58.

———. "Regionalism and the Politics of Landscape Preservation in the Third Reich." *Environmental History* 4.3 (1999): 384–404.

Lekan, Thomas, and Thomas Zeller, eds. *Germany's Nature: Cultural Landscapes and Environmental History*. New Brunswick, N.J.: Rutgers University Press, 2005.

Leopold, Aldo. *A Sand County Almanac*. New York: Oxford University Press, 1949.

Lichem, Heinz von. *Gebirgskrieg, 1915–1918.* Bozen, Italy: Verlagsanstalt Athesia, 1980.

Lidtke, Vernon. *The Alternative Culture: Socialist Labor in Imperial Germany.* New York: Oxford University Press, 1985.

Limerick, Patricia Nelson. *The Legacy of Conquest: The Unbroken Past of the American West.* New York: W. W. Norton, 2006.

Lipp, Anne. *Meinungslenkung im Krieg: Kriegserfahrungen deutscher Soldaten und ihre Deutung, 1914–1918.* Göttingen: Vandenhoeck and Ruprecht, 2003.

Liulevicius, Vejas G. *The German Myth of the East: 1800 to the Present.* New York: Oxford University Press, 2011.

———. *War Land on the Eastern Front: Culture, National Identity, and German Occupation in World War I.* New York: Cambridge University Press, 2000.

Löfgren, Orvar. "Natur, Tiere und Moral: Zur Entwicklung der bürgerlichen Naturauffassung." In *Volkskultur in der Moderne: Probleme und Perspektiven empirischer Kulturforschungen,* edited by Utz Jeggle, 122–44. Reinbek Rowohlt, 1986.

Loveland, Thomas, and James Merchant. "Ecoregions and Ecoregionalization: Geographical and Ecological Perspectives." *Environmental Management* 34 (2004): 1–13.

Lukan, Karl. *The Alps and Alpinism.* London: Thames and Hudson, 1968.

Luža, Radomír. *Austro-German Relations in the Anschluss Era.* Princeton: Princeton University Press, 1975.

Macfarlane, Robert. *Mountains of the Minds: Adventures in Reaching the Summit.* New York: Vintage, 2004.

Maier, Charles S. *Recasting Bourgeois Europe: Stabilization in France, Germany, and Italy in the Decade after World War I.* Princeton: Princeton University Press, 1975.

Mailänder, Nicholas. "Jüdische Beiträge zum Alpinismus." In *Hast du meine Alpen gesehen? Eine jüdische Beziehungsgeschichte,* edited by Hanno Loewy and Gerhard Milchram, 240–57. Hohenems, Austria: Jüdisches Museum Hohenems, 2009.

Mathieu, Jon. *History of the Alps, 1500–1900: Environment, Development, and Society.* Translated by Matthew Vester. Morgantown: West Virginia University Press, 2009.

———. *The Third Dimension: A Comparative History of Mountains in the Modern Era.* Cambridge: White Horse Press, 2011.

Mathieu, Jon, and Simona Boscani Leoni, eds. *Die Alpen! Zur europäischen Wahrnehmungsgeschichte seit der Renaissance / Les Alpes! Pour une histoire de la perception européenne depuis la Renaissance.* New York: Peter Lang, 2005.

Mazohl-Wallnig, Brigitte, Hermann J. W. Kuprian, and Gunda Barth-Scalmani, eds. *Ein Krieg, zwei Schützengräben: Österreich-Italien und der Erste Weltkrieg in den Dolomiten 1915–1918.* Bozen, Italy: Athesia, 2005.

McNeill, John R. *The Mountains of the Mediterranean World: An Environmental History.* New York: Cambridge University Press, 1992.

———. *Something New under the Sun: An Environmental History of the Twentieth Century.* New York: W. W. Norton, 2000.

Mendelson, Edward. "Baedeker's Universe." *Yale Review* 74 (1985): 389–90.

Minghi, Julian. "Boundary Studies and National Prejudices: The Case of the South Tyrol." *Professional Geographer* 15 (1963): 4–8.

Mitchell, B. R. *International Historical Statistics: Europe 1750–2005*. 6th ed. New York: Palgrave Macmillan, 2007.

Mittermaier, Johann. *Der Schrecken des Krieges: Die Erinnerungen eines Südtiroler Kaiserjägers aus dem 1. Weltkrieg*. Brixen: Suedmedia, 2005.

Moranda, Scott. *The People's Own Landscape: Nature, Tourism, and Dictatorship in East Germany*. Ann Arbor: University of Michigan Press, 2014.

Morgenbrod, Birgitt. *Wiener Großbürgertum im Ersten Weltkrieg: Die Geschichte der "Österreichischen Politischen Gesellschaft" 1916–1918*. Vienna: Böhlau, 1994.

Mosse, George L. *The Crisis of German Ideology: Intellectual Origins of the Third Reich*. New York: Grosset and Dunlap, 1964.

———. *Fallen Soldiers: Reshaping the Memory of the World Wars*. New York: Oxford University Press, 1990.

———. *The Nationalization of the Masses: Political Symbolism and Mass Movements in Germany from the Napoleonic Wars through the Third Reich*. Ithaca: Cornell University Press, 1975.

Müller, Alfred M. "Geschichte des Deutschen und Österreichischen Alpenvereins: Ein Beitrag zur Sozialgeschichte des Vereinswesens." Ph.D. diss., Westfälischen Wilhelms-Universität zu Münster, 1979.

Murdock, Caitlin. *Changing Places: Society, Culture, and Territory in the Saxon-Bohemian Borderlands, 1870–1946*. Ann Arbor: University of Michigan Press, 2010.

———. "Tourist Landscapes and Regional Identities in Saxony, 1878–1938." *Central European History* 40 (207): 598–601.

Murphy, David Thomas. *The Heroic Earth: Geopolitical Thought in Weimar Germany, 1918–1933*. Kent, Ohio: Kent State University Press, 1997.

Netting, Robert. *Balancing on an Alp: Ecological Change and Continuity in a Swiss Mountain Community*. New York: Cambridge University Press, 1981.

Nicolson, Marjorie Hope. *Mountain Gloom and Mountain Glory: The Development of the Aesthetics of the Infinite*. Ithaca: Cornell University Press, 1959.

Nipperdey, Thomas. *Deutsche Geschichte 1800–1866: Bürgerwelt und Starker Staat*. Munich: C. H. Beck, 1983.

Norton, William. *Historical Analysis in Geography*. New York: Longman, 1984.

Oberwalder, Louis. *Franz Senn: Alpinismuspionier und Gründer des Alpenvereins*. Innsbruck: Tyrolia-Verlag, 2004.

O'Donnell, Krista, Renate Bridenthal, and Nancy Reagin. *The Heimat Abroad: The Boundaries of Germanness*. Ann Arbor: University of Michigan Press, 2005.

Olábarri, Ignacio. "New, New History: A Longue Durée Structure." *History and Theory* 34, no. 1 (1995): 1–29.

Olsen, Jonathan. *Nature and Nationalism: Right-Wing Ecology and the Politics of Identity in Contemporary Germany*. New York: St. Martin's Press, 1999.

Olwig, Kenneth. *Nature's Ideological Landscape*. London: George Allen and Unwin, 1984.

Oxaal, Ivan, Michael Pollak, and Gerhard Botz, eds. *Jews, Antisemitism and Culture in Vienna*. New York: Routledge and Kegan Paul, 1987.

Pauley, Bruce F. "Political Antisemitism in Interwar Vienna." In *Jews, Antisemitism and Culture in Vienna*, edited by Ivar Oxaal, Michael Pollak, and Gerhard Botz, 153–73. New York: Routledge and Kegan Paul, 1987.

Peukert, Detlev. *Inside Nazi Germany: Conformity, Opposition, and Racism in Everyday Life.* Translated by Richard Deveson. New Haven: Yale University Press, 1982.

———. *The Weimar Republic: The Crisis of Classical Modernity.* Translated by Richard Deveson. New York: Hill and Wang, 1989.

Philpott, William. *Vacationland: Tourism and Environment in the Colorado High Country.* Seattle: University of Washington Press, 2013.

Pils, Manfred. *Berge Frei! 100 Jahre Naturfreunde.* Vienna: Verlag für Gesellschaftskritik, 1994.

Pircher, Gerd. *Militär, Verwaltung und Politik in Tirol im Ersten Weltkrieg.* Innsbruck: Universitätsverlag Wagner, 1995.

Pois, Robert A. *National Socialism and the Religion of Nature.* New York: St. Martin's Press, 1986.

Pretes, Michael. "Tourism and Nationalism." *Annals of Tourism Research* 30 (2003): 125–42.

Price, Larry W. *Mountains and Man: A Study of Process and Environment.* Berkeley: University of California Press, 1981.

Puschner, Uwe. *Die völkische Bewegung im wilhelminischen Kaiserreich: Sprache, Rasse, Religion.* Darmstadt: Wissenschaftliche Buchgesellschaft, 2001.

Radkau, Joachim, and Frank Uekötter, eds. *Naturschutz und Nationalsozialismus.* Frankfurt: Campus, 2003.

Rapp, Christian. *Höhenrausch: Der deutsche Bergfilm.* Vienna: Sonderzahl Verlagsgesellschaft, 1997.

Rechter, David. *The Jews of Vienna and the First World War.* London: Littman Library of Jewish Civilization, 2001.

Rentschler, Eric. "Mountains and Modernity: Relocating the Bergfilm." *New German Critique* 51 (1990): 137–61.

Reulecke, Jürgen. *Geschichte der Urbanisierung in Deutschland.* Berlin: Suhrkamp Verlag, 1985.

Richter, Karl. *75 Jahre Sektion Osnabrück des Deutschen Alpenvereins, 1888–1963.* Osnabrück: Deutscher Alpenverein, Sektion Osnabrück, 1963.

Riechers, Burkhardt. "Nature Protection during National Socialism." *Historical Social Research* 21, no. 3 (1996): 34–56.

Rigele, Georg. *Die Grossglockner-Hochalpenstrasse: Zur Geschichte eines österreichischen Monuments.* Vienna: WUV-Universitätsverlag, 1998.

Ring, Jim. *How the English Made the Alps.* London: John Murray, 2000.

Riordan, Colin, ed. *Green Thought in German Culture: Historical and Contemporary Perspectives.* Cardiff: University of Wales Press, 1997.

Rödel, Jarl. *100 Jahre Sektion Nürnberg des Deutschen Alpenvereins. 1869–1969. Festschrift.* Nuremberg: Deutscher Alpenverein, Sekt. Nürnberg e. V., 1969.

Rohkrämer, Thomas. *Eine andere Moderne? Zivilisationskritik, Natur und Technik in Deutschland, 1800–1933.* Paderborn: Schöningh, 1999.

Rollins, William H. *A Greener Vision of Home: Cultural Politics and Environmental Reform in the German Heimatschutz Movement, 1904–1918.* Ann Arbor: University of Michigan Press, 1997.

Root, G. Irving. *Battles in the Alps: A History of the Italian Front of the First World War.* Baltimore: Publish America, 2008.

Rotenberg, Robert. *Landscape and Power in Vienna*. Baltimore: Johns Hopkins University Press, 1995.
Rothman, Hal K. *Devil's Bargains: Tourism in the Twentieth-Century American West*. Lawrence: University of Kansas Press, 1998.
Rudolf, Richard. *Banking and Industrialization in Austria-Hungary*. New York: Cambridge University Press, 2008.
Rudwick, Martin. *Bursting the Limits of Time: The Reconstruction of Geohistory in the Age of Revolution*. Chicago: University of Chicago Press, 2005.
Rumley, Dennis, and Julian V. Minghi. *The Geography of Border Landscapes*. New York: Routledge, 1991.
Sahlins, Peter. *Boundaries: The Making of France and Spain in the Pyrenees*. Berkeley: University of California Press, 1991.
Salked, Audrey, and José Luis Bermúdez. *On the Edge of Europe: Mountaineering in the Caucasus*. London: Hodder and Stoughton, 1993.
Schama, Simon. *Landscape and Memory*. New York: A. A. Knopf, 1995.
Schindler, John R. *Isonzo: The Forgotten Sacrifice of the Great War*. Westport, Conn.: Praeger, 2001.
Schlaffer, Heinz. *Der Bürger als Held: Sozialgeschichtliche Auflösungen literarischer Widersprüche*. Frankfurt: Suhrkamp, 1973.
Schöning, Largot. *Festschrift zur Hundertjahrfeier der Sektion Frankfurt des Deutschen Alpenvereins, 1869–1969*. Frankfurt am Main: Deutscher Alpenverein, Sektion Frankfurt, 1969.
Schorske, Carl E. *Fin-de-Siècle Vienna: Politics and Culture*. New York: Vintage Books, 1980.
Schrepfer, Susan R. *Nature's Altars: Mountains, Gender, and American Environmentalism*. Lawrence: University Press of Kansas, 2005.
Schultz, Hans-Dietrich. "Fantasies of Mitte: Mittellage and Mitteleuropa in German Geographical Discussion in the 19th and 20th Centuries." *Political Geography Quarterly* 8 (1989): 315–39.
Schulze, Max-Stephan. "The Machine-Building Industry and Austria's Great Depression after 1873." *Economic History Review* 50 (1997): 282–304.
Scott, James C. *Seeing Like a State: How Certain Schemes to Improve the Human Condition Have Failed*. New Haven: Yale University Press, 1998.
Semmens, Kristin. *Seeing Hitler's Germany: Tourism in the Third Reich*. New York: Palgrave Macmillan, 2005.
Sheehan, James J. *Museums in the German Art World: From the End of the Old Regime to the Rise of Modernism*. New York: Oxford University Press, 2000.
———. "What Is Germany History? Reflections on the Role of the Nation in German History and Historiography." *Journal of Modern History* 53 (1981): 1–23.
Short, John Rennie. *Imagined Country: Environment, Culture, and Society*. Syracuse: Syracuse University Press, 1991.
Shoumatoff, Nicholas, and Nina Shoumatoff. *The Alps: Europe's Mountain Heart*. Ann Arbor: University of Michigan Press, 2001.
Sieferle, Rolf-Peter. *Fortschrittsfeinde? Opposition gegen Technik und Industrie von der Romantik bis zur Gegenwart*. Munich: C. H. Beck Verlag, 1984.
Smith, Helmut Walser. *The Continuities of German History: Nation, Religion, and Race across the Long Nineteenth Century*. New York: Cambridge University Press, 2008.

Smith, Paul. *History of Tourism: Thomas Cook and the Origins of Leisure Travel*. New York: Routledge, 1998.

Sperber, Jonathon. *Kaiser's Voters: Electors and Elections in Imperial Germany*. New York: Cambridge University Press, 2005.

Stachura, Peter. *The German Youth Movement, 1900–1945*. London: Macmillan, 1981.

Stern, Fritz. *The Failure of Illiberalism*. New York: Columbia University Press, 1992.

———. *The Politics of Cultural Despair: A Study in the Rise of the Germanic Ideology*. Berkeley: University of California Press, 1961.

Stone, Norman. *The Eastern Front, 1914–1917*. London: Penguin, 1975.

Stradling, David. *Making Mountains: New York City and the Catskills*. Seattle: University of Washington Press, 2007.

Strauss, Gerald. *Sixteenth-Century Germany: Its Topography and Topographers*. Madison: University of Wisconsin Press, 1959.

Suval, Stanley. *Electoral Politics in Wilhelmine Germany*. Chapel Hill: University of North Carolina Press, 1985.

Taylor, Joseph E. *Pilgrims of the Vertical: Yosemite Rock Climbers and Nature at Risk*. Cambridge, Mass.: Harvard University Press, 2010.

Terray, Lionel. *Conquistadors of the Useless: From the Alps to Annapurna*. London: Bâton Wicks, 2001.

Thaler, Peter. "Fluid Identities in Central European Borderlands." *European History Quarterly* 31 (2001): 519–48.

Thompson, Mark. *The White War: Life and Death on the Italian Front, 1915–1919*. London: Faber and Faber, 2008.

Torpey, John. *The Invention of the Passport: Surveillance, Citizenship, and the State*. New York: Cambridge University Press, 2000.

"Tourists' Heavy Alpine Toll." *BBC News*, 30 August 2001.

Uekoetter, Frank. *The Green and the Brown: A History of Conservation in Nazi Germany*. New York: Cambridge University Press, 2006.

———, ed. *The Turning Points of Environmental History*. Pittsburgh: University of Pittsburgh Press, 2010.

Uekoetter, Frank, and Joachim Radkau. *Naturschutz und Nationalsozialismus*. Frankfurt: Campus Verlag, 2003.

Urbanitsch, Peter. "Bürgertum und Politik in der Habsburgermonarchie, eine Einführung." In *Bürgertum in der Habsburgermonarchie*, edited by Ernst Bruckmüller, 165–75. Vienna: Böhlau, 1994.

Urry, John. *The Tourist Gaze*. New York: Sage, 1990.

Viazzo, Paolo Pier. *Upland Communities: Environment, Population and Social Structure in the Alps since the Sixteenth Century*. New York: Cambridge University Press, 1989.

Wachtler, Michael. *The First World War in the Alps*. Bozen: Athesia, 2006.

Weigand, Katharina, ed. *Heimat: Konstanten und Wandel im 19./20. Jahrhundert, Vorstellungen und Wirklichkeiten*. Munich: Deutscher Alpenverein, 1997.

Wettengel, Michael. "Staat und Naturschutz 1906–1945. Zur Geschichte der staatlichen Stelle für Naturdenkmalpflege in Preußen und der Reichsstelle für Naturschutz." *Historische Zeitschrift* 257 (1993): 355–99.

White, Richard. "The Nationalization of Nature." *Journal of American History* 86 (1999): 976–86.

Whiteside, Andrew G. *The Socialism of Fools: Georg Ritter Von Schönerer and Austrian Pan-Germanism*. Berkeley: University of California Press, 1975.

Wiese, Bernd, and Norbert Zils. *Deutsche Kulturgeographie: Werden, Wandel, und Bewahrung Deutscher Kulturlandschaften*. Herford: Busse Seewald, 1987.

Wigen, Kären. "Discovering the Japanese Alps: Meiji Mountaineering and the Quest for Geographical Enlightenment." *Journal of Japanese Studies* 31 (2005): 1–26.

Williams, John A. "The Chords of the German Soul Are Tuned to Nature: The Movement to Preserve the Natural Heimat from the Kaiserreich to the Third Reich." *Central European History* 29, no. 3 (1996): 339–84.

———. "Ecstasies of the Young: Sexuality, the Youth Movement, and Moral Panic in Germany on the Eve of the First World War." *Central European History* 34, no. 2 (2001): 163–89.

———. "Protecting Nature between Democracy and Dictatorship: The Changing Ideology of the Bourgeois Conservationist Movement, 1925–1935." In *Germany's Nature: Cultural Landscapes and Environmental History*, edited by Thomas Lekan and Thomas Zeller, 183–206. New Brunswick, N.J.: Rutgers University Press, 2005.

———. *Turning to Nature in Germany: Hiking, Nudism, and Conservation, 1900–1940*. Stanford: Stanford University Press, 2007.

Wiltschegg, Walter. *Österreich—der "Zweite Deutsche Staat"? Der nationale Gedanke in der Ersten Republik*. Stuttgart: Leopold Stocker Verlag, 1992.

Winiwarter, Verena. "Nationalized Nature on Picture Postcards: Subtexts of Tourism from an Environmental Perspective." *Global Environment* 1 (2008): 192–215.

Wistrich, Robert. *Antisemitism: The Longest Hatred*. New York: Schocken Books, 1994.

Withey, Lynne. *Grand Tours and Cook's Tours: A History of Leisure Travel, 1750 to 1915*. New York: William Morrow, 1997.

Wozniakowski, Jacek. *Die Wildnis: Zur Deutungsgeschichte des Berges in der europäischen Neuzeit*. Frankfurt: Suhrkamp Verlag, 1987.

Wyss, Jörg. *Berge und Soldaten*. Munich: Ott Verlag Thunn, 1963.

Zahra, Tara. "Looking East: East Central European 'Borderlands' in German History and Historiography." *History Compass* 3 (2005): 1–23.

Zebhauser, Helmuth. *Alpine Exlibris: Sinn und Bild in einer grafischen Kunst von 1890–1930*. Munich: Bruckmann Verlag, 1985.

———. *Alpinismus im Hitlerstaat: Gedanken, Erinnerungen, Dokumente*. Munich: Bergverlag Rother, 1998.

Zeller, Thomas. *Straße, Bahn, Panorama. Verkehrswege und Landschaftsveränderung in Deutschland 1930 Bis 1990*. Frankfurt am Main: Campus, 2002.

Zimmer, Oliver. *A Contested Nation: History, Memory and Nationalism in Switzerland, 1761–1891*. New York: Cambridge University Press, 2003.

———. "In Search of Natural Identity: Alpine Landscape and the Reconstruction of the Swiss Nation." *Comparative Study of Society and History* 40 (1998): 637–65.

Index

Allgeier, Sepp, 154
Alpine Club Austria, 59
Alpine Library, 54–55
Alpine Museum, 54–55, 219
Alpinen Referenten, 102, 113
Alpine publications, 53–54
Alpini, 96, 97, 104, 111
Alpinism, 14, 216, 221; and anti-Semitism, 13, 64, 121–22, 145, 151, 219; and *Bildung* (personal development), 48, 51, 53, 55, 58, 66; and danger, 47, 51–52, 81, 87, 90, 182, 184, 186; and health, 21, 49, 73, 147, 185, 203; and inherent tensions, 26, 35, 51, 68, 87, 118, 214, 217, 218; and *Kampf* (struggle), 49–50, 68, 72, 76, 81, 87, 90, 117, 159, 168, 172, 182, 183, 185–87, 206, 215; and mass tourism, 17, 21, 69, 76, 155, 159, 181; and National Socialism, 6, 187–88, 209, 211; and national unity, 2, 31, 56, 66, 147; and war, 91, 96, 117, 186; and women, 178, 180; and youth, 79, 81
Alps, 2; agriculture in, 18–19, 22, 46; Allgäu, 38; Arlberg Range, 22; automobiles in, 3, 77–79, 85, 160, 166–75, 203; Carinthian, 37; Carnic, 13, 97; commercial development in, 69–71; Dolomites, 13, 78, 89, 91–92, 93, 97, 101, 103, 104, 124, 125, 127, 166–67, 202; Eastern, 2, 4–5, 7, 12, 13, 17–18, 20, 22, 26, 34, 46, 66, 67, 75, 77, 78, 86, 89, 92, 112, 123, 131, 152, 175, 207, 218; Julian, 13, 97; Karwendel Range, 38; mass tourism in, 19, 67–68, 71, 82, 152, 180–82; Ötztaler Range, 22; railways in, 4, 19–20, 21, 22, 47, 70, 76, 77, 104, 109, 159, 215, 216 (*see also* Cogwheel trains); scientific research on, 40–44; Stubaier Group, 37; urbanization in, 20–21, 48–49; Venediger, 86; Western, 9, 20, 46, 76, 78; Zillertal Range, 38
Andreas Hofer Bund, 125–26
Anschluss, 13, 64, 65, 128–31, 137, 146, 150, 184, 194, 204–9, 214, 218
Anti-Semitism, 4, 6, 13, 58, 63–65, 66, 121–22, 148, 187, 217, 219; in Alpine Association, 132–44, 146, 149–50, 153, 176, 195; and "Aryan paragraph," 64, 121, 133–38, 140, 183, 190–91
Arndt, Ernst Moritz, 61, 122, 146
Arnold, Karl, 137, 141
Association for the Protection and Care of Alpine Plants, 84
Austria, 2–7, 12, 14, 17, 21, 26, 28, 31, 34, 48, 49, 50, 55, 57–60, 62, 64–65, 67, 72, 78, 83, 84, 89, 91–92, 94, 97, 101, 102, 103, 115, 116, 122–23, 125, 127–30, 133, 135, 141, 146, 147, 149, 151, 157, 163, 166, 170, 183–84, 186–88, 193–98, 202, 204–8, 211, 213, 214, 218
Austrian Alpine Association, 10, 17, 21–28
Austrian Mountain Association (ÖGV), 64–65, 132, 146, 147
Austrian Nature Reserve Association, 85
Austrian Ski Association, 72
Austrian Tourist Club (ÖTC), 59, 84, 132, 136, 146, 147
Austrofascism, 194
Austro-Prussian War, 55, 57
Autobahn, 201, 203

277

Bacher, Sepp, 206
Bad Reichenhall, 199
Baedeker, Karl, 8–9, 45, 89
Battle of Königgrätz, 61
Battle of Solferino, 89
Bauer, Otto, 55, 128–29, 130
Bauer, Paul, 189–90, 192
Bavaria, 26, 36, 44, 76, 83, 148, 161, 164, 182, 195, 201, 220
Bavarian Botanical Society, 84
Beer Hall Putsch, 187, 196
Benz, Karl, 78
Berchtesgadener Land, 5, 198, 200, 201, 204, 220
Bergfilme, 13, 152–59
Berghof, 204
Berlin, 27, 60, 63, 74, 80, 92, 97, 123, 131, 144, 155, 159, 164, 189, 192, 209
Bezold, Gustav von, 27
Bismarck, Otto von, 48, 55, 59, 62
Blaueis Glacier, 198–99, 201
Bleichert and Company, 76, 161
Bludenz, 22, 28, 40, 196
The Blue Angel (film), 154
Bocca di Brenta, 92
Bolzano, 20, 27, 45, 75, 78, 100, 125, 167
Borderlands, 3, 7–8, 13
Bregenz, 22
Bremen, 20
Brennerbahn, 20
Brenner Watershed, 18, 25, 92, 121–24
British Alpine Club, 9, 23, 26, 177

The Cabinet of Dr. Caligari (film), 153
Cable cars, 3, 11, 75–76, 108, 153, 160, 161, 163–67, 172, 180, 216
Cadorna, Luigi, 97–99, 104, 105
Carinthia, 18, 28, 34, 37, 43, 116, 220
Carpathian Mountains, 97, 102
Catholicism. See *Kulturkampf*
Center Party, 44
Central Association for German Citizens of the Jewish Faith, 138
Chasseurs Alpins, 96
Christian Socialism, 133, 147–49

Clausewitz, Carl von, 95–96, 107
Coblenz, 8, 61
Cogwheel trains, 76–77, 160–62, 216
Col di Lana, 109–10
Convention on the Protection of the Alps, 221
Cortina d'Ampezzo, 78, 167
Czánt, Hermann, 109, 186–87, 189

Dalmatia, 91
Danube River, 26, 61
Dellmensingen, Konrad Krafft von, 99
Deschmann, Rudolf, 89
Desor, Edouard, 17
Deutscher Alpenverein. See German Alpine Association
Deutscher Bergsteiger- und Wanderverband (DBW), 189, 192
Deutsche Reichbund für Leibesübungen (DRL), 188–89, 192
Deutscher und Österreichischer Alpenverein. See German and Austrian Alpine Association
Deutsches Museum, 54
Deutschtum, 56, 102, 125, 187. See also Greater German
Deutschvölkische Bund, 137, 140
Dietrich, Marlene, 153
Dinkelacker, Paul, 190, 208
Dollfuss, Engelbert, 170, 193–94, 197
Dolomite Highway, 78, 109
Dolomites. See Alps: Dolomites
Donabaum, Josef, 62, 65, 122, 133, 136, 195
Donauland, 133–46, 149, 150, 176, 183, 187, 217, 219; Glorer-Hut, 138; Mainzerhut, 141
Dreisprachespitz, 105
Dreitorspitze, 69–70
Dresden, 131

Ecoregion, 7
Eiger, 184
Emmer, Johannes, 30
Enzensperger, Ernst, 80–81

Falkenhayn, Erich von, 99
Fanck, Arnold, 154–59
Fatherland Front, 194
Fenzl, Eduard, 21, 24
First World War, 12, 13, 28, 30, 34, 38, 50, 65, 67, 75, 80, 87, 89–91, 97, 122, 153, 185, 202, 214, 216, 217; Alpine Front, 90, 97–99, 103; Austrian High Command, 97–100; Austrian mobilization, 99–100; avalanches during, 112–14; Battle of Caporetto, 115; Battle of Piave, 115; Battle of Vittorio Veneto, 115; combat in the Alps during, 102–4, 112–13; Entente, 97, 123, 129; environmental impact of, 108–11; German High Command, 95; home front during, 100–101, 106–7; memory of, 116–18; and mountain troops, 96–97, 101–2; prewar tensions and, 91–94, 97; and prisoners of war, 105–6; Swiss General Staff, 97; and Swiss mobilization, 95; and women, 107
Five Finger Peak, 45, 78
Font debate, 62–63, 100
Franco-Prussian War, 56
Frankfurt a.M., 27, 62
Freikorps, 147
French Alpine Club, 10
Frick, Wilhelm, 192–93, 196, 200
Friedrich, Caspar David, 204
Friends of Nature. See Naturfreunde

German Alpine Association, 10, 26–27, 55–56, 129, 192, 207, 219
German Alpine Association Berlin, 145–46, 189
German Alpine Corps, 99, 110
German Alpine Road, 184, 201–4
German and Austrian Alpine Association, 2, 10, 26–28; democratic practices of, 30–31; and First World War, 100–102, 106, 117; membership in, 28, 30; and mountaineering group, 175–77; and patriotism, 61–63; and scientific research, 41–44; and *Winterfest*, 31–33; and women, 30, 177–80; and youth groups, 81–82
— Chapters, 30–31; Academic Section Berlin, 36, 101; Academic Section Dresden, 144; Academic Section Graz, 34; Academic Section Munich, 63–64, 74; Academic Section Vienna, 65; Augsburg, 48, 136; Austria, 28, 35–36, 65, 67, 74, 85, 133–37, 139, 141, 148, 179, 219; Bamberg, 101; Bayerland, 69–70, 141, 143; Berchtesgaden, 144; Bergfried, 127, 135; Berlin, 10, 27, 30, 31, 32, 37, 40, 63, 74, 135, 136, 143, 144–45, 177, 179, 192; Bozen, 124–25; Bremen, 92–93, 127, 141; Breslau, 135, 139, 141; Cassel, 124; Chemnitz, 127; Donauland (see Donauland); Essen, 135, 137, 141; Frankenthal, 136; Frankfurt, 27, 141; Freiburg, 40, 74, 190–91, 192; Gastein, 36; Graz, 132, 208; Hamburg, 10, 31, 136, 141, 149, 190–91; Hanover, 135, 137, 190–91; Heidelberg, 27; Hochland, 82, 135, 136, 137, 185; Hohenzollern, 136; Innsbruck, 27, 31, 36, 38, 62, 70, 82, 86, 94, 129–30, 182; Kaiserslautern, 136; Karlsruhe, 124; Kiel, 136; Klagenfurt, 78, 138, 140–41, 165; Landshut, 124; Leipzig, 27, 101, 135, 137; Lienz, 27, 138; Lindau, 36; Linz, 24, 127, 140; Lungau, 36–37; Magdeburg, 124; Mainz, 135, 141; Mannheim, 136, 141; Mark Brandenburg, 63–64, 135, 136, 146, 177; Munich, 10, 30, 31, 35–36, 63, 77, 82, 123, 144, 179, 190–91, 195–96; Nuremberg, 101, 141; Oberland, 135, 137; Pforzheim, 127; Radstadt, 140; Rhineland-Cologne, 191; Rosenheim, 136; Rostock, 136, 190, 191; Traunstein, 135; Villach, 37, 138; Wien, 65, 13; Zwickau, 124

— Huts, 35–40; *Arbeitsgebiet*, 34–35, 177; Berliner Hut, 37, 38, 40, 41; Bremer-Haus, 92–93, 94; Committee for the German Huts in the Lost Regions, 124; Dresdner Hut, 36; Franz Senn Hut, 36, 38; Freiburger Hut, 40; Glockner House, 58; Hofmann Hut, 58; Hut and Trail Committee, 35–36, 70–71, 78; Johannes Lodge, 58; Kemptner Hut, 38; Klagenfurt Resolution, 36; Lamsenjoch Lodge, 38; Lindauer Hut, 36; Meiler Hut, 69; Münchner Haus and Observatory, 43–44, 77, 163, 165; Nürnberger Hut, 37; Ortler-Hochjoch Hut, 67; Payer Hut, 87; Stüdl-Hut, 25

German Ski Association, 72

Germany, 1–7, 11–14, 17, 21, 26, 28, 31, 43, 48–49, 50, 55, 57, 62, 64–66, 67, 80, 83, 94, 99, 101, 116, 122, 125, 128–31, 135, 137, 141, 143, 146, 151, 153, 157, 163, 166, 177, 183–84, 186–88, 189, 193–94, 196, 198–200, 204, 207, 210–11, 214, 219

Ginzkey, Franz Karl, 116

Gleichschaltung, 13, 187–91, 193, 199, 208–9

Gmünd, 20

Goebbels, Joseph, 218

Göring, Hermann, 200

Graubünden, 91, 97

Greater German, 2–3, 6, 13, 48, 56, 59, 62, 63, 65, 82, 150, 183, 187, 194

Grohmann, Paul, 17, 23, 26, 45

Grossdeutsch. *See* Greater German

Grossglockner, 25, 58, 78, 205–7, 218

Grossglockner High Alpine Road, 153, 160, 165–72, 174, 175, 202

Guttenberg, Adolf Ritter von, 85–86

Habsburg Empire, 55, 64, 91, 115, 123, 128, 166, 208

Hamburg, 20, 86

Hannover, 20

Hauptner, Rudolf, 145

Heiligenblut, 20, 78

Heimat, 5–6, 48, 56, 73, 81, 82, 123, 188, 215, 216

Heimatschutz, 30, 67, 83, 132

Heimwehr, 147–48

Heritsch, Franz, 152

Hess, Heinrich, 100

Himmler, Heinrich, 193, 218

Hitler, Adolf, 6, 13, 144, 182, 183–84, 187–88, 190–98, 200–208, 210, 211, 215

Hofmann, Karl, 26–27, 57, 58

The Holy Mountain (film), 155, 158

Innsbruck, 20, 22, 27, 35, 44, 70, 82, 122, 133, 136, 149, 157, 195, 208

Irredentists, 13, 91, 93–95, 101, 122, 131

Isonzo River, 94, 97, 99

Italian Alpine Club, 10, 123, 132

Italy, 11, 78, 84, 89, 97, 103, 166, 202, 220; border disputes with Austria, 122–23, 126, 127; negotiations with the Central Powers, 94; property disputes in the Alps, 91–93

Ittlinger, Josef, 215

Jenny, Hans, 121

Jews, 1, 4, 60, 62–64, 121, 132–39, 143–46, 176, 185, 190–91, 219. *See also* Anti-Semitism; Donauland

Jungfraubahn, 76–77, 161–62

Kaiserjäger, 96

Klebelsberg, Raimond von, 136, 195, 207, 208

Kleindeutsch, 55

Kohlererbahn, 75–76

Königspitze, 97, 109

Kracauer, Siegfried, 154, 155

Kuhn, Franz, 96

Kulturkampf, 4, 48, 57–60, 195

Lake Constance, 22, 201

Lammer, Eugen Guido, 73

Landesausschuss für Naturpflege, 84
Landesschützen, 96, 97, 99
Lang, Fritz, 153
Lansing, Robert, 128
Lebensraum, 2
Leipzig, 27, 66, 76, 161
Leuchs, Georg, 191, 195–96
Liberals, 24–26, 44, 55, 58–60, 62, 65, 133, 187, 217
Lienz, 27
Linz, 20, 24, 205
Lombardy, 89
Löwenbräukeller, 31, 162
Lower Engadin, 85
Lüneburger Heide, 86

Magdeburg, 20
Mallnitz, 20
Mann, Thomas, 47, 152
Marcus, Siegfried, 78
Marinelli, Giovanni, 91–92
Marmolada, 103, 109, 114
Marmorek, Oskar, 143
Marr, Wilhelm, 64
Matterhorn, 12, 17, 85, 162
Melingo, Achilles, 23
Mendelssohn, Felix, 61
Merano, 76
Metropolis (film), 154
Mojsisovics, Eduard von, 23, 26
Moltke, Helmuth von, 59
Müller, Gustav, 136, 137, 185–87, 189, 190
Munich, 10, 20, 26, 31, 54, 63, 69, 72, 82, 85, 96, 136–37, 141, 146, 149, 161–63, 219, 222
Mussolini, Benito, 121, 125, 131, 203, 205

Nanga Parbat, 183, 190
National Park Hohe Tauern, 220
National Socialism, 1, 4, 6, 12, 13, 142, 143, 148, 149, 154, 170, 183–84, 187–91, 193, 198–201, 209, 211, 215, 219; outlawed in Austria, 194–95

Naturalist Society, 84
Nature conservation, 13, 68, 71, 79, 83–87, 118, 164, 188, 198–200
Naturfreunde, 50–51, 139, 147–50, 189, 194
Nazis. See National Socialism
New Deal, 169
Niederösterreichischen Gebirgsverein, 53, 65
Nordkette, 82

Ortler, 76, 87, 97, 105
Österreichischer Alpenverein. See Austrian Alpine Association

Pan-Germanism, 64, 65, 125, 150, 187
Papen, Franz von, 193, 196
Pasterze, 172
Patscherkofel, 82
Penck, Albrecht, 92
Petersen, Ernst, 156, 158
Pfister, Otto von, 65–66, 71, 79
Pichl, Eduard, 64–65, 102, 132–41, 144, 148, 150, 153, 176, 182, 183, 190, 191, 192, 208, 211, 219
Pinzgau region, 86
Prague, 25, 31, 193, 208
Preber Lake, 37
Protestantism. See *Kulturkampf*
Prussia, 22, 27, 55, 57–60, 83, 89
Pustertalbahn, 20

Ratzel, Friedrich, 66
Regensburg, 82
Rehlen, Robert, 208
Rehrl, Franz, 170, 172
Reich Nature Protection Law, 199–200
Reich Sports Office, 188
Renker, Gustav, 102–7, 111, 113, 116
Renner, Karl, 128
Republican Defense League, 147
Reuter, Philip, 137–38, 141
Rhine River, 4, 26, 61, 122
Richter, Max, 183
Rickmer-Rickmers, Willi, 54

Riefenstahl, Leni, 155–56, 158, 178
Riehl, Wilhelm Heinrich, 56
Rigele, Fritz, 193
Roon, Albrecht Graf von, 59
Rosenheimer compromise, 140–41. See also Donauland
Rothpletz, August, 84
Rudoff, Ernst, 67
Ruhr Valley, 137–38, 143
Ruthner, Anton von, 23, 25

St. Gallen, 22
Salzburg, 18, 20, 24, 27, 34, 36, 37, 43, 56, 57, 58, 86, 129, 198, 220
Salzkammergutbahn, 20
San Lorenzo, 93
Sautner, Johannes, 45, 78
Schalek, Alice, 99, 107
Schaubach, Adolf, 24, 79
Scheiber, Alois, 209
Schlieffen Plan, 95
Schmidkunz, Walter, 104, 108, 113
Schmitt, Robert Hans, 45, 78
Schneeberger, Hannes, 205–6
Schönerer, Georg von, 64
Schuschnigg, Kurt, 170, 172, 197, 202, 204–5
Schweizer Alpenclub. See Swiss Alpine Club
Second World War, 213–15, 216, 218–19, 220
Seipel, Ignaz, 147
Semple, Ellen Churchill, 66
Senn, Franz, 21–26, 44
Senners, 18–19
Serbia, 94
Serles, 82
Seyss-Inquart, Arthur, 204–5, 207–9
Simony, Friedrich, 23
Skiing, 12, 13, 71–76, 186; Alpine Association tensions with, 73–75
Social Democrats, 50, 55, 80, 128–29, 147, 150, 194, 202
Society of Trentino Alpinists (SAT), 93, 123, 124, 125, 131

Sommaruga, Guido von, 23, 26
Sonnblick Peak, 43
South German Alpine Association Munich, 145–46
South Tyrol, 25, 34, 45, 76, 89, 96, 97, 102, 122, 123, 124, 150, 202; tensions in, 13, 91–93, 121, 125–28, 130, 131
Steinbeis, Otto von, 77
Steinitzer, Alfred, 96, 178
Stelvio Pass, 20, 78, 105
Stephen, Leslie, 6, 9, 45
Stresemann, Gustav, 128
Stüdl, Johann, 25–26, 136, 141
Sturmabteilung (SA), 188, 196
Stuttgart, 27, 85, 86
Sudetenland, 208
Suess, Eduard, 21–23, 44, 47
Swiss Alpine Club, 10, 26, 131–32, 177
Swiss National Park, 85, 86
Switzerland, 20, 50, 60, 84, 85, 91, 95, 97, 104, 105, 106, 162, 202, 213, 220
Sydow, Reinhold von, 208

Tessin, 91, 97
Tölzer Guidelines, 176–78, 180
Tonale Pass, 97
Tour guides, 18, 25–26, 39, 51, 58, 60, 86, 155
Trautwein, Theodor, 10, 26, 27
Treaty of St. Germain, 123, 129
Treaty of Versailles, 123
Trenker, Luis, 109, 154, 156, 157, 159
Trentino, 89, 91, 92, 94, 97, 123, 233 (n. 2)
Trieste, 98, 99
Triple Alliance, 94
Tschammer und Osten, Hans von, 188–89, 192, 207
Turner, Frederick Jackson, 7–8, 216–17
Turnverein, 64
Tyrol, 1, 18, 20, 25, 36, 37, 57, 58, 59, 60, 69, 91, 94, 96, 99, 107, 129, 161, 163, 195, 220, 233 (n. 2)
Tyrol Farmers' League, 133

Ullman, James Ramsey, 213–14

Venetia, 89
Vent, 21–22
Verein Naturschutzpark, 85–86
Vienna, 5, 20, 21, 23, 24, 25, 26, 28, 30, 50, 58, 59, 62, 63, 65, 66, 85, 91, 93, 98, 106, 107, 116, 123, 129, 132–33, 136, 144, 145, 147, 149, 157, 179, 193, 195, 205, 206, 207

Waffen-SS, 215
Wagner, Richard, 61
Wallack, Franz, 165–66, 170, 172, 202
Wandervogel, 80, 82
World War I. *See* First World War
World War II. *See* Second World War

Yellowstone National Park, 85, 86
Youth development, 13, 68, 79–80

Zdarsky, Mathias, 72
Zell am See, 20
Zugspitzbahn, 77, 160–65, 168, 170, 175, 220
Zugspitze, 43–44, 77, 160–65, 220, 222

Printed in Poland
by Amazon Fulfillment
Poland Sp. z o.o., Wrocław